THE NATURAL & THE SUPERNATURAL

THE NATURAL & THE SUPERNATURAL

BY

JOHN OMAN
Principal, Westminster College, Cambridge

WIPF & STOCK · Eugene, Oregon

Wipf and Stock Publishers
199 W 8th Ave, Suite 3
Eugene, OR 97401

The Natural and the Supernatural
By Oman, John
Softcover ISBN-13: 978-1-6667-3476-8
Hardcover ISBN-13: 978-1-6667-9096-2
eBook ISBN-13: 978-1-6667-9097-9
Publication date 9/3/2021
Previously published by The Macmillan Company, 1931

This edition is a scanned facsimile of the original edition published in 1931.

PREFACE

It was said of William James that he derived undue credit for originality by ignoring his intellectual ancestors. But I confess to sympathy with his true reason, which was not a desire for undeserved merit, but a dislike to burdening his pages with the display of learning, preserving names, as he puts it, like flies in amber. Moreover, many references were not necessary for my purpose: for, though I use the classical forms to state positions in preference to abstract questions, I am not concerned with the history of philosophy. For example, I refer to Kant and Hegel with considerable frequency, yet it is not to expound either, but because the former was concerned with the central problem of the eighteenth century, what I have called the *Individual*, and the latter with the central problem of the nineteenth, what I have named *Individuality*: and I have referred to them so often because a large part of my contention is that both problems should be taken together and that they are not two problems but one. As little have I attempted to write the history of religion. Though I use the religions because they are the concrete and illuminating presentation of the problems, my concern is with the problems, and in particular with the one problem of the relation of the Natural and the Supernatural.

At the same time I should willingly acknowledge my obligations were it possible after a somewhat extended life spent in reading and thinking on the subject. A long list of authorities could be compiled, but the proper place for them is a text-book, like Dr Galloway's, where it is given with learning and discrimination. Also I have read a great deal of the recognised literature without much sense of obligation, and many other works with more profit. In any case, to attempt to distinguish what I might claim as my own from what is due to the suggestions of others would at this time of the day be a hopeless task. The obligation I am most conscious of is to those from whom I have most differed. For example, I mention Siebeck thrice to disagree with him. But of all the *Religionsphilosophien* I have read—Rawvenhoff's, Hoffding's, Pfleiderer's, Runze's, Seydel's, Eucken's, and one or two others—I incline to regard Siebeck's as the most profitable. Again I have seldom referred to Prof. Leuba except to disagree with him, but though I judge his acquaintance with religion to be mainly with a rather crude type of evangelism, he knows what he is talking about, and I have learned more from him than from any other psychologist of religion, though mostly by way of differing.

Mr Francis Healey and Mr George Alexander read the whole MS, Dr Alexander Wood the scientific part and Prof. Welch the Old Testament part. To all of them I am indebted for suggestions about the form of presentation. Miss Wolstencroft's interpretation of my palimpsest into lucid type made this help possible. Mr Alexander has read all the proofs, and the Rev. H. C. Carter read the earlier part and the Rev. B. R. H. Mein the later. To all these I desire to express my warmest thanks.

JOHN OMAN

WESTMINSTER COLLEGE
Cambridge, May 1931

CONTENTS

PART I

SCOPE & METHOD

Chap. I. The Field of Inquiry . . . . *pages* 2–14
    (*a*) The Test of Interest, 3–8
    (*b*) The Insufficiency of the Test of Interest, 8–11
    (*c*) Justification of the Inquiry, 11–14

II. The Seat of Religion 15–28
    (*a*) Religion as a Mental State, 16–21
    (*b*) Religion as a Social Phenomenon, 21–23
    (*c*) Religion as Theology, 23–28

III. Theories of Religion as Illusion . . 29–46
    (*a*) Theories of the Hegelian Type, 30–35
    (*b*) Theories of the Schleiermacher Type, 35–37
    (*c*) Theories of the Kantian Type, 37–42
    (*d*) Psychology and Metaphysics, 42–46

IV. Theory and History 47–57
    (*a*) Quasi-historical Views, 47–51
    (*b*) Universal Scepticism, 51–54
    (*c*) Fact and Theory, 54–55
    (*d*) Origin and Beginning, 55–57

V. The Religious Environment . . . 58–73
    (*a*) The Experience of Environment, 58–59
    (*b*) The Sense of the Holy, 59–65
    (*c*) The Judgment of the Sacred, 65–69
    (*d*) The Supernatural, 69–73

VI. Standpoint 74–98
    (*a*) In Respect to Bad Religion, 74–82
    (*b*) In Respect to Religion and Environment, 82–86
    (*c*) In Respect to Evolution, 86–95
    (*d*) In Respect to Theology, 95–98

CONTENTS

Chap. VII. Method and Problems . . . . *pages* 99–117

    (*a*) Illuminism, 99–102
    (*b*) Rationalism, 102–104
    (*c*) The Method of Descartes, 104–108
    (*d*) How a Method should be determined, 108–110
    (*e*) The Problems, 110–114
    (*f*) The Order of Inquiry, 114–117

PART II

KNOWING & KNOWLEDGE

VIII. Awareness and Apprehension   120–143

    (*a*) Four Types of Knowing, 120–124
    (*b*) A Poet's Awareness and Apprehension, 124–132
    (*c*) The Child's Perceiving, 132–137
    (*d*) A Poet's Child, 138–140
    (*e*) Sincerity, Sensitiveness, Unity, 140–143

IX. The Individual and Individuality   144–167

    (*a*) The Unities, 144–147
    (*b*) Danger and Necessity of Theory, 147–149
    (*c*) Religious Outlook and Theory of Knowledge, 149–151
    (*d*) The Two Aspects of the Problem, 151–152
    (*e*) Kant's Theory of Knowing and the Individual, 152–155
    (*f*) The Individual Frontier and the Natural, 156–160
    (*g*) The Individual Frontier and the Supernatural, 160–165
    (*h*) Rationalism and Romanticism, 165–167

CONTENTS

Chap. X. The Form of Perception . . . *pages* 168–184
- (a) The Method of Inquiry, 168–170
- (b) Berkeley's Divine Visual Language, 170–172
- (c) Speech and Perceiving, 172–174
- (d) Symbol and Meaning, 174–176
- (e) The Context of Fixed Ideas, 176–178
- (f) Oneness of the Senses, 178–180
- (g) Space and Time, 180–184

XI. Sensation 185–200
- (a) The Physical and Physiological Medium, 185–188
- (b) The Function of Interest, 188–192
- (c) Quality of Sensations, 192–195
- (d) Sensation and Awareness, 195–199
- (e) Impacts, 199–200

XII. Value and Validity . . . 201–216
- (a) Theoretical and Value Judgments, 201–204
- (b) Natural and Ideal Values, 204–207
- (c) Logic, Ethics and Aesthetics, 207–212
- (d) Agnosticism and Value, 212–214
- (e) True Enlightenment, 214–216

PART III

NECESSITY & FREEDOM

XIII. Cosmologies of Freedom and of Necessity 218–240
- (a) The Two Kinds of Reliable Sequence, 218–221
- (b) The Cosmological Law of Award, 221–226
- (c) Karma and Positivism, 227–230
- (d) The Cosmological Law of Inertia, 230–236
- (e) Inadequate Theory, 236–240

CONTENTS

Chap. XIV. Concordats between Necessity and Freedom . . . *pages* 241–257
- (*a*) Phenomenon and Noumenon, 242–244
- (*b*) Quantity and Quality, 244–246
- (*c*) Concrete and Abstract, 246–253
- (*d*) Symbol and Meaning, 253–257

XV. Evolution as a Process of the Natural 258–280
- (*a*) Progress, 258–260
- (*b*) Problems of Evolution, 260–261
  1. The Place of Organism, 261–264
  2. Life and Meaning, 264–271
  3. Meaning for the Individual, 271–277
  4. Environment, 277–280

XVI. Evolution as a Process of the Supernatural 281–297
- (*a*) Selection by Environment, 281–282
- (*b*) The Truth in the Conception, 282–284
- (*c*) Necessity as Freedom, 284–286
- (*d*) Responsibility, 286–289
- (*e*) Process and Evil, 290–292
- (*f*) Natural Process and its Theory of Sin, 292–294
- (*g*) Metaphysical Process and its Theory of Sin, 295–297

XVII. Freedom 298–311
- (*a*) The Will to live and the Will to live better, 298–300
- (*b*) Determination by Character, 300–302
- (*c*) Freedom in respect to the Natural, 303–305
- (*d*) Freedom in respect to the Supernatural, 306–311

CONTENTS

Chap. XVIII. Conscience and Conscientiousness . . . . . *pages* 312–329
  (*a*) The Scope of Conscience, 312–314
  (*b*) The Infallibility of Conscience, 314–318
  (*c*) The Individual and the Content of Conscience, 318–323
  (*d*) The Individual and Conscientiousness, 323–326
  (*e*) Absolute Good and Evil and Evolution, 326–329

XIX. The Ideal and the Real . . 330–343
  (*a*) Freedom and Environment, 330–332
  (*b*) A Just World, 332–335
  (*c*) The Natural as Award, 335–336
  (*d*) The Ideal and Experience of the Natural, 336–339
  (*e*) The Personal, 339–343

PART IV

THE EVANESCENT & THE ETERNAL

XX. History and Experience . . 346–357
  (*a*) Tradition, 346–350
  (*b*) Anthropological, 350–352
  (*c*) Religious-historical, 352–354
  (*d*) Prophetical, 354–357

XXI. Classification of Religions 358–371
  (*a*) Standpoint, 358–360
  (*b*) Intellectual and Ethical Principles of Valuation, 360–363
  (*c*) A Natural and Supernatural Principle, 363–368
  (*d*) A Classification on the Natural and Supernatural Principle, 368–371

CONTENTS

Chap. XXII. The Primitive . . . . *pages* 372–389
- (*a*) Beginning and Origin, 372–373
- (*b*) Historical Perspective, 373–375
- (*c*) Religion of Nature, 375–376
- (*d*) Views of Primitive Religion, 376–378
- (*e*) The Primitive Unity of Fixed Idea, 378–380
- (*f*) The Animistic, 380–383
- (*g*) Magic, 383–385
- (*h*) Primitive Monotheism, 385–387
- (*i*) Religion and Morality, 387–389

XXIII. The Polytheistic . . .   390–404
- (*a*) Gods as Anthropomorphic Inference, 390–392
- (*b*) Property and the Concrete Individual, 393–395
- (*c*) Polytheism and Civilisation, 395–397
- (*d*) Elements of Progress, 398–400
- (*e*) Limitations and Defects, 400–404

XXIV. The Mystical   405–426
- (*a*) Two Types of Religions, 405–408
- (*b*) Ways of describing their Difference, 408–412
- (*c*) Early Indian Pantheism, 412–416
- (*d*) Pessimism, 416–418
- (*e*) Common Elements, 418–420
- (*f*) Christian Mysticism, 420–426

XXV. The Ceremonial-Legal . .   427–445
- (*a*) Common and distinguishing Elements of Apocalyptic Religions, 427–432
- (*b*) Dualism as a Problem and as a Solution, 432–433
- (*c*) The Persian Situation, 434–436
- (*d*) Two Elements of Progress, 436–438
- (*e*) Dualism as a Theology, 438–440
- (*f*) Good and Evil as a Problem, 440–442
- (*g*) Law and Prophecy, 443–445

CONTENTS

Chap. XXVI. The Prophetic . . . . *pages* 446–471
 (*a*) A Religion of Reconciliation, 446–448
 (*b*) Prophetic Monotheism, 448–449
 (*c*) The Prophetic Faith and Polytheism and Legalism, 449–453
 (*d*) The Rule of God, 453–455
 (*e*) Suffering and Sin, 455–459
 (*f*) The Present and the Future, 459–466
 (*g*) Religion and History, 466–469
 (*h*) The Rule of Good and the Rule of Evil, 469–471

APPENDICES

A. The Holy	474
B. Kant and Hegel	475–477
C. The Unity of Awareness	477
D. The Origins of Modern Science	478–480
E. Biological Principles	480–481
F. An Ethical Classification of Religions	481–482
G. Some Primitive Ideas	483–485
H. Primitive Monotheism	485–488
I. The Primitive in Indian Religion	488–494
J. Mysticism	494–500
INDEX	501–506

PART I
SCOPE & METHOD

CHAPTER I

THE FIELD OF INQUIRY

SEEING that the world is one and our experience of it 'one universe of discourse', there is no ultimate separateness either in what we study or how we study it. Absolute frontiers no subject has, and the better we know a subject, the more debatable its frontiers become, till it seems to be very little more than a selection according to a particular interest. An inquiry into the Natural and Supernatural would in any case seem to include all things in heaven and earth. All special studies, as Prof. Hobson says, depend on the fact that experience is made up of approximately isolated systems, and that these, for practical purposes, can be isolated still more.[1] Thus natural science limits its field by ignoring everything, even in the world of the senses, outside of a system of measurable quantity; politics by ignoring everything, even in the world of society, except a certain organisation of it; and ethics by separating conduct from much else that goes with it. But, as one of the most important aims of our discussion is just to see this unity, and to try to pass beyond arbitrary divisions of experience, we cannot hope to limit our field by assigning to it a special system and ignoring the rest.

Yet, though the Natural and the Supernatural include all environment, and an inquiry into their relation can involve nothing less than a view of the universe, the mere division of environment into natural and supernatural shows that the inquiry is limited by the particular interest of religion. We might, therefore, describe our subject as the concern of religion with environment. This involves very large questions, but, as they have a definite purpose, they have definite limits.

The interest of religion in the Supernatural may be more apparent than in the Natural: and it might seem that we

[1] E. W. Hobson, *The Domain of Natural Science*, pp. 44 ff.

should limit our field of inquiry by confining ourselves to it, as many studies of religion have done. But it will be maintained that there is no possible study of anything apart from the Natural, and least of all religion, and that not only has religion to do with our relation to all environment, but that by its view of the Natural the quality of religion is determined, even if it be also true that the view of the Natural is determined by the conception of the Supernatural. Therefore we may not limit our field by ignoring the Natural and concentrating on the Supernatural, as science ignores quality and concentrates on quantity.

The field, therefore, cannot be limited, but our special business in it can be: and, as this limitation is by its interest for religion, we must begin by determining the scope of religion, with as much definiteness as its width and variety allow.

(*a*) THE TEST OF INTEREST

So wide is the scope of religion that it has been maintained that its essential quality is to be concerned with the mind as a whole and the world as a whole. In that case, it would be a hopeless task to try to distinguish what embraces everything from anything else and, from the start, any attempt to define religion would seem doomed to failure. Nor do the variety, the contradiction, the generality of the many attempts already made afford much evidence that a better result awaits us.

Runze, after reviewing a long list of them, says that no definition, no description even, can include all the manifestations of religion, without becoming too general to be of use as a criterion for distinguishing from other phenomena those specially religious. He proposes instead to accept the fact that the boundaries of subjects are determined purely by interest; and his prescription is: Have the right interest in a subject, and you will see what belongs and what does not belong to it. Given the right interest in religion, which is to have a soul at peace with itself, so as to be responsive to the great things of life, then, without needing to define the sphere of religion, you will know practically what is within it and what without. If this be thought vague guidance, no other central human activity, he maintains, has better, nor is more required to show what concerns it and what does not. Even natural science, definite as it seems to be, can no longer be defined so that all belonging to it shall be included and all else excluded, yet no one with a scientific interest and a scientific habit of mind has any difficulty in distinguishing what does and what does not belong to natural science. And, though art is even more impossible to define than science, an artistic interest and an artistic attitude of mind can determine even more certainly what belongs to art and what does not. Religion may be still more difficult to define, but with a religious interest and a religious attitude, he maintains, we can still more surely distinguish what does and what does not belong to it.[1]

The importance of this equipment of a right interest and a right attitude for discernment, except, singularly, in religion, is rarely questioned. We do not expect persons, whose only standard of a scientific truth is the number and confidence of its advocates, or whose standard in art is the price in the catalogue, to be able to distinguish what belongs to science or art, even with the aid of any amount of description or definition, while we generally assume that, given a scientific or artistic interest and habit of mind, there will, even without the help of definition or description, be no grave mistake.

In all other subjects students are approved as they have sympathy, insight and enthusiasm for their study. In religion alone, it would almost appear that complete lack of interest, and even positive distaste, are necessary qualifications Religion is apparently thought to be so peculiar that interest in it is necessarily bias.

This prejudice against religious persons, in contrast with scientific or artistic persons, has, it must be admitted, not been wholly without justification There have been religious people whose interest in religion was largely prepossession, and who,

[1] Georg Runze, *Psychologie der Religion*

instead of regarding truth as the supreme religious interest, rather treated religion as a germ to which daylight is fatal.

But, though religion offers larger scope to the wrong kind of interest than any other sphere, it is far from having a monopoly; and no more than in any other subject do the errors of individuals justify identification of interest in religion, forthwith and without discrimination, with bias. True interest in religion, as in all else, is just interest in what is true concerning it: and when we speak of interest in religion, we ought to mean this right kind of interest, as when we speak of interest in art or science.

Without interest man never achieves clear consciousness of anything. The study of the development of mind, hitherto, has been mainly concerned with the progress of man's power of reasoned explanation, but a still more important chapter, could it be written, would tell how he came to his present reach and quality of awareness, for it would be little less than the whole inward story of life: and it is almost entirely the story of his interests. Nor has anything done more to stir higher interests than religion.

Religion is, above all else, concerned with 'moving about in worlds not realised'. We may be living by this higher environment as fishes in the water live by air, and be equally ignorant of the fact: and the reason may be lack of interest, not of capacity. To inquire into such a possibility without interest in it is obviously futile. Supposing that the task which gives religion its unique character is not to secure what man's present interests reveal to him, but to stir in him interests which will make him aware of still higher environment, the turning away of interest from the highest we know would obviously be fatal to any effective consideration of this even as a possibility.

This question of interest goes back to the relation of feeling to reality. As Prof Whitehead says, the insistence in the Platonic culture on disinterested intellectual appreciation is a psychological error. But there is the still graver objection that it is also an objective error. We cannot know without interest. But is there not an interesting world to be known, which is the interest of some other mind before it can be ours? All life, at all events, has dealt with the world only by interest, and the world does not seem to have responded to anything else all down the ages. And to the higher interests of truth and beauty and goodness it has responded most. Even the scientist, to quote Prof. Whitehead again, is a kind of artist, sustained in his labours by the ideal of finish and perfection in his work. And, on the lowest grounds of utility, science would have no uses were there no validity beyond the mere mechanical world which science has been supposed to prove to be alone real.

A further reason for the need of interest for any study is that, if we have not the right interest, we introduce interests, which, being alien, are certain to be misleading.

This is true of every subject. Science, when there is no interest in knowledge for its own sake, comes to be regarded as a mere commercial or military asset; poetry, when the true interest of imagination is wanting, is judged as epigram, rhetoric or philosophy; art, when there is no interest in beauty, is esteemed only as decoration or as an evidence of wealth. But, of all subjects, religion is most confused by lack of its own interest, because almost any interest can be dragged into it, till it comes to be treated as a quasi-science or a popular philosophy or as a buttress for morality.

Rationalism, for example, conceived religion mainly as an intellectual affair of evidences about God as the maker of the world, and providence as the direction of it, and immortality as compensation for its injustices and imperfections. The reason was not that religion ever seemed anything of the sort to those really interested in it, but that interest in religion was replaced by interest in scientific discussion, which, in that age, was the one dominating interest. Art, for example, fared no better than religion.

Because religion is often studied by persons who are better equipped intellectually than religiously, this danger of introducing intellectual interest illegitimately is always with us.

It is a danger of the same kind as criticism is for poetry, when it proceeds as if criticism were poetry.

But interest in mere intellectual evidence is not the only misleading interest in the study of religion. In our day there are two ways of regarding religion which seem to be utterly unlike the old Rationalism, and to be wholly anti-intellectual. The one is the study of psychology and the other of history, especially the history of primitive religion.

It was not left to our time to discover that the proper study of mankind is man, but in our time this study has moved from the consideration of the mind in its normal and logical functioning to the study of life-impulses, instincts and complexes, with a tendency to concentrate on the non-rational, and to emphasise the abnormal. Religion, because it magnifies the defects as well as the virtues of human nature, offers large scope for this kind of psychology, which, by the selective working of its special interest, tends to revive an old view of religion as due to mental characteristics of a rather morbid practical type. But in religion, as in all else, we ought to distinguish what belongs to it as such from what is merely imported into it by the imperfections of human nature. Nothing that has so central a place in man's life and has played so large a part in his history can be due purely to what is abnormal in man's mind. No more in religion than in anything else is there justification for ascribing to it in particular what is due to human nature in general. But this means an interest in religion itself and not merely in matters connected with it.

Yet the real cause of a view of religion which makes it all explicable by a certain kind of psychology is still due to the substitution of scientific for religious interest. Religion is not found to be what Rationalism thought it, but there is still the same idea, that, if it deals with any objective reality, it ought to be· so that while the psychology is not rationalistic, the psychologist still is.

The same is true of a view of religion which makes it all explicable by primitive ideas. The reasoning is that, as most primitive ideas have religious associations, and primitive ideas are outlived ideas, therefore religion is outlived ideas. Here again, while the history is not rationalistic, the historian is, for it rests on the rationalist view that all religion, as Sir James Frazer expresses it, is just 'theories of thought'.

True interest in religion, as in any other subject, should start with a sense of the importance of positive, constructive knowledge of it. This a study which is purely external, negative and critical resents, but if the Supernatural should happen to be an actual environment, and interest in it central for man's mind and the driving force in his history, we ought to be supremely and positively interested in it, and, for a right study of it, lack of interest is bias of the most obstructive kind.

(b) THE INSUFFICIENCY OF THE TEST OF INTEREST

But, while in religion, no more than in any other subject, is right interest bias, or indifference love of the truth, interest only approves itself when it is ready to spare no pains in seeking truth. Interest even in religion cannot justify itself merely by appealing to its own value, for the value of any interest is in the reality and importance of its object.

In respect of religion, more than any other subject, we can say that, without the right interest and attitude of mind, all attempts to distinguish its sphere by definition or description are vain. Yet it does not follow that, with them, discussion can serve no purpose and that the labour of attempting to define or at least to describe its sphere can be escaped. Even if we could show that all theories of religion have depended on the attitudes and interests of the minds that produced them, there is still the question of the right attitude and the right interest: and in any case it would not deliver us from the necessity of discussing what religion really is. It will not suffice to say with Runze: Have a soul at peace with itself, and be responsive to the high things of life, and you will know what religion really is and what it is not, because the vast differences of opinion which have been held by serious and able workers in this field, to the great confusion of understanding and co-operation, cannot be thus easily settled.

In the first place, neither could we determine when this condition of right interest and high response is fulfilled, nor could we bring our differences to the test of it, even if we had it. Therefore, it matters not how unsatisfactory the long discussion may have been, we cannot escape the necessity of continuing it and making the best of it. Unfortunately, in this troubled life, tasks are usually necessary in proportion as they are difficult.

In the second place, the difficulty of riding the marches is, as a matter of fact, not as great, either theoretically or practically, as Runze affirms, because, while it is true that there is only one world known in our experience, it is equally true that, the more we see the world as one, the sharper are the distinctions we draw in it; and the more we bring it within the unity of our thought, the more definitely we distinguish one part of our knowledge from the rest. All advance in experience, knowledge and thought has meant discrimination and differentiation. If we see the closer relations of things, we also have a deeper sense of the reality, significance and independence of the things themselves, so that, however we may conceive them to be in one universe, it may not be by the easy process of shunning the drawing of clear distinctions. Religion too is no less something apart at any stage because it is so intimately related to our whole world without and within· and it also becomes more clearly differentiated with progress. Both in practice and in theory it has, with the process of time, been ever more clearly distinguished from other concerns.

In primitive beliefs and practices it is difficult to say what is religious, and it is almost impossible to say what is not. Yet the extremest difficulty of the task cannot save us from trying to distinguish even primitive religion from primitive science, or magic, or social custom On the contrary, the greater the confusion, the more an attempt to bring clear distinctions into it is necessary. But, as mankind advances, it becomes plainer that religion has its own sphere, and that, though it touches, ever more widely, all aspects of human life, it does so in a way which is quite distinct from the ways of science or philosophy or social custom or even magic. It ought, therefore, to be possible to distinguish the sphere of religion, if not by such a mark as would be a definition, yet by such characteristics as would set it apart from all else.

Finally, even supposing that the confusion were so great throughout, that, from first to last, it seemed impossible to discover any mark by which religion might be defined or any description which would include all religious phenomena and exclude all non-religious, a discussion of the problem would be the more necessary. When we differ because we are not all considering the same object, the mere discussion of our differences at least helps to turn our attention in the same direction, even if it do not at once determine what is to be seen.

The sphere even of natural science is not so determined by scientific interest as to make discussion of it unnecessary. More recently there has, as a matter of fact, been a great deal of discussion which cannot be thought to have been superfluous. To the casual thinker, physics, for example, seems to be a science of the things of sense, at once taking them naively as we perceive them and displaying a deeper reality than we perceive. But to the philosophical scientist it is plain that physics abstracts both from the changing incidents of nature and from the mind which experiences them. It is far from being finally determined what this may mean of restriction in the sphere of natural science, yet the discussion of the problem has been of great value, because it has helped to clear away misunderstandings which have long been misleading dogmas.

Granting that the sphere of religion is less definite than the sphere of physical objects, and that the study of it touches, at more points, the whole world of human interests, and that its sphere is, therefore, still more difficult to distinguish than the sphere of natural science, so much the more is it imperative to distinguish as clearly as we can, and to discuss any reasons there may be which hinder our further progress in definiteness.

For example, the Evangelical Movement, by its interest in

religion itself, realised much more in it than was possible for the merely intellectual interest of Rationalism, yet it was a weakness in Evangelicalism, the gravity of which the years have increasingly shown, that it merely dismissed as human perversity the problems of Rationalism. Rationalism was limited by its special interest, yet the problems it raised remain: and still, even if its view of religion be wrong, it is more profitable to find objective reasons for this conclusion, than to dispose of it easily as a mere error of an alien interest. Theories of religion as psychological illusion we might, in view of what religion is and all it has done, feel ourselves still freer to dismiss as due to lack of interest. Yet, here also, we may not answer merely by setting up one contempt against another, for the good reason, even were there no other, that from those with whom we most differ we usually learn most, and especially in religion. Religion, though the last subject on which men exercise forbearance, is the first that requires it: and, as an essential part of this forbearance, we must discuss our differences about its nature as well as about its grounds, as purely objectively as we can.

(c) JUSTIFICATION OF THE INQUIRY

Without interest in a subject, it is impossible to maintain the sustained application necessary for understanding it. The right use of interest, however, is not as a substitute, but as an inspiration for this application. From lack of it, conscientious laborious investigation in this department has, in our day, rather fallen into disrepute, and any other kind of knowledge, from biology to business, is taken to be better equipment. Religion would seem to have come to the state in which we lay hold of a brother who has any kind of intellectual clothing and say: 'Let this ruin be under thy hand'. That it needs to be under someone's hand we must admit; and we must also admit that the graver inquiries often require a more laboured attention than such interest as exists could be expected to provide. Few studies more amply illustrate the saying of Horace Walpole: "How dull one may be, if only he will take pains for six or seven and twenty years together": and this may be only another example. Moreover, there may be special studies in any subject which so narrow attention as to make it impossible to see the wood for the trees, and religion is no exception. Here also the specialist is sometimes as narrow as he is dull. It may be unfair that this should be more resented in the study of religion than in the study of any other subject, but it has this justification, that religion is every man's business and nothing human should be alien to it. For the study of religion, therefore, to blear one's eyes with the dust of books may be a dehumanising process of a specially disqualifying kind. And no doubt it would be better to hear men who have met life in the spirit of high adventure in the field of action, rather than those whose adventure has been mainly in the field of thought and learning. But, though such persons may very vigorously concern themselves with the living of religion, they do not occupy themselves with the study of it. Therefore we have to do our best with the student who does, by making allowance for his intellectual bias.

Yet the only compensation for the limitation of the student is that his studies have been applied to the subject in hand, and that he has used books to enlarge experience, not as a substitute. In this study, as in others, it is true what a wise Greek has said, that "Not to know what was done in the world before we were born is always to remain a child". Therefore we may not dismiss lightly anyone who has thought religion to deserve and require the highest interest, and who has accordingly given it his most serious and diligent attention, even if we have reason to believe him wrong, because, even if he has interpreted his experience wrongly, it does not follow that there is nothing in his experience or even that he has shed no light on its interpretation. As Copernicus did not arrive at a better explanation of the movement of the heavenly bodies by dismissing all the astronomers had said about it and all their theories of it, but by understanding and using both more effectively than others, so we ought to know and, if possible, understand better what has been done

Respect for our subject and respect for those who have studied it are both necessary, and the many studies of religion which are conspicuously marked by the absence of both are somewhat on the same level of value as a report on the natives of South Africa by a sailor who, having seen them in a seaport, dismisses them all as 'niggers'.

Yet, with the best equipment, we cannot hope to set religion in any clear light, unless we distinguish what belongs to it as such from all that may be found mixed up with it, any more than the qualities of gold can appear, undistinguished from alloy. The same human nature works in religion as in all else. Yet, in religion, as in all else, we ought to distinguish what belongs to it as such from what is merely imported into it by imperfect human nature.

Just because religion, like every human concern, depends upon human nature, there is bad religion as well as good. But this does not justify us in ascribing to religion in particular the evil that is due to human nature in general.

Class opinion, for example, and even mass passions have often assumed the authority of religion, just as they have assumed the authority of patriotism. But, as in politics we distinguish good government from graft and wire-pulling, so in religion we ought to distinguish what is genuine from what is mere corruption. Our study of religion should be wide enough to include both. As, in a study of politics, Abraham Lincoln and Boss Croker should be included as politicians, so in a study of religion St Francis and the Grand Inquisitor should be included as religious men. But in neither case ought it to be without distinction. Devotion to the Church as a state—which is not really different from devotion to any other impressive visible institution—does not belong to religion in the same way as devotion to the poor and ignorant, any more than the employment of corruption and wire-pulling for party ends—which is in essence the same as any kind of selfish business—belongs to the conduct of government in the same way as courageous self-sacrifice for a high patriotic purpose.

A vast number of dubious intents and practices profess to

be religion, and our conception of religion must be hospitable enough to include them, just as a vast number of doubtful principles and deeds profess to be politics, and our study of politics must not be too prudish to admit them. Nay, it is in the highest degree necessary to keep it constantly before us that religion, like all else, suffers from the imperfections, weaknesses and errors of human nature, and that, in consequence, there is bad religion as there is bad business or bad science or bad morals. Nothing gives more unreality to the study of the subject than forgetfulness of this fact and the expectation that everything claiming the name of religion ought to be admirable and capable of being defended. Yet as we should realise the ideal originally expressed in the term politics, so we ought to have a standard of what is genuinely and normally and rightly religion. Or, if a standard prove to be too exact a measure to obtain, we must still face the question and do our best to answer it of what religion ought to be, as well as of what it is. But to do this, we must not ignore what it is, or forget that, as mankind deals with it, it is, like all our higher environment, opportunity for abuse as well as use. This is no disproof of its reality, yet the way in which it is misused may shed light upon the kind of reality it is.

CHAPTER II

THE SEAT OF RELIGION

IN order that we may not simplify our task by the easy process of narrowing its scope, we shall take Windelband's account of the manifestations of religion.

"In the first place, religion is a life within, a transaction of the soul; and as such embraces all the psychical functions. It is not only an idea, a discerning and knowing, or, if we speak critically, an opinion, a conviction, but also a consciousness of worth, a feeling, a sense of being taken possession of and of self-surrender, and further, in accord therewith, a willing and accomplishing.

"From this it follows that it is also a life without, not only an acting according to the particular values of feeling and will, but as a complete manifestation of that inward life, as ritual and worship.

"Therewith it oversteps the limit of the individual life and appears as a doing of the community, as a social phenomenon, historically conditioned, and embodied in real institutions as an external organisation.

"And religion will be yet more than all this that is empirically given. It always reaches beyond the earthly experience, being a relation to higher powers, to the inmost nature and ground of all reality, a life with God and in God—a metaphysical life."[1]

The substance of this is that religion is (1) an attitude of the spirit—a reverence and a trust, (2) a cult—an adoration and worship, (3) a social bond—an organising force, (4) a concern with the Supernatural—in some sense a theology.

Three criticisms may be made. First, these aspects are never really apart. Discerning and knowing within, for example, cannot be separated from a relation to higher powers without.

---

[1] *Praeludien*, 2nd edit. p. 357.

Second, the creation of religious institutions is not the only or even the most important social effect of religion. Finally, a metaphysical life is not one point among others, but is what qualifies all the rest.

Yet equally great objections might be found to any other description: and, for our immediate purpose, these defects are rather virtues, because practically all attempts to find a mark common to all religious phenomena, and not applicable to anything else, emphasise one or other of these aspects as central and distinctive. We shall, however, take religion as a cult and as a social bond together because, though quite different theories have been based on them, both are social.

(a) RELIGION AS A MENTAL STATE

While the tendency has been more and more to deny that there is any distinctive power of the human mind specially concerned with religion, more and more the characteristic mark of religion has been sought in a special mental attitude. Attention is directed to motive rather than to practice, to the manner of believing rather than to the object of belief.

In support of this view it is argued, first, that the inward marks of a religious spirit must be simpler and more certain than any property common to the amazing and multitudinous variety of outward forms, and, second, and more important, that a person's worship may be a form, his ecclesiastical connexion an accident, and the object of his belief a tradition, and that they are religious only as they express his faith or piety or some similar inward state.

The first argument is that the inward marks of religion are clearer and more definite than its external manifestations and beliefs. But this does not seem to be borne out by facts. At no time has there ever been much more agreement about the essential nature of faith or piety than about the essential nature of the outward manifestations of religion or its objects of belief. Even on so elementary a question as the department of the mind to which religion is to be assigned, opinions have been as different as the possibilities of the case allow.

Nor has this been through haste or shallowness, for the most earnest and profound thinkers have radically disagreed. Kant held religion to be essentially belief in the reality and sovereignty of the moral order, and, therefore, to be dependent, in the last resort, upon a right attitude of the will. Schleiermacher denied that such an appendage to morality was of the nature of real religion at all, and found the sphere of religion in piety, which he described as a feeling of dependence that is absolute because it places us in immediate relation to the absolute, universal, final reality. Hegel rejected both views and regarded religion as intellectual exaltation into the region of eternal truth. Thus Kant placed religion in the sphere of will, Schleiermacher of feeling, and Hegel of reason. Such wide divergence between thinkers so serious and profound does not encourage the hope that the essential mark of religion will be easier to discover in the peculiar quality of religion in the soul than in its manifold outward manifestations; and, in point of fact, the question of what belongs to religion in history has never received quite such divergent answers as the question of what belongs to religion in psychology.

These three theories exhaust the possibilities, because there is no fourth aspect of mind. But, seeing that ethics rules in the first, aesthetics in the second, and logic in the third, if we could reduce religion to any aspect of mind, we should have made it subordinate either to logic or ethics or aesthetics.

A way out has been sought by making the essential quality of religion to be the employment of all our powers.

The first form of this view is to be found in the statement of James that religion is our total reaction upon life.[1] But if we might argue that this is what religion ought to be, we certainly could not maintain that it is what everything usually accepted as religious, or even every genuinely religious frame of mind, always is. Nothing less than our whole outlook upon everything is our total reaction upon life. From this relation of our whole selves to our whole environment religion, of course, cannot escape; and we may go farther and say that our religion

[1] William James, *The Varieties of Religious Experience*, p. 35.

is identified with ourselves and concerned with our whole experience in a way nothing else in our experience is. This doubtless is highly important, and suggests weighty matter for the study of religion: and James himself did not mean more. But, as an account of religion, it has all the defects of not covering the subject, of being applicable beyond it, and of being a test impossible to apply.

First, there is a great deal of religion, and that the most genuine, which is a very specialised kind of reaction to a very special kind of reality, with a conscious and deliberate limitation of itself to wait on its particular ministry. Second, for many, and these not always non-religious, the wholeness of their experience is often connected with other experiences than their religion, their religion having rather the contrary effect. Third, it is not a test we could apply to anyone's religion except our own, for how are we to determine who fulfils the condition? And even to apply it to our own would require a self-knowledge not granted to the children of men. Nor would this be the end, for, if we could decide that our reaction was total, we should still have to ask whether it was to a properly representative reality, because religious reality, even if it be not all reality, seems to be a much greater matter than what occupies the attention of most people. We, therefore, come in the end, not to the totality of our reaction but to the question of the particular kind of reality to which we react, which is to say that the essential quality of religion is an objective reference.

The other form of this generalising view of religious faith is that it is the harmony of all our powers. Though different in form, this theory is an attempt to express the same truth about religion, that it is very widely concerned with experience and touches our minds in many ways. This theory also is probably rather a judgment of what religion ought to be than a definition of what it is: and religion no doubt is the spring of all efforts after harmony both in our souls and in our world. But, while this may be a matter of moment in the study of religion, as a mark of religion it could only be useful to minds more anxious to shun excess than to understand enthusiasm. As a psychological mark, who is to say when the powers of mind are in harmonious balance? And if we succeeded, would not a vast amount of very vital religion be excluded? And with this care about the balance of our powers, would what remained be particularly religious?

Probably both theories are determined by the same idea, which is not so much to find a mark of religion, as to discover a standard of validity: and what they set forth is the view that we have a right to believe in anything which has on its side our whole experience and which we have tested with all our powers. This is important in its own place, but it is not a mark by which we can distinguish religion. Rather it is a confession of inability to find any special aspect of mind which would serve as a test. Thus it also directs attention to the objective reality with which religion deals as the essential mark of religion, and away from anything that is merely in the mind.

The second argument is that the essential quality of religion belongs to the soul that cherishes it, because no kind of religious belief would be of any religious value unless it were entertained by a conviction of a peculiar quality, and no rite truly religious except as it is done with piety.

This dependence of religion on what we may describe generally as piety is not only to be admitted, but cannot be too much emphasised. Even in studying the religions of the past, we ought not to be content with the mere outward relics, but should try to realise what inward forms of faith and trust they expressed, and know that if, as in most cases, the monuments left to us embalm only the outward forms from which the spirit has fled, we do not recover the religion.

But, while nothing is so utterly a mockery as a religion which has no reality of the spirit, this dependence for its reality on the response it evokes in the heart is not so unique as to be a distinctive mark of religion, because there are other things which are equally dead if they are mere outward forms. Nothing is really truth for us except as it is our own conviction, or beauty for us except as we truly perceive and feel it, or goodness except as it is good to our own insight. Truth, without our conviction of its truth, would be mere facts in an encyclopaedia; and morality, without our own conscience of right, mere rules of good form. Nevertheless, the special quality of truth is to be objectively valid, and of goodness to be concerned with the actual moral order. And, in the same way, the special quality of religion is to be concerned with what is regarded not merely as real, but as the ultimate reality; and this is in no way altered by the importance of our personal relation to it.

Ritschl's view, that religion is concerned with the maintenance of the worth of the personal spirit against mere extension and mass, might seem to find the special character of religion in its significance for the whole personality, and this as an inward experience. But he himself states that the essential concern of religion is with the world and the working, in the world or above it, of the exalted spiritual powers for this victory of the personal over the mere course of nature and the natural forces of society.[1]

There is one way, however, which would seem at first sight to make the essential seat of religion our own mind, which is the radical denial that it has any other reality than subjective ideas and emotions. If the whole idea of spiritual powers concerned with the value of our spirits is a pure illusion, a mere straw man has clutched at in his terror at going down in the whirling, turbid flood of irresistible events, which will ultimately swallow him up with all else, must not the only mark left be in the mind?

But, even were religion all illusion, the matter would not be settled. We should still have to ask what distinguishes religion from other illusions: and this must be sought in what is believed and not in the way of believing. To believe what we desire is not in any way confined to the religious sphere, nor

---

[1] "In all religions man seeks, by the aid of the exalted spiritual power he reveres, the solution of the contradiction in which he finds himself as part of the natural world and as spiritual personality claiming to rule it." Ritschl, *Die Lehre von der Rechtfertigung*, 3rd ed vol. III, p. 189.

does it work there differently from anywhere else. Therefore, illusion cannot be, in any special way, a mark of religion.

The views of religion as illusion, moreover, have all the psychological differences of the views of it as reality. In some theories, religion is intellectual error about gods; in others, emotional error about our hopes; in others, practical illusion from the struggle for existence. We have, therefore, still the old difficulties about the particular place religion occupies in the mind: and in none of them is illusion, as mere psychology, different from illusion about anything else. In all the theories alike, it is the objective reference which is characteristic; and that cannot be determined psychologically.

(b) RELIGION AS A SOCIAL PHENOMENON

A more concrete and definite mark than anything in the unseen, either in man's heart or in the universe, would be some rite or institution or sphere of action, what broadly we might call an ecclesiastical mark. So satisfactory would it be that, in spite of the certainty that religion may be one thing and its rites another, more recently the observance of some kind of worship or cult has been regarded as the distinctive characteristic of religion. For example, it has been argued that there is no common element in all forms of Christianity except that Jesus has been the centre of all forms of its cults, and that, so long as this continue, Christianity will remain, in spite of all its variety, one religion. And this importance of the ritual could be maintained with still more certainty for other religions, such as Confucianism or Brahmanism.

But, even if the cult could be regarded as the mark of a particular religion, it could not, by any narrowing of the meaning of the word, be made to exclude all that is not religious. There are elements in many cults which are mere social traditions. Still less can it, by any stretching of the meaning of the word, be made to include all that is religious. There have been beliefs which have been the more religious for remaining a secret of the heart, except in so far as they may work a visible change in the believer, and there are practices which have been the more religious for turning attention from public ceremonies to common human relations. The most conspicuous example in history is the religion of the Hebrew prophets, who constantly declared that a religion marked only by the cult was mere profane trampling God's courts, and who made no attempt to replace the existing cult by a better, but declared that true religion was to do justly and love mercy and to walk humbly with one's God. Nor, though Jesus visited the synagogue and the temple, can it be said that his religion had much to do with either. In face of these examples to the contrary, it cannot be, as has been maintained, that what makes doctrines religious and not merely philosophical, and practices religious and not merely ethical, is their relation to the cult.

Just as little can we find the mark in any social embodiment. The farther back we go the more religion is embodied in rites and is a social function, and the more its sphere is a visible political group and not a fellowship determined by belief in things unseen. But, in more advanced religions, even the most spiritual church could not comprehend all the essentials of religion. Besides, the church then is largely an idea which itself depends on the idea of religion.

These views of the central significance of the cult and the society have been emphasised by recent theories which explain, or rather explain away, all religion by them. The gods are regarded as mass ideas generated by congregationalised emotion in the cults, which originally were mere festive doings; or the emphasis is laid on the wider and more orderly influence of society, which is said so to impress its mind upon men as sacred as to be the essential element of all religion.

But, first of all, even if the true origin of religion were in either or both, it would be no guide to determine what are religious phenomena and what are not. And, in the second place, it matters not how the beliefs arise, the distinctive religious element is a belief in gods or at least in a sacred reality which is not human society.

All these theories, therefore, direct attention away from

merely psychological or social marks of religion. Quite as clearly by regarding it as illusion as by regarding it as the ultimate reality, they show that the essential quality of religion is the claim to deal with a special kind of environment, which has its own particular sanctions. If this environment do not exist, religion has no basis. And, even so, it would not be a mere psychological state to be described as illusion, but would be a wrong objective reference, due to misunderstanding, not about our own minds, but about our environment, so that it ought rather to be described as delusion. Wherefore, any theory of religion as illusion brings us to the view of religion as essentially a dealing with an unseen environment of absolute worth, which demands worship If this environment were proved to be non-existent, religion would be shown to be baseless, but its essential character would still depend on this supposed objective reference and not on some peculiar quality of belief, or pious feeling, or practical trust. And, as it is the same human nature which deals with all environment, if the environment do not exist we should the less expect anything peculiar in man's way of dealing with it, because, while every real higher environment stirs higher faculties and affords larger opportunities for displaying them, an imaginary one cannot be the source of a development of a peculiar quality of belief, feeling or even practical trust.

(c) RELIGION AS THEOLOGY

Our discussion so far has tended to show that, whether this environment be real or not, religion is an affirmation of what we may call broadly the Supernatural, and that its quality is determined by this outward reference and not by any particular kind of subjective feeling or attitude, while its validity wholly depends on whether such an invisible world exists or not.

But, if this question of validity must be supreme, it might seem that we are brought so near to the Rationalist view of religion, as a matter of evidences for the existence of God, providence, and immortality, that the difference would not be worth discussing. Where difference does exist, the advantage might even appear to be on the side of a theory which states what its Supernatural is and establishes the existence of it by inference from the Natural. And undoubtedly we have, in its insistence that the essential question about religion concerns its truth, the reason why the Rationalist view of religion has been so widely held and why it endures to this day: for unless the object of religion is real, nay, the ultimate reality, religion is a vain and most unnecessarily distressing illusion. Moreover, Rationalism was right in insisting that this question may not be evaded, and also that we may not escape the demand to answer it for ourselves: and it was wrong only in its view of how the task is to be carried out.

If we had to fix upon any one particular object of belief as the mark of religion, it would necessarily be belief in gods or divine beings; for, in most religions, this belief occupies a large place. But, in spite of the fact that many theories accept it as the distinctive mark of religion, it is not universal in religion, and much less is it inclusive of all that is religious.

If we keep strictly to the idea of gods as personal beings, there is at all events one religion without it. Primitive Buddhism replaced at least all effective idea of gods by a rigid law of requital: and we may not exclude a religion which has claimed so many adherents for so long a time. Nor can we include all the objects of worship in other religions under the conception of personal gods or even of their dwelling-places. Yet, on the other hand, should we define gods more vaguely as unseen powers, while our definition would then cover all religion, it would include much else. Magic is also belief in unseen powers, and mere magic has been distinguished from religion by the most profoundly religious persons from the Hebrew prophets onwards. Further, there is a wide range of belief in vague unseen influences, such as have recently been called the 'numinous', which may be merely the 'spooky' and have no necessary connexion with religion.

Providence and Immortality—the other two beliefs in the Deist Triad—would seem at first sight to have still less promise than belief in gods. The most spiritual of ancient religions—Prophetic Judaism—made no use of the doctrine of immortality, and certainly did not conceive it after the manner of Deism. Also, the deistic providence, as manifest benevolent management of the world, no religion has ever found. Yet we could interpret both ideas in a way to make them universal elements, not indeed in all religion, but at least in all religions. All religions are concerned with a reality not subject to time's destruction and contempt, like the things seen. Even the most primitive religions have a belief in souls which links man's hope to this reality and connects religion with the unseen and eternal. Finally, while no higher religion is optimistic, in the sense of finding the world obviously well and benevolently ruled, all concern themselves with the problem of the order and rule of the world, and seek to discover wise, righteous, good and permanent ends by which its immediately unreliable and distressing course may be interpreted. In the higher religions this last is a central interest; and some dim groping, some feeling after a deeper interpretation than the immediate convenience or inconvenience of what happens, if not yet a considered idea, is manifest even in the lowest fetishism. From this it might be argued that, wheresoever this victory over the world is sought, and not evaded as in early Buddhism, God becomes the supreme mark of religion. Whereupon it might further be maintained, as has been done, that Primitive Buddhism was not a religion but a rationalising ethical society, and that its failure to meet the real religious needs only resulted in a revival of the most superstitious ideas about divine beings and their operations. Then everything concerned with religion might, by generous interpretation, be included under some aspect of these three beliefs.

But in no religion is any of these beliefs an inference from the seen, a conclusion proved logically from the world of the senses. Deism, following this method, only arrived at (1) God as the creator or rather manufacturer of the world, and moral governor or rather Lord Chief Justice; (2) providence as a very skilful designer of a benevolent mind, who, the better he had done his work at the beginning, the less he had to interfere with it—all his dealings after creation being interference; (3) immortality as the necessary court of assize, of which a morality depending on reward and punishment stood very much in need, but by which it was only made less moral.

Seeing that we can now start from a somewhat less mechanical and more flexible view of the world, we might arrive at something a little freer and more expansive than this. But it would have just as little to do with anything mankind has ever really experienced as religion; and, moreover, our greater freedom would be more than counterbalanced by our greater uncertainty.

On this view, it should follow that, when we rationalise most, belief in God is best proved; that, when things go best with us, we are surest of providence; that, when we are most dissatisfied with the rewards of our goodness, we look with most confidence for the future award. But no religion, even when it holds these beliefs, ever has arrived at them or continued to hold them by this way of argument from the beneficence and justice of the world, or by inference from a happy state, or by an assurance that our virtue deserves reward. On the contrary, the moment they become mere reasoned, comfortable or self-approving conclusions, they cease to be specially religious

Of this view of religion we can say, that it is both farther away than the others from any appreciation of what religion really is, and nearer to the heart of the question. The basis of religion, whatever it may be, is not intellectual argument. Yet religion is an illusion, unless it has an objective reality which has a witness convincing to ourselves, and not merely heard of from others. If, in the meantime, we take the Natural to be what appeals to our senses, and the Supernatural to be what is above it, we can say that the essential mark of religion is concern with whether there is such an environment as the Supernatural, and that what at least religion ought to be depends on what the nature of this environment is. The question of religion, therefore, is a question, not merely of reality, but of the ultimate reality.

If we look more closely at the theories of religion as essentially of reason or feeling or will, which have been considered above, we shall see that there is one point on which they are agreed. They are metaphysical and not merely psychological. They ask how environment is known, and the presupposition of them all is, that it is not by arguing from something else, but that the ultimate reality is known by what is the really creative element in all knowledge.

This, as a matter of fact, is the only point on which Kant, Schleiermacher, and Hegel are agreed. The difference in their opinions about the seat of religion in the soul is as complete as the possibilities admit, seeing that there is only intellect, feeling, or will to which it could be ascribed. But they are at one in seeking religion where they think they discern the creative element in experience, so that their real divergence is not first about religion, but about how ultimate reality touches the human spirit, because for all alike the intercourse with the universe which creates all our experience is, so to speak, a religious intercourse.

Schleiermacher definitely held this view. The universe is a great aesthetic unity all of which touches us in the creative moment before intuition divides into thought and feeling. We may call this intuition feeling, because feeling is the stem, yet it is not feeling in the sense of conscious emotion, but is that moment before consciousness divides into thought and action which is the contact between the universe as one and the soul as one. This is so essentially a religious intercourse that religion would naturally develop out of it, alongside of the reality which comes in by this channel, were not the progress arrested by false worldly prudences. To say generally that, for Schleiermacher, religion is feeling is to miss his central conviction, which is that religion has its source in the peculiar feeling or intuition which is the contact with the universe that creates all experience of reality.

Hegel, though denouncing Schleiermacher's view as a confusing of religion with mere personal emotions, does not really differ from him in relating it to the creative element in experience. For Hegel this is reason, as the channel of the universal reason, which thinks in us and through us. Philosophy is the highest and purest manifestation, but religion also is philosophy, even if it be in popular and picture form; and its task, too, is to emancipate the spirit from the merely individual, and to show, amid the changing shadows of time, the calm and steady sunshine of the eternal light.

Kant is somewhat less definite in stating this relation of religion to the creative source of experience, but it is quite as deeply embedded in his theory. The necessary forms of the theoretical reason, he held, are imposed by itself, and, therefore, may not be valid beyond its own ordering of phenomena, but the real world is the world of freedom, which approves itself to us as we deal with it in freedom by obedience to our own moral reason. And to this world of reality, this realm of free moral ends, religion belongs, and indeed its reality is one with the existence of such a realm.

All these theories, therefore, though ascribing radically different origins to religion in the mind, agree in seeking them where reality manifests itself to us. Their views of what religion is also differ with the seat to which they ascribe it, yet all agree that it is, or ought to be, victory and peace through providing for us a right relation to the ultimate reality. For Kant this reality is the moral order, for Schleiermacher the artistic harmony of the universe, for Hegel the cosmic process of reason: but, for all, it is that which is absolute in its claim, and, for all, religion is the recognition of this claim and, through it, is emancipation from the fluctuating values of sense, and victory over all that is changing and accidental.

CHAPTER III

THEORIES OF RELIGION AS ILLUSION

IN contrast to the view that where we touch reality we have intercourse with the Supernatural, we have theories which seek to show how, from the very nature of the human mind determined mainly by its history, the illusion of such an environment arises. As nothing shows more fully the universality of belief in the Supernatural and the extent to which mankind has lived in the power of such a belief, we might be content with the practical answer, that, if this is unreal, nothing else can be proved real. But, if we go a little deeper, we can see that these theories raise negatively the relation of our knowledge of the Natural to the Supernatural, as Kant, Schleiermacher and Hegel raised it positively.

What professes to find in psychology the ground for regarding the object of religion as illusion is a negative objective conclusion about the existence of an outside reality, which must go as much beyond a mere consideration of purely mental states as the most positive. This is made plain by the fact that there is no psychological difference from the theories which maintain that it is the ultimate reality. The former are of the same types and naturally divide on the same principle as the latter. Thus we have intellectualist types like Hegel's, emotional types like Schleiermacher's, and volitional types like Kant's. The only difference is that, instead of ascribing religion to what is ultimate in mind, they ascribe it to aberration; instead of ascribing it to the primary, creative contact with the universe, they ascribe it to delusions wrought by our individual feelings; instead of ascribing it to a realm of free moral ends, they ascribe it to self-interested practical prepossessions. The older thinkers took this question to be metaphysics, and, seeing that the sole difference concerns validity, which plainly must depend on what is presented to the mind, and not on the mind's mere mode of acting, it cannot at least be merely psychology.

(a) THEORIES OF THE HEGELIAN TYPE

All theories which explain away religion as a mere primitive stage in man's intellectual development are of this rationalist type. The general idea is that religion is a kind of science, and we have only to show that, judged by the method of modern science, it is primitive and anthropomorphic science, to prove its world to be utterly unreal.

The general type is fairly well represented by Comte's view of the order of human progress. First, when the happenings of the world were thought to be purely accidental, they were ascribed to the caprices and interferences of personal beings like men themselves, only more powerful. Religion is thus a theory of gods, which, though man's earliest view of his environment, is explained by his thoughts about himself. Second, after the idea of some kind of order had arisen, the religious stage was followed by the metaphysical, which explained the world on abstract mental and rational principles. Third, with the discovery of the fixed order of events, metaphysics gave way to science. As its explanation by mechanical sequence is the final method, this is the final stage.

Few theories have ever been enunciated more pontifically: and this rests on the confidence that it is a true history of the mind, or what in our day is called a genetic psychology. First, man transfers his own will into his world; second, he imposes his own abstractions upon his world; and only after failing in both does he proceed to learn from his world But what is really done is to make the method of the Newtonian physics the measure of reality. Were this a true and complete cosmology there would be no place for anything in nature above motion or for minds that could have the least concern even with motion. But men still continue to ask whether reality, in the last resort, is rational or merely mechanical, and whether even scientists could get along without the freedom and purpose they find it convenient to ignore. In our day, moreover, the idea that physics either proves or presupposes any such cosmology is as antiquated as primitive anthropomorphism itself.

The same criticism applies to all the other explanations of religion as mental illusion. They all end in the same way, not with the psychological proof they promise, but with a world measured by the Newtonian physics and a mind which is the pure product of history, usually interpreted by the Darwinian theory of evolution.

Two more recent forms of the theories of illusion are still more akin to Hegel's determination of the whole process of reality by the process of mind. But, while Hegel starts from the assumption that at least what is universal in the mind gives real knowledge and that the standards of truth and beauty and goodness are of universal validity, these theories profess to show that there is a mechanism of mind which creates a sort of mirage of the Supernatural. Hegel took his view to be a necessary presupposition of all thinking about reality, but, if error can be part of the mind's normal functioning, this would still be a metaphysical question, with the only difference that there would then be little use discussing metaphysics or anything else.

Yet, just because they raise this question of mind as the functioning of a certain organism which has been developed among other organisms by the age-long working of the struggle for survival, it is necessary to deal with them at greater length than their intrinsic merit would by itself justify.

Any psychology which enters into the matter at all is after the pattern of Wundt's theory, that the effort to know is mainly an exercise of the imagination, making sympathetic transference of ourselves into the object. Religion, it is held, merely makes this process complete by ascribing to the universe a personality.

Such a psychology by itself proves nothing about any reality, unless it be some justification for assuming that there must be something of personal quality in a world which so fully responds to our sympathetic transference of ourselves into it. But the denial extends to the reality of the ascription of personality even to ourselves, beyond the mere functioning of a unified organism.

The first theory is A. E. Crawley's. He attacks the central citadel, by trying to show that all belief in a soul is a sort of double of its ideas made by mind in its ordinary working.[1]

Soul, he says, is nothing in the world except the memory-image of the object. All knowledge depends on the retention of perceptions: and this has been greatly forwarded by the vitalising of the images of them into ghosts. By this process the mere gold-dust of experience was coined and stamped and hoarded and used for exchange. Thus the notion of the soul has been the creator of all knowledge, and not alone of religion. It is, to use another figure, the necessary scaffolding for building man's experience, which we have now built high enough to be able to take down. But religion, as it were, sticks to this scaffolding and is nothing else. In religion soul continues to be everything—the lower religions providing all sorts of things with souls and all higher religions depending on a belief in a soul in man not perishing with his body and in God as the soul of the world. But science has dispensed with all need of any kind of soul, and vitalism is disposed of by organic chemistry, and science recognises only what it sees.

Yet, being a universal belief, it cannot be explained, as in the usual theories of animism, by sporadic causes. Nor can it be merely an abstraction, for the savage cannot abstract. This last ignores the fact that even a child can know very well what life is without being able to talk of a principle of life. But the broad criticism is right. If we are to explain a universal cause by mind, it must be by what is universal in mind, and it must have experience of something to go upon.

To this theory, however, it is easier to raise objections than to almost any other theory of animism. First, there is no evidence that there ever was a time in all human history when the memory-image was so visualised as to be thought as real as the percept. Second, a ghost, he says, is the mental image of a person as modified by the fact of death, death being ascribed to the

[1] *The Idea of the Soul*, 1909.

absence of the soul. But why should the memory-image create fear when the percept itself did not? The explanation that the fear is lest the memory-image should become a percept, which is to say that the ghost should become a living person, is untrue in fact, and is absurd in reason when there would be no fear of the percept.

As an example of another form of explanation by the structure of mind I take de la Grasserie's theory.[1] His reason for resorting to it is the same, that a universal effect must have a universal cause, and so, if religion is not created by any reality without, it must be produced by some universal quality of the mind itself.

Religion, we are told, is the product of twelve mechanical laws of mind. But, as one of them—the law of the unity of the human spirit—dominates them all, we can ignore the other eleven. This does not, however, have the usual meaning that each mind is a unity to which there is no other parallel. It means that all minds have a sort of physiological uniformity like all human bodies, and that they think the same thought because they are all turned off the same lathe. Hence the laws are called mechanical: and it is the mechanical uniformity of their action which is the point of the theory.

From this alone, it is argued, can we explain the extended, practically universal presence of the same beliefs, observances, myths, monuments of religion. Pillars, totems, fetishes, curious common tales, and practices like mutilation and asceticism, cannot be explained either by communication, or common sense, or the long arm of coincidence, or anything save a uniform mechanical working of the human mind.

But, first, not one of these is universal in the absolute way required by such a theory; second, the world is small and the chances of communication various and the time for it long, therefore it might all be by imitation; third, as in primitive society interests are limited and the means of expressing them also limited, it is not remarkable that the same forms are repeated; finally, people can arrive independently at identical

[1] *De la Psychologie des Religions*, 1899.

conclusions for similar reasons For example, stones to mark places and asceticism as a duty may have had good reasons, at least for the primitive mind. In many cases we know why men did these things; and no inquirer doubts that there was some kind of reason for the rest. The professed mechanical cause, moreover, constantly becomes selfish and material motive: and the most selfish material motive is as little mechanical as the most altruistic and spiritual.

The whole position appears in the kind of reality the author ascribes to religion. "There exist perhaps", he says, "between the subjective and the objective mysterious and reciprocal bonds, such that, if the subjective produces the objective, it is because previously the objective has produced the subjective." Here we see where we are. Knowledge is not knowledge in any real objective sense: and this is as true of the natural world as of the supernatural. It is the effect of a cause, and we may hope that the effect is like the cause. But, on the other hand, it might be as unlike as the soil to the cabbage: and this blind trust that the mental series we know may correspond to the real series we do not know must be weakened in proportion as we find in the series we know a universal cause of what we are in a position to know is not knowledge.

The theory, moreover, has nothing to do with psychology, which tells us only of a knowledge which is meaning, based on insight and interpretation The whole discussion only makes more evident Hegel's contention, or rather the postulate of all knowledge as he assumed it, that there can be no knowledge of any reality if we assume that our absolute values and our ideal standards are mere singularities of a particular biped and not manifestations of the ultimate reality. Hegel also does not overcome the temptation to fall back on mechanical uniformity, but at all events his method is not discredited from the start as a means of explaining knowledge

This view of knowledge as caused by another series outside of the mental series is the ground of all agnosticism, and the only difference from de la Grasserie is that it much more naively assumes that we can know the mechanical physical series to be real, while we regard the consciousness by which we know as a mere effect of a cause which may have no resemblance to it.

(b) THEORIES OF THE SCHLEIERMACHER TYPE

Of the type of theory of religion as illusion akin to Schleiermacher's the best known is Feuerbach's.

Feuerbach is too slashing a writer to be a very consistent thinker, but, in the main, his contention is that religion is purely concerned with feeling and that any objectivity it professes to have is a mere projection of our desires delivered from the limitations of reality. As his commentator Jodl expresses it: "The specific quality of the religious outlook is phantasy winged by human desire".

In Feuerbach's earlier work, *The Essence of Christianity*, this projection of desire to infinity is demonstrated by a kind of Hegelian logic of the absolute. Though purely subjective, the infinite quality of the religious projection is a necessary outcome of man's mental constitution, because, unless he had another consciousness to provide the qualification, there would not be anything to qualify it. How this exactly creates the idea of the infinite is at least not self-evident. But, anyhow, man has this idea, and it makes religion a stimulating embodiment of his best ideals. Our God is nothing beyond our unlimited imagining of what we ourselves would be if we could, and depends on ourselves and can only be as good as we wish to be, yet, as the idea grows with our growth and may even be an ideal to reach up to, it is a goal and a stimulus, and helps to free us from our individual limits, and to keep before us our true nature and reprove our deficiencies. Thus religion, though it is only psychology of desire, has psychological justification.

But in Feuerbach's later writings, especially *The Essence of Religion*, religion has become a purely desolating illusion of self-regarding desire. Any marks of nobleness it may have in contemplation become in practice mere desire to make God just a tool for realising our wishes, so that miracle becomes the heart of the whole business of religion. Yet, in manifesting this deep-dyed egoism, religion does not differ from anything else. If in religion man loves himself in God's name, outside of it he loves himself in his own name In that case, one form of knowledge would seem to be as much an illusion of desire as another, and we need not bother about truth anywhere. And this is the plainer that the formula about the absoluteness of consciousness is really the demand for another consciousness to tell us that we are conscious of truth: and unfortunately we have been left in all departments to worry along with knowing what we can with the one consciousness we have.

There is some pretence of historical proof, but it merely consists of unproved large deliverances. Thus he says of asceticism: "The more the sensuousness is denied, the more sensuous is the God to whom the sensuousness is offered". That is to say, we create a God to satisfy our desires, and then we invent a reason for sacrificing to him the desires for the sake of gratifying which we created him. As any admission of reality in any demand of a man to deny himself would be fatal to the theory, we are offered the old view that good could be done by Beelzebub: and we can only offer the old answer that, if we choose to call good evil, there is no more to be said. The appeal of any goodness cannot be supported by the verdict of another goodness beyond it, any more than the witness of our consciousness by the testimony of a consciousness beyond it.

Religion, we are told, is not theology but anthropology, not ontology but psychology. The ground of this is that, as with Schleiermacher, Feuerbach makes the point of contact feeling. But, for Schleiermacher, the creative feeling is intuition of reality, an intercourse between a universe, present always in all its meaning, and a spirit, responding with all its understanding, as, for example, when we read poetry there is a sense in which all the poet's mind and all ours are present in the intercourse. To Feuerbach, on the other hand, feeling is pure sensation, a patter of impacts upon the senses. Beyond them, there is no contact with reality, and, even to them, all meaning is given by our feeling, with the result of presenting a view of experience which is as if we held speech to be a mere jumble of sounds and its seeming sense what it pleased our phantasy to ascribe to it.

From this sensationalism we are led on to selfish motive, as though it were also a mere impact upon the senses, and no explanation were needed of how, in the midst of this universal scheme of mechanical, levelling impacts, anything like a self should ever have arisen. Thus we come to the real importance of the theory, which is that it raises for us sharply the question of the relation of feeling to reality, and shows again how impossible it is to ascribe religion to any universal aspect of mind and regard it as illusion, without exposing all knowledge to the same charge.

A great deal of English thinking has been of the same type, the usual basis of it being Hume's sensationalism. But it is Hume turned dogmatist, which Hume was far too shrewd a person to be. He was quite aware that he was merely upsetting abstractions, whereas his followers, taking abstractions for the ultimate reality, imagined that they were upsetting experience.

(c) THEORIES OF THE KANTIAN TYPE

As our example of a theory of religion as illusion of the Kantian type we shall take Leuba's,[1] but, in these days of volitional psychologies, he has plenty of companions.

Like most other writers of this school, he frequently gives as psychology what is deduction from the Darwinian theory of evolution Kant's emphasis on will is now the will to live, and its concern is not with a realm of moral ends as the ultimate reality, but with the struggle for physical survival.

For Leuba, as with Kant, religion is belief in a personal order in the universe. But this is for Leuba a pure illusion, created on the pattern of our own actions and kept going by its biological value, the notion of a being, who gives man the impression of companionship and backing in the battle of life, being of the utmost value in the struggle for existence Though the gods are non-existent, belief in them gives an invigorating sense of control over nature, is stimulating "suggestion",

[1] James Leuba, *A Psychology of Religion*, 1912.

helping the rule of mind over body; supports intelligence and feeling by the idea of having to do with spirits, and not mere dead things; and, so far as these spirits are conceived as benevolent, engenders a feeling of confidence and optimism of high dynamic value. Even communion with God is sought for the purpose "of dismissing the worrying complications of this world, of escaping a dread sense of isolation, of entering into a circle of solacing and elevating thoughts and feelings, of forgetting and surmounting evil". Finally, religion gives an exalted sense of keeping superior company, thus it is what we might call high-society fiction.

Besides being of this value for the individual mind, it has social value. The ideals of the community are unified, socialised, consolidated by being embodied in gods, and the many social doings associated with the ideas of religion have even more effect than the ideas themselves. Religion, therefore, both by conserving and by expanding life, is a biological factor of the highest importance.

This he thinks the more certain, in that the special character of religion does not depend on any special religious instinct, faculty or organ in the mind, but on the kind of power it would make use of for practical ends.

Man has three types of behaviour, corresponding to the types of powers he has always believed in. These powers are the mechanical, the coercitive, and the anthropopathic. To make use of them he has produced science, magic and religion. The purpose of religion is to make use of the anthropopathic kind of power for the practical ends of life. As science has once for all disposed of such a reality, religion is reduced to what we may call a pick-me-up, manufactured purely in the crucible of imagination, but man needs it till he becomes strong in the scientific faith.

Even within Leuba's own limits the difficulties are obvious.

First, if man, as is maintained, has always known the mechanical mode of behaviour, and if, as Leuba holds, reality, outside of our fellows, corresponds to it alone, how did he come to apply so extensively the wrong method to the world, when he knew the right one? Moreover, this aberration is not confined to man, but, as every living creature has dealt with the world as meaning and not as mechanism, this mode of behaviour is as theriopathic as it is anthropopathic, and much more exclusively.

The second difficulty is just about the practical value so strongly emphasised. Imagination is a practical faculty of incalculable value so long as it anticipates what experience will confirm; but, as a mere weaving of phantasies, what is more disastrous? Sincerity in the conduct of life is surely the first requirement in conducting it effectively. If a type of behaviour, which works with meaning and assumes its environment to have qualities of knowledge, wisdom and justice which give meaning, succeeds so well in the battle of life, how are we to know that any power is real if this kind of power is unreal? Were paper money thus honoured day by day in life's business, with nothing behind it, the problem of how to live at the rate of ten thousand a year on nothing would be solved. And what would such a religion be but money that is nothing save paper?

The third difficulty is how this anthropopathic person, who succeeds so amazingly in modelling a world, fashioned on a wholly different pattern, to his own pet mode of behaviour, was ever produced? Is he not also a part and product of the world? What were the mechanical ways of the world doing when they created him to contradict them?

Finally, while psychology is supposed to be arbiter in religion, no psychology ever discovers us dealing with the world except by way of our ideas and interests and purposes, or knows anything by itself of any reality which is not in this sense anthropopathic The actual court of appeal is scientific theory. But that ought not to be determined by the nature of mind. It is to be proved right or wrong on grounds presented to the mind.

A still larger problem of knowledge, moreover, is raised by the theory, which Leuba himself does little more than mention. For Kant, the practical reason is the final testimony to an ultimate reality of meaning and purpose, to a realm of moral ends, and not of mere mechanical forces; for Leuba, it also creates a belief in this world of ends, but only as a vast illusion. Right living apparently has no relation to right knowing. Yet this biological psychology does not seem to leave any other basis for any kind of knowledge of our environment except our use of it for practical ends.

This cannot apply to religion alone. If mind is developed in the struggle for life, and if, in this struggle, illusion will serve as well as truth, what assurance is left of any reality? Why, for example, in spite of the utility of science, is not the object of it as much an illusion as the object of religion? Pragmatical grounds are worthless, for the assumption of Pragmatism is that reality alone will work in the end, and that even illusion only works up to the measure of reality it contains. Are the senses alone reliable? But they work with meaning and not mechanism, and have been very largely developed for practical uses.

Leuba does make some kind of attempt at an answer. Like Hume, he distinguishes between a rational scheme of the universe—to which, however, he would not, as Hume does, give the name of religion—and religion as belief in anthropopathic forces. His creed, he says, is empirical idealism, not materialism. As all experience works not with impact but with meaning, the basis of empiricism is not evident; and, as the essence of idealism is that the standards of truth and beauty and goodness express the nature of ultimate reality, one can only suppose that the idealism is, like religion, merely a working illusion. Apparently his rational scheme of the universe is a vague idealistic pantheism. But for it he offers no better support than the prevailing opinion of philosophers, just as he has no better support for his mechanistic view of the world than what he takes to be the prevailing opinion of scientists. And this naturally worthless mode of establishing truth is made more worthless by the certainty that none of these philosophers would have imagined that they could affirm anything about the universe on Leuba's theory, or have dreamt of calling themselves idealist if they had not held valid what he denies.

The theory disposes even of de la Grasserie's dim hope that

what is produced in our minds may have some resemblance to what has produced it. Real knowledge we might perhaps not hope to obtain with powers which have been evolved for so purely practical ends, but if we could believe, as might seem natural, that success in the struggle would be determined by the extent to which our real environment was accepted, and that illusion about it would be the most certain of all causes which blot the living creature out of existence, we might have assumed that the processes of our mind, even if they did not rise to the level of knowledge of reality, must run an effectively parallel course with it. But if a vast illusion about it prove to be the most effective way of dealing with our environment, even this confidence is baseless.

Apart from this unreality of its reference, Leuba's theory of religion is not very different from Ritschl's, that the beginning of religion is a distinction in value between personal beings and extended things, and that its concern throughout is to secure this worth in face of the mechanical forces of nature or society, or, in other words, that it is essentially personal victory over the mechanical world: and it is certainly not any kind of psychological argument which would prevent us from concluding with Ritschl that, if this victory is possible, it can only be because there is a reality in the world and above it akin to the personal

Another form of this theory of religion as an illusion of the will ascribes religion to man's social consciousness. Leuba also holds that the ideals of the community are unified, socialised, consolidated by being embodied in gods. This is, however, only a slight extension of his theory, because society is considered by him mainly for its value as support in the struggle for survival. But the French anthropological school, of which Durkheim is the best-known representative, makes the authority of the social group itself the source of all religion.

Religion, Durkheim[1] says, has been too enduring and dominating a factor in human history to be regarded as a mere mental illusion. Some objective reality, he thinks, it must have.

[1] Emile Durkheim, *Elementary Forms of the Religious Life*, p. 2.

This he finds in the sanction of the social group. The authority of the group is what makes anything sacred, and so distinguishes its sanction from all other sanctions of various degrees of force.

But, first of all, a social sanction is not the kind of sanction which religion itself claims, and in point of fact a social sanction is not by itself more sacred than a personal one, nor is it recognised, at least by any advanced religion, as being so. This theory, therefore, would seem to reduce religion to illusion quite as much as Leuba's, and, even less, to cover all religion.

It also quite as definitely raises the question, why such an illusion should have wrought so long and so effectively. If there is actually a sacred world and man belongs to it, human relations may be sacred and sacred obligation be the pillar and ground of them; but if society is merely an extension of the herd instinct, the idea that its relations are sacred is an illusion, the rise of which is difficult to explain and the obligation of which all progress in understanding must undermine.

The recognition of the sacred as the religious element is important, but it is precisely this sacredness which is, on the theory, illusion. And the question is how such an illusion could arise out of mere mass feeling, and still more, how it could later develop into the only sanction which could be set up effectively against the mass mind. If the sense of the sacred were already there, it would naturally attach itself to the society in which we live and by which we live; but how, out of mere social, variable, and comparative values, could the idea of an absolute value, in the might of which man can stand alone over against his whole society, ever arise? Nothing is more certain than that the sacred claims to have its sanction in itself, and that it is corrupted when its sanction is submission to public opinion.

(*d*) PSYCHOLOGY AND METAPHYSICS

Psychology, interpreted as imaginative, sympathetic insight into other minds and other conditions, is no doubt a help to understand religion along with other things, facts being mere dust and ashes unless the glow of life is still in them. But the real meaning of the claim of these theories is that a certain biological theory of the origin of mind is arbiter. Facts are accumulated on peasant religion, diseases of religion, physiological influences in religion, men's religion and women's, adolescent and adult religion, conscious and subconscious influences, conversions sudden and otherwise, much of it interesting, but, as E. W. Meyer says, with a right liberal use of the privilege which Schopenhauer called the brevet of nobility of genius, the prerogative of producing the useless.[1]

The ways of theologians and philosophers are set aside, and generally not without displaying in the process palpable evidence of ignorance of what these ways are. The result is to leave us very clear about the claim of psychology as a sort of intellectual Lord Chancellor, but without any definite idea of its decisions or its method of reaching them. Starbuck,[2] for example, claims that the mind is absolutely subject to law: and it might appear that some psychology has achieved the formulation of it in a form which a great deal of vague and generally irrelevant physiology seems intended to prove to be just physical law. But, when we come to the facts, we are presented with statistical averages, under which we see the individual working out his own problems, so as to make it plain that thus to lose the individual in the crowd is a mere myopic effect of limited understanding. And this is the more certain, in that religious experience is admitted to be a real widening of our relation with a larger spiritual environment, and this just through using our minds to discover it by insight and obedience. And that this is a normal dealing with experience is further confirmed by the cumulative evidence that a vastly greater number of people are religious than we imagine, and that even the extremest forms of religion cover a quite normal need of the personality in living relation to a higher world.

But, with most psychologists of this type, the claim that

[1] *Zeitschrift für Theol. u. Kirche*, vol. XVIII, p. 305
[2] E. D. Starbuck, *The Psychology of Religion.* "There is no event in the spiritual life which does not occur in accordance with immutable laws," p 3

psychology is sovereign is equivalent to a denial of any supernatural influx into experience. Usually the polemic is against William James, and not infrequently by means he has himself provided. Irving King[1] even lays it down as a postulate that supernatural elements must be ruled out, because, if the various reactions on the human side require completion on the existential side by superhuman elements, no science is possible. "No science", he says, "can be built upon the assumption of an interaction between two unlike worlds, one of which is knowable and the other unknowable or subject to different laws and categories from the first."

But are not the laws of consciousness and of motion just such different laws, and yet apparently they interact in a way unknown and possibly unknowable; and is the influence of another personality upon ours as different an order as the influence of a material world? The sole ground is the assumption that physical law alone is science, and that psychology can only be made scientific by being reduced to it. But even physical laws may not all be mechanical, and psychology may have to be content to be as scientific as all its facts allow. "Every known element", we are told, "must be susceptible of some sort of explanation in terms of the rest of the world." Does this mean the rest of the world without that element? It cannot be science to ignore supersensible elements any more than sensible, if they by chance exist, unless science and knowledge of reality have different meanings. Finally he sums up, "A scientific statement has no meaning except within a closed system of definite relations". But does any science work in such a system, and has not it also to be content constantly to be as scientific as it can?

Ames[2] claims that psychology dominates all philosophical studies, philosophy being a mere extension of psychology. This would apply to an aesthetic or an ethic as much as to a philosophy of religion. All alike would be the outcome of a structure of mind which itself is the direct outcome of the

[1] *The Differentiation of the Religious Consciousness.*
[2] *The Psychology of Religious Experience,* 1910.

struggle for existence, the norms of our thinking and feeling and acting having no other necessity than practical experience. In that case, not merely would our truth be relative to our state of progress and the limitation of our minds, but our minds would not be instruments at all for the truth of anything except the convenient. Ames, seeing that, however it originate, mind is all we have as a means for reaching any reality, does not, like Leuba, single out religious truth as biological illusion, but he seems even more to lay us open to the wider fear that everything may be biological illusion.

Mind is defined as the means whereby adaptations occur in novel and complex situations to smooth the way for action, and we only perceive what we mean to use. "The intellectual processes arise when the impaired or faltering activity needs them, and the emotion is an accompaniment of the hesitancy, testing, issue or inhibition in the action."[1] This is as much as to say that a signpost turns into a policeman when the traffic becomes complex enough to need him. Even logic is a mere practical faculty, governed apparently by no other necessities. But when we ask why we must reason, if we are to reason successfully, in one fixed way, we are face to face with the question whether it may not be because it is the way of reality. If not, logic must be as much an illusion as religion.

As it would be some confirmation that the Supernatural is an actual environment, if it could be shown that the mind acts normally in respect of it, so it would be some disproof if it could be shown that, in all dealing with religion, the action of the mind is abnormal or morbid, though even this would be far from final, for the greatest minds have seldom satisfied the average standards of normality. But no such proof is attempted. On the contrary, it is admitted that the belief is practically as wide as humanity, that it has been held by the sanest minds, and that it has had a very deep and continuous influence on human affairs. This type of theory is, therefore, compelled to derive the illusion from the ordinary working of the human mind under the actual conditions set by the universal

[1] E. S. Ames, *The Psychology of Religious Experience*, p. 20.

experience. Psychology, therefore, so far as it can determine validity at all, would seem to be on the side of a belief that has arisen from the normal mind, dealing with a universal experience.

For psychology everything is within the mind, and it can only say that some things are also regarded as outside the mind. Whether this be reality or illusion can only be determined by whether the evidence for it presented to the mind is good or bad. But illusion is by no means confined to religion. Wherefore, if what the mind takes to be objective knowledge can, from the nature of the mind itself, be shown to be illusion, all knowledge must be suspect.

The theories of religion as illusion, therefore, bring us again to the view of religion as a concern with environment, natural as much as supernatural, in the same way as, we saw, was done by the theories which relate religion to what is ultimate in experience.

CHAPTER IV

THEORY AND HISTORY

(a) QUASI-HISTORICAL VIEWS

How far any theory is psychology and how far it is history is not always easy to decide. Does a view like *Timor fecit deos* or

> Courts for cowards were invented,
> Churches built to please the priest,

profess to be an account of man's history or an analysis of his mind? Formerly it only professed to be psychological theory, but in our time some attempt has been made to prove it historical fact. The other ancient view, known as Euhemerism, which ascribes the rise of gods to more or less deliberate deification of individuals, though it looks like a historical explanation, was formerly only psychological theory, inferred from the spell cast over the human mind by fear or favour As Hobbes put it: "The strong boasted of supernatural powers, the deserving were honoured as divine from thankfulness". Though this is placed in the past and looks like history, it was only what he took to be the ways of human nature. But even the earlier, more definite aspect of the theory, as Critias set it forth at the end of the fifth century B.C., that the rulers ascribed supernatural powers to themselves as a protection against opponents of law and order, anthropologists of our day have sought to establish as history.

It was not left to modern times to discover that there were other elements in religion besides intellectually attained conceptions about gods or inferences from the Natural to the Supernatural. Nor was it assumed for the first time in the seventeenth century that, while even the intellectually demonstrated elements may be baseless, all the rest must be But in the seventeenth century, the first serious attempt to deal with the unreasoned elements in religion was made by Hobbes

As religion is only found in man, he argues that it must be due to some characteristic human quality. Starting from anxiety, which is his modification of the old Lucretian explanation by fear, Hobbes says this causes man to be inquisitive of the causes of the events upon which his good or evil fortune depends, and, having come to observe the order, sequence and dependence of things, and how there is regular antecedence and consequence, he either imagines himself, or receives on the authority of others, causes of his fears, which, as he is too ignorant to find in things seen, he ascribes to some power or agent invisible, which he naturally took to be of the same nature as his own soul, the idea of which he derived from dreams and reflections. But, not knowing how these invisible agents effect anything, he did not look for any connexion between events, save that they had happened together before and might again, upon which expectation all superstitions depend. Naturally, he invoked their aid by such gifts and prayers as he would use to his fellows. "And in these foure things, opinion of Ghosts, Ignorance of second causes, Devotion towards what men fear, and Taking of things Casuall for Prognostiques, consisteth the natural seed of Religion; which by reason of the different Fancies, Judgments, and Passions of several men, hath grown up into ceremonies so different, that those which are used by one man, are for the most part ridiculous to another."[1] Even the modern name of Animism for this very modern theory is not lacking, for he says there is nothing that has a name which has not been feigned to be 'inanimated', inhabited or possessed by some spirit or other.

Whether the cultivation of this religion was done by man's own invention or by God's direction, the purpose was to make men more apt to obedience, the people being led to lay "the fault on neglect or errour in their ceremonies" for any evil that might arrive, rather than to mutiny against their governors. As religion thus forwards the contract by which men are supposed to have resigned their liberty and, for the sake of

[1] *Leviathan*, ch XII.

protection, to have accepted implicit obedience, it is a useful superstition. Yet, alongside and quite independent of this religion derived from solicitude, there is a belief in a First and Eternal Cause, derived from reasoning upon the causes of natural bodies, which is truth.

This theory was reproduced with some changes by Spinoza in his *Tractatus Theologico-politicus*. There are, however, two marked differences. First, the kernel of truth is ethical, second, the end is freedom, not subjection.

But the suggestions of Hobbes were first taken up with full appreciation by Hume, who still more clearly distinguished between the foundation of religion in reason and its origin in human nature.

In respect of the foundation of religion in reason, Hume added nothing to the ordinary rationalist view of his time. The religion of reason consists of a purely intellectual deduction of an Intelligent Author from "the whole frame of nature". This is the sum total of rational religion. But he maintains—and this is the vital point—that what appears as religion in history is not of this intellectual type at all. It is due neither to a primary impression of nature, on the one hand, nor to an original instinct, on the other, nor to any form of speculative curiosity or love of truth.

His argument we may reduce to three points. (1) Such impulses were no part of the mental furniture of primitive man, who was "a barbarous, necessitous animal...with some grovelling and familiar notion of superior powers". (2) As the universe is evidently of a piece, man could not, had he followed the way of intellectual inquiry, have ascribed such a single effect to several causes, yet, "so far as writing and history reaches, mankind were universally polytheists". (3) Had man once attained so magnificent an opinion as an Author of Nature, the power which attained it must have more than sufficed for its maintenance.

The true source of religion was not intellectual curiosity but concern with the events of life. This kept men in incessant hopes and fears. "In this disordered scene, with eyes still more disordered and astonished, they see the first obscure traces of divinity." The imagination, kept active by feelings excited by perpetual alarm, formed ideas of the powers on which the issues of life depended. Being "unable to penetrate the purely mechanical scheme which governs events, men naturally conceived them dependent on powers after their own image".[1]

Fundamentally this is still Hobbes's scheme—anxiety, ignorance of the laws of nature, and an extended use of the analogy of our own wills. But there is an advance upon Hobbes which may be summed up in four statements: (1) The psychological aspect of the question is much more clearly distinguished from the question of what truths religion may contain. (2) The emotional character of religion is more fully realised and the impossibility of understanding it as a merely intellectual scheme more clearly stated. (3) Development in religion is plainly indicated. Even polytheism is said not to be founded on caprice or accident, but on the tendency of our human nature to ascribe our good or ill to intelligences like ourselves, only greater in power. Yet man's religion rises with man's mind. "The mind rises gradually from inferior to superior: by abstracting from what is imperfect, it forms an idea of perfection: and slowly distinguishing the nobler part of its own frame from the grosser, it learns to transfer only the former, much elevated and refined, to its divinity." (4) A hint is given of the possibility of a deeper intercourse between human nature and reality than the only channel so long recognised—reasoning from the data of the senses. In itself, popular religion is by no means the high-road of reason. If this religion of our hopes and fears is harmonised with the religion of reason, it is at best by accident. When, through fear and the desire of favour, flattery can go no further, it arrives at the infinite and perfect, and so reaches "the attributes of unity and infinity, simplicity and spirituality". Yet this instinctive trust in an invisible intelligent power may be a kind of mark or stamp which the

[1] How little religion is a first principle of mind or thought appears, he says, in this—that Anaxagoras, who was the first philosopher to suggest Supreme Intelligence as the First Cause, was the first we know of to be accused of atheism

Divine workman has set on his work, a mark which dignifies all mankind, for, if a people destitute of religion could be found, it would be little removed from the brutes.

To arrive àt the pinnacle of reason by way of the abyss of flattery may seem so strange a road as to deprive the suggestion of all value. Yet it may be misunderstanding of Hume's scepticism to question the seriousness of the suggestion, for it is a mistake to regard him as, like Mephistopheles, one who *stets verneint*. In any case, and however it was intended, the view that religion is an essential element in human nature, and that essential human nature must reflect the reality which gave it birth, has much to say for itself, and has played no small part in later discussions.

(*b*) UNIVERSAL SCEPTICISM

But Hume's most important contribution was to set the experience of the Natural on exactly the same footing as the experience of the Supernatural, or rather to raise such scepticism about the Natural by itself that all hope of rescuing it seemed to be by giving it order, meaning and value from the Supernatural.

Because the Supernatural is not manifest to the senses, it had been assumed, both by those who maintained its reality and by those who denied it, that it must be proved from the Natural, which is. As the result was either complete rejection or a Supernatural so attenuated that it was not worth upholding, there came to be a common opinion that a supernatural environment is wholly out of court, and that the purely natural environment rules alone by reason of having no rival. Yet this conclusion is only possible for those who overlook what happens when the Natural is subjected to the same test.

Among Western thinkers from Descartes onwards attempts have been made to prove the existence of a material world by other evidence than the way it environs us, but the result was no more reassuring for the reality of the natural world than the same method has been for the reality of the supernatural, and the questions raised were even more embarrassing

Descartes himself started with the conviction that the mental is nearer and must be more certain than the material: and if we doubt that we know ourselves as knowing, we shall seek in vain for better evidence of reality. The inevitable conclusion was drawn by Hume. If we are not prepared to take the quality of the mind's experience and the meaning of its order as proof of reality, we are left with a mere stream of impressions, amid which knowledge and reality are indistinguishable from dream and phantasy.

On the principle of proving the reality of our environment from something else, the sceptical conclusion is at least as inevitable in the case of the Natural as of the Supernatural: and in both for the same reason, which is neither remarkable nor recondite. It is simply that we cannot prove the reality of any environment while omitting the only evidence it ever gives of itself, which is the way in which it environs us. If this count for so little to us that we need to have its existence proved, it would not seem to matter much whether it exist or not: and, in any case, no environment presents further testimonials besides its own witness. So far is reality from feeling obliged to meet all our objections that it only dimly unveils itself to our most sympathetic and far-reaching insight. This may be highly unphilosophical on the part of environment, yet the fact remains, and even philosophy can only accept it.

On this method of proof from something else, men's belief in the visible world is much less certain than their belief in the invisible, because, when we betake ourselves to this kind of proof of reality, the world of the senses is necessarily called in question earlier and more radically than the world of the mind. All things, even though known by the senses, are known only in thought, whereas thinking is at least a direct experience. Hence, for many centuries, the Indian philosophy, making use of this method, has denied all reality to the world of the senses. Its only external reality is a sort of nightmare of Brahma, and the witness of our senses about it is *maya*, illusion. Yet, with all this scepticism about the natural world of the senses, the existence of a great spiritual, unseen reality, both without in the universe and within in the soul, has never been so much as questioned.

To us practical people it may seem impossible that any sane person should regard the visible world as more unreal than the invisible, but the fact remains that there are such persons and that their conduct proves this estimate to be no pretence. As practical people we give a practical reason for our conviction. We go about our business in the world sensibly, and this leaves us in no doubt about the world's reality. Were we asked to explain why the Indian is not equally convinced, we should say that, having withdrawn from the world, he has deprived the world of the power to witness to itself by its uses. That is to say, we take the reality of the visible world along with the employment of its natural values, and do not go on to ask for some reason outside of what it means for us whereby to establish its reality.

The way that all environment manifests itself is precisely by keeping men "in incessant hopes and fears", and, until it does, we seem to be incapable of being aware of it, and to be without any sustained motive for investigating it. Probably our awareness of the material world even more than of the spiritual was due to "the imagination kept active by feelings excited by perpetual alarm". We may even take Hobbes's whole scheme—anxiety, ignorance of the laws of nature and an extended use of the analogy of our own wills—and find it apply as much to awareness of the visible world as to any possible invisible. How else have we ever been interested in it at all? Why, then, should we not have as real knowledge of a supersensible world in the same way as we have of the sensible?

The result of this reasoning is that religion is a concern with a special kind of environment, in the same way as any other experience, which is to say, by dealing with it and not merely by arguing about it. If it is real, we can think about it and even argue within it, as well as order our actions in respect of it, and the more successful we are, the more it will approve itself to us in one experience which is in one universe of discourse. No kind of thinking ever reveals any kind of reality, yet no experience comes without an active dealing with it in thought and action. It comes as meaning, not as impact; and meaning is value; and value in the end depends upon feeling: yet it is not upon mere feeling, but upon right thinking and acting in relation to it.

(c) FACT AND THEORY

Does not all this show that we should start from the facts of religion as they are found, and especially with the facts of Primitive Religion?

Sir James Frazer and some of his disciples seem to think that, when we get back to primitive forms, every element of religion is so simplified that any difficulty there may be in distinguishing them disappears. But even in Sir James's own description, unfortunately, we find an enormously complicated confusion of beliefs and practices, which so far from giving an impression of simplicity, confirms Turgot's saying, *Les hommes grossiers ne font rien de simple*. Moreover, religion is mixed up with everything else. Even in later, more developed forms, in which religion is much more clearly differentiated, we have great need of some principle whereby to distinguish the religious part from the rest, for history as well as present experience shows that much ostentatiously professing to be religion may not concern religion at all, while much that makes no such profession may be effectively religious. Only the great geniuses have ever achieved anything like simplicity in religion, yet, even in them, some standard is needed to distinguish what is specially religious.

The real reason for thinking that the primitive simplifies religion is drawn, not from its simplicity, but just from its welter and confusion. As almost all primitive ideas have religious associations, and primitive ideas are outlived ideas, it is concluded that all religion is outlived ideas. Then we are merely back at Comte.

"The comparative study of the beliefs and institutions of mankind", says Sir James, "will lay bare the weak spots in our foundations, showing that much we regard as solid rests on the sands of superstition rather than the rock of nature."[1] But all the rock of nature was once sand, or mud or lava, which was still less stable, yet that our house now stands firm on it is evidence enough that it is no longer in its former state. In the first place, we cannot really tell what is in any beginning except by what comes out of it; and, in the second, we have no right to assume that nothing has been added since the beginning.

(d) ORIGIN AND BEGINNING

There are two questions which ought to be kept apart, but which are constantly confused. By distinguishing words more than in common usage, we shall call them the questions of the *origin* and of the *beginning* of religion. The former concerns man's whole sense of the Supernatural; the latter only the particular forms of belief or practice in which this sense first expressed itself.

The origin of religion, so understood, cannot be a historical question. There is no knowledge which goes behind the time when man responded to his experience with a feeling of awe which was more than fear, the admission of claims which oppose the clamour of his senses, and the assurance of an environment which is above what merely offers physical resistance.

At the lowest stage we know, man is already, in some measure, walking by faith, with his religion as a going concern in all its aspects of higher feeling, higher values and higher environment and surely Hume is right in thinking that man would not have reached the human stage at all, with no feeling save what stimulated his nerves pleasantly or unpleasantly, no value save the immediately convenient, and no thought of any environment except what was manifest to his senses.

At all events, we know of no stage of human development without a sense of the holy, which, even in its most superstitious form of awe, is still distinct from mere dread, a judgment of the sacred, which, even as the crudest mana or taboo, makes a quite different demand from any claim of profit or convenience, and a belief in the Supernatural, which, even in its grossest

[1] *The Magic Art*, I, p. xxv

material embodiments, evokes a reverence and a trust not to be explained by any exaltation of the Natural. That he was still unable to conceive this except in material forms or respond to it in any way we might now call spiritual, no more calls in question the reality of such an environment and its significance for man's progress, than the absence of any clear idea of the world of the senses in the first beginnings of life calls the existence of this world in question or disproves the importance of it for the development of perception. Nor can awareness of either environment be explained except by the quality of the environment to stir response and a kinship of life and mind to respond to it.

The beginnings of religion, as an account of its early manifestations—thus distinguished from the origin of religion as an explanation of man's awareness of a higher endowment—we can make some pretence of treating as a historical question. Yet history does not carry us anywhere near an absolute beginning of the story. What professes to reach this goal is merely psychology masquerading as history.

For facts the main authority relied on is anthropology, and the main source of its information is the study of backward races. But it suffers from two disturbing elements, which do not become less evident, with the increasing volume of information and the multiplication of treatises which discuss it, than they were in the days when Max Muller first drew attention to them. Nor are his criticisms less applicable.

(1) Travellers note merely what strikes them as odd, without going on to ask what lies behind. Thus fetishism comes to be regarded as the primitive form of religion, whereas an inquiry into what lay behind it might perhaps show that it never was an essential element in any religion. Again, we know that, in many languages, the word for soul means shadow; but when we are told that the Benin negroes regard their shadows as their souls, we are not informed at all what, under this figure, they take their souls actually to be.

(2) Travellers constantly reflect learned theory. In the days of Rousseau, the savage was seen in a halo, as Tacitus saw

the Germans, who, he says, call by the name of gods only "that secret something they perceive by reverence alone". In the days of Darwin, on the contrary, the doubt is whether the savage even deserves the name of man, being lower than the Germans to Caesar, who said that they "reckon gods only what they perceive and visibly profit by".[1]

Besides, there is the great difficulty of making any inquiry which shall go deeper than outward customs and tradition.

Even about these same Germans to-day, though their religious attitude is nearer to us than that of any other race, a student who speaks with them in their own tongue, reads their theology and attends their services, might still have to speak with more hesitation of their real religion than of anything else about them. On a matter regarding which it is somewhat of a sacrilege to intrude upon a brother, there is naturally a closed door to a stranger, and, more especially, if the investigator, instead of being able to talk to the savage in his own tongue, goes about with an interpreter and a camera. Yet broadly it is with the savage as with the rest of us. Those who speak his tongue most freely, whose intercourse with him is most friendly, and who do not court wrong answers by asking inquisitive questions, have the highest opinion of both his piety and his morality. The individual picture at least is never as irrational and repellent as the sort of witches' stew of elements collected from various writers and cooked together in the cauldron of the comparative anthropologist.

Plainly there are no results here from which we may obtain a view of religion, but we very much need a view of religion to know what are the relevant facts and how far they have significance. If we do not know already what religion is, we can no more hope to reconstruct a living religion out of a mere welter of facts than if we had never seen a tree to reconstruct it out of sawdust. If religion is an actual experience of an actual environment, we can only hope for an answer as to what that environment is by asking with all our knowledge and capacity how it environs us.

[1] F. Max Müller, *On the Origin and Growth of Religion*, pp. 52 ff.

CHAPTER V

THE RELIGIOUS ENVIRONMENT

(*a*) THE EXPERIENCE OF ENVIRONMENT

WE know all environment, not as impact or physical influx, but as meaning: and this meaning depends on (1) the unique character of the feeling it creates; (2) the unique value it has for us; (3) the immediate conviction of a special kind of objective reality, which is inseparable from this valuation; and (4) the necessity of thinking it in relation to the rest of experience and the rest of experience in relation to it.

In all experience these four aspects are indivisibly joined in one, and each loses its significance in isolation. The feeling depends on the value, and the value on the feeling; the conviction of reality is not an additional inference, but the valuation depends on the conviction of reality, and the conviction of reality on the correctness of the valuation, the thinking of it in its place in our whole experience is not after we have received it, but is necessary for receiving it, and essential to the conviction of its reality. These elements are the same for the experience of things physical as for the experience of things spiritual. What distinguishes religion from all else is the unique quality of the feeling, of the valuation, of the nature of the object, and of the way of thinking things together.

There is, however, a constant necessity to distinguish what we may not divide, nor is it specially difficult with the world of religion, because, as with every other environment, there is (1) a reflexion of it in a feeling of its own special quality, (2) an immediate judgment of worth of a kind different from all others; (3) a conviction of a peculiar kind of reality; and (4) a special way of thinking it all together as one experience. For the first two I propose to distinguish two words which are only vaguely distinct in our language and, as is often necessary in the use of terms for more technical purposes, to differentiate them somewhat more precisely than is done by common usage. These words are the 'holy' and the 'sacred'. The 'holy' I propose to use for the direct sense or feeling of the Supernatural, and the 'sacred' for its valuation as of absolute worth. The special object I shall call 'the Supernatural', and the thinking together 'theology', both words, however, having a somewhat more specialised meaning than they have in popular usage. By the sacred, in particular, all religion is distinguished; and all religious thinking is right thinking only as it is about what is truly sacred. The Supernatural is not a further inference from it as from effects to a cause, but is felt and valued in it; and, when separated from this manifestation, it is without content and deprived of all reality, because it no longer deals with an environment, but is mere abstract argument about the universe.

(b) THE SENSE OF THE HOLY

In every Western European language, as well as our own, the term 'holy' used by itself would be understood to mean what stirs moral reverence. But this is not its original meaning. In the oldest parts even of the Old Testament, it is used for what stirs a mysterious dread, a 'holy God' not meaning a God "of purer eyes than to behold iniquity", but one apart and awe-inspiring. The more religions are primitive, the more the holy has to do with awe, and the less with moral reverence. Yet expressions like 'the holy edifice', 'the holy sacrament', still embody the same awed, non-ethical feeling.

This we shall call 'the awesome holy' In its most primitive form, it is so difficult to distinguish, as mere feeling, from dread, that fear has been regarded as the spring of all religion. But it can also rise to the sublimity of the vision of Eliphaz.

> Now a thing was brought me by stealth
> And mine ear received a whisper of it,
> In thoughts from the visions of the night,
> When deep sleep falleth on men
> Fear came upon me and trembling,
> Which made all my bones to shake
> Then a breath passed over my face;
> The hair of my flesh stood up.

> It stood still, but I could distinguish its shape—
> A form it was before mine eyes.
> A voice of silence I heard:
> Shall mortal man be just before God?
> Shall a man be pure before his Maker?   Job iv. 12-17.

Prof. Otto holds this awesome holy to be the one essential religious feeling; and he describes it as *mysterium tremendum et fascinans*. But, though such great poetry speaks of a profound and heart-shaking experience of it, the whole book of Job is a passionate challenge to the idea that awe is the last word in the conception of the holy. Otto does his best to argue that Job repents of his boldness and, through the monstrous, weird products of creation, has this feeling again revived in him. But it is a vain effort: for what Job is summoned to do, in face even of the most terrible works of nature, is, in repentance and humility yet in boldness, to gird up his loins like a man, not only to hear God but to answer him.

We have here two different kinds of religion, one a surrender of awe and one a challenge and adventure of reverence.

Because religion magnifies all experiences, the sense of *mysterium tremendum et fascinans* may be more frequently recognised in religion than elsewhere, but it is by no means confined to the sense of the holy. Any environment sufficiently great and strange may evoke it. It accompanies all life's high adventures; and it may go as far back as conscious life. Some overwhelming sense of an 'other' may have been the first conscious experience. Still more clearly, the reptile that first ventured out upon the land—a creature of enormous significance for all higher evolution—must have had a sense of a tremendous mystery in what it yet hoped to find its own. Fear and fascination, therefore, may not even be confined to man. But of man's whole spirit of adventure it is the nerve and sinew. He hazards his cockle-shell upon the roaring tides, penetrates Arctic snowfields and the barren Sahara, precisely because he feels himself so small as he is shaken by awe, overshadowed by majesty and reduced to nothing before the resistless energy of the powers of nature, yet also feels himself so great as he dares to face them. But he is there to face them, and his true response, which teaches him what they are, only rightly begins when he has won calmness of feeling and a serene sense of being at home in the midst of the sublimity.

The sense of the holy can be the most overwhelming of human emotions, even to the abject sense of nothingness as a creature. But it may also be the calmest of all responses to a reality in which we find our true independence. Intensity of the feeling, moreover, is in inverse ratio to value for experience, as sensation, in the same measure as it has value for perception, ceases to be conscious feeling, the significance in both cases being in the quality, not the vehemence.

Prof. Otto relates the holy to what he calls the *numinous*. The name will serve as well as any other, for it is the mere impression of an awe-inspiring something, the mightier for stirring intense feeling the vaguer it is. The object of primitive religion is largely of this kind; mystical religion also deals with it; in all religion it is perhaps a general basis, as the world of touch is to the other senses. It plays a specially important part in creating what we call 'the undifferentiated holy'. This is somewhat parallel to undifferentiated contact; or to seeing the sunshine and not what it illumines.

As mere feeling taken by itself, we cannot rightly interpret the sense of the holy, but must relate it to sacred value and the existence of the Supernatural, because we cannot explain one feeling by another, but only by the judgment of value which depends on it and the kind of environment into which it introduces us. Ideas we can more or less explain by other ideas, but we have little success in describing feelings, because, the moment we start, they become ideas. We can, however, distinguish them by the values that arise from them or the objects to which the values are ascribed. As mere feeling, the sense of the holy would be impossible to distinguish from the mere spooky feeling which is magical, at one end, and from the sense of the sublime which is artistic, at the other. But, when we relate it to the absolute value of the sacred, we see at once that its awe has a quality different from dread, and its reverence from the sense even of the sublime. Especially this distinguishes its lower forms from everything else. If it is a feeling which is wholly directed towards our own advantage, it is not the sense of the holy: if it has to do with incomparable value, to which desires, convenience and profit must be subordinate, in the presence of a reality before which one may not seek his own pleasure or walk after the imagination of his own heart, it is.

For this reason holy awe, even when most akin to abject fear, is never utterly abject, because, if it crush man with the sense of being the creature of a day, it also speaks to him of the eternity 'God has set in his heart', so that the most primitive man who responds to it could say with the poet, "I felt myself so small, so great". And, as there is in the poorest awe a certain quality of moral reverence which distinguishes it from fear, so, at the other end, there is in the highest moral reverence an element of awe which distinguishes it from a purely intellectual judgment. At the lowest stage, the object of this awe may be so confusedly conceived that we may discern little but crude dominating feeling; at the highest, its object may be so clearly conceived through the true, the beautiful, and the good, that Kant could regard it as delivering us from the domination of all feeling whatsoever. Nevertheless, the feeling throughout has its own essential quality, in which there is no break anywhere in its evolution. Being original, it is not to be described by something else, but, being the same feeling throughout, all the stages of its progress shed light on each other.

In the earlier stage we may have some difficulty in discovering what we regard as moral, but we have no difficulty in seeing the sense of something absolute in value from which all morality springs. Historically, too, the awesome holy has developed into moral reverence. Perhaps there is no surer measure of progress, yet there is no stage at which one form passes wholly into the other. On the one hand, the crudest awe has a quality from which moral reverence can evolve, all morality being a religious development springing from this sense of the holy; and, on the other, no truly moral feeling is ever wholly without something at least akin to awe.

Prof. Otto, more perhaps than any other writer, has put the emphasis on the awesome holy as the essential religious characteristic, and he divides it entirely from the ethical, which he regards as a quite separate development alongside of it. Yet so undeniable is the close and apparently necessary connexion, that, after distinguishing them sharply, in the interests of his theory, he maintains, in the interests of experience and common sense, that they are related *a priori*.

Such a position hardly needs refuting, and would not have been taken up had it not been necessary, in order to afford support to a non-ethical and non-rational view of religion, without denying, as a consequence, the dependence of all higher religion upon both ethics and reason. But how two quite separate developments should be connected *a priori* is difficult to conceive, for it does not seem to be in accord with any known form of development. In every development, it matters not what may be added in its course, when we look back, we can detect the germ of it long before it appeared in separate, clearly distinguishable form. And, when we thus look back on this evolution of the sense of the holy, it is not difficult to discover, in every stage known to us, the germ at least of the moral developments

The ethical and rational, Otto says, is added as *schematisation*. So they are always by legalists and often by metaphysicians. But is there then any development of religion itself? Apart from this blessed effect of schematisation, what are we to think of all the amazing list of holy things such as the *quedeshah* or the temple prostitute? If the essential element of religion is an overwhelming emotion, without ethical or rational quality, measurable by mere vehemence, how are we to deny that the natural religion is the Phoenician, with its unbounded licence and its unbounded terror? Was it not precisely by an appeal to a higher sense of the holy that the prophets set up against it the first truly rational and ethical religion?

This confused result is reached, both by not distinguishing

rightly and by not relating rightly the feeling and the valuation. The holy is used to include also what we have called the sacred, which means that it is only the kind of valuation springing from awe. As there is obviously another valuation based on reverence, this is merely appended. This scheme really assumes two Supernaturals. One we realise only by awe and value by the shuddering of the creature; and one only by moral reverence and moral value in the liberty of God's children. That, in realising the Supernatural, we develop from one feeling and value into another is certain, but, in the end, if there is one higher environment, there can only be one right relation to it. Again, in respect of the rational, are there two supernaturals—one a numinous might, before which the creature has no claims and no rights, and one a moral order which speaks to us as to children? Ought we never to have the perfect love which casts out all fear? If not, how are we to condemn the terrorised piety which cut itself with knives in a delirium of surrender, and sacrificed the fruit of its body for the sin of its soul? Is it not the placid mirror of holy calm, clearer perhaps after the storm, which, reflecting the heavens above, shows all the height and depth of what is greatest? This is not schematisation added to the holy, but the sense of the holy itself, directed to its real values and its true environment.

At the same time, the sense of the holy is not mere moral reverence which follows a moral judgment. It is the sense of the Supernatural, and only becomes moral reverence because of the moral nature of this environment. Moreover, it is not primarily applied as ethical feeling. The 'undifferentiated holy' has already been mentioned. But alongside of it we have what we might call 'the particularising holy'. The one is a general sense of the supernatural as one absolute reality, and the other the feeling of this in almost any conceivable manifestation. The former is like having a general sense of infinite force, and the latter like running your head so hard against a brick wall that the wall seems to embody the whole power of the universe. One effect is to associate the feeling, as nothing else, with the sense of unity in all our environment, yet, as nothing else does, to separate its embodiments into sovereignties independent each in its own right. Another and kindred effect is to make it both the most exclusive and the most diffusive of human emotions. On the one hand, it seems to set an impassable barrier between the holy and the profane; on the other, it can draw almost everything into its circle. Thus the holiness of the Koran extends to its binding.

In consequence the holy manifests itself in all kinds of degrading superstitions, and also passes from one thing to another. This might show that the feeling has no basis, or the continual change might be the best evidence that no particular thing fully manifests the reality, and that man is in continual pursuit of a more adequate form of what he feels in many things.

Anyhow, and whatever we make of it, we have to recognise the effect of the feeling of the holy in localising the Supernatural and pouring its absoluteness into particular objects, making each a world in itself which reflects something absolute and even infinite. Nor is this feeling wholly past even in the civilised. The popular preacher is not a person who influences by his teaching, but one who, at the highest, makes people feel that surely God is in this place, and, at the lowest, creates the impression of something mysterious and awe-inspiring, which has the emptiness but also the sublimity of the void.

In a sense both the particular and the general feelings are justified. Everywhere there is one reality in all its potency, yet there is only one unity which harmonises all difference into one universe, and the true question about the sense of the holy is, which unity does it challenge us to seek? We can sink back into its mere undifferentiated unity, or we may find it a challenge to seek an ideal which does not suffer us to rest anywhere in the effort to harmonise all our experiences.

(c) THE JUDGMENT OF THE SACRED

The sacred, as here used, just means absoluteness of value, that which is of incomparable worth, and incomparable is not merely super-excellent, but what may not be brought down and compared with other goods. The moment we ask how this sacred value compares with pleasure or ease or prosperity, it ceases to be sacred.

The interaction between the sense of the holy and this valuation as sacred is not all in one direction. On the one hand, the valuation may immediately follow the feeling, or, on the other, the feeling may immediately follow the valuation, though it is not, in either case, mere sequence. We value things because they appeal to our feelings, but we also feel about them largely as we value them. Yet, more frequently perhaps than any other feeling, the sense of the holy follows and depends on its value; and, on the whole, this becomes increasingly the case as the mind develops. We might even regard it as at least one mark of progress, that, while the more primitive the life the more the feelings determine the value, the more advanced the development the more the values determine the feelings.

This relation of feeling to value is not confined to the feeling of the holy and the value as sacred. All development of mind is marked by the growing power of the rational in feeling over the merely impulsive. But a rational feeling means one dependent on and proportionate to the actual value it regards. This transformation can be resisted by the mere vehemence of the sense of the holy as feeling, but the moment it is attached to anything sacred, the absoluteness of the feeling is quite apart from its intensity, and appeals by a tone and quality of its own, which opposes mere submission to it as overriding, dominating emotion.

Moreover, it is a question whether all difference of tone in feeling, possibly all transfusion of it with rational value, is not more or less directly related to the sacred value. At all events, take this kind of valuation entirely out of experience, and all higher feelings would be affected, if not debased out of existence, even while it still remains true that it is the feeling which gives original experience, and value depends on it. Yet the root lives and grows by its foliage, even while the foliage is wholly dependent on the root.

The sacred, as thus defined, might seem to afford a very exalted test of religion, entirely different from the feeling of the holy, which mixes itself up with all kinds of crudities. But, unfortunately, history is far from confirming this expectation. Even as absolute valuation, such as we have defined it, we still find that it includes the most weird and even debased objects, and, moreover, to such an extent that even the most dread sense of the holy is easier to understand as a stage of human progress than the grossness of the sacred. The task of conceiving how absolute value should have been ascribed to birds and beasts and creeping things, even by the most primitive minds, baffles, not merely our knowledge, but our imagination. Of how the vault of heaven and certain aspects of the spirit of man should be sacred we have some understanding, because, with Kant, we revere the starry heavens above and the moral law within, and perhaps understand better than he did that it is because they speak to us by what cannot be measured by mathematics or the categorical imperative. But, for this very reason that we have attained so exalted an idea of the manifestations of the sacred, we have difficulty in understanding how it could be embodied and expressed in cows and cats.

This inability to explain why the sacred was embodied in such strange forms should not, however, blind us to the enormous significance of the entrance into human life of a valuation not to be weighed or bargained with, a valuation which spoke to man of another reality than that which he knew by his senses and judged by his appetites.

But the problem of these queer, gross sacreds still remains: and it is impossible to be satisfied with the usual explanation that the whole scale of values of primitive man was different from ours. As the surest measure of progress is the higher quality of our values, this is doubtless part of the answer. But it cannot be the whole, because, on the one hand, primitive man had much more reverence for the higher things of the spirit than the material forms of his worship would show, and, on the other, as mere material objects, his reverence for his sacred things does not seem to have been much greater than ours.

Here we meet another important aspect of our inquiry. Things are sacred not merely because they belong to a higher reality without us. The claim to our absolute reverence depends also on what in ourselves belongs to it, on spirits which find their true worth by loyalty to its sacred requirements. But this belief too had material beginnings.

The singular connexion between sacredness and life, so that to be above life in value is the measure of sacredness, while at the same time life itself becomes sacred, is only a material form of the singular relation to our own souls which goes with every valuation as sacred. This also could only be conceived materially as the life. But the life which is a manifestation of the claim of the sacred by a worth within us which belongs to us, and which we only win by being ready to lose it, is more than the material life. Even life was at first too immaterial an idea. Wherefore, the blood was taken to be the life, and was esteemed sacred. Other things, and above all the peculiar physical impression made by blood, especially on primitive minds, went to intensify the experience. But this does not hinder the fact that in its sacredness was felt something of higher meaning and value than can be explained by mere blood, something which is the real explanation of the blood-sacrifice, the whole impression and valuation of which is not explicable by rational arguments about totem-animals or feasting with the god, or even upon the reasoned idea that life is the noblest gift of the gods and must be offered them again. No one of these explanations suffices for a sacredness which is raised above all comparison. Especially a sacredness felt in the blood, and not the mere blood, is needed to explain human sacrifice, which confers sacredness on human life as well as sacrifices it to the god.

Later, man conceived this sacred nature in himself in the form of a soul, a half-material, vaguer, swifter, smaller image of himself. This quasi-material form again was necessary because of the inability to think without material association; but again, though there was more of argument and inference here, such reasoning does not account for the peculiar feelings about the soul or for the value set upon it, a value which, in its rudimentary way, is of the same quality as the estimate that it would not profit to gain the whole world and lose one's soul.

If we are to have one mark of religion, it could only be this sacred or absolute valuation: and, on the whole, it fairly adequately satisfies the requirement.

Everything that is sacred is in the sphere of religion, and everything in the sphere of religion is sacred. Unless dogmas express beliefs valued as sacred, they are mere intellectual formulas; unless rites are the worship of a power valued as sacred, they are mere social ceremonies; unless God himself embody all we value as sacred he is a mere metaphysical hypothesis. Only when the valuation as sacred accompanies the sense of awe and reverence have we the religious holy; and only a reality having this absolute value is the religious Supernatural. Therefore, if there be any one mark of the sphere of religion, it is this valuation of everything within it as sacred. But, as we had the problem of the awesome and ethical holy, so we have the problem of the material and ideal sacred.

(d) THE SUPERNATURAL

If the valuation as sacred is the mark of religion, it might appear that there is no need to seek farther for its sphere, and that it is only necessary to relate this valuation to the sense of the holy But the sphere of religion is not the value or the feeling or both, but the environment known by means of them. Just as we are concerned, in our daily life, with the natural world, and not with our way of knowing it, so are we concerned with the supernatural. Yet both the Natural and the Supernatural are distinguished by the way in which they make themselves known, which is by the meaning or, in other words, the value they have for us. As the natural world is known by sensation and its varied comparative values, so the supernatural world is known by the sense of the holy and its sacred or absolute values; and for practical purposes, the distinction between the Natural and the Supernatural is between comparative value and absolute. This is not, however, different from the division into 'things seen and temporal' and 'things unseen and eternal', because, though in the end this may mean the fleeting and the enduring, immediately 'temporal' and 'eternal' are not distinctions of time, but of value.

Here at length there may seem to be hope of escaping the gross, material, crude elements in religion. If we are dealing with the Supernatural, and this means what is above natural values and stirs more than natural feeling, are we not necessarily set free from all that is not high and spiritual?

Unfortunately there is not yet any such deliverance. The conceptions of the ultimate reality may not have been as gross as the objects in which its presence has been felt, but they have been even more conflicting and more perplexing. To one it is an almost material force; to another a purely spiritual influence. To one it is indivisible unity; to another it is gods many and lords many. To one it is the most personal of all that is conceivable and the source and goal of all freedom; to another it is a fixed cosmic process of which the individual is merely the vehicle, and freedom is only compulsion from within and not from without. To one it is the meaning, goal, completion of the natural world; to another the natural world is a mere veil to hide it. To one it is a world to be entered by "building up the pyramid of our individuality"; to another we enter it as we lose even our identity. To one it has depths which we cannot, by any searching, find out and where our wisdom is faltering humility; another it makes omniscient enough to know that those who differ from him should be burned for the good of their souls. To one it is the immovable pillar of an unchanging world, secure in recognised authority and venerable custom; to another it is wholly concerned with worlds unrealised as yet, requiring heroic venture and the challenging of the obsolete and effete. For one it concentrates its fierce light on a single purpose and a few austere demands; for another, like the morning sun, it seems to turn muddy pools and common window-glass into flaming diamond.

No reality, it is often assumed, could manifest such protean variety. Hence when the variety is admitted, the reality is dismissed, and when the reality is admitted the variety is dismissed, or at least minimised.

This minimising is a common kind of apologetic for religion; and the effect of it is to give the impression merely of hiding one's head in the sand and refusing to look reality in the face. Yet to pass directly from the amazing differences in man's response to the Supernatural to the conclusion that there is no reality, is a superficial and hasty judgment. Both in nature and in history, it is the illusions which have shown mechanical uniformity. A mirage sun is merely a shining disc the same for all and changing nothing of what anyone is observing; the natural sun is a constantly varying object, giving to each observer a different impression of the world it shines on. To no real experience do all men react in the same way; and only when dogmas are mere forms of words can they be held with identical meaning. The question of the misuse of this environment will come up later, but the worst misuse does not prove it non-existent.

Even about the material world people can have the crudest ideas, and they can feel towards it unnaturally and misuse it sadly. But we do not argue that there can be, in that case, no stable reality, and that it is a mere phantasmagoria of man's changing moods. The variety of impression, on the contrary, is a very important part of the manifestation of reality, for we rightly know any environment only when we have a mind to perceive it aright and a will to use it well.

But, while the Supernatural would have no meaning were there only sensations and the values of physical pleasure and pain, in the end the validity of religion depends neither upon the feeling of holiness nor upon the judgment of sacredness, but upon the reality to which these belong—the existence of the Supernatural. The Supernatural is the special concern of religion, and nothing else is concerned with it in the same way as religion.

As here used, the Supernatural means the world which manifests more than natural values, the world which has values which stir the sense of the holy and demand to be esteemed as sacred. This is the only way in which the distinction can be drawn, but in this way we draw it quite simply every day.

We cannot distinguish the Natural as the mechanical and the Supernatural as the free, for we do not know how much freedom there is in the Natural or how much law in the Supernatural; nor can it be divided as between the ordinary and the miraculous, for the Natural is sometimes the more miraculous, and the Supernatural the common stuff of our daily experience. The two are not in opposition, but are so constantly interwoven that nothing may be wholly natural or wholly supernatural. Yet our interests in them are different and very definitely distinguish two aspects of our experience. Part of what we experience is natural, in the sense that its values are comparative and to be judged as they serve our needs; and part of it supernatural, in the sense that its values are absolute, to which our needs must submit.

We know the Supernatural as it reflects itself in the sense of the holy and has for us absolute value directly and without further argument: and the question is not that it exists, but how it exists in its relation to us and our relation to it. We can make no more out of arguing abstractly about it than we should out of arguing abstractly, as men long did, about the Natural. The supreme task, the task which has more than any other marked human progress, has been to discover the true Supernatural, and this means again to exercise the true sense of the holy and have the right judgment of the sacred. Only as we are related to it and it to us by the right judgment inspired by the right feeling, can we with profit ask· What is the Supernatural?

Thus awareness of the reality of the Supernatural is not something added to the sense of the holy and the judgment of the sacred by some kind of argument, say from the natural world. Where they are divorced, religion is identified with theology, and theology hung up in the air without any world of its own to work in; and the reality is sought in the theology, instead of theology being, like other sciences, the study of a reality already given. The Supernatural must be inquired into, like the Natural, as a world in which we live and move and have our being, if it is to be inquired into with profit.

Nor can we so easily separate the reality of the natural world from the reality of the supernatural as we imagine. The reality of the former is not proved merely by the violence of its assault on the senses. The difference between us who take it to be the most solid reality and the Indian to whom it is *maya* is no mere matter of the senses, for the witness of the senses is the same for him as for us. The difference concerns a different valuation of the world the senses reveal and a keener response to it in feeling. And these valuations are not, argue as we may, exclusively by natural values, but consciously or unconsciously by a different sense of their place in our higher life, being far more a difference in our religion, and the place the natural world plays in it, than in our science. Did we betake ourselves to the same kind of religion as the Indian, we also should live in the world as in a vain show, and no kind of physics could in the slightest degree make the world appear less of a dream.

From this the importance both of our standpoint and our method is apparent. They ought to be determined by the reality we find; but constantly the reality we find is determined by them. and if at the start we set off in the wrong direction, we are not likely to reach the right goal. Therefore, the first question concerns our standpoint and the second our method.

CHAPTER VI

STANDPOINT

(a) IN RESPECT TO BAD RELIGION

Of any environment we may be unaware, either because we have not developed the interests which it serves, as space to a creature without motion, or because it so constantly serves them as not to stir any reflexions, as space to the animals that rove about in it. Also it is possible to deny in theory what is believed in practice, as one might argue that the atmosphere is a mere factory of disease germs, yet set wide open his windows first thing in the morning. For any of these reasons the Supernatural can be ignored. We may not be seeking anything it provides; we may so live and move and have our being in it every day and all day that, because it has never failed us, we have not reflected on it; the belief we profess may be one thing, and the belief we act on another.

What is peculiar and in need of explanation is the zeal, the only parallel to which is religious enthusiasm, with which sensible and honourable persons have denied the existence of any environment except the Natural. The question is, why does the Supernatural, which stirs the most passionate enthusiasm, also stir the most passionate antagonism?

Part of the answer is the view taken by both parties of the absoluteness of the Supernatural. The mood of neither conduces to calm inquiry, and they are not so very unlike, because for both the Supernatural is an absolute, infallible, external authority, wholly good or wholly bad, utterly to be rejected or utterly to be accepted. Therefore, the findings of both are radical, and the difference is only in the tipping of the scales, because the weight in one is that, as some things claiming to be sacred are good, all are, and, in the other, as some are bad, all must be. Both are mistaken, and it is largely the former mistake which has justified the latter.

Yet this is not the sole reason for the bitter antagonism stirred by religion or any mention of the Supernatural. Another is the vast evils which have masqueraded under the name of religion. Of part of this it is quite right to say that the name is misappropriated, and that it is not religion merely to say, 'Lord, Lord'. But it is also true that 'Lord, Lord' can be said very religiously, yet be itself made a defence, as nothing else in the world can be, of insincerity and unreality. The sole hypocrisy is not in invoking religion as a pretence. A more subtle and dangerous hypocrisy invokes it genuinely to defend unteachableness and to approve self-satisfaction. To regard our opinions and practices as sacred is indeed the only quite impenetrable barricade against the assaults of chastening experience.

This does not mean merely that we are all given to deceiving ourselves about what we wish to believe, and that we are none of us so open-minded, resolute not to be deceived, and sensitive to truth as we might be, and that such shortcomings limit and pervert our experience of all environment. But the absolute value of the Supernatural can be used so to justify our belief and to defend our judgment as to make tradition or preconception the very pillar of the truth; to give crude, hard, legal action, and even cruelty and wrong the witness of a good conscience; and to clothe the unrealities of sensuous emotion and vapid sentimentality with the armour of piety. Refusal to inquire may be identified with faith; refusal to move outside the beaten track with virtue, and refusal to give reality any hand in our feelings with devoutness. Men have, not only in the name but by the power of religion, done things which, if not more terrible in outward manifestation, are, at least, more appalling in the turning of good into evil and evil into good than can be matched elsewhere, while they sunned themselves not only in their own approval, but in God's.

The conscious and deliberate hypocrite, who makes capital of his neighbour's belief in the Supernatural and has none of his own, is rarer in life than in fiction· and he is useful in fiction just because he is obvious. Save for their obviousness,

Tartuffe and Pecksniff, for example, would be problems of tragedy, not amusing figures of comedy. But the dangerous hypocrisy, to which perhaps only sharing in it can make us feel quite superior, is to live in the Supernatural as the most important, most real and possibly the most insistent environment, yet to use its sense of the holy and its sacred values, not to judge our own emotions and actions with humility, but to glorify them in our own eyes and to make them appear angels of light to others, even to the extent of the suppression of truth, shady conduct, and rancorous feeling, and be wholly unconscious of the travesty. Nor do we necessarily escape by denying in theory that any such environment as the Supernatural exists, for agnosticism itself may be a thanking God that we are not as other men. Something similar can be done with almost any environment that has human value of an impressive kind, such as wealth or rank, but nowhere so effectively or disastrously as in religion, because nothing else has the same impressiveness as what is sacred, though these lower goods can themselves become a kind of supernatural, and the worship of them a religion. This hypocrisy can pervade every part of human nature and block up every avenue to reality.

In matters of overt action we are less apt to be imposed upon than in matters of belief and feeling, especially if it be the actions of other people. Yet, even in action, we are not always so penetrating when the religious mask is in the form of accepted, profitable custom, or the upholding of the particular caste or sect to which we have given the absolute value of religion. More particularly the negative, legal moralist justifies his narrow, external rules by making them legislation from the throne of the universe, till he can tithe mint and anise and cummin and neglect the weightier matters of the law, and even withhold what is due to human need by calling it dedicated to God, and that with a satisfied conscience and entire self-approval. Moreover, there is no kind of conscience so comfortably elastic about the end justifying the means as a certain kind of dehumanised religious conscience.

Intellectual hypocrisy is still more subtle. It is easy to have an ill-founded assurance both that we can discern it and that we most utterly repudiate it. But there is hypocrisy, even now not entirely unknown, which can regard it as a sacred duty to be a manipulator of the truth, which, as Job puts it, speaks wickedly for God, because it is armed by religion itself against truth. But the more familiar intellectual hypocrisy is so highly punctilious about verbal veracity that Washington himself would not have been more upset by the mildest fib. Yet in matters of belief it is almost entirely convinced by impressiveness, while the idea of truth has never disentangled itself from the accepted and the conventional. While vastly concerned with correct belief, there is no idea that a belief is truly correct only as it corresponds with reality. The Supernatural is not that which challenges all our search for the real, but that which is too sacred to be investigated. Then intellectual honesty, though it is the first requisite in face of reality, and the first guarantee that our truth may correspond to it, is held in horror as impiety, till there is only the tradition which makes void any original witness of any possible word of God.

Yet even this is not the subtlest hypocrisy or that which most gives the impression of religion as unreal. What makes religion most repellent and arouses against it the most vehement antagonism, and is the really desolating hypocrisy, destructive of all true experience of any reality and more particularly of the Supernatural, is insincerity of feeling. If not in the hidden recesses of his spirit, at least in all outward bearing, a man may, in intellectual matters, be honest, and, in moral doings, upright, and yet be wholly unreal and disingenuous. This may so corrupt the primary witness of reality that, while all a man thinks may be according to logical rule and all he does according to moral law, none of his ways of feeling about anything may be right. From this an atmosphere of insincerity pervades all his views of the world, all his dealings with men, all his estimation of himself, in short, all his relations to everything. He may revel in dialectic and be eminently didactic in morals, and yet his mind and conscience be as elusive for earnest thought or moral insight as a ghost ᵢfor cold steel. This manipulation of feeling to make reality say, not what it wants to say, but what we want to hear, is the ultimate insincerity.

Manipulation of feeling is by no means confined to religion. The very senses can be made artificial; and we shall see later that this is a very important question for sense-perception and so for our whole theory of knowledge. But there is another reason why the sense of the holy can be more entirely divorced from the reality to which it witnesses and be indulged in as an emotion which may cloak over the deepest insincerity. This is in the nature of the feeling itself. All feeling, by its special quality of intensiveness, tends to diffuse itself, and the sense of the holy has this quality in a high degree. But it has also an exaltation, which seems to make it all-sufficient in itself, and to consecrate whatsoever is in any way related to it.

The antipathy this creates is often due to unfortunate personal experience. Even in the pursuit of science, prejudice due to circumstances and personalities is not wholly unknown. But in religion it seems to be more justified, because no other sphere is so personal, nor is there any other in which it is so easy to be personal in the wrong way.

For the abiding influence of what he calls the religion of a beautiful soul let us take Goethe. It is the more impressive that, in any formal sense of being a religious man, he left much to be desired. His description of what influenced him is primarily of absolutely transparent sincerity of feeling and of the impression this made of touching a higher reality than his spirit was always attuned to know. This assurance remained as an atmosphere, in which he saw all life with breadth, depth and clearness of vision, and it was also the chief source of his large serenity. The ignoring of this by his best known English biographer, is a good illustration of the effect of the adverse, the repellent influence. But it is easy to find examples among much more naturally religious minds than G. H. Lewes. It needs very little reading between the lines of some American psychologists of religion to see the effect of revivals or camp-meetings or some other kind of wrought-up religious emotionalism. Nor is the effect of a certain kind of Catholicism, which deliberately cultivates the stimulation of mystical, if not magical, feeling, difficult to discern in some French brethren of the same craft. Having experienced the effect and left it behind, they take the whole sense of the holy thereafter to be a mere befogging of common sense, revealing nothing except man's capacity for mass-impressions and auto-suggestion.

Sensitiveness of feeling, nevertheless, is the only gateway to reality: and the higher the reality, the greater must be the sensitiveness which responds to it. To be obtuse in feeling is merely to be wall-eyed before every kind of reality; and to have no keen sense of the holy would mean that, however we lived and moved and had our being in the Supernatural, we never could realise it. Moreover, the Supernatural is precisely the environment which is always calling us into new territory, so that there is no religion except religion in the making. Therefore it is the country which is most apt to overwhelm us with dread and mystery. This tempts us in two ways. The first is to sit down in the sun and merely bask in it and adventure no more. The other is to think, because intense emotion, and not least when it is painful, may be a window open upon a wider world, that to welter in a flood even of harrowing emotions is to be specially real. Both lead on to the idea that to keep ourselves in what we regard as a higher world, we must work up our feelings, till we land in a sentimentality which can be as delusively sensuous in its own way as sensuality itself. And under the influence of mass emotion this happens without effort, because, in an ordinary way, we all rely on comparison with the feelings of others about any experience to confirm our own, and this can pass into a vicious circle, where there is no experience of any reality, but one merely responds to the emotions of others and passes it on, till, returning with accumulated effect, it becomes an overmastering passion, resembling a sort of material whirlwind and having a resonance in the body, of an actual physical violence. This may then come to be regarded as the only true experience of religion, till the life becomes a cult of artificial and auto-suggested emotion. Then the main impression of religion from this particular kind of experience, upon anyone who has escaped from it, is naturally of the utter unreality of the whole business.

While feeling is the gateway of reality, feeling as mere subjective emotion may only be the gateway of unreality. Only as we consider what we feel, and ask what is it's real value, and make this steadfastly a question of what actually exists, do we pass through feeling to the truth of existence. And, when this is done, feeling always changes its character from turbulent subjective feeling into the calm witness of reality, till it may entirely cease to be conscious emotion. Therefore, it is pure misunderstanding to fail to follow the sense of the holy into the judgment of value, and to follow that again into the witness of the ultimate reality, and to suppose that true religion only exists so long as it remains an overwhelming emotion of tremendous mystery.

By what we have called the sense of the undifferentiated holy, this purely emotional alienation from experience of life can still further be turned into a city of refuge from all life's conflicts. We shall see afterwards that this sense of the undifferentiated holy has an important place in our sense of the world as one universe, but it can also be used to empty our spirits of everything except this feeling of oneness, in which we can wrap ourselves away from all moral and intellectual problems and live in a sort of blue void in undistracted calm In its complete form, this is a rare achievement of the practised mystic, but, in less obtrusive forms, it gives the impression of religion as seclusion from the world and not of victory over it, which is naturally repellent to minds deeply concerned with life's problems. Nevertheless, as we shall see, all standards of truth and beauty and goodness belong to the Supernatural, and there is a sense in which beauty, understood as the perfection of form to which feeling responds, is the most fundamental of the three.

Upon the long story of the degrading superstitions, the

magical practices, the bloody rites, the cruel persecutions, the devastating wars which have borne high over themselves the banner of religion, it is not necessary to enter, because it is the same problem of invoking the sanction of the sacred, not to subject the soul to what ought to be, but to subject what ought to be to one's prejudices, lust of power and arrogance of place. Hypocrisy we often regard only as a cringing vice, but, though of a voluntary humility, it is usually the blindness of arrogance. It is not in the Gospels only that it flaunts itself as God's chosen vessel of power as well as of righteousness and truth.

This is of the first importance for all true knowledge of the Supernatural. It ought to prevent us from even attempting to prove that all evil arises from the Natural. Moreover, it would serve no purpose if we could, for the Supernatural cannot thus disown the Natural. It may be the Natural which makes the lion rend the lamb, and not lie down with it: but it is the Supernatural, with its sense of tremendous, dominating reality, which has created sacrifice, and more particularly human sacrifice. It may be the Natural which has slaughtered multitudes in panic and fear: but only the sense of serving an absolute good could suggest burning a fellow-creature alive with circumstance and high solemnity as a religious duty.

This is a difficulty which ought not to be evaded or minimised. To solve problems by not raising them is futile in any case, but it is as foolish as it is perverse, because it is usually the difficulties which are most important for directing our understanding, and, in the end, for resolving our perplexities. Therefore, as the very first condition of our inquiry, we must not only admit, but set before us as a matter of the first importance, that the Supernatural is the one reality about which, in the deepest sense, we can think erroneously, feel basely and act wrongly, the one environment in respect to which we ought to speak of error, coarseness and sin, while, in the merely natural sphere, we should not speak of positive evil, but only of dullness of thought, lack of sensitiveness of feeling, mistakes of judgment and action as defect. Instead of evading this fact or minimising its significance, we ought to realise that, concerning the Supernatural, the question which may be the most illuminating, even as it is certainly the most difficult, is: What is the particular quality of this environment which makes it one in which we can positively and perversely go astray?

There is no doubt that, with Carlyle, we must say that faith has done much evil, and even say that, without faith, evil would not in the strict sense be evil: and the only question is, whether we can add, as he does, that faith has done all the good, and add also that, without it, there is not, strictly speaking, any good.

(b) IN RESPECT TO RELIGION AND ENVIRONMENT

Man has been defined as a rational animal, as a tool-using animal, as a laughing animal, as a religious animal. If the purpose of a definition is to include the whole class and distinguish it from all else, they are all good definitions. All apply to at least all normal specimens of the race, and are not found, at least in any clearly recognised form, in any other species. But these four characteristics are quite amazingly different, so different as to seem at first sight wholly independent: yet four quite independent parallel lines of development would border on the miraculous. The greater the difference, the greater is the necessity to look for a common root, or to see in one the stem and the other the branches; and the probability would be that there is both a common root and a main stem.

The common root is not difficult to discover. All alike show that man does not accept his environment in the way it is accepted by all other animals. To be rational is to think no longer of things merely as they happen, but to inquire about their permanent relations; to use tools is to accept no more the arrangements life made for him, but to think of altering them to suit himself; to learn to laugh is not to submit to the immediate impression of what threatens, but to determine his own impression by twitching off its mask; to be religious is to face the immediate and convenient, even when he could not reason, or work, or laugh himself out of them, and to look for something more reliable in them and more permanent beyond them. Thus all are phases of the one peculiarity in man, that, somehow, he was able to gain a footing amid the mere flux of his experience.

This power to seek, amid the flux of experience, the true order and relations of events, to direct their current for his own ends, to stand above their impressions and smile at their threats, to pass beyond their immediate and face value and ask what is beneath them and beyond them, transforms man's whole relation to his environment: and this determines, on the one hand, all that is characteristic in human development, and, on the other, the character of the environment which creates this independence and responds to it.

But it is very improbable that man won four separate and unconnected victories over his environment. One must have been the stem and the other the branches, and the stem must have been what gave him faith to stand on his own feet in the changing flood of circumstances.

Most earlier explanations regarded reason—the power to seek real relations beyond habitual associations—as the original, immediate gift, the special mark in man of the image of his Creator. Then it seemed possible to explain his use of tools by reasoning about the means of livelihood, and his religion by reasoning about the order of the world and the causes of things, while humour was explained also as in some way an affair of reasoning, even if it were only a sort of reasoning of reason out of countenance.

More recently the fundamental postulate has been activity; and, in accord with this view, Bergson takes the distinctive quality of man to be the use of tools. This it is, he says, that has turned man's attention from his own life in the world to the world itself, as an objective possession to be cut up into parts suited to his needs. By this task reason has been developed. Being the intellect of a tool-using animal, it is merely an analysing instrument, and is, therefore, unsuited for understanding any reality of a creative nature, and rather stands in the way of the direct intuition by which alone we can discern it, just as, because a sheep can be cut up into chops, we are apt to think it came into being for this purpose. Humour, he argues, is merely a neater tool than digging your elbow into his ribs for adjusting your relations with your neighbour.

But, with regard both to reason and the use of tools as the stem of the specially human development, we have the same difficulty. How was man able to stand far enough back from the stream of passing events, with its associations by repetition and its immediate appeal to his desires and fears, to inquire into its real and abiding relations, and to deal with it by working changes in it? How did he win the required forethought and patience and postponement of his desires? How, in short, did he escape from the mere flux of his experience?

No one, so far, has sought the main stock in laughter. Yet nothing shows more plainly the marvel of the victory by which man has refused to accept his environment at its face value than the transformation of fear by making its object ridiculous. It is at least as great an achievement as starting off with a hoe or even making a beginning with a syllogism. The most blundering attempt at either was only made possible by a measure of emancipation from immediate impression; and when man could grin back in the face of life's menaces, he was in a position to begin thinking about the abiding relations of things and altering their course to suit better his own convenience and to set above them his own purpose. Nor does anything better show the peculiar quality of man as a creature that does not accept the immediate impression of his environment or submit to the domination of its mere sequence of good and evil in a subjection which is vulgarly described as lying down, than the power to meet ills with laughter.[1]

But while humour shows that the essential victory is an attitude of the spirit, even humour cannot be regarded as the stem of man's development, for the power to turn the menace

[1] Probably laughter is physiologically just a checked and transformed gasp of terror, as it were the scream of the pebbles when the billow is cast back by the beach. This theory was first suggested to me by Mr H. H. Farmer, one of my old students, who had thought of it himself, but I have since found it in one of Peacock's novels.

of his environment into absurdity is even more in need of explanation than the power to revise its associations and alter its arrangements. It is a transformation of the vastest consequence in man's dealing with his experience, but it presupposes a very great victory already won over environment, and cannot be invoked to explain it. Moreover, as a matter of fact, humour in any true sense is a late attainment, just because it presupposes a very large measure of victory over the world. So long as man is bound by immediate association and immediate advantage, he may be a somewhat uproarious, but he is at bottom, like all other animals, a solemn creature, though any kind of laughter is at least a holding in check of fear.

Reason, tool-using and laughter, therefore, presuppose and do not explain man's victory over immediate association and immediate advantage and immediate impression.

Only one thing in life challenges in its own right man's submission to his environment, and that is the sacred. But he obtained firm footing to deal with his environment the moment he regarded anything as sacred, because he could say 'No' and was no longer its mere creature. Without this foothold, no extension of his associations, no adjusting himself to his surroundings, no resolve to grin and bear it would have set him free: and without this freedom reason would not have gone beyond mere association, or working changes in his environment taken the place of mere adjustment to it, or laughter lightened grim endurance. But the moment he said, 'This is sacred, this is not in the realm of ordinary values', even granting that it was said of what to us is the insanest of taboos, he had said to his world as well as to himself, 'Thou shalt not'. Forthwith he began to be master of himself, and, thereby, master in his world. Then, in some true sense of the word, he began to be free. Thus by the judgment of the sacred, man was set free from the leading-strings of nature, the nurse which, with the immediate values of the visible world, had hitherto nurtured all living creatures.

Doubtless it was an exchange of much peace of mind and easy acceptance of life for larger hazard and conflict and agony of soul; and it afforded the possibility of degradations and evils which are wrongly called bestial, because creatures guided wholly by nature cannot fall into them. But it also meant entering on the battle in which man has become a reasonable soul, and, in a very marvellous way, lord of creation, and a being capable of vastly higher enjoyment, even if this mean also the possibility of greater folly, greater abuse of life, greater sorrow. And, as the Natural has responded to the reason within him and the purpose before him, it too must be of the quality of the rational and meant to be the mother of the free and not a mere nurse of creatures tied to the apron-strings of its necessity. But, if this reflects a higher environment, the deepest question about religion is, whether it is the supreme call and inspiration and power for fulfilling the task it first imposed on man, or the supreme device for evading it.

(c) IN RESPECT TO EVOLUTION

If there is evolution in our awareness and understanding of any environment, there must necessarily be imperfect stages, and this should not be confused with conscious, positive, regressive evil. And more particularly, if, as has been maintained, it is by the claim of the sacred that man has found footing amid the flux of experience, and, thereby, been enabled to develop reason and conscience, we should expect to find more in the lower that offends the higher stages in the history of man's mind in what concerns the Supernatural than in what concerns the Natural. What has not arrived at the stage of being rational, refined or moral, as we now understand it, is not to be judged as though positively irrational, bestial and immoral. What is due to the progress of religion is one problem, and what religion has to answer for in the way of misuse is another. They may not be easy to distinguish, but they are different problems, and we shall begin with the former.

One of the commonest charges against religion is the appeal it seems to make to self-interest. Yet why should self-interest be a strange thing in religion? Is it not the accepted appeal in the sphere of the Natural? Why is there the constant assumption that it ought not to be so in the sphere of the Supernatural?

Let us take something which is naively business, like most of the Vedic Hymns. "May that be ours which we desire when sacrificing to thee: may we be lords of wealth." "We always are their servants, that we may live even the whole of life." Or the writer of a hymn reminds his patron that it will have material benefit and that this should be shared with the author. Why, when this is in religion, does it evoke a superior smile? Men sacrifice pleasure, ease, health, to be lords of wealth; they are servants for a livelihood; they send in their bills for work done.

Even in those early monuments of religion the answer begins to appear. There is a sense of something overshadowing man's littleness. "Worship the hosts of the Maruts, the terrible, the glorious, the musical. May they be magnified here among us." This and countless other passages show us that some other sense of the world is stirring than can be given by mere selfish desire. This surely should have our regard, however vigorously ordinary human nature maintain itself alongside of it. It may be mixed and imperfect, but in it a nature which lives by more than bread alone begins to respond to a nature which speaks of more than the Natural alone. And if we live in a world in which our souls cleave still less to the dust, it does not become us, if we have climbed higher, to look down with contempt on the ladder by which we climbed. Herein we see that the continuity of ethical reverence with numinous awe and of the ideal sacred with the material sacred concerns not mere psychology, but the continuous dealing with one supernatural reality. If the experience is real, it can only be because such reverence cannot be any combination of mere natural feeling, and that such an absolute valuation cannot be built up by any addition of natural, comparative values.

Here we have an example of how the very progress in reaching higher standards by continuous dealing with the Supernatural is used against the reality of this dealing. It is thought of as some sage people do of education. Because this **only imperfectly** changes people from ignorance, all the faults of half-knowledge are ascribed to it, so that one might imagine that everyone would have been innocent and wise, had not this angel with a flaming sword driven him out of paradise. And ignorant subservience is an Eden of a sort.

Similarly it is assumed that all higher ideas and ideals are somehow produced by material and social interests from the Natural, and that it would all be very beautiful and simple and charming, had not this welter of ideas about the Supernatural mixed everything up into hopeless confusion.

This is a superficial view, not only of religion, but of all history. Hegel's great conception of history as the furnace in which we can see the bricks glowing hot in the fire of fresh experience, which are now built cold into the structure of our thinking, is still very imperfectly understood. Instead, there is much of the old, shallow, unhistorical rationalism, which looks down in contempt on lower levels, ignorant of the fact that they are the hole of the pit from which it was digged. Then, of course, there can be no conception of what Schleiermacher means when he calls history the greatest and most general revelation of the deepest and holiest, and says that religion begins and ends with history. History, he adds, is for religion prophecy. All true history takes its origin in religious ideas and serves a religious purpose; and all that is finest and tenderest in it is to be comprehended only by a religious disposition. It is the prophecy of the abolition of dead mass moved by impact and by blind instinct, which is akin to death—the death-slumber of freedom and humanity, and is the calling into existence of a life, free, individual, exalted. "To this the work of the minutes and the centuries is directed: it is the great ever-advancing work of redemptive love."[1] But, granting that the sense of the holy may have been essential in developing the rational and moral, and that it may have itself been very imperfectly rational and moral, what of the amazing gallery of queer objects which have been regarded as sacred?

This we may take as the whole problem of the material sacred. It is mainly determined by fixed ideas; and escape from

[1] *On Religion*, trans. Oman, p. 82.

it is mainly by the acquisition of free ideas. As this will play an important part in all the discussion which follows, we must try to have a clear conception of what is meant by the terms.

Usually the decisive question is thought to be the freedom of the will. And it is a decisive question, not only about man, but also about the universe. As it has been put, If there is no freedom in the microcosm, we have no reason for ascribing it to the macrocosm. But there is a previous question, and one which sheds even more light on the whole nature of our environment as well as on man's whole career in it. This is the question of fixed and free ideas. There is part of the order around us given as fixed idea, and there is part to an understanding of which we attain only slowly and with much perplexity and error by free idea. Here the immediate consideration is that, while the absolute requirement of the sacred is the source of the mastery over environment which has enabled man to have free ideas, a large part of the history of religion is to be explained by the slowness and difficulty of this achievement, and is to be ascribed to the persistence of fixed ideas.

The main point to be borne in mind is that 'fixed idea' has nothing to do with 'idée fixe', that is morbid obsession. It does not even mean fixed in its meaning. Here it is used exclusively for an idea fixed in its context, a thing normal in all minds and dominating in some. Possibly no idea, at least of the higher animals, is quite fixed in its meaning, but all their ideas seem to be fixed in their context. When they come up they bring with them their whole experienced setting, somewhat in the same way as, at a rudimentary stage of reading, we might be able to think our own thoughts with the author, but be incapable of any thinking without him. So nothing can be reproduced except in the original form and context, even though there be some power of altering thought in relation to it.

A free idea, on the contrary, is one separable from its context in any kind of special experience and from any particular material embodiment, and which we can take by itself and apply to any set of circumstances. This is only possible when by firm footing in the flux of experience there is escape from mere immediate impression and natural desire. But, because, as we have seen, this triumph over mere happenings is by the power to oppose them given by the sacred, it does not follow that, though all free ideas depend on the sacred, all judgments of the sacred are free ideas. On the contrary, what evolves them as reason and insight and conscience naturally has to do without them till they arrive. By this is explained what we shall call the 'material sacred'. It is just an idea fixed in the particular material conditions which stirred the sense of the holy and gave occasion for the valuation as sacred.

If this be a right account of the material sacred, there is no more difficulty than with any other higher development in explaining how it passes into the ideal sacred, which also had a long progress before it could be summed up as the absolute value of the true, the beautiful, and the good. The rudimentary presence of the higher in the lower form is not more difficult to discover, nor are the stages of the evolution of the lower into the higher less closely linked than in any other kind of human progress. In the first place, the most primitive and material valuation of anything sacred manifests the three abiding forces of spiritual advance: (1) the affirmation of a reality of absolute value; (2) the subordination of all else to it; (3) a tendency to regard its nature less materially. Therefore, ideal quality was there from the beginning. In the second place, we have in all history a singular insistence that nothing is ever new in religion, that it is in man's world and man's heart already, that he has always been rejecting it, and that it is not something only recently brought to his notice. The prophet in all ages speaks as though he were merely reviving an old religion, and the more rational and ethical the newness is, the greater is the assurance that it merely comes out of the old. Nor is this either convention or historical illusion, because there is no sacred which does not have something of ideal value in which the rational and ethical are potentially present.

This is not hindered by the fact that the sacred may, besides being material, also be irrational and immoral, because a possibility of good is, in all human uses, always a possibility of evil. And in this case we have an explanation in the very close dependence both of reason and conscience upon the sacred. This will require fuller justification, but how can we conceive them developing with no restraint upon desire beyond fear of consequence? And, if so, how could religion use reason and conscience at the start for determining its character, when it had to develop them in the process of exploring its territory?

We may not always be able to say what is positively a breach of truth and beauty and goodness and what is merely negatively crudeness of conception and grossness of action inevitable in the course of development, but we should never think them the same problem.

Even in our own better ordered minds, our deepest feelings and our highest thoughts are often stirred by the trivial and not infrequently by the repellent, and are by no means rigidly reserved for sublime occasions. The experiences of primitive man apparently were much more accidental, sporadic, unarranged and uncriticised even than ours: and to the extent in which this was so, the difference in his view of the sacred depended on different experiences. Yet it was only to this extent. The real difference was not due to anything in the experiences themselves, but to the absence of power to deal freely with them; and the main reason why his higher experiences remained embedded in crude material things is simply that, lacking free ideas, he was unable to separate any part of his experience from the whole context in which it happened to him. Emancipation entirely depends on this freedom, which enables man to set his ideas apart from their accidental associations: and without this power, we too should have had few sacred things free from bizarre material associations. Even as it is, we are, perhaps, not quite so superior to the savage as we imagine, but the lack of this power of free ideas, this power of selecting from his experience and thinking it as his own generalised thought, and so of finding what is to be revered in it apart from its material embodiments, is precisely what makes man primitive. His experience, being as it were solid with its context, was necessarily material in form. Moreover, this form was cherished, because his sole method of seeking to revive his experience of higher reality was to return as much as possible to the material conditions in which it first came. This explains not only why primitive religion has many crude sacred objects, but why it is so much occupied with particular places, marking them with pillars or stocks or such like. It was in order to return to the exact spot and thereby to revive the presence of the sacred formerly felt there. Though the amazing pantheon is not only of the sky and the hosts of heaven and of river and mountain, but of birds and beasts and creeping things, when we think of the way of arriving at it, we should not be wholly without understanding, or doubt that the experience may concern high matters which are really and truly sacred, while the embodiment of it is, so to speak, rather gargoyle than seraph. And with this should go his queer and, to us at least, absurd and irrational taboos, for they are all ways of respecting the presence of sacred powers, of powers not at any cost to be brought down to the convenient.

This limitation, which tied his conception of higher ideas to material objects, is not at all confined to religion or to ideas of the sacred, because primitive man could no more conceive sharpness apart from a cutting instrument than sacredness apart from material embodiment. Yet, as he knew what sharpness is, so he knew also what sacredness means. Therefore, if the absence of free ideas left the sacred unemancipated from a sporadic and unreasoned and material experience, we ought not to conclude that there was nothing in it besides the accidental and material. On the contrary, the recognition of anything as sacred, as of an absolute value above desire and even above life, was the well-spring of all endeavour after emancipation from a material world merely appealing to his appetites, because this alone in his life was not measured by them. Even in its most material forms, therefore, he was finding a higher power which made this victory over the material world possible, and this he made plain by revering it above all might of visible things and obeying its requirements at all cost of loss or hazard.

This valuation as sacred, therefore, we ought to esteem as the spring of all self-mastery and all mastery over the world, as the sublime attainment by which man became truly man. Man with a taboo, which he would not break for any earthly gain or even to save his life, was no longer a mere animal whose only inhibition was the threat of suffering or the fear of death. He might still fear what could only kill the body and his judgment of sacredness might still relate itself to this fear, but if there was something in his experience more sacred than life, the fear of death as the final ill was conquered in principle: and this victory is the condition of all progress, for there is no real spiritual good possible at lower cost than the hazard of our material life, nor any impossible at that price.

This relation of the judgment of the sacred to human progress is obscured by the frequent use of its sanction to defend reaction. A belief or custom is fixed with all its present material associations by being regarded as sacred. Then it becomes a sort of fenced city from which it is hard to escape and which can resist attacks both of right and reason. Instead of leading men into a world of free ideas in which the sacred liberates itself from material bonds, sacredness is invoked on behalf of these associations. Thereupon, we have an idolatry which is the worst form of reaction and a 'yoke of bondage'.

But men can misuse anything, and the possibility of good is usually the measure of the possibility of evil. Moreover, it is on the steepest road that the temptation to make our progress the justification for resting where we are is strongest. Wherefore, the misuse of the sacred to arrest progress is no disproof of its importance as the spring of the specially human evolution. Nor does the fact that reaction is mainly a return to its material form, or at least a maintaining of it when greater freedom offers, disprove the importance even of the material sacred as a necessary stage of progress, because influences are like persons who have the more power to arrest progress if they have been effective to advance it.

Both results we can see plainly in the religion of Israel. The prophets, just because their higher truths were sacred and required all their devotion, emancipated religion from material associations in a way unparalleled elsewhere. These associations, which were sacred in the popular mind and were defended as such, the prophets denounced as idolatry and the chief hindrance to the discernment of what they regarded as the true sacred. Nevertheless, even the prophetic religion had itself travelled through a stage at which the judgment of a sacredness above life had been embodied in material objects like the ark.

The ark is a specially interesting example of the material sacred. It stirred an awed sense of the holy which made the touching of it sacrilege; and yet part of its contents could be destroyed when it became itself an object of worship. It represented a value which was above life and killed the profane person who would steady it as though it were a mere box, yet the natural life alongside of it was also becoming sacred, and that through the religion embodied in the ark.

Whether we can speak, as some writers do, especially some French writers, of a prelogical mind, within the scope of human history, may admit of question, but certainly there must have been a prelogical mind somewhere in human development. And to this day there are persons, even in civilised countries, for whom logic is merely a device for giving an appearance of plausibility to what they wish to believe. Still more plainly logic in the large sense of utter loyalty to all objective truth, and the standard of it as an absolute standard of veracity in all our understanding, has had very manifest and comparatively recent extension of its scope, yet is still, in many minds, at a stage which can only be described as rudimentary. But so long as there is a sense of the absolute claim of truth in so far as we see it, we must be advancing in the power to think: and when this fails no increase of information serves any high end.

Still more manifestly the ethical standard has grown with the generations, though, even yet, moral judgments are not always free from material taboos. But if we are loyal to the claim of what is sacred, we must be advancing in the power to discern what it is and to act upon it with more freedom. And this will be, not by reasoning, but by a finer discernment of the beauty of the holiness.

(*d*) IN RESPECT TO THEOLOGY

If the Supernatural is the sphere in which man can become only a little lower than the angels, it offers also the possibility of sinking much lower than the brutes. The reason of this is that the Supernatural is the possibility of all that ought to be and not the fixed ground of what already is. Hence the possibility that the Supernatural is the most certain reality, in which alone man's higher achievements have so much as come within the range of conception, is in no way refuted by the fact that it is the only sphere in which we can properly go astray. Yet this is so only on one condition, which is that the Supernatural is an order for which the personal, independent understanding, appreciation and consecration of the individual is essential. This is the vital question, not only about human freedom, but about the nature of the world in which we are free, and this may be summed up by saying that both the heights and the depths depend on the significance of the individual. The Supernatural derives its quality from being the order which neither asks nor receives any other than individual loyalty. Moreover, only as man receives it or rejects it is it either good or evil a true choice. This it is that makes good religion the possibility of all higher experience and achievement, and bad religion the worst source of stagnation, of unreality, and of self-satisfied iniquity.

This is not merely a question of the Supernatural. The misuse of the Natural is by means of the emancipation of free ideas from our fixed dependence; and this is given by the Supernatural. But, if the freedom is to be true and emancipating, it must be a call to think them rightly together, and to ask what is their true relation to us and our true relation to them Otherwise, it merely allows us to substitute what we wish to believe for what we ought to believe. And while this concerns right thinking, right thinking, in such matters, is never apart from right feeling and acting.

All environment deals with us and we deal with all environment as meaning, and for this our thinking about it is of the utmost importance. We know a reality not, as some seem to suppose, when we do not think about it, but only when we think about it rightly, which is when our meaning corresponds to its meaning. Thus a vast amount of thinking and valuing, which is a kind of science, is embedded even in our perceptions And, in the same way, a vast amount of thinking and valuing, which is a kind of theology, interpenetrates our higher intuitions. For this reason we can argue ourselves out of any experience and, without right thinking, we cannot rightly receive the plainest facts.

This is sometimes obscured by the difference between our speculative and our practical thinking. Just as we may be sceptics with regard to the material world in profession while all our actions in it prove our theory to be mere intellectual gymnastic, so we may be materialists in theory while we show that our real faith is of a quite different quality. But this does not make theory of no importance, because it always in time works back into our experience and comes to determine the kind of experience of which we are capable. If we are not continually seeing our theory through our experience, we shall come to see our experience through our theory. Thus the theory of the Indian, about the world of the senses being illusion, makes the world to him in time a dream and paralyses his practical dealing with it. In the same way, what we may call our theology is of vital importance, for though our practical spiritual world may long continue very different from our theoretical, the theoretical will gradually bring it to its own level, so that, as a matter of fact, nothing has more determined the history of the race than men's conscious, though not necessarily their formulated, theologies, meaning by that their ideas about the Supernatural. Thus, even for seeing the highest, we may say that the greatest need of every age is a true theology.

Religion is not theology, any more than life is science, the Supernatural, like the Natural, being known only by direct experience. But, man, at least as he develops, cannot regard any environment as real, unless it is reasonable. This does not mean that he must assume it to be one rational unity, but it does mean that he must think it real, if the more he is able to think things in it together the better ordered they seem to be. Moreover, rational man at least cannot even feel or judge aright except in relation to this pursuit of objective knowledge. Not merely is he debased by wilfully perverting the truth, but unless he is consecrated to a whole-hearted purpose to know his environment as it exists, he cannot be penetrating or even genuine. Feeling it through, living it through, and thinking it through all go together.

The greatest question about anyone is his theology, or even his no-theology in this sense; and in the history of man's progress the theologies of his religions have been of primary importance. At the same time, we have only to think of them to know that we no more arrive at pure and undefiled religion in the theologies than anywhere else. They are all, as we shall see, attempts at thinking together the Natural and the Supernatural, but there have been constantly ideas of both which are neither exalted nor reasonable. And again we have both reasons, partly backward development, partly unreality and perverseness, especially lack of courage to explore and colonise, or, in other words, failure to follow the requirements of sincerity, courage, and endurance, in thinking as in acting, to the end.

Much theology is like much science, a mere exercise in the pleasing assurance that the Almighty would have too much sense to depart from our views of how the world should be run. Even matter and motion can be, for this highly gratifying end, a kind of cheaply rational Almighty. Unless theology is, like true science, about experience and not in place of it, it is worthless. But, if it has been so occupied, however inadequately or even mistakenly or even foolishly, we shall, if we realise how large the problem is, and how it involves all progress of heart and purpose as well as mind, not be too readily repelled by its crudities; nor shall we too hastily condemn the departures from the ways of what may be in us an all too pedestrian common sense, which prides itself on its reasonableness because it has neither imagination nor courage.

This inquiry is not a theology, even in this very general sense: but it springs from a conviction of the supreme importance of thinking on high matters; and is an attempt to lay a foundation for theology, by considering its method and its problems. It does not aim at defending the theology of any religion, but its purpose is to discover what should be settled, before any particular question is raised. Yet, as nothing is settled by abstract reasoning apart from experience and history, the theologies of the religions are an important part of the material of our inquiry, only it is vain to deal with them till we have seen first what the inquiry involves.

CHAPTER VII

METHOD AND PROBLEMS

THE question of method naturally follows. This whole inquiry is concerned with it, but, as the main contention is that no other method than surveying our environment from the highest standpoint we can reach, with all our experience and all our insight as well as knowledge, can be applied with any profit, we can best begin by settling our relations to the opposite method, which seeks to start as low as possible and build up on this foundation by reasoning. The task is the more necessary that this method was grounded on a right principle, which has to be maintained, even when the particular application of it is rejected.

As the movement which is sometimes called Rationalism, or, as it called itself, The Age of Reason, and sometimes the Illumination or Illuminism, which is the equivalent of the French *Illuminisme* and the German *Aufklarung*, illustrates both what is right and what is wrong, with it we shall begin.

Rationalism expresses its temper and method and Illuminism its attitude and principle. As it was the latter which made it a crisis in the history of thought, possibly the greatest in all the centuries, we shall take it first.

(*a*) ILLUMINISM

No more than any other movement of thought did it come as a bolt from the blue. The Greeks had long before said that "Man is the measure of the universe", and all down the ages men were found bold enough to question traditional authorities They grew in number and boldness in the twelfth century and from the Reformation the volume and daring of this revolt steadily increased. But the Illumination stated as a principle, with universal reasons, what had hitherto been felt only in connexion with particular situations and it is always a great event, when what men are only feeling after in practice, is definitely presented as a principle.

It affirmed that truth is not truth for us, except as we ourselves see it, and that right is not righteous, except as we ourselves determine it; and that to determine our own beliefs by our own reason and our own duty by our own conscience, is man's highest and most personal concern, which he may not delegate with honour. Thus, although it was too negatively stated, the result was to set up, against all authorities external to it, the authority of the witness of reality to itself, and to make it our duty to defer to it alone. For this reason Kant regarded it as man's arrival at intellectual manhood.

This principle is far from having been always accepted in practice. Even science has frequently been retarded by setting up persons like Newton and Darwin and making them the standard of orthodoxy. But in science it has never been questioned in theory, whereas in theology it has been rejected in theory as well as in practice.

As a positive principle, it rests on the faith that the witness of reality will not deceive us, if we approach it with the right questions, and if, in sincerity, we spare no pains to understand its answers. However much this may be used in science, it is a religious faith; and there is no sphere where we ought to be surer of it than religion. Moreover, as science may not be every man's business, while religion is, the obligation to determine our own religious beliefs, and the actions which accord with them, must be, as nowhere else, a universal personal requirement.

On this matter a great deal of dust has been raised by confusing authority as a secondary means of knowing truth with authority as the basis of it. For example, it is said: "You believe the astronomer, when he says the earth goes round the sun, though he is a fallible man and all your own observation shews the sun going round the earth. How much more should you believe the inspired authorities, through whom the Spirit of God speaks, even if they tell you things alien from your reason, or possibly opposed to it!"[1]

[1] This thesis I once heard defended in a sermon in Cologne Cathedral.

The answer is that the astronomer only professes to be a secondary authority, while the evidence of the motion of the sun and the earth is the primary authority, to which every inquirer is free to appeal if he will take the trouble: whereas the Pope or the Fundamentalist Bible, let us say, professes to be the primary authority, with nothing behind to which anyone could dream of appealing.

In contrast to this, what made the Illumination a portent was, not that it challenged this or that particular authority, which had been done before, but that it said, truth is not truth for us unless we see it, and righteousness not righteousness unless we judge it; and that, even if there were such authorities, we could not, in loyalty to the image of God in us, give our minds and consciences into their keeping. Wherefore, if theology is ever to be a convincing pursuit, it must accept four principles which belong to all inquiries into the nature of any kind of experience:

(1) Religion, like all else that claims to deal with a real world, must submit to open investigation. It is of the nature of all reality to challenge investigation: and fear of investigation can only arise from doubt about the reality.

(2) A right investigation seeks to know only what exists, so as to have a full awareness of it, and, as far as possible, an understanding of it, and we may not set any limit to the inquiry.

(3) We have at least as much right to assume that man's mind is made in the image of the Supernatural as in the image of the Natural, and that, rightly used, it is in this sphere, at least as much as in the sphere of the Natural, the measure of the universe.

(4) True humility is not submission to human authority, but total disregard of it when the reality speaks to us. And this must be at least as true of the Supernatural as of the Natural. Here too the only objective authority is the authority of the object.

As nothing else, religion sets a man alone. The recognition of this fact, as final and decisive, is the watershed of all thinking, and more particularly of religious thinking. Though science is concerned with truth valid for all, no one has a scientific mind till he has emancipated himself from scientific fashion, treats the greatest scientists only as his teachers, and acknowledges no ultimate authority save the witness of reality to his own mind. Religion is equally concerned with universal truth, and still more with harmony in the love of it, but no one is strictly a religious person till he has realised the utter loneliness of his spirit and desires to hear nothing but what speaks in this aloneness, and no deliverance from it except harmony with the reality of this sacred world which sets him in this isolation.

This independence we may call the form of freedom: and we shall find it to be of such high importance for estimating all spiritual value as well as for investigating facts, that we owe a great debt to the Illumination for showing so clearly and insistently its place.

(b) RATIONALISM

The repudiation of this debt, and the idea of the movement as a denial of our spiritual heritage and the impoverishment of all our higher values has not, however, been wholly without justification. The form was so exalted that it seemed a matter of indifference what it might contain. Insight into the whole depth of reality and consecration to the whole requirement of the highest had no place accorded to it compared with the mere negative insistence on being independent. So long as we did not believe anything not forced on us by mere logical argument, or did not do anything except what was imposed on us by rationalised imperatives, it seemed not to matter how much we missed of truth and righteousness, in complete disregard to the saddest of all failures in life, which is just what we miss of its fullness. Thus man was made a much poorer measure of the universe than he has it in him to be, and it was forgotten that, while his own knowing is the only measure man has, it is used to profit only when he realises how very far the universe is beyond his measuring, and how with his best knowing and groping, he is, as Newton said, only a child gathering pebbles on the shore of the great ocean of truth.

Thus we might say that Illuminism remains right about the form of freedom, while its rationalistic temper and outlook have proved to be an impoverishment of its content. This form may test, but does not replace, a positive faith in a witness of reality which is above all other witness, and a positive duty to lay ourselves open in every way to its testimony. From lack of this the movement failed to provide a right method for studying either the Natural or the Supernatural.

(1) It did not proceed to ask, what is the Natural or what is the Supernatural, but it imposed on the former the conclusions of its science and on the latter the conclusions of its theology. Thus it reduced religion to intellectual doctrines about God, providence and immortality, as it reduced nature to a mechanical scheme of matter and motion.

(2) It did not seek understanding by full awareness, but reduced all truth to what could be proved by abstract reasoning. Instead of realising that each kind of reality has its own witness, which alone can determine the true method of investigation, it determined beforehand the method, and limited its inquiry to what this could include.

(3) It regarded nothing in man's mind save the understanding, and failed to realise how much is assumed in making even it more than the accidental equipment of a certain kind of animal. In assuming the validity of our reasoning, it accepted something like Descartes' idea of a perfect being. But, when it tried to get truth out of the mere notion of abstract universality, and goodness out of abstract laws, and beauty out of abstract utility, mind was conceived neither in the image of the Natural nor of the Supernatural.

(4) It failed to develop the humility which realises that man is small and the universe great, but assumed itself to be great by making the universe small. Perhaps the root of all

these limitations was just this temper, and we shall see later how grave the limitation was for all higher insight into the Natural as well as the Supernatural.

(c) THE METHOD OF DESCARTES

The ideal of its method, both in science and philosophy, was to start as near to nothing as possible and to build up by reasoning a whole cosmogony. Theology continued to set its heart on starting from the other end with our widest and highest experience, but it was unhappy in the sense of working with a method which the age had decided was not scientific, and it had to face results which science and philosophy appeared to have won from the other method, which denied not only its method but its province.

Though Descartes did not create this method or expect this result, he gave it the most impressive historical expression: and, as the influence of it is not yet wholly of the past, at the risk of repeating what has often been repeated before, we must again consider his *Discourse on Method*

Descartes' motive we can accept as the inspiration of all inquiry. He earnestly desired to know how to distinguish the true from the false, that he might be able to discern the right path in life and proceed in it with confidence. To this end he sought to emancipate himself from haste and prejudice, that he might neither reject truths because they are strange nor accept errors because they are familiar. This emancipation he sought in travel and intercourse with men of other traditions: and he had more hope of finding truth in the reasonings of persons intimately and practically involved in life's business, who have to bear the brunt of judging amiss, than in those of arm-chair speculators, who are so sheltered from life that they might indulge mere conceit of cleverness and remoteness from common sense without patent disaster.

The relevancy of this to all inquiries is apparent. It must be common to all that they search for truth and hold truth to be what corresponds with reality. In seeking this reality, we have to guard against accepting our presuppositions and prejudices as right thinking: and we may not allow even right thinking to determine right observing; while the test of right observing is in use and not in mere contemplation. Nor are the prejudices against which we must guard ourselves merely what are known as popular. In every department we can docilely look with spectacles provided by the pundit, and not measure our dogmas by the universe, but the universe by our dogmas. Nor is there yet any better device for giving us freedom than the experience of practical men in the actual, strenuous conduct of life. Mistakes and omissions which cost nothing in the study are always dearly paid for in life; and no right thinking can afford to ignore the test of practice.

Descartes' method may be summed up in four rules:

(1) To accept only what presents itself to the mind so clearly and distinctly as to exclude all grounds of doubt.

(2) To divide the difficulties into as many parts as possible.

(3) To commence with the simple and ascend to the more complex: and to observe this order even when the sequence in time is different.

(4) To revise carefully, that nothing be omitted.

These rules show that the ideal of method was geometrical reasoning: and its persistence is not due to its arguments, which have often been refuted, but to the view that geometrical proof is the ideal of evidence.

Descartes begins with the postulate, that a truth is that which is *clear*, in the sense of being self-evident, and *distinct*, in the sense of being dependent on nothing else. Then, upon this foundation, all else is to be built by consistent and consequent reasoning.

His ambition is to rebuild the whole edifice of his knowledge by this method. He begins by taking, as it were, the most respectable lodgings in what he finds accepted around him, being determined in his choice mainly by moderation of opinion and by what will enable him to persist in one line of inquiry without persisting in one set of opinions. Then he proceeds to pull down the whole edifice of his own opinions, razing it to the foundations, with the resolve only to use the old material, for rebuilding, as it endures the test of his method.

In his knowledge of himself as a thinking being he thought he found what is clear and distinct, in the sense of being self-evident and not depending on anything else. Nothing in the outward world has this evidence, because it is known only indirectly through our knowing, and might be mere dream and phantasy. But his own existence as a thinking being seemed to be given in the very fact of thinking, and to be beyond doubt, shining in its own certainty, having much depending on it, but itself depending entirely on its own witness.

The merely logical form, by which the method then proceeds, exposes it to merely logical difficulties. From the idea of a perfect being in his mind he proceeds to the actuality of such a being, because what exists is more perfect than what does not exist. He then brings back the certainty of the reality of our experience of an objective world by the certainty that such a being would not deceive us.

As argument, this is exposed to Kant's criticism that a hundred dollars are as large in imagination as in possession, but not as real. Yet the contention, apart from its scholastic form, is not quite so cheap. When we seek the meaning behind the geometrical form of argument, we see that it lays hold of the important point that even doubt goes beyond any mere product of nature Mere nature does not question itself and cannot be other than it is, but doubt springs from some sense of what is true beyond our questioning, which gives confidence that truth can be found and that our search for it will not deceive us.

Yet this call of the beyond, of what he calls the perfect, though it is the only means whereby the method can start working, has no real place accorded to it even in his own reasoning. For him that alone is convincing which comes out of what is already given As we can only produce in this way mechanically, that is by mere alteration of parts, only mechanical explanations come to be accepted. His chief illustration is from Harvey's theory of the circulation of the blood, which he finds convincing just in so far as it can be understood mechanically. As he then extends this explanation to all organisms, he plainly regards it as the one self-imposing type of explanation. Thus the perfect ahead, always waiting to be realised, disappears, and its place is wholly taken by mere transformation of what exists and acts as impact from behind.

In science, for a long time, this seemed to be the only adequate method: and on it was based a view of the universe as all a manifestation of one law of motion. Newton's laws of motion seemed to fulfil the requirements of clearness and distinctness which make them postulates, because they can all be reduced to the one law of inertia, the law that everything continues in the same state of rest or motion except in so far as it is altered by the impact of other forces. This seemed to be a postulate, because the forces do not seem to be doing anything except merely continuing as they are. Then the ideal of all explanation in science seemed to be the reduction of all phenomena to forces acting after this simple fashion, in short to be explanation of all change as a mere change of appearance.

There was a gain for the human mind in this attempt to arrange its experience of the world, for we only know what is new as we relate it to our experience of what is old and already known to us. But the idea that the new was in any way explained by being made merely the old was an illusion And now, in science, as we shall see later, the method is proving inadequate even for arranging knowledge, and is being set aside as a hindrance to progress.

In philosophy we have had an application of the method which still more closely follows Descartes. Spinoza alone has attempted the geometrical method, but there has been a long succession, down to Hegel and his followers, who, also starting with the postulate of thought, seek by a process of dialectic to manifest the cosmic process by which the Universal Thought unfolds into the universe. This also has proved barren, and we are waiting to-day for some change in philosophy away from Hegelianism and the process of thought as the key to the universe, corresponding to the movement of science away from

Newtonism, with its assumption of the laws of motion as the efficient cause of all things.

(*d*) HOW A METHOD SHOULD BE DETERMINED

From Descartes' own *Discourse*, we can see what is omitted. What makes him question the truth of what he believes and gives him assurance of finding right beliefs, if rightly sought, is an idea of perfection which he is led to ascribe to a perfect being. This we can interpret as an ideal of truth and goodness, which is not a mere natural product, because a natural product, at least as he understands it, cannot be ahead of what has produced it or require aught different from what the forces working in the past have brought about.

But there is a still further and even more important consideration. If there are such things in the world as a freedom which reaches beyond itself, and values not yet realised, and a purpose which makes things as they are have their meaning beyond them, they cannot be dealt with by a method which looks exclusively to what is lower for the manifestation of the higher, and to dividing up difficulties. If this method assume itself to be the only valid method of knowledge, it will already have ruled out the possibility that the universe has any supernatural aspect, or at least that this could have any significance for us. All that it could mean would be that, without inquiry, the reality of the Supernatural, and of the Natural as the means for its realisation, had been disposed of. Rationalism never asked itself how a reality of this kind could be known, but adopted a method which could not know it, however evident it might be, because it is a method which does not look in the direction in which such a reality could be found.

While every study must lay its foundation in awareness of all the facts, and should determine its explanations by them, and not its facts by its explanations, Rationalism shows not only that theory may be blinkers upon our awareness, but also that man at least cannot be aware without some right understanding. Hence the value of a right and adequate theology, as well as of a right and adequate science.

METHOD AND PROBLEMS

But Rationalism more than almost any other movement increased the danger of a wrong theology by identifying religion more entirely with theology. Like all other real investigations, theology must depend on the nature of the object of its inquiry, which in this case is the Supernatural, and must also be secondary to the experience of it, which, in this case, is religion. By so doing, Rationalism was only following what it was already doing in another sphere, by making science the measure of nature, not nature of science. The effect in both cases was to deny the reality of the experiences by which we know them; and it ended in questioning all reality whatsoever.

Each kind of reality has its own kind of witness, and this must determine its own kind of method. This cannot be laid down beforehand: and the chief requirement is an open mind to learn as we go on our way. But it is evident that the witness of a sphere which is mainly concerned with what ought to be cannot be the same as that of a sphere which is wholly concerned with what is. We have not only to consider its facts in the light of all the aspects of reality we cannot escape, but to be aware, to the utmost limit of intuition and anticipation, of the whole reality. If this is a higher reality, which is seeking to reveal itself through our whole experience in this present world, it requires us to reach out after our farthest vision and follow even the dimly discerned beckoning of its requirements, as they speak to us of what is beyond demonstration and only discerned in moments of deeper insight and higher consecration. It thus deals with life's supreme business of progress: and this is its justification.

Humanity will have fallen out of the march when its dominant interest in knowledge and enterprise ceases to be a reaching forward to the things that are before.

Even physical science, though it looks backwards, is for the guidance of the future. But as it concerns itself only with what will be the same in the future, it leaves out everything except the uniformities it is sure to meet again. The Supernatural, however, from its very quality, is the yet unrealised. Therefore, a study of it is interested, not in the uniformities of the past, but in the new, the exceptional, the experiences above our own. And, as it hopes to find the unseen manifested in the things that do appear, it may not concern itself merely with abstractions or omit anything of the present, concrete, varied world that is within our finite grasp.

(e) THE PROBLEMS

While every study should lay its foundation on awareness of all the facts, its business is the interpretation of facts. This means that it must face the problems raised by the facts. But, just as we should judge our explanations by facts, and not measure our facts by our explanations, so we should determine our method by our problems, and not limit our problems for the convenience of our method.

As our study concerns the Natural as well as the Supernatural, no problem life raises may be wholly ignored: but the main problems which face us are three, though each has two aspects, which may appear to be contradictory, but cannot be separated.

1. All experience is the particular experience of individual minds. It is grouped round one centre, which, in the deepest sense, is ourself It is arranged according to one meaning, which is the more perfectly objective as it is truly our own. The one organ of it is that very imperfect instrument, our own mind, and there is a sense in which it must be all a mental construction Yet, on the other hand, nothing we know presents itself as merely our knowing, but affirms itself to be reality entirely independent of it. Moreover, our knowing is taken to be an actual awareness of this reality, and not a mental copy of it. Finally, a large part of it affirms itself to be not of a mental texture at all, but to be a physical universe of which we ourselves are only a very insignificant part.

No solution which disregards either aspect of the problem can ever be satisfactory. On the one hand, our knowledge cannot be a purely mental creation, and, on the other, it cannot be a mere effect of an outward cause or a mere reflexion passively, as in a mirror, of an outward reality. Neither the appeal to mind, nor the affirmation of objective reality may be permanently ignored without distorting our view of the Natural; and the study of the Supernatural has been still more disastrously affected by regarding only one aspect. Knowledge is taken to be exclusively a mental construction, any correspondence it may have with reality having to be proved by something apart from our experience itself; or our knowledge is taken to be imposed wholly from without, and to be true in proportion as it requires no task of awareness and understanding or any kind of active dealing with it on our part. In neither case can our knowing be truly knowledge

Nor is it enough to hold these two aspects together and not to neglect either. In our active life they are intimately one. The more our minds are active, the greater the assurance that our knowledge is objective; and the stronger and more direct the impression of the reality, the more our minds are stirred to activity concerning it. Only in this intimate unity can we ever hope to find any light on our knowledge of reality, natural or supernatural.

2. Underneath all the change and continual movement of the world as we experience it, there seems to be a rigid framework of some kind, capable of being quantitatively measured and presented in mathematical formulae · yet, even the discovery of this order has been the achievement of minds which work by meaning and, therefore, not by mechanism or anything capable of quantitative measurement. The interests of freedom are the spring of the whole enterprise of science; upon free ideas and free experiment all its methods depend, and only for its uses by freedom has measurement or mechanism any value.

For generations it has been the habit to take one of the aspects of this problem and regard it as the explanation of all things. For one person the universe was a meaningless system of measurable vibrations, a mere mechanical change of a blind force, working in a determined process, the present in such equivalence with the past as to be merely another form of it, however strangely different, all of it so entirely of impact that there could be nothing of purpose. The very knowing by which we know any reality and the purposeful activity by which alone we prove it were a sort of vapour hovering over the stream of material forces and wholly determined by it. For another person, freedom and meaning and purpose were the explanation of all things. This no doubt was truer, but its value was lost when the question of the measurable, quantitative, mechanical nature of things was passed over dry-shod. Then freedom was too near mere arbitrary action to have purpose, and the universe too unreliable to have meaning.

In the world and in our experience mechanism and freedom are never apart, much less antagonistic. The rigidity of the spade has its significance and purpose in the freedom of the hand, and the efficiency of the hand has as its instrument the mechanical working of the spade. Plainly the two are mere aspects of one problem and belong together: and the inability of our knowledge to compass their union is no manner of reason for setting them apart or in any kind of opposition. Even for science it is folly, for light on the problem may come from considering the two aspects together, and certainly can never come from denying what the whole method of science, as well as of experience, presupposes. Only as man has achieved freedom of thought and independence of action, has he discovered the world to be ordered and secure; and the more he has discovered what is fixed in it, the more it has been for him the sphere of freedom. Scientific conclusions which would deny the experience by which any science could be reached and the only conditions under which it could be applied refute themselves. Yet the Natural, though, if it were nothing but the necessary it would be meaningless, when regarded as merely the shadow of acts of freedom, has neither order nor reality.

Yet this union of order and freedom is of still more importance for the study of the Supernatural, because there the two aspects of the problem can be more utterly and more calamitously divorced, and theory may far more gravely pervert, not only our understanding, but even our awareness of our environment.

In spite of the obvious concern of the Supernatural with freedom, the tendency here too is towards a rigid, necessary order, either of the fixed fate or of the foreknowledge absolute type, just because this is what man himself could manage. Then it really ceases to be supernatural in any higher sense of reverence and spiritual judgment and purpose. Nor is the case better when nothing except freedom is considered, when man is taken to be free purely by making up his mind, apart from all question of the mind he makes up and the nature of the world about which he makes it up. This also takes all order and reality from the Supernatural. If we look back upon the history of the human spirit, we find that the idea of an arbitrary world and of fatalistic determination in it went together, and that the idea of an ordered world and of a world which challenges and supports our freedom have advanced together. Plainly, therefore, freedom and order can neither be alien nor apart.

3. All our awareness of any kind of reality—natural or supernatural—and all our power to judge it, interpret it, use it, have come to us in the continual stream of change, in which no two moments are alike, but, as the old Greek said, "all things flow". We may no longer say that there is nothing new under the sun, for, when we look back far enough, we see that the solid earth and all the life upon it, and our thoughts about them and our sense of their value, and even the standards by which we measure them, have all arrived through the process of change. The question is whether this is merely

> Time's thievish progress to eternity

or a manifestation of the unchanging, amid which we may hope that the marks we set up may themselves be progress in its realisation. This is not a question of change or permanence but of both.

Not only is the task made easy by taking one aspect of one of these problems and using it as if it were the whole, but this can be proclaimed as an emancipation and set up as a cult.

In contrast, it is even matter for gratitude to find writers in our time, who insist on the necessity of giving a place in our consideration to all the elements involved. Yet our gratitude is moderated when we find that the only solution offered is to lump them all together. We are told that we must find a place for something of necessity and something of freedom, something traditional and something independent, something of the mind itself and something of the external world. We are treated to the well-worn illustration of life as an ellipse with two foci, and not a circle with one centre, and then incompatible things like a faith which is a relic of tradition and one that is of living insight are yoked together, so that the universe comes to look like a bench of unruly boys who have to be kept very carefully in their places lest they push one another off into the void.

We only begin truly to face our problem when we begin to ask how all these aspects of one reality go together and make a universe, embracing the Natural as well as the Supernatural.

(f) THE ORDER OF INQUIRY

The problems, therefore, are not one before the other, either in a chronological or a logical order, but are together, as it were problems of each other, being only aspects of one living organic interest. The order of treatment, therefore, depends solely on the needs of our understanding, and not on the nature of things.

The quest for the method that shall be adequate to this task may be more difficult than the quest for the holy grail. But we learn more by asking large questions than by answering small ones, for the right questions, asked comprehensively, are not merely steps towards understanding, but are themselves interpretations. At all events, if it provide nothing else, it can increase our sense of the depth and mystery of things, which is no small gain when superficiality is the supreme ignorance and misunderstanding.

For this task none of Descartes' rules can be of any value. If we are only on the verge of our problem at the outmost limit of our knowledge and experience, we cannot be helped by setting aside everything except what can impose itself on us after the fashion of a mathematical postulate; if our supreme difficulty is to see all our problems as one, it is only an evasion to attempt a solution by dividing up our problems still farther; if what we may see is a deeper reality and a greater purpose foreshadowed only in our largest experiences and highest aspiration, we cannot be helped by merely revising piecemeal, to see that we have not omitted details.

Whether any method that can deal with such a task as has been sketched can be called scientific is mainly a question of definition. If scientific method mean only the method of physical science, then it is not scientific. But if science mean all inquiry into any sphere of reality by the method appropriate to it, with the one purpose of knowing what it actually is, then it is, or at least it ought to be, scientific.

Here, at all events, we frankly abandon all pretence that we are capable of applying any form of the Cartesian method, of starting from a simple fact or a self-evident postulate and of building up, by facts which seem to come out of the original fact or reasonings which evolve from the original postulate, and recognise clearly that we have no hope of success with any problem except as we bring to bear on it all our powers and all our knowledge.

This is at least easier to do, if we take these problems in the order above, beginning with the widest—the problem of knowing and knowledge, the problem of how all knowing is meaning in our minds, yet all knowledge affirms itself to be of a reality which is not dependent on our meaning, but is that on which our meaning, if it is true meaning, depends

To begin either with facts about the Supernatural furnished by the history of religion or with the view of the Natural furnished by science, or with some philosophical process of reason which professes to include both, would be to assume the capacity for using the Cartesian method of evolving, by reasoning, some germ of fact or thought into the world and the fullness thereof.

This is plainest when the starting-point is an abstract principle like the scientific co-ordination of cause and effect The usual course is to assume gradually what is supposed to be explained, explaining away the long struggle for meaning and value which gives interest to history and turning aspiration and purpose into an illusion accompanying a fixed mechanical nexus. But it is not much better when we start with a fixed process of reason. There is no means of arriving at the variety, individuality and originality of the natural world, on either scheme; and the supernatural world is determined from the beginning by the mechanical scheme as the Unknowable and by the rational as the pantheistic Absolute, without any room for it to show itself to be just what it is.

More could be said for starting with history. During last century all problems became historical. Scientific explanations were an account of how things came to be; philosophy was largely a theory of history; religion seemed to be at the mercy of critical historical questions, and there was an active school which taught that all its problems could be determined wholly on grounds of historical evolution.

But a historical scheme constantly turns out to be merely what we might call an illustrated edition of the Cartesian method. It is thought that, if we can get far enough back, we can begin with simplicity, and then from this we pass to all the elaboration of the world by seeing that everything in a new age is merely a little rearrangement of what existed in the age before. Moreover, it has exactly the same effect of minimising events down to the level of our ability to explain them.

Throughout last century the accepted means for using the Cartesian method was just history. The dominating idea of explanation was simply an account of how the thing to be explained came into being. This arrangement of our knowledge about it is useful for two good reasons. First, all that exists has made its appearance in process of time; and to know this history is an aid to understanding as well as memory, because we pass to new knowledge, not merely from the old, but by it and with it. Second, it further shows a close relation between events, meaning by events beings as well as happenings, which reveals an expanding order of complexity, at once more elaborate and more perfectly adjusted. This at least suggests that the work of time has a progressive purpose. Yet the notion that thereby the new is any less new, and that it can be shown to be an easily explained rearrangement of the old, only tends to minimise its originality, so that it may not too obtrusively pass beyond the limits of our explanations.

It is never more than a pretence to start anywhere else than in the whole actual present, or with anything less than the conclusions of our experience. All we can do is to use the fullest capacity of mind which has been developed in us by the highest training of its powers, with all its knowledge and all its insight: and from the historical position in which we find ourselves, not to seek to empty ourselves of our convictions, but to be ready to revise them. That we can start from nothing and end with everything is plausible only because where we are to arrive is there all the time. Thus it is an illusion that we can work with any merely analytic method. Nothing is explicable about any environment except from the highest experience of it and the fullest knowledge of it we have. The only truly empirical inquiry works with all experience possible for us to have, and the other kind of empiricism, which is supposed to start with sensations, starts not from facts but from hypothesis.

At all events, the method of the former empiricism is here adopted, and we shall see what comes out of it. We shall not start even from the facts of the changing and the evanescent, as if we could know them without all our knowledge, but try, if possible, to discover what they mean when we are in a position to consider them in relation to the highest conception of our environment we can reach. Therefore, we shall end with them, and begin with the largest problem, the question of our whole world and our whole experience, or in other words the problem of mind and environment, or, in technical language, of Knowing and Being: and even with it we shall not attempt to tell the story from the beginning onwards, but, starting from the widest scope and the highest reach of our perception, consider how far we can work back to its elements.

PART II
KNOWING & KNOWLEDGE

CHAPTER VIII

AWARENESS AND APPREHENSION

(a) FOUR TYPES OF KNOWING

FOUR types of knowing are to be distinguished. These we may call awareness, apprehension, comprehension, explanation. Like everything unique and only known by experience of itself, they are impossible to define; and, like all that belongs to one mind, they ought not to be divided. Yet they are sufficiently unlike to be distinguished and sufficiently apart to be illustrated, if not described.

While walking in a dreamy mood along a country road, we may have a vivid sense of all that is about us, without attending to anything in particular. Our knowing is then a general field of *awareness*, including scent and sound as well as sight. The more we are entirely in this state of pure awareness, the more all our senses are active, so that we may even have vague realisation of the taste of the apples in the orchards and the coolness of the waters in the streams.

Something in this field arouses particular attention, say an object moving toward us on the road. If it specially interest us, as, for example, by being unfamiliar, we concentrate attention on it to see exactly what it is, seeking to *apprehend* it as one object by what appears to be its more relevant and important details. Let us say that we apprehend it to be a man riding a bicycle.

Then, supposing we have none of the information we afterwards learn to include under the name bicycle, but have everything to learn about it, we try, as it approaches, to *comprehend* it. This we do by considering the machine in relation to the man as a means of locomotion: and we think we comprehend it when we understand how it is the means for gaining this end.

Finally, as it passes, we are faced by the problem that it seems to have no support from its breadth, yet keeps upright while travelling along a line. This singularity we must try to *explain*: and we do it with such general principles as the scientific knowledge we happen to possess provides.

At each stage the scope of knowing is less. Awareness alone takes in the whole field, with the man and his bicycle in proportionate place as a moving object within it. In apprehension, all save the object of interest has become a mere background. In comprehension, we attend only to what embodies its purpose, as it were to its skeleton, while the details by which we apprehend it again fall into the background of attention. In explanation nothing remains but a sort of geometrical diagram, illustrating gravitational or centrifugal forces or whatever be the principle employed. Yet our comprehension may be deeper for our explanation; our apprehension more precise for our comprehension; our awareness more individual for our apprehension: and so large a place has this in the educated adult mind that it almost looks to us as though, by explaining anything, we could know everything about it. Nevertheless, there is no other source of concrete knowing than awareness and apprehension and, if we fail to realise this dependence, it is because we fail to realise that, as we return, we simply pick up again what we omitted on the outward journey.

But what is of still greater importance for us to notice here is, that we do not always return from our comprehending and explaining better equipped by awareness and apprehension for perceiving. Instead, we can make our perception both partial and perverse by seeing only with the eyes of our theory. Besides, there is a sense in which no return is possible even with the utmost openness of mind, because there is a simple penetration in awareness which is lost when mixed with apprehension, and something is always lost in apprehension when mixed with our understandings and explanations.

The true gain of comprehending and explaining is not for perceiving our environment, but for using it. The man who invented the bicycle may not have been able to state his explanation of its working as an abstract scientific theory, but he knew it in some effective practical form when he comprehended the general conception of a machine which would embody it. Thereafter, he apprehended it in all the details which would express attractively his understanding. Finally, he may see as his end the voyager interested in the whole field of awareness. But this he does by a knowledge which is not included in his theory, and had he not this knowledge, his theory would remain a mere abstract principle of dynamics.

The knowledge of adult civilised man is of this mixed character. He is active in applying explanations; he helps out his comprehension by ready-made concepts and fits his explanations on to them; then he fits these concepts on to his apprehension and is often content to see nothing more.

In this process directness of knowing is diminished. This is evident from the account of it already given, but it is still more evident in practical matters of skill. A boy rides a bicycle best by direct comprehension, unhampered by the attempt to ride according to a theory of centrifugal forces, or by any theory of how he does it.

Mr Lloyd Morgan speaks as though this were not knowing at all. Ask a boy, he says, how he turns a bicycle in a particular situation, and he will probably give a wrong answer, and he may act wrongly in consequence of trying to explain.[1] But this gives no reason for arguing that the boy is acting without any knowledge. His knowledge is understanding, which, being the kind of knowledge relevant to what he has in hand, is disturbed by the other kind of knowledge, explaining. For his purpose, understanding is the full knowledge, theory a mere diagram of it.

Again, direct apprehension may be disturbed by introducing into it some question of comprehension. This is not well illustrated by a bicycle, because all its parts are, as it were, a frame of comprehension. But the apprehension of a beautiful horse would be disturbed and limited by regarding it only as an animal for riding. Another of Mr Lloyd Morgan's illustrations is a still better example.[2] He argues that, because a chicken has no comprehension of an object as food, it pecks at

[1] *Life, Mind and Spirit*, p. 204.   [2] pp. 100 ff.

it, and even, after trial, rejects it as unsavoury, without any kind of knowledge whatsoever. Instead, he finds the explanation in a number of accompanying actions, which he regards as automatic. But the actions, on a common-sense view, seem to be accompaniments merely of pecking and testing its food, and to afford no kind of explanation of why it should peck. The plain explanation would seem to be that, without being able to comprehend the object as food, the chicken apprehends it as an object in some relation to hunger, which, for its purpose, may be the most useful kind of knowing. What we call its instinctive action may be all the more certain and rapid that it is not disturbed by any attempt at comprehension. In any case, it is wrong to maintain that there cannot be apprehension which is real and useful knowledge without comprehension, or that, even with man, it cannot be more effective for its special purpose. The chief reason why we apprehend so much more rapidly and completely in youth than in maturer years is that our minds are given wholly to the object and are not partly in the back of our heads looking for understandings and explanations.

Our experience does not go back to pure awareness, because memory does not begin till we apprehend things in some ordered context of awareness. Or rather, to be more correct, we should speak of recollection, because, as there is growth of experience from the earliest awareness, there must be memory. But for recollection there must be an individual apprehension to recall, and a context by which to recall it. We can, however, recall a time when we lived in a continuous, lively awareness, with apprehension only as a brighter light always moving across its field, without ever keeping one object long in the foreground, and when comprehending and explaining did not trouble us.

The rapidity, sureness, completeness and penetration of apprehension at this stage are for us, in later years, almost inconceivable. The objects of it still stand out uniquely in our memories, and what we now apprehend is vague in comparison, and, even so, is largely dependent on this youthful experience

This experience, which we must try to isolate if we are to make any guess as to how we perceive, is apprehension in a general field of awareness. Comprehension, in the sense of taking the object out of its place in this field and looking round it, and explanation, in the sense of taking it to pieces and looking inside it, are not only not necessary but are hindrances for simple perceiving. As both understandings and explanations are woven into our adult perceptions, the task of isolating what is pure perception is difficult, perhaps hopeless. But it must at least be attempted.

Yet the attempt will be doomed to failure, unless we begin from the highest awareness and the greatest world that can be apprehended. Our contention all along has been that we cannot work to any profit except by starting from the fullest development we know, and then, after trying, with all our powers of knowing and all our knowledge, to understand it, working back from it. The attempt to analyse out of experience some rudimentary beginning and build up on it by theory never is in any subject more than an elaborate device for evading the problems piecemeal. But it is bound to be specially misleading in this question of perception, because the function of theory is to give us general guidance by enabling us to omit the detailed and individual and concrete, while the function of perception is to provide them. Even with the best effort to avoid such a result, every theory of perception is in danger of substituting understanding and reasoning for awareness and apprehension, till the theory, instead of explaining the facts, replaces them.

(b) A POET'S AWARENESS AND APPREHENSION

In order to avoid this as far as possible, we must try to realise how the world looks to a supreme seer and how he sets to work in the seeing of it.

From this we are more likely to understand even the most rudimentary perception, because we cannot see what is in any beginning except by what comes out of it. And there is the still more important question of the nature of the environment we perceive This we must be nearer coming within sight of by dealing with the world of concrete realities of infinitely varied interest and value of the poet, than with even the best and truest abstract cosmological principle of the philosopher. Possibly the chief difficulty in our understanding of perception is just the poverty-stricken nature of our idea of the environment and its power to make itself known, which the reduction of awareness and apprehension to comprehension and explanation is apt to give. The simplifications may be just what make the problem difficult. We understand how we learn the enormously complicated thoughts in another mind, if we start with it as a whole mind, perhaps greater than our own, as we do not know how we perceive a stone as colour and form, if we start from some abstract notion of it as vibration of material particles. The question therefore involves the world which makes itself known, and not alone the way of knowing, because both the knower and the knowing could only have been developed in relation to what is there to be known.

We shall, therefore, not betake ourselves to the scientist and the philosopher as authorities on what is known by awareness and apprehension, because they are precisely the persons whose eyes are most turned to the back of their heads, looking for understandings and explanations, and who, even when they do look at their environment, are most in danger of seeing it only with the eyes of their judgments and theories, but to the poet and the child whose gifts are for perceiving and not for explaining.

Any great poet might serve our purpose, even the austerest of them, such as Dante or Milton, being in a very high degree sensuous. But sensuous is not sensual. Sensuous means masters of keen senses, great perceivers; sensual means slaves of sense, prisoners in the cell of subjective sensations. Sensuousness means an alert, interested aesthetic objectivity; and this every great poet has. Sensuality, on the contrary, which turns sensation into channels of subjective gratification, blunts and ultimately destroys fineness of perception: and with this no one can be truly great in any way, and least of all as a poet

It is better, however, to take one example than to discourse at large on great poets. For selecting Shakespeare it might suffice to say that he is widely regarded as the greatest. But at least two further reasons can be given. The first is that no other poet shows more plainly the poet's special way of knowing, and the second, that no one else with equal clearness and fullness shows the poet's world: and these are what concern the question of knowing and knowledge.

First, then, we ask, how does the poet see?

The question of the poet's way of knowing concerns, first of all and most of all, his aesthetic sincerity, using aesthetic in the wide sense of the response of feeling to all experience of environment.

Carlyle seems to think that Shakespeare could have done everything as well as he could imagine it, and might have been a great statesman or a great general, or a great scientist or philosopher, had he not happened to occupy himself with being a poet. Not only is this very improbable, but, as all great practical achievements are by comprehension and explanation, had he given himself to them, he would not have been a great poet. He himself knew that the task of the poet is to "hold the mirror up to nature" and that his equipment for it is to be "of imagination all compact", which means the power to see and to interpret. Yet Carlyle is so far right that only a great man can write great poetry: and Lee's biography frequently gives the impression of a good business man and clever playwright, who could produce profitable goods to order without feeling anything deeply or in any way personally experiencing them, and that, in his multifarious investigations, the biographer has somewhere mislaid the poet. The poetry is the chief biography, and it speaks of a nature sensitive as an Æolian harp to every breath of feeling.

When sensuousness is taken to be sensuality, the chief appeal is to *Venus and Adonis*. Certainly the poem is sensual. But, if Shakespeare plays any personal part in it, it is as Adonis, which accords with all we know of his youth and with the interest throughout his plays in open-air activities and the abundant and accurate observation of natural phenomena. One might suspect something of an *apologia pro vita sua*, were not its companion *Lucrece*. Taken together, they are seen to be studies of opposite types. Probably neither was very attractive to him. But this would only be another example of what is abundantly evident in all his work—the catholicity of his interest in human nature. In any case, no sensual nature ever saw women with the clear, penetrating vision he did. Moreover, very little knowledge of contemporary drama will show how rarely he condescended to what was plainly a very easy appeal to the theatre-goers of the day. His supreme characteristic, and the spring of all the rest, is his aesthetic sincerity, his objective, unrestricted, unflinching facing of every kind of feeling, and all it revealed to him.

With this objective sincerity of feeling all inquiry into perception ought to begin. Because of its perfection in Shakespeare, Schiller, with a curious lack of insight for a poet, felt him to be cold, Olympian, impersonal, distant. It is true that he does not use his poetry as a confessional. Never, except in the *Sonnets*, do his feelings appear as personal emotion, and elsewhere we only glean some idea of what he felt most deeply in this way from what have been called 'his recurrences and fervours'. In the *Sonnets*, in spite of Lee's contrary opinion, most people will feel that the emotion is personal, wrung from him by some event which had caused him great distress: and of this the change in the character of his whole work at this period is further evidence. That this power of intense feeling was always there we may be sure, for nothing he ever wrote could have been written without it, yet in his work he arrests it before it becomes subjective emotion, and turns it to artistic appreciation, governed by the one passion for artistic truth and reality.

Hamlet is particularly instructive. The hesitation which marks the play is not due to any doubt about the facts. The function of the ghost is to make them certain. Nor is it due to incapacity for action in the hero, because he acts with force and decision when it is a mere question of action. But, in playing the part of judge, he commits the very crimes he condemns. Thus the hesitancy is whether man may play this part of judge in life at all. In short, the real personal aspect of the play is the recovery of the author's artistic soul to see 'life steadily and see it whole', after it had been shadowed by days of fierce condemnation and sense of wrong. And from this time his serenity is an ever surer possession.

Lust is still an occasional motive. Apparently he himself introduces it into the story of Lear's daughters. But it is always as a blind and cruel passion. That he should look this in the face only shows that he is never determined by the mere pleasantness of feeling, nor in any way selects or limits its witness, but lays himself open to its whole testimony. Thereby he reaches the gayest comedy and the saddest tragedy, and introduces melancholy into his comedies and absurdity into his tragedies. No writer is more concerned with realities, yet his work is not mere realism, because the impulse of it is a great sense of the wonder and depth and beauty which shine through all things and even the worst of men, a great awareness of what, in spite of every defect and evil, is a beautiful and above all an interesting world of men and things. Like every true poet he loves beauty, but he loves truth more, and without this the mere love of beauty is apt to be impoverished and to be narrowed to some kind of preconceived theory of art. The essential point is that feeling is not determined by pleasant or unpleasant sensation, but by objective interest in an interesting world.

Here we have a condition of perception which sheds light on its nature. If we think of this, which, in all its forms, we may call poetic sincerity, as merely an idiosyncrasy of a unique and, to many people, not very real quality called genius, we must remember the audience as well as the poet. Its members were far nearer the child than the genius, yet they too could respond to sensitiveness of emotional response, determined by a general response to the whole interest of environment. By introspection we could no doubt discover in this response subjective feeling, and could argue that the whole power of appeal is due to the enjoyment of it. But this would be mere theory. The poet doubtless is a person in a very high degree responsive to feeling, but, if he is a true poet, he changes it into interest in objective creation, and it is by doing this that he interests his hearers: and this fact is of the utmost importance for showing how sensation functions in perception and how its meaning comes from its objective context.

Just because Shakespeare works so entirely with perception, and expresses everything in forms of awareness and apprehension, he can make the common simple person see and feel what the thinker could not make him even understand.

His way of knowing has two aspects, which are never separated, yet are, as it were, never telescoped, but help to make each other more distinct and independent. We might describe them as an almost omniscient quality of individual apprehension, and an almost omnipresent quality of general awareness.

His world is of endless concrete individuality. There are no abstractions, no generalities. Everything has "a local habitation and a name". The commonest natural object is as accurately presented as in Wordsworth. Yet its special quality is not felt alone, but as it is informed by a wider interest, and he never, like Wordsworth, isolates nature in a way that is more of the understanding than of perception. In Shakespeare nature is never apart from the whole interest of the perceiver. She does not provide mere similes to illustrate what man does or thinks, but is a body of living metaphor through which all his thoughts and actions shine. Yet the individual quality of everything gains by being thus held together in one field of awareness. Precisely because of this human meaning in it, nature is so individual and objective; and precisely because of this embodiment in nature, man is an individual of the utmost distinctness and yet of a measureless range of character and relations.

In his presentation of man nothing 'stales the infinite variety'. It comes as near omniscience as the mind of man has ever reached in any department. Even two anonymous persons, speaking out of a crowd, have special characteristics. If there is one model for several characters, as there may be for Rosalind, Beatrice and Maria, this only shows more clearly how each is herself and no one else who ever lived.

And this is the more astonishing that he does not need to exclude the small in order to appreciate the great, or the mean and base in order to exalt the sublime and pure. "Unaccommodated man is but a poor forked radish." This is one aspect. Yet though man is "this quintessence of dust", no one ever better met Matthew Arnold's test of the true poet, that he takes a serious view of life, meaning that man himself, and what concerns his real life and inward experience, are of infinitely more interest to him than any outward good or material possession. The great description, beginning with "What a piece of work is man", is not mere dramatic rhetoric. All his insatiable interest in man sprang from the vision of him as the beauty of the world, noble in reason, infinite in faculty, angelic in action, god-like in apprehension. Yet all this is brought out by the individual's intimate interaction with his world, and still more with other equally individual persons, usually not of any heroic stature. Scenery was dear, and was done without, but titles on the stage were cheap; and Shakespeare may even have had the proverbial English respect for them. But the only one of his characters he seems to have strongly disliked was a king, and he would not pay any tribute to the Queen who had betrayed his friend; and if at times he makes ordinary people ridiculous, he never makes them unpleasant, while the loving care he bestowed upon his fools shows what a large place there was in his heart for the waifs and strays of humanity.

This interest in the vast variety of human nature sprang from the clearness with which he saw everyone as an individual and his value just as man. Working mainly with awareness and apprehension, he does not group men together by general conceptions and relations. His whole idea of tragedy depends on the sense that everyone is alone in the depths of his soul, with his own responsibility and destiny; which is both man's greatness and his sorrow. Though he works with no rules or regulations, whatever may have been his own moral shortcomings, he has a deep and sincere moral insight, informed by something deeper than mere moral approval or disapproval, which sees that the defects which bring tragedy are of a man's greatness, even if it be by misuse of it. Nor does anyone ever meet his final catastrophe till he stands alone. Thus it is, for example, with Macbeth and Othello and Lear. It may be more the insight of the publican than the regulated judgment of the Pharisee, but it is none the less faithful to the deepest reality.

Though his dominating interest is apprehension, and not comprehension and explanation, there is a supreme intellectual sincerity in the whole character of his awareness, which shirks nothing and never shields itself from the stress of life by average opinions or conventionalities. This is important, because, though truths may be many, the spirit of truth is one.

Most clearly this appears in what is usually called his melancholy, and more especially in his continual occupation with the idea of time. This idea is not of reflexion and the effort to comprehend, but is also part of 'the vision and the faculty divine'. It is a baffled effort to apprehend, not to comprehend; and he cannot apprehend it, because it is not an object of perception, but a form of the general awareness which is the ground of the whole impulse to aesthetic apprehension. Scientists and philosophers, thinking of time as quantity, argue about it, but are not obsessed by it. Only for poets and children, who perceive keenly and discuss little, is it a quality of dominating insistence and impressiveness. It might almost appear as though there were no genius of the poetic type not shadowed continually either by the idea of space or time; and perhaps there are few children who live much under the open heavens who do not share the experience.

With Shakespeare this burden of the sense of time has little to do with any idea of quantity, but is a quality which comes very near to what we have called the undifferentiated holy. He does not speak of ages. Ancient and modern seem to have little meaning for him. Three hours suffice to express it, as when the fool says very wisely "it is ten o'clock, and but one hour ago it was nine and one hour hence 'twill be eleven". It is this tale of our ripening and rotting, the tale of our terrible aloneness, which has in it the qualitative difference of the finite and infinite. Or he feels it as the waves make towards the pebbled shore, as in "sequent toil all forward do contend". And it is this quality of time, surrounding the spirit's loneliness, which makes the glory and splendour of all he is aware of and apprehends appear "such stuff as dreams are made on". In all like Goethe, "he feels himself so small so great".

(c) THE CHILD'S PERCEIVING

The question is whether this is the most adequate way of perceiving, and the true world to be perceived. Is the poet merely a phantastic dreamer, or is he the supreme seer? Is his world the concrete reality for us all, had we eyes to see it, or is it mere vain imaginations?

At least it is very simply and universally human, having the widest as well as the deepest human appeal. Nothing moves simple folk and children like the idea of aloneness in the ever-moving vastness of time, if this be filled with concrete individual forms on the one hand, and invested with what we have called the feeling of the undifferentiated holy on the other. A vivid, concretely apprehended world is, at the same time, a world of one general awareness, which the seer, who does not confuse himself with efforts to comprehend and explain, is conscious of as his own, and by which he is in a direct way conscious of himself. Even to a child this often raises the question of whether he perceives as others perceive, and whether it is not all 'the baseless fabric of this vision'. The notion that the perceived is not just the perception of the perceiver, and that subject and object are merely poles in one experience never arose out of perception, but is a purely sophisticated introduction of theory. The difference between using Shakespeare in this connexion and, let us say, Hegel is that, while both are thinking about experience, Shakespeare's thinking springs spontaneously out of perceiving and is more likely to illuminate the process than Hegel's thoughts which are dialectically introduced.

It has been said that a poet is one who remembers his youth. But Shakespeare did something more. He retained his youth. These are 'the long, long thoughts of youth' only brought to depth and adequate expression by 'the vision and the faculty divine', which is still, as with the child, not understanding and explaining, but awareness and apprehension. In the poet it is singular in having the reach and perfection of genius, but it is not in essence and quality different.

If this could be shown, it would go a long way towards proving that this is the real world of perception, and that the imagination of the poet is not a weaving of phantasies, but a juster, wiser and profounder perception.

Unfortunately, the only experience available for the purpose is one's own. But an average sort of child, living under the conditions in which man has developed his powers of perception, with nature's work much in evidence around him and man's little, often alone under the open sky, and about as much on the sea as on the land, among simple stay-at-home people and some far-travelled folk and wandering gypsies, is at least as near the conditions in which man's perception developed as this Western modern world affords.

The most noticeable feature of my earliest view of the world is of how minutely, definitely, decisively everything in it was individual. My language being an advanced Aryan tongue, I had abstract terms, and no doubt made some use of them. But they were luxuries and not necessaries. That to their owner a flock was only sheep, which he did not know one from another, seemed to show an incredible blindness. The birds were too numerous and rapid and changing for personal acquaintance, but a flock of them was an object by itself, with its qualities of flight and grouping; and when birds were nearer and few enough for separate attention, they were always particular living creatures, each with some singularity of colour or form or behaviour. Life of every kind fascinated: and there was a different quality of apprehension of it which is lost when interests are in another direction and classification has to be used to save the trouble of individual apprehension. Probably life was the essential individualising idea. This may explain why animism, or the ascription of life to everything we treat individually, is a general, if not a universal stage, towards objective apprehension. Yet the person who has once had this power will scarcely doubt that it is perception, not mere weaving of his own phantasies into what he perceives, and will always be much more ready to believe that reality is at least nearer to pan-psychism than to pan-mechanism. At all events he will not readily believe that later ideas, regulated by what we comprehend and explain, are a better means of perceiving the whole of reality than his earlier simple apprehension and awareness.

Akin to this, or rather the most striking exercise of it, was an astonishing rapidity, sureness and penetration in directly apprehending other minds. Later experience, though it has added something of intellectual and moral judgment, has added little or nothing to this kind of aesthetic knowledge, which is more certain and often more just. Moreover, only as we carry this kind of knowledge with us from our youth, has any other kind of knowing our fellow real insight.

As I recall it, the judgment was independent both of approval and of liking. Personal feelings indeed rather interfered, one's own relatives being taken for granted. But the idiosyncrasies of a gypsy, who, on his wife's testimony, was to be five score his next birthday ever since I could remember, though I understood his character of very mixed shades of grey downwards, no more troubled me than when I read of Falstaff to-day. I had just the same artistic interest in what might be called a consistent character of inconsistencies. With this mind Shakespeare saw Falstaff, and with this mind we read of him, though perhaps, if we met him in the flesh, our adult reflexions would have nothing but disapproval.

Along with this detailed, concrete, individual apprehension went a general awareness, from the peculiar qualities of which the sustained interest in apprehending everything in it individually was derived. While my apprehensions of the countryside continually varied with sunshine and shadow, day and night, summer and winter, my general awareness of it was neither of a changing scene, nor of the aspect I preferred, nor was it of an average impression or a composite picture, but of something one in all its moods and aspects, much like awareness of a friend. From this, and not from pleasure or pain given by the separate objects themselves, the insatiable thirst for apprehending everything in its individuality came. This general, sustained aesthetic impulse, and not a series of individual impulses which had to be changed as attention moved from one object to another, caused the restlessly inquiring nature of attention.

The significance of this is seen in the singular relation of interest to feeling. All awareness must be aesthetic in the sense of having its source in feeling and manifesting itself by meanings which at least could not be apart from values for feeling, while an immensely lively interest must mean active feelings. Yet I cannot recall any memory of attending to anything because I liked it or of turning away from it because I disliked it. On the contrary, in particular apprehensions the conscious purpose of gaining pleasure or shunning pain was conspicuously absent, or at least it was over-ridden by something of general import which was much more powerful.

It may of course be argued that the only possible motives are subjective pleasure and pain, whether we recognise them or not; and that when we say they are not, we ought only to say that youth has not reached the time of reflexion. But this is to settle a question of experience by a general conclusion of comprehension, which is precisely what is here being challenged. As a matter of fact, we boys knew perfectly well when people shrank from looking at anything, say blood, because the sight pained them. Our seniors did absurd things and they might if they liked, but in boys we regarded this as highly reprehensible.

Nor was it different with action. For daring, large liberty of conduct was allowed, but, for mere subjective pleasure, none.

No language could have expressed our opinion of a boy who consciously and habitually made this his motive, could we have conceived such a person to exist. And at any age is not desire of pleasure or fear of pain a morbid and reflective and even artificial motive?

In one sense, it may be that every motive must be feeling, but, if so, it is feeling passing over into knowledge and mastery, and the dominating motive is interest in this general dealing with environment and not particular preferences. Thus all our knowing and doing is a dealing with our whole environment by means of a feeling which is a universal impulse of all awareness. In youth especially, it is so effective as to dominate feeling as pleasure or pain, except under a violent attack of pain, which even then gives the sense of being weak and abnormal; and this is soon forgotten, and, except by the sage injunctions of seniors, does not act as a warning. This is spoken of as the thoughtlessness of youth, whereas it is really the simple objectivity of interest.

Connected with this and rising out of it, not as a reflexion introduced into it, but as an actual insistent form of this general awareness and what one might call the possessive power of its appeal, was a very early and insistent and dominant obsession with infinity. It expressed itself in time and space, but even space was qualitative, absolute, in the sense we have attached to the word rather than the idea of extension. Strictly perhaps it was not an idea at all, not being an experience of something, but a form of experiencing everything.

To the very long sight of one who constantly looked from horizon to horizon, the depth of the sky was overwhelmingly impressive, and was the first object I think ever to hold my attention immovably. It compelled me to think of travelling on and on for ever and ever without being any nearer the end. Thus though space was, as it were, the illustration, the real impressiveness was in time: and perhaps time is always what gives the impressive quality. Through this first came the idea that I was alone. I had been to church. I think the preacher had been expressing the absolute difference between good and evil under the material forms of heaven and hell. I went down to the edge of the water alone, and stood, a very small child, with the full tide at my feet. Along the smooth waters of the sound a path of sunshine carried the eye out to the open sea. It flashed on me that, if I dropped in and floated out, with endless sea around, I should be alone for ever and ever.

The result was a consciousness of myself which set me thinking, yet not about myself. Instead, it caused doubt about whether the world I saw was in the least like the world other people saw. I tried hard to find out, but words were like the measuring rods of the relativist—their use was regular, but this might conceal any difference of meaning.

Theoretically no very small boy should have any such notions: nor would he, if they were problems of comprehending and explaining. But the contention here is that they rise up spontaneously from the form of our awareness. This is what gives them their extraordinarily intense character, quite different from our later days when, by understanding and explaining, we have reduced time and space from fascinations to formulas, and ourselves, in the midst of them, as bearers of the same strange impressive quality, to an argument about the existence of the soul.

This question of the existence of the soul does come up later, and under very much the same images as a savage uses. But this is plainly an attempt to comprehend something the child has already apprehended. Tennyson's view is that

> Through the frame that binds him in
> His isolation grows defined.

But the normal experience rather is that the child has little idea of his body binding him in: and he certainly does not reason from this to his aloneness. His discernment of himself is one side of the whole aesthetic nature of his early awareness: and its peculiar quality, which leads to questions about the soul, is the feeling of something of the same absolute quality in himself as that which he feels in the sense of time and space. Through both he perceives how utterly he is alone.

(d) A POET'S CHILD

At first sight it might seem as irrelevant to the explanation of the perception, let us say, of a beetle to introduce the mind of a great seer like Shakespeare as to introduce the mind of a great thinker like Kant. But, in the first place, the great danger of explaining anything is that we take it to be of the understanding. With Kant we simply walk into this trap, because his whole world is a product of the understanding; with Shakespeare we are kept in touch with the real world of our experience and know that it is by the concrete fullness of awareness and apprehension. In the second place, it is one thing to explain even the lowest form of perception, if its full environment is this unity and individual quality of meaning, and another, if it is a chaos of impressions wrought into meaning and unity by the mind that perceives. Though the living creature may have no consciousness of it, if this environment has the values realised by the poet, the whole development may have a tendency wholly different from what it would be, if there were no objective values at all, or if these were only for pure animal persistence. In the third place, if perception arrives at the vision of the poet, something of the same quality must have been in it all along, and by reading back from the highest perception we are far more likely to understand the lowest, than if we try to work up from some curious transformation of mere physical energy, because mind, from its lowest beginning, perceives by meaning and not by impact.

But it plainly has more relevance to ordinary perception if the poet's insight is only the maturer, more penetrating, better equipped perception of the child. Unfortunately for most people's understanding, their childhood was spent in communion with the dead buildings of man's erection, not with a living nature; and in crowds, who perceive as well as think alike; and with schoolmasters' tabulated information, instead of independent observation.

But we have a very important document in Wordsworth's *Excursion* on the opening mind of the boy much alone in

AWARENESS AND APPREHENSION

communion with nature, which shows still more plainly how the context of perception is unity of feeling, touching a unity of the world on one side and a unity of the mind on the other, with an absolute sense of value, at least akin to what we have called the 'undifferentiated holy'.

This boy, from his sixth year
> In summer, tended cattle on the hills,

and, in winter, from his distant school,
> In solitude returning, saw the hills
> Grow larger in the darkness; all alone
> Beheld the stars come out above his head.

By this experience the foundations of his mind were laid.
> In such communion, not from terror free,
> While yet a child, and long before his time,
> Had he perceived the presence and the power
> Of greatness; and deep feelings had impressed
> So vividly great objects that they lay
> Upon his mind like substances, whose presence
> Perplexed the bodily sense.

With this came
> An active power to fasten images
> Upon his brain,

gathered by incessant, lively, varying attention to all things. In this he traced
> ...an ebbing and a flowing mind,
> Expression ever varying.

This was sustained and crowned by what the poet calls love.
> Far and wide the clouds were touched,
> And in their silent faces could be read
> Unutterable love

Then with this vividness of apprehension came, in a still higher degree, what the poet calls the *perception*, but what we have been calling the *awareness*, of "the presence and the power of greatness".
> ...his spirit drank
> The spectacle: sensation, soul and form
> All melted into him.
> Thought was not; in enjoyment it expired,

> Rapt into still communion that transcends
> The imperfect offices of prayer and praise
> His mind was a thanksgiving to the power
> That made him; it was blessedness and love.

To this we may add the poet's description of his own experience, even though it may not be wholly unaffected by theory.

> I have felt
> A presence that disturbs me with the joy
> Of elevated thoughts; a sense sublime
> Of something far more deeply interfused,
> Whose dwelling is the light of setting suns,
> And the round ocean and the living air,
> And the blue sky, and in the mind of man;
> A motion and a spirit, that impels
> All thinking things, all objects of all thought,
> And rolls through all things.

(*e*) SINCERITY, SENSITIVENESS, UNITY

That even Shakespeare always saw life steadily and saw it whole may be more than can be said, but no one known to fame was more concerned to do so, or went so far.

Both his conduct and his learning may have been defective, but he had the profoundest moral insight and the most transparent love of all truth, and these were not unimportant for his supreme equipment, the direct unblurred mirror of his feeling, with its pure objectivity. This objectivity was essentially right valuation. There are two kinds of values, which we may call the natural and the ideal, which will have to be discussed fully later, but it is already plain that the ideal values, which we may sum up as the true, the beautiful and the good, are not separable from the sincerity of feeling by which anything is rightly valued and so rightly known. In both alike it is sincerity of feeling which arrives at right and objective values, there being for anything an appreciation which is according to nature and a perversion which is not. And a true objective sense of the natural world is as dependent on this as a true objective sense of the supernatural.

The understanding, within limits, allows us to judge natural values by convenience and preference and requires us to choose among them; while by the understanding we judge consciously that to introduce convenience and preference into ideal values is by that very act to corrupt them. On the one hand, the basis even of a moral judgment is sound natural values; and, on the other, we cannot have sound natural values quite apart from right ideal values. We sometimes speak of a man as having only animal senses. This may not even be fair to the animals. But no true human perception of the world, at least, is ever purely natural, and certainly not the perception of any great poet. It is a poet's perception precisely because of what he perceives through the physical and not merely in it, and this is the basis of everything he may ultimately see of truth, beauty and goodness. Thus the way to receive the witness of all reality would seem to be a mind concerned to know the object by valuing it aright, and this goes back even to sensation, making it a true response to the witness of reality.

Possibly we have no right to limit this to man. The whole evolution of the senses may be the history of a long series of living creatures responding sincerely, or, as it was not of conscious purpose, we may say really, to the aesthetic quality of their environment. At all events it is in all men more or less, and in men like Shakespeare preeminently, the source of the vivid, accurate, objective, concrete apprehension of every object around them and the impulse to see all apprehensions steadily and as a whole.

But, besides sincerity, there is also sensitiveness. As the former has more to do with apprehension, this has more to do with awareness, though insincerity may affect the message even of our commonest sensations, and obtuseness may blunt every apprehension. Wordsworth says that "he that has nothing to confer has nothing to perceive", and the first thing he has to confer is alert and interested sensitiveness, which is not merely great and keen activity of the senses but an awareness through them of what is beyond them. It means a joy in our whole awareness of environment, which Wordsworth calls love, though it is much nearer artistic appreciation of the whole than any selective liking for any part of it.

This alone would mark the difference between the mere submission to impression and the insight of the poet and the child into other minds. The senses are keen and active, the mind is alert to interpret, there is sympathy and understanding, and the effect, as for example in Shakespeare's characters, is not of odd thoughts picked up here and there, but of seeing the whole character in all its bearings and relations. It is through the senses, and what is beyond them is just this unity which expresses itself in all its manifestations. We have all something of this in our knowledge of any friend. Through his manifestations of himself we know a person who is more than all his manifestations. It has to do with a unity which is as a whole in all its manifestations.

We have already spoken of a child's awareness of his environment as if it were one mind with varying manifestations. Moreover he continually feels about some objects in a way which explains how the savage regards them as sacred. Animism is usually regarded as a mere transference by the understanding of man's idea of himself into things. But when we resort to the understanding to explain savage ideas we are probably on the wrong track. No doubt it is a crude way of grasping the individuality of things, but is it not some attempt to get at a unity which is through the senses but not in them, and is it not a step towards a really objective apprehension? By thus going beyond mere physical perceptions, man wins the interest in them which enables him to pass beyond their mere profit to himself to concern with them as existing in their own right. Here, and not in what is merely material, we have the spring of the poet's joy in all he sees and his gift of making it interesting to other people.

The reaching out to the unity of all environment in all awareness is in the same way akin to what we have called the undifferentiated holy. In Shakespeare we saw it specially in the sense of time. In every genius whose special gift is perception, either time or space seems to be a dominant intuition. In Dante and Milton it is space, but it has the same significance of a form of the infinite.

We have seen how that, specially through this, the aloneness of the individual in the universe is realised, giving the sense both of worth and isolation in the midst of it. That the savage has it as well as the poet and the child appears from the fact that primitive ritual appears to have no end except to express it, and as rhythm of song and of movement have come out of it, clearly it is connected with the idea of time

With this goes the other appeal to heaven and hell. The mere mention of this may seem to be an introduction of crude and even horrible superstition. But it is one thing to reach the middle of a ladder by climbing and another by falling. The material forms through which man has reached out to his higher knowledge of his environment are important and illuminating, while a return to them is mere disaster and degradation.

One of the singular things is that Dante and Milton, who were so much occupied with the idea of space, were also dominated by the ideas of heaven and hell. Whatever other connexion there may be, they are both material ways of conceiving something infinite and of absolute apartness. The connexion also shows that these ideas arose out of the form of perception and are not a mere introduction from tradition and reflexion of the contemplation of horrors. It is an attempt to conceive under the material forms of inconceivable happiness and misery absolute difference in value felt in perception. In spite of being glorified by their imaginations, it still belongs to the stage at which man realises the spiritual through the material, but no stage is more important for understanding man's higher perception, and possibly something of it reaches down to the lowest animal perception.

CHAPTER IX

THE INDIVIDUAL AND INDIVIDUALITY

(*a*) THE UNITIES

If our method is to start from the highest human knowing and to try to penetrate through it to its elements and its beginnings, we must take as our first question the unities which are the most general character of all knowing.'

We might set out from what has been not very accurately called Wordsworth's nature mysticism. But, for our purpose, it is not mystical enough, and we take instead mysticism of the extremest type, because though useless for knowing the content of experience, it is a valuable laboratory experiment in isolating the form.

From the disturbing content of the senses it seeks escape by asceticism, and of thought by contemplation and ecstasy, until, beyond experience and beyond thought, there is nothing save oneness with the One. Nothing is then left save the empty form of unity. But, as this is the form of the environment of which we are aware, of the mind by which we become aware of it, and of the feeling which embraces both, it works with something which has psychological and metaphysical and emotional reality.

With respect to the metaphysical aspect, there is a reflexion of the unity of all things in everything. This unity, by continual effort, can be emptied of all content. What remains is little more than blank space. Yet, as the embodiment of infinity, this can be realised as the one Supernatural in which division is unreal.[1]

The result has rightly been described as reaching mere unity with empty hands, yet it is not as though the unity were nothing. It contains nothing, and therefore no description of

[1] It is an interesting, and perhaps a relevant fact, that there is a faith-healing society in China which works entirely with meditation on blank space.

it can be given; in a sense it is nothing, as no form has existence apart from all content: and yet, even in this emptied state, it is felt as the universal form of awareness of a universe which is one.

This is even plainer about time. Time is for us the element in which everything happens: yet, if we exclude all happenings, though it is no longer time experienced as change, it is still felt as the universal form of a present eternity, a sort of changeless awesome holy. This would seem to support Durkheim's contention that the ideas of time and space are religious in their origin: but what concerns us here is that what is left is an empty form of the oneness of the Supernatural.

The psychological basis is the bare unity of the mind. The natural function of the oneness of the mind is to bring all we know into one varied meaning, but by effort the mind can be made a sort of 'vacant interlunar cave'. The supreme task of this kind of mysticism is to be rid of the multitudinous conflicting elements of the concrete personality, by suppressing desire, purpose and self-affirmation, and seeking to reach unity by ecstatic vision, beyond sense and beyond intellect. Being an attempt to have oneness of mind without the burden of the sacred task of thinking all its thoughts and experiences together, it is, as all form without content is, unreal. Yet again, it is not mere negation, but has, as one blank sacredness, the unity of mind, which is, as a matter of fact, its form.

The unity of environment and the unity of mind the mystic emptying of content only isolates and emphasises, but in practice at least we all assume them. The third element, however, which is the essence of this mysticism, even if we do act upon it, is usually overlooked. We might call it a unified frame of love emptied of all content. This is the joy unspeakable, which is spoken of by all the mystics with every conceivable superlative. In essence it is just the undifferentiated holy. The challenge of true unifying reverence, with one joy in all things in spite of pain, is for endless awareness and apprehension, and of exhaustless variety. This may mean endless conflict as well as endless learning: and to seek to escape from it into mere superlative-ness of undifferentiated feeling, impresses ordinary, practical people as artificial and morbid and unreal; and it is a right impression. But one of the first lessons of life, or at least of this inquiry, is not to be impatient with what we dislike or even rightly reject because it does not deal with what we know to be the whole reality, as if it had in it no aspect of reality from which we may learn with profit. And here we have a very important isolation of the unity of feeling which works in all awareness. It is merely the wish to enjoy light without being disturbed by the world which light manifests, but it works with the fact that there is one light. Hence this unity of feeling, though being empty it reveals no reality, is not merely nothing, but is the form of feeling which is operative in all awareness, and which is the motive to seek in all our world harmony and peace, and which sustains us against discouragement from their absence.

The right content of these forms is not emptiness, but a world of infinite variety, harmonious to the feelings, like the poet's; a world challenging to understanding and in relation to one mind, like the philosopher's, a world to be explained as one on a consistent principle, like the scientist's; of one sphere of active victory, like the moralist's, of one reverence, like the religious thinker's. Even the poet and the philosopher, and still more the theologian, can fall into a satisfaction akin to the unity of the mystic, and be as blind to what cannot be included in their particular kind of unity, and as hostile to its intrusion. But their partialities also show that the whole context, by which the varied qualities of sensation come to mean awareness of an actual world of one meaning to one mind, is a unity of feeling, which embraces the unity of the environment which is known, and the unity of the mind which knows, and of a world of what in some sense is one value for thought and action.

From this alone can we hope to understand how environment makes itself known and how our minds know it. Man's true destiny is not to renounce his call to adventure, but to respond to his environment by valuing it aright by simple, open,

THE INDIVIDUAL AND INDIVIDUALITY

genuine feeling, thinking it through, and living in it with steadfast purpose and humble courage, yet one self, one environment and one relation are the unities which direct his way, and he misses it when he fails to maintain any of them.

(b) DANGER AND NECESSITY OF THEORY

If the poet's vision is the truest and most adequate perception, and the Natural is as he sees it, and not as abstract explanations limit it, is not Wordsworth right in thinking that theory can add nothing, and may take much away? A theory of perception is specially exposed to this danger. The particular is the essential object of apprehension, but the particular is precisely what does not lend itself to the kind of understanding which produces theory. Therefore, it is apt to disappear into a general abstraction of the understanding, till perception appears to be mainly a work of the understanding itself. It is not explained, but reduced to explanations, till it seems that we have discovered the trick of the whole contrivance, with the result of making the universe appear to be a very cheap and soulless affair. As soon as we start to explain anything, it is difficult for our limited minds not to substitute what is easy to understand for the fullness of experience. and theories of perception, it must be admitted, are often the merest dry bones of what we know by perceiving. May we not, therefore, with Wordsworth, pass it by as a limitation and a desecration? Should we not be content with the poet's knowing and the poet's knowledge, and not shut out the light of day and make the world appear a human dug-out, where we grow blear-eyed, and where in any case nothing great or beautiful is to be seen?

For not entering upon theories of knowing, and especially of perception, in any study of religion, there might seem to be the further reason that, even if science or philosophy does show another world, it is in the world of the senses that religion has to do its business. And it may also be admitted that one of the impoverishments of religion has been that its world is not sufficiently the poet's world, but one seen too much with eyes bleared and blinkered by theory.

Philosophers, like other people, use reasoning a great deal more to justify what they already believe than for making discovery of new truth. Yet there are good reasons, both negative and positive, which require us to deal with their theories.

In the first place, as limited interest impoverishes theory, defective theory justifies this limited interest, and so impoverishes experience. People can be so self-enclosed by theory that they cannot see, any more than they can think, outside of it. Kant is interested in the world mainly as a sphere of action; Hegel mainly as a sphere of knowing; Schleiermacher mainly as a sphere of artistic feeling: whereas it is a sphere for all three, and perhaps for a great deal more. But even these interests were blinkered by theory. Action, for Kant, was a business of rules; knowing, for Hegel, a business of abstractions; feeling, for Schleiermacher, a business of rather artificial harmonies.

In the second place, the possibility of accounting for the kind of knowing, and, more particularly, the kind of perception we actually have, is a very important test of a view of the world. If a theory does not need to modify experience to suit itself, but makes some reasonable approach towards showing how experience, as we actually have it, is possible, the view of the world on which it is based would be so far confirmed; whereas, in so far as a theory of knowing could not by any possibility account for the kind of experience and, in particular, for the kind of perception, which we actually have, the view of the world on which it is based is called in question.

In the third place, a theory is not necessarily of no value for our inquiry because it is determined on a partial basis. On the contrary, the isolation of a particular aspect of reality may be, as it were, a useful laboratory experiment. Laboratory experiments are all partial, and, if we take them to be the measure of the universe, all misleading, but, if we use them in their proper place and for their proper purpose, their partiality is their value. And these theories do emphasise the elements in our experience, both of the Natural and of the Supernatural, which are most essential. Kant emphasises the importance of the individual for all experience; Hegel the importance of the unity of experience, and of thinking things together; Schleiermacher the unified character of our awareness and the importance for it of one feeling as the source of intuition.

In the last place, in spite of differences, almost any theory of knowledge raises the decisive question for our inquiry, because, in the end, every theory of knowledge comes to be a theory of the Supernatural, even if it be that the Supernatural has no existence.

(c) RELIGIOUS OUTLOOK AND THEORY OF KNOWLEDGE

We have already seen the close affinity between views of religion and theories of knowing, because both are determined by what is regarded as the essential contact with reality, which again is determined by what we take the essential nature of reality to be. Theories of knowing are not first demonstrated, and then the nature of reality deduced from them: but philosophers, like other people, form their views of the world from their whole intercourse with it and according to their widest knowledge and highest knowing; and, like other people too, they only use their reasoning powers to test, and sometimes merely to maintain, what, on other grounds, they already believe. Hence their religious, or perhaps their non-religious outlook, is primary, and their philosophy, even when sincerely used for its true end, is only a touchstone of it. As the thinkers we have already considered are the most distinguished representatives of the most diverse ways of regarding religion, they will best serve as examples.

Kant's use of the old logic, suggestive as it often is, is mainly a parade of demonstrating each position step by step, and continually confuses his readers, and not infrequently himself, about his real purpose and method. His task was determined by his acceptance of the Newtonian theory of the Natural as universal, fixed, mathematically calculable process. But the influence of the moral and religious dignity of the humble people among whom he was brought up and of the teaching of Rousseau on the dignity of man as man was still earlier and deeper: and his supreme purpose is to find room in this Newtonian world for a realm of ends and the Supernatural as universal self-imposed moral legislation, in which the individual, as an individual, should realise in freedom his rights and his responsibilities. Thus, in the moral way in which he conceived religion, his dominant interest was religious.

Dilthey's *Early Life of Hegel* makes it plain that the interests out of which Hegel's philosophy arose were religious; and Hegel himself tells us that he thought the work thereof was peace, being a reconciliation with the universe, which was a higher religion, or beyond religion.

No other philosopher has ever professed so confidently to deal only with a logic which creates, as well as orders and demonstrates, all it affirms. Yet his use of it is a mere device for stating a general view which was already there; and the device is convincing for no one who does not share the same outlook. Like Kant he also accepted the view that science has shown the universe to be a scheme of fixed and necessary sequence· but he could not regard the Natural as a mist of impacts, ordered by the individual mind, nor could he regard the Supernatural as a mere scheme of moral legislation. Such a natural world was hard and bare, and a supernatural of such a type was mere striving and crying: and, in an artistic age, he needed variety and warmth and colour, and, in a troubled age, he needed peace

But the philosophical dialectic is mainly window-dressing, and rather a frigid scheme at that. The real source of his philosophy is a religion by which he had rid himself of the individual as understood by Rationalism, for the peace of his soul and the enjoyment of his world, before he jettisoned it as a nuisance in a philosophical scheme of Cosmic Process But again the question is, whether fixed Cosmic Process is, or is not, the real world, and whether the problem of knowledge can be solved merely by merging the individual in the process.

That Schleiermacher's theory of knowledge was determined

by his religion of aesthetic mysticism is not only plain, but was openly acknowledged. He himself speaks of it as making him a mystic of a higher order. The essence is that, by feeling and in a kind of mystical oneness, the spirit, which is an artistic whole, has intercourse with a universe, which is also an artistic whole. The idea of the individual has more meaning for the universe and for man himself than with Hegel, but has none of the importance for thought and action that it has with Kant, its freedom being merely harmony with the universe. Thus perception is for Schleiermacher a unified aesthetic knowing, because the essence of his religious faith is that the universe is a unified artistic whole.

Wherefore, though he finds the source of harmony in feeling while Hegel finds it in reason, the difference is more in form than in substance.

(*d*) THE TWO ASPECTS OF THE PROBLEM

Our problem is that knowing seems to be entirely within the individual mind yet knowledge to be of reality existing independently. On the one hand, there is no knowledge which is not our knowing, the more likely to be knowledge the more the knowing is our own; on the other, there is no knowledge except it is of an object existing apart from our knowing and in its own right, the more likely to be knowledge the more knowing is wholly concerned with the object.

The common device for making the explanation easy is to emphasise one aspect and minimise the other, till it seems to be merely a question either of the world that is known or the mind that knows, not of both But, in experience, or rather as the possibility of experience, both are at once distinct and harmonious, neither identical nor conflicting, and we must, as it were, neither divide the substance nor confuse the persons. No inability to explain, therefore, justifies the denial or even the subordination of either part To gain unity by absorbing one into the other is merely the common but futile device of fitting facts to theories, not theories to facts. The very partiality of the theories may make them of special value for showing us how far either aspect can carry us, yet the problem is their rights as well as their relation.

This problem we may, by again distinguishing words more definitely than in popular usage, call the *Individual* and *Individuality*. By the Individual is meant the peculiar character of being one person. The problem of the individual concerns what belongs to man as man, and is common to all. By Individuality is meant what is distinctive, what makes each man a special kind of personality. Person and Personality might seem better terms, and so they are for the highest and fullest situation with which the problem is concerned. But the whole range of the question is wider than the moral person, and affects our whole view of reality: and this is better included in Individual and Individuality.

The essential interest of Rationalism being the individual and the essential interest of Romanticism individuality, we have in these movements the material necessary for the discussion, though we shall also have to consider a naturalism, which did not so much sit on both stools, as between them, with the usual result. It will suffice to take Kant and Hegel as representatives, the former of the rationalist interest in the individual and the latter of the romanticist interest in individuality.

(*e*) KANT'S THEORY OF KNOWING AND THE INDIVIDUAL

As no one has dealt more profoundly with this idea of the individual than Kant, we take as our example his theory of knowledge. Like the rest of his philosophy, his theory of knowledge is an attempt to reconcile a supernatural world, which requires us to legislate for ourselves and act in freedom, with a necessary natural world, by which we and our actions alike seem to be determined: and his answer, in both cases, entirely concerns the place of the individual.

Kant is merely developing the rationalist view of the individual when he makes the form of the moral law a maxim which can be applied universally, and the substance of it to treat every man as an end in himself, and never as mere means to other ends. That this works by reverence is only another way of saying that the individual is of absolute value and, therefore, his frontier a real distinction in the Supernatural. To bring the Natural into accord with this, Kant goes to work still more drastically with the idea of the individual. What he calls the Pure Reason is as individual for him as what he calls the Practical Reason. Thus, even in perception, everything essential is done within the frontiers of the individual. Its content is no doubt from sensations, but they are only as clay is the material of pottery, mere raw chaotic material, about which he troubles himself very little, taking the real interest to be in the rules and processes of manufacture.

First, this material takes shape by being received into what he calls "the two pure forms of sensuous intuition"—space and time. By a pure form he means what is entirely contributed by the mind. For this reason they give universal, exact, mathematical results. All the rest is done by thought, and the essential aspect of its working is the imposing of concepts upon intuitions. To these are then assigned permanent relations by the categories of judgment; and the whole is finally wrought into unity by the ideas of reason. The result is necessary and is mathematically calculable *a priori*, because the mind has so constructed it.

This theory at least faces the first aspect of our problem, that, as Kant himself expresses it, "the object can be given only (to human beings at least) through a certain affection of the mind", and that the mind does not merely receive its knowledge passively, but knows only in the measure in which it actively deals with it.

Something might even be said for time and space as pure forms of intuition, as well as for the concepts, as our way of grasping intuitions, and for the categories, as our way of relating them, and for the ideals of reason, as our way of unifying them, because there is a selecting, interpreting, arresting which does belong to mind. Yet all sense of reality in our perception depends on the belief that this is directed by the order of reality which determines directly the context in which we receive sensations and indirectly the forms in which we arrange them. The forms may be more abstract and uniform as we use them than in reality, as all forms of our mind are apt to be, but, seeing how we deal with our environment by means of them, they must be adequate to it so far as they go.

Kant ascribes so incredible a creation to mind, because he did not start, as Reid had already done, by criticising Hume's account of the contribution of the senses. As grammar is already in speech, the forms of mind are already in the context of sensation. The mind simplifies, arrests, groups under ideas, but does not create. Thus concepts are a very important way of ordering our knowledge, but concepts, in their ordinary meaning, are merely useful ways of omitting details of apprehension, based on resemblances already existing in awareness, and not a way of making apprehensions into presentations which are mainly mental structures.

What Kant says of the forms with which mind works in knowing is true and important, but as he conceives their working, it is incredible. If we see an object at a distance by means of a system of physiological and physical vibration, we must in some way have a representation of the message, as we have of what is communicated to us by speech Yet, in both cases, the communication may be a link establishing direct understanding, and not a mere vehicle of a message, first translated into symbol and then translated out of it. In any case, re-presentation from what conveys a meaning which exists and from which it is conveyed in a context of meaning which interprets it, is one thing; and representation as an original creation of the mind which gives meaning to what otherwise has none, is another. Thus by his indifference to the other side of our problem—the existence, in its own right and independently of our minds, of what we know—he makes incredible even what is right in his view of the aspect of it in which he is interested.

For the same reason, the rest of his account of how the mind works in the kind of knowing which is perceiving is misleading. It is as though we should think that we understand what is said by distinguishing the parts of speech and applying the rules of syntax. His categories of judgment and ideals of reason are only the analysis, by reflexion, of what is given as one context of fixed idea in awareness and apprehension, and which has its ultimate origin in the context of reality, and not in the ordering of the mind, which only perceives it and does not create it. By understanding and reason we can discover that our environment is reasonable, but we perceive even this by awareness and apprehension, and not by understanding and reason. The result of Kant's theory would be, that not only is perception what James described as faked by the mind, but so little remains to be faked that it is merely what the mind imposes upon itself.

Moreover, there is the further difficulty about the theory that, while, in knowledge, it works with a mind, which, entirely by its own fixed forms, provides a rigid, mathematically calculable mechanical world, in action it works with another mind, the essential quality of which is freedom, and which gives a world of ideal purposes, a realm of ends to be determined purely by reverence for their worth. A mind which works in perception by fixed ideas determined by the order of the environment it perceives, but which attains to free ideas by its further dealing with the whole environment in which it lives is credible, but this fundamental dualism is not.

As frequently happens, extremes meet. Fichte's conclusion that, if the mind provides so much, it may as well provide also the little that remains, readily follows Then we have merely acosmic individualism. In spite of the extreme contrast in temper between rationalism and mysticism, this is not very far from the mystic's acosmic pantheism, because, apart from a world of reality in which they act, there is nothing to distinguish God from our mind, or our mind from God.

Yet in spite of all this criticism, the relation of the mind to its knowing, and the significance of the frontier, within which it is knowing, is as Kant conceived it: and this remains the most important contribution ever made to the subject.

(f) THE INDIVIDUAL FRONTIER AND THE NATURAL

The other side of our problem is how our knowing can be knowledge of a reality which exists in its own right and independently of our knowing. This is not only entirely unsolved, but is more evidently than ever shown to need a solution.

The obvious device for gaining what Kant had failed to provide was to deny the reality of the frontier of the individual.

This was at once adopted, but the denial took opposite directions. One, starting from Kant's Newtonian phenomenal world as the sole reality, conceived it to cross the individual frontier somehow as a physical cause of which knowledge was the effect. Thus the individual was merely a form in the Natural. The other, starting from the absolute, noumenal world as the sole reality, conceived it to pass the individual frontier as universal reason. Thus the individual was merely a form in the Supernatural. The one was a continuation of Rationalism, without Deism; the other still maintained the method of Rationalism, but was in substance a new departure under the banner of Romanticism.

These theories are as unlike as possible in outlook and temper, but as both alike discarded what was most important in Rationalism—the significance of the individual, the boundary between them is not always impassable. The former theory constantly helps itself out in difficulties from the latter, and the latter is not always as different from the former as its form might lead us to suppose.

The naturalistic theory regards the individual as continuous with a universal mechanical system of cause and effect. In mind this energy is transformed into knowing, somewhat as an electric bulb transforms into light which is seen, the current which, though it is not seen, is continuous with it in the wire. Thus the individual mind, though as a form within the world it is of some consequence, has no real frontier across which knowledge of the world can only come as its meaning, but is continuous with physical energy, so that knowing is an effect of it as flame is of heat.

THE INDIVIDUAL AND INDIVIDUALITY 157

Plainly, then, naturalistic theory is based on a theory of the world we perceive, and not on any concrete study of how we perceive it. No one, from the consideration of his own knowing, would ever imagine that the world it knows is a mechanical arrangement of atoms, with merely quantitative motions and without all quality, and that knowledge of it is an effect of such a cause. The ground of the theory is not anything in the nature of awareness and apprehension, but is a structure by the understanding of a sub-microscopic world of this mechanical nature which science is supposed to have revealed, and which is taken to be more real than the world we perceive, or rather to be the sole reality of it. Later this conception will fall to be considered, but a very important and relevant objection to it at this point is that out of it no possible theory of perception which has the least accord with the perceptions we actually have could ever be won.

We can argue from effects to causes only when we have knowledge of similar causes and effects from which to argue. When we argue from an explosion to dynamite, we do so with the knowledge that this particular substance has this special effect: and, were this entirely unknown, we could not have the dimmest conception of a cause so utterly unlike the effect. Therefore if *ex hypothesi* knowledge is only an effect, there can be no knowledge of any reality as its cause. The idea that science proves the cause to be matter and motion ignores the fact that science also would only be an effect which cannot know its own cause. The only logical conclusion would be agnosticism, but it would begin with the Natural. The kind of agnosticism we are familiar with is not agnostic at all, but is pure dogmatism about the importance for the knowledge of reality of what has quantity and can be interpreted as mechanism, compared with what has quality and must be interpreted as meaning.

But perception deals with the world just as meaning, and the dealing with it as measure and mechanism is a later work of the understanding, which itself depends on the meaning given in perception. Moreover, this meaning depends on an active valuing by the mind itself, and is not a mechanical effect of the object in respect of which the mind could only be passive.

Furthermore, as this meaning has inconceivable variety of value, it cannot be the effect of one kind of motion, which has no variety except of quantity which again is reducible to one unvarying quantity of force.

Mechanical explanations will always be attractive, because they appeal to our understanding, seeing that they are our way of managing our environment. But, apart from the fact that the universe does not seem to be constructed to the end of being easily understood, there is the difficulty of the understanding itself, which can only set up its purposes, even when it achieves them mechanically, by the meaning of the world. The result is not an interpretation, but what we may call a schoolmastering of the universe, which is not a profitable way of dealing with anything. Mechanism may have meaning, and, as the symbol of it, convey meaning, but it is because the meaning is already there. From pure mechanical vibration without meaning there is no possible opening into knowing, which is all meaning.

The simplicity of the theory being outdone by its futility, something more has to be sought to give at least the appearance of life to its valley of dry bones, and resort is made to Psychophysical Parallelism. In its cruder forms it is purely mechanical. The mental series is merely like the ticking of a clock, accompanying the revolution of the wheels, or like the mist, which follows the course of the river. But such parallelism affords a still more dubious passage back from effect as knowing, to cause as known, and, if possible, gives us even less right to speak of knowledge as corresponding to anything. Only the mental series is known, and we cannot stand outside of it to know what it corresponds with. No theory is more entirely based on its own presupposition, which is that our physical environment cannot deal with mind or mind with it. On what other ground Mr Broad thinks it may still be true, though he denies the necessity of its presupposition, is, to say the least

THE INDIVIDUAL AND INDIVIDUALITY 159

not evident, for what else is there to contradict experience except this presupposition?

But, being in possession of a mental series from which meaning can by no device be banished, Scientific Naturalism can modify itself into Artistic Naturalism.

This is not the same naturalism, nor does it work with knowledge as the effect of a physical cause. It is merely illegitimately adopted from the other theory of the world as universal mind and of knowledge of the world as participation in the universal mind. Man and his universe as the World-Spirit unfolding himself for his own artistic satisfaction, has nothing to do with a universe of the endless diffusion and mutation of mechanically determined, purely continuous forces. But Goethe can be dovetailed into Spinoza, and the decay of Newtonism, with its explanation of everything by inertia, and the rise of a more organic view of reality, has put new life into the theory which is the work of this combination.

The essential contention, that the physical and mental series run parallel because they are both modes of one being, is Spinoza's contribution This can still be imagined in a mechanical form. Spinozism, indeed, when stripped of what belongs to the humanity and religious spirit of its author, is just a mechanical scheme of bullets keeping abreast, because they are fired with the same charge, at the same moment and in the same direction, from one revolver.

As this does not bring us much nearer the concrete world of varied quality in which we live, Goethe is laid under contribution, and the bare absolute of the unity of knowing and being is transformed into the artistic World-Spirit. As an artistic spirit actively fashions himself and his work at the same time, by his own idea of unity and in accord with his own forms, an artistic World-Spirit might be building up what Goethe calls "the pyramid of his own individuality", by the process of fashioning his world into artistic perfection. But this possibility would at once endanger the mechanically secured unity of the universe, and upset the theory that knowledge is one aspect of it continuous with the rest, and thereby destroy any advantage to be gained from the mere parallelism of the mental and physical series. His artistic quality, therefore, shrinks into a mechanical unfolding of what is immanent in himself, with a necessary parallel projection of it as knowing and being. Thus it is none the less mechanical for part of it being a necessary mode of spirit.

Perhaps the most moving appeal for this theory since Spinoza himself is Mr Lloyd Morgan's. He clothes it also with his large-minded, gracious and religious personality. Yet all that has happened to Spinoza is that, in turning biologist, he has a little more room for the spirit of Goethe and his varied, historical world. But, when Mr Lloyd Morgan beseeches his readers to believe that, in spite of the fact that his theory seems to leave mind only a specially complex kind of biological arrangement, whose knowledge cannot be really knowing and which cannot affect its environment by any power of its own, it, nevertheless, does all that we know it does, his argument turns into an excess of technical terminology, which at least is not fitted to increase faith in the simplicity of his meaning. All one can gather is a general impression, and it is of a man, interested in a large world, with a small theory of it, being drawn into the hopeless task of trying to show that a thing can be and not be at the same time.

(g) THE INDIVIDUAL FRONTIER AND THE SUPERNATURAL

But, with Goethe himself, we come definitely to Romanticism, and with Romanticism to the theory which opens the frontier of the mind towards the Supernatural. This as fully identifies the individual with his environment as the theory we have just been considering, but it does so in another way, and is enormously interested, as the former theory is not, in individuality, as of endless variety, reflecting an endlessly varied universe.

The term Romanticism is often confusing, not only because it is used with different meanings, but because there is a constant habit of slipping from one meaning into the other. In its wider meaning, Romanticism covers the whole poetical movement of the early nineteenth century; in its narrower, it means a special school of which Goethe was the divinity, Friedrich Schlegel the high-priest, Hegel the philosopher, and Schleiermacher the prophet. Here we are dealing with the latter kind of Romanticism, especially with its philosophy: and we shall confine ourselves to Hegel as the representative of it.

The limitation of Rationalism, with its concentration on the individual, Kant merely made more obvious: and Hegel is only to be understood and his value rightly appreciated as the philosopher of a movement which was a revolt against it. For Kant man was what George Herbert calls "a well-trussed pack, a shop of rules", and his world little more than a system of rules, imposed by himself, of necessity on his knowledge, and in freedom on his action. To this, whatever Hegel may have done or failed to do, his philosophy was a resounding challenge.

As Kant's position was in accord with the spirit of his age, it is no wonder that few ages have been so barren either in artistic feeling or artistic achievement. But the supreme interest of the Romantic age which followed was, in the class at least which fashioned its temper, aesthetic, which meant interest in the endless variety of man's individuality and the infinite variety of environment therein reflected. The individual was, for it, little more than the frame, valuable only for the picture it contained, not something of worth in everyone, from which all that gives individuality—especially beauty and goodness—derives its worth. Interest was confined to the individuality which made the individual what Schleiermacher calls "a particular thought of God".

The whole outlook of the age was determined by what was felt to have been lacking in the previous age: and if, like other ages, the new age ignored the importance of what the previous age had contributed, there was large justification. Having an artistic and historical sense, it could not regard the Natural as related to us only by a mist of sensations, or ascribe all ordering of it to the individual mind however transcendental, or ignore history and its significance for evolving the fullness of experience, or be satisfied with the Supernatural as purely transcendent, abstract moral legislation.

Hegel, sharing in this dissatisfaction, concentrated on the other side of Kant's theory—the practical reason. But Kant's idea of freedom he changed from self-determination by the individual's own ends into an artistic sense of being exalted above a mechanical into an ideal world. This artistic unity was extended to being as well as knowing, and came into operation as universal rational cosmic process. On this view individual knowing is knowledge because it is merely a pattern in the universal web, with warp and woof running, uninterrupted, through it.

This process unfolded itself by Being, Not-being and Becoming. One of his own followers has described this unkindly as "an unearthly ballet of bloodless categories". But there is no use working with a process, if no suggestion can be made of how it works: and Hegelianism, as the final solution Hegel thought it to be, is buried with its scheme.

The important part of the process, which is called Not-being, shows that Hegel did not ignore the problem of the individual. A genuine individual frontier would be a denial of any scheme of scientific pantheism, but at all events it appears to exist: and this suggestion of inward stress in the Universal Reason, which is apparent in its finite vehicles, is at least the most plausible device yet hit upon for explaining, even if it be only explaining away, the fact that knowledge is meaning in the mind of the individual and progress dependent on his purpose and striving. Possibly it is the best that could be devised.

The trouble is that even this concession to the individual has no right in the system. Doubtless the human reason suffers plenty of negation: but that is precisely because it is individual. From the Universal Reason we might confidently expect it to be absent, for, if the frontier of the individual is not a boundary which the universal meaning can cross only as it becomes our meaning, it presents no barrier against which its smooth current should break into this bewildering foam. Nor does a mere logical negative really explain how the Universal Reason, in

THE INDIVIDUAL AND INDIVIDUALITY   163

its passage through us, gives rise to error, which is a creation of the individual mind, and has to be corrected by its activity, if corrected at all. Were this painful struggle confined to "the labour of the notion", we might regard it as mere growing pains, but unfortunately it extends to every aspect of existence.

The system is largely concerned with truth, beauty and goodness as universal standards, the universality of thought being precisely what the scheme is produced to provide. But, as we use them, they are not mere diffused qualities of the universe, which, as Hegel thinks, could have their highest manifestation in Prussia. Unfortunately, they are only possibilities for the Prussians. Prussia as the sublimest vehicle of the Universal Reason for the manifestation of itself, however excellent the Prussians, is merely mythology. Truth, beauty and goodness exist only as they are realised with conscious purpose and in freedom; and while the standards of them belong to the nature of the universe, and, as Hegel rightly thinks, there is no knowledge without them, man only realises them as he sets the highest he knows before him and seeks to fulfil it. The reality of ideal standards vanishes with the reality of the individual, for then they lose their true significance, which is not for what is, but for what ought to be. This may not, as with Kant, be striving and crying, but still less is it a mere mirroring of Universal Reason.

For Hegel, the victory of the whole system was peace. In the introduction to his *Philosophy of Religion* he speaks of it with a moving eloquence as though it were

> Rest after toil, port after stormy seas,
> Peace after war.

The only fear is that we should have to conclude, as the verse does, with

> Death after life

for the question is whether this, more than any other pantheism, is victory in life or escape from it. What it appeals to is what psychologists call the mother-complex, and what it promises is rest on the broad bosom of the universe. Seeing how many seek this from philosophy, as others from religion, this philosophy has had many adherents; and in spite of Troeltsch's confidence that it, as well as Naturalism, is a dead issue and a waste of time to discuss, new forms of it will doubtless have many more.

But the question for us at present is how far this view of the world approves itself by its theory of knowing. There are three main criticisms.

The first is that from abstract reason we can never arrive at a concrete world. No system professed more confidently to apply the Cartesian method and to show how, from mere potentiality as an abstraction, we arrive at the concrete varied world of our experience. But it is just as much a begging of everything new as it goes along, as any other system which substitutes understanding and explanation for awareness and apprehension. While it starts from the aesthetic world of poetic Romanticism, and keeps up the appearance of never losing it, it loses everything concrete by the way, and at the end has to appropriate again from awareness and apprehension what it makes a parade of demonstrating.

The second is that perception may be 'picture thought' as Hegel describes it, but to be anything resembling perception as we know it, this should at least be from the object and not merely of the object as the Universal Mind thinks it in us; merely allotting a certain part of itself to the individual. This may be knowing as a sample of the whole, though even that is a large assumption on these premises, but it is not knowledge of what is not itself, being merely a part of the general consciousness. It does not give a subject who knows an object, but only subject and object as poles of one universal process.

The third is that knowing by mere fixity of cosmic process, embracing knower and known, in the end is as mechanical as any scheme of cause and effect. Indeed the attraction of the theory is just that the idea of whole and part can be understood mechanically, as simply as the idea of cause and effect. Therefore, what has been said of the worthlessness of simplicity for the understanding, as determining the nature of the universe, is equally relevant here.

Yet this solution of the problem of why knowing in the individual mind should be knowledge of what exists apart from it and in its own right, by regarding both as continuous and the individual frontier as no real distinction in the universe, is too simple and obvious to pass easily. Even after the conception of the whole as fixed cosmic process has followed the categories which profess to explain it, the idea still remains that knowledge is an infusion of what is in suffusion around us. Thus Prof. Pringle-Pattison says that all difficulties about perception disappear, if we hold steadily by the two ideas of immanence and continuity.[1] The exact reason for this faith would depend on the meaning given to the words, but it is at least not obvious how these ideas remove difficulties, unless immanence means identity of the mind without and the mind within, and continuity the flow of the mind without into the mind within in such a way that the individual nature of knowledge is set aside as mere appearance. Then, of course, the difficulty disappears, yet only because it has not been raised, and knowledge remains in the hopelessly inadequate category of pattern and web.

(h) RATIONALISM AND ROMANTICISM

These problems of Rationalism and Romanticism correspond to the two aspects of our problem, that knowing is meaning for the mind that knows, yet is knowledge of reality existing independently and in its own right. We have taken Kant as representative of the former and Hegel of the latter: and, as the two sides of the problem are not considered, the result is that Kant, regarding only one, gives what may be knowing but cannot be knowledge, while Hegel, regarding only the other, gives what might possibly be knowledge but could not be described as knowing. While we recognise the value of the emphasis each put on the aspect he saw, the one way is as barren as the other. The real problem is how the individual has a genuine frontier towards the world, across which nothing

[1] A. Seth Pringle-Pattison, *The Idea of God*, pp 110 ff.

should come except as his own meaning, and yet has an individuality which is a reflexion of the world's infinite variety, which has produced him and not he it So they are not apart, nor is the one the mere shadow of the other.

This is the true problem, whether we can make any approach towards solving it or not. It is the glory of kings to search out a matter, but it is also the glory of God to conceal it: and our understanding is not the measure of reality, or even of our experience of it. The moment we put these two aspects of our problem together, it is obviously futile to attempt to solve the problem either by the idea that the mind manufactures its own knowledge, or by the idea that knowledge is somehow other than the thinking of the individual mind. The idea that the universe has its qualities purely from the thinking of the individual mind, and the idea that the individual mind is not a real distinction in the universe and an essential manifestation of its qualities, are equally inadequate to explain knowing as we know it and knowledge as the reality it claims to be.

Hegel's position has this truth in it that the environment with which we deal must be the whole of reality, so that even what we call physical is not a fact in isolation; and we have also so far to agree with the naturalistic position that we must in the end attribute, not alone all knowing, but also the mind that knows, to environment. But, then, the question which arises is, What is the environment which is equal to this task? The moment we introduce the individual as a distinction in the universe, of supreme importance for its economy, because no knowledge of it passes to us except across the frontier of the individual's mind as his meaning, it is evident that environment cannot be mere diffusion of any process, whether physical or metaphysical.

Kant, in whatever else he may be wrong, is wholly right in maintaining that all knowledge is given by an affection of the individual mind and all dealing with it by the thinking of the individual mind: and all inquiry into knowing is vain of which this is not the starting-point. Where his theory fails we shall see later, but that it does fail as a theory of perception would appear from this fact alone, that the mind assumed in it is the human mind, whereas all animals have some perception, and many would appear, in some ways at least, to perceive better than we do. We can only argue from our own perceptions which we know, and not by some genetic method from animal perception which we do not know, but a theory which could not be extended in some general way to lower perceptions than human would lack an important confirmation. Also apart from this and merely as a theory of knowledge, it is like a theory of writing which regarded conversation as a jumble of sounds till it was reduced to paper: whereas the obvious presupposition of perception is an intelligible sensory, as the presupposition of writing is intelligible conversation.

There is a sense in which space and time are forms of the mind, but not in the sense that we merely manufacture them and impose them upon reality. Our minds probably simplify them to the absence of difference, in time as measured in two directions and space in three, and our way of working them may only be a kind of useful perspective from our point of view, as it plainly is in our picture of room: but, even so, our forms must have a practical correspondence with the forms of external reality, even if it be only as the perspective of a picture, and be an interpretation of it and not merely imposed upon it. Nor do we divide reality into individual things without any corresponding individuality in the things themselves, even though we may stereotype their distinctions by categories of substance and such-like, in a way more fixed than they are in the flux of experience. Nor, though the idea of cause and effect may be largely derived from our own activities, can an order in some way corresponding to it be absent from the relations of actual environment. Finally, our ideas of reason, though there may be simplifications which are useful because they are more static than reality, are not mere inventions of our own, which we impose on our world, but are useful in experience because our experience is of a world as an ordered whole.

Wherefore, the essential question of perception is precisely what Kant dismissed as a mere welter of sense impressions, the question of what we may call the context of sensations and the coherence of the reality which witnesses to itself by it.

CHAPTER X

THE FORM OF PERCEPTION

(a) THE METHOD OF INQUIRY

On few other questions than this of knowing and knowledge has the Cartesian method been more constantly employed, and perhaps for none is it less adequate.

"To accept only what presents itself to the mind so clearly and distinctly as to exclude all grounds of doubt" would, as Descartes himself saw, not even leave us with the fact that we actually perceive. Unless we accept knowing as the way to knowledge, there seems to be no possible beginning; and unless we trust the most enlightened knowing as giving the truest knowledge, no hope of progress in it. What we may call the minimal attitude of mind never reached any great truth in any department: and it is least of all likely to understand what embraces the universe as well as the individual.

"To divide the inquiry into as many parts as possible" is likely to be merely a way of evading the difficulties of any problem, which are usually just in the relation of the parts to each other and to the whole. But this is specially true of our inquiry, because if there is anything which ought to be one it is knowing.

"To commence with the simple and ascend to the more complex" has also been an order extensively followed in this inquiry. A start is made with physical impacts; then somehow sensations are their passive effects; then sensations are somehow associated into perception, and perceptions somehow into judgments: till we arrive at rational beings in a rational world, all fashioned out of the clay of physical impacts. This conclusion is Empiricism, but it is very far from being what it claims to be, empirical, because we do not experience sensations in perception, and there is no possibility of starting from sensation and arriving at a poet's perception. The best we can do is to start from the highest perception we know and to ask what part sensation may be thought to play in it.

Nor in respect of this empiricism would it be the slightest use "to revise carefully that nothing be omitted". Impacts, sensations, awareness, apprehension may be the whole story of perception. What is omitted is not details but their whole significance in a rational experience. Of sensations in relation to a world of varied meaning we can be reasonably sure and can with equal confidence relate them to mechanical impacts, but sensations and physical impacts, as discrete isolated facts, are unknown, for all that gives them significance is just the part they play in the world of meaning and rational experience. Even if science reduces the physical facts to vibrations, what is most important about them must be that they are in a context of meaning, and that between them and sensation there is not mere passive subjection but active interpretation of them as meaning. Physical science may ignore this, but it is fundamental for our inquiry: and though seen clearly only in the highest perception, may shed light on the lowest. What the field of awareness for any being save ourselves may be we cannot tell, yet even the lowest sense of touch must be some sense of its environment, some dim prophecy of the awareness of the child and the poet, which is more like the awareness of one mind and its manifestations than anything else we know.

We cannot even limit ourselves to what is psychological, for what ultimately determines our way of knowing is the nature of the world we know If it is a world in which the Natural mirrors the Supernatural, the perception of the lowest living creature is a very different business from what it would be if its environment were merely a world of hurtling physical impacts. And, even for the highest perception, what may be most important may also be far beyond our perceiving. All we can do is to be awake to the largest possibilities of the dependence of knowledge on the nature of ultimate reality. This may seem to be a very roundabout way, compared with a direct method which has in it from the start the solution of empiricism.

But the difficulty about a problem is usually from not conceiving it widely enough, the larger problem being in the end the simpler. We know at least a great deal better how we know the varied world of thought and feeling, which is in the mind of another person, than how we could perceive a stone from mere discrete impacts.

(*b*) BERKELEY'S DIVINE VISUAL LANGUAGE

Apart from touch, which has a general relation to all the senses, and from taste, which is a specialised form of it, the function of the senses is to give us knowledge at a distance.

We might begin by trying to work back to some dim first beginning and to guess at a development. But it would be a guessing which never could be knowledge. What we do know is how we have extended still farther than the senses this power of knowing at a distance: and it is at least probable that this is an extension of the kind of knowing we have in perception, and not a completely new invention.

The most important and general means is language. By it man has extended his knowledge far beyond the range of his own senses and to times remote from his own experience; and by making his experience a universe of discourse with his fellows, has come to a conscious knowledge that it deals with an actual universe which is rational and ordered.

Some helpful analogy between speech and perception has long been admitted, but Berkeley's denial that there is any essential difference between the kind of reality dealt with in speech and the kind of reality dealt with in perception has made men shy of admitting any closer resemblance. Yet Berkeley has not been shown to be wrong in thinking, as one of his critics expresses it, that "sense experience has the intelligibility of a language whose conventions are one and all determined by a spirit akin to our own"; and his argument against a reality that is matter without meaning is valid to this day.

Where he goes astray is in assuming that there is no difference between these two kinds of communication: whereas, it is plain that we ought always to be alive to the possibility that the extension even of the same kind of knowing does not necessarily give us the same kind of knowledge.

His first error is in overlooking the difference between the nature of the symbols.

While a large part of the symbolism of speech is arbitrary and, in principle, may be so entirely, the symbols of perception are entirely fixed by the nature of things. Therefore, he has no right to assume, as he does, that the symbols of perception may be, at least in God's mind and, therefore, in their real nature, as arbitrary as speech is for ours. Our whole belief in an objective world assumes that the symbols by which we interpret it belong also to its natural order, and that their objectivity is not covered by the bare fact that they are not under our control, as Berkeley affirms.

His second error is in overlooking the difference between the context of perception and the context of speech.

The context of speech has only to do with the consistency of thought, whereas the context of perception has to do with the consistency of reality or, if we will, of our whole environment. No doubt this also alters continually, yet in such a way as to show that it has a quite different kind of consistency and permanence from speech. This might be regarded, with Berkeley, as due merely to the greater consistency and continuity of the Divine thinking. But, though a continuity of inert matter may be a mere mistaken inference, our belief in an objective world assumes an environment there in its own right, linked together by cause and effect and other continuous relations and not merely by thoughts imposed upon it from moment to moment and it could be no work of the Divine mind to impose upon us an illusion.

His third error is in overlooking the fact that the universe we perceive is not merely consistent for our thinking, but has significance for itself; and that if so, this must be between us and the mind of God. Were this not so, the universe would be a very poverty-stricken affair, and objective knowledge an

172   THE FORM OF PERCEPTION

illusion. He rightly thinks it all meaning, but it is meaning in itself and by itself, and, probably to a larger extent than we know, for itself, as well as for us and for God.

(c) SPEECH AND PERCEIVING

This does not, however, prove that language is not a continuance of the same kind of knowing as perception and that the former sheds no light on the latter. On the contrary, the history of language enables us to get back to two facts which show how near the origin of speech is to apprehension.

We begin with the fact that originally there was no arbitrary use of sounds, but all were purely imitative. That is to say, their meaning depended on the already fixed context of perception. Only as man attains free ideas can he determine his symbols freely or, if we will, arbitrarily, so as to have at his disposal all sounds to which meaning can be attached, and use them independently of particular immediate situations.

The second point is that words originally expressed whole unanalysed situations. In primitive languages still one term may include the subject, the object and their relations. The subject, the object, the time relation, the kind of activity, the qualities of the subject, the qualities of the activity, the kind of bearing on the object, the various forms of sequence, are only gradually analysed out of the one situation, and developed into parts of speech. That is to say, they are only slowly taken out of the scheme of fixed ideas in which they are apprehended, and which is the context of apprehension.[1]

How near this speech of imitative signs and unanalysed situations is to the use of the mind in perception appears from the fact that people who are still at the stage of fixed ideas

[1] Jespersen thinks that language sprang from the poetic, not the prosaic side of life, and that originally singing and speaking were not distinguished, which is to say that it was rather an expression of an inward state than an outward interest; that speech started with complicated sounds which were sentences and that "the bigger and longer the words, the thinner the thoughts". Thus it was only a slight advance on the fixed context of perception. But as speech advances, it becomes not a method of conveying our thought, but of selecting what we wish to convey, so that there is a sense in which speech is for concealing thought.

seem to have the greatest difficulty in distinguishing memories and even imaginings from perceptions, and even conceptual words from percepts. Even so great an abstract thinker as Plato often speaks as if we ought to be able to see everything we can talk of.

So advanced a literary language as Hebrew has the conjunction as sequence, the pronoun as subject, the verb as action, and the pronoun as object, all in one word. Moreover, the subjective as dominating the objective interest in the happening is shown in the tenses, which are not objective time relations but merely an order of happening in relation to the person, and in the moods, which are not modes of objective happenings but impressions on the subject, such as intensives, causatives, reflexives—even actives and passives not being objective as in Aryan tongues. The Hebrew prophet was the first to conceive that he lived in an ordered world, and he saw all things in it with an apprehension which was both practical and poetic, but his interest in it was as a human environment. And the highest poetry continues to see the world most clearly and beautifully in this same relation to human interest, mere description of nature being apt to be rather reflexion than pure perception.

Yet the Hebrew prophet saw this objectively because he had emancipated himself from the sense of the mere awesome holy. But we see this sense abundantly in his contemporaries, everything being, so to speak, in its atmosphere. And though no doubt the source of idolatries, was it not also the source of higher human perception, being the stage at which man said that there is more in our experience than we can touch and a higher value than heat and cold and satisfaction and hunger? This sheds the more light upon perception that he could not say it except in a particular material context, in which this sense of absolute quality was at least the beginning of feeling all his apprehensions to be in a universe.

In the Aryan languages we have another kind of development, which shows an interest in the world by itself. Conjunctions mark various kinds of objective sequence, tenses objective time relations, moods modes of happenings. But these languages have embedded in them the most abundant, the most imaginative mythology. Max Muller took this to be an outgrowth from speech, the imaginative person calling the river by metaphor the runner, and the dull person turning poetry into prose and taking it to be an actual runner. But the working of the human mind would seem to have been in the opposite direction. First, men had about the river, coming from the unknown and passing on to the unknown, a sense of the awesome holy; and so it became a sacred object, a real, living, ceaseless runner. Thus they became interested in it for its own sake, with the same kind of objective interest as they had in their neighbours, and apart from supplying their fish and watering their fields. They watched it glowing in the sun or shining mysteriously under the stars or feeble in heat and strong and violent in spate, and listened to it rippling gently over the stones or making the woods echo with its mighty voice. As they learned to set their own surroundings over against themselves, they came to separate the god from the river. Finally, as they were emancipated from the material sacred, they could see it objectively in a world which they related as a whole to the Supernatural. We now may be stirred with the river's mighty voice and be impressed by "the silence which is among the everlasting hills" without mythology, but should we have won the interest to perceive, save for those before us who passed in this animistic way beyond the stupid animal gaze?

Two things this is intended to show. Man won a lively objective perception by active human interest, stirring a lively and penetrating imagination; and what did rouse interest in the world in its own right was a sense of the Supernatural, both as a feeling of the holy and as a valuation of the sacred.

(d) SYMBOL AND MEANING

If speech is thus an extension of perception, the mind acts in all our senses as in hearing. Suppose we are listening to the playing of a violin. We know that without there are vibrations in a system of meaning, because we know that the player

THE FORM OF PERCEPTION

creates them in accord with his melody· yet of this we are not conscious, but are aware only of sounds corresponding to them. These sounds we may be aware of as pleasing, but, when we are rapt in the music, we cease to be conscious of the pleasure of the sounds, and are conscious of the music only as continuous melodious meaning.

If all perceiving be of this nature, at the frontier of the individual there is a system of symbols of vibration without and a corresponding system of sensations interpreting them within, and the significance of the individual frontier is that knowledge can pass it only as our meaning. Thus knowing is not knowledge as an effect of an unknown external cause, but is knowledge as we so interpret that our meaning is the actual meaning of our environment.

That in perception we should thus be working with a double system of symbols, and not be aware of it, may seem incredible. But this differs only in completeness from the unawareness of the symbols of speech and even the still more artificial symbols of writing. In reading, we always see the print as letters and never as peculiar black marks, and we can be so absorbed in a book as to be entirely unconscious; not only of letters but of words; and when listening we may be still less conscious of the special nature of sounds in speech, but, under the spell of the speaker, pass directly to his meaning We can even use apprehensions as symbols of other apprehension in such a way that, though we must have attended to them intently, we have great difficulty in recalling them as objects. For example, from no feature do we read character so much as from the eyes, yet there is no feature, and especially in familiar faces, which most people have greater difficulty in recalling. But that we are aware of them appears from the fact that nothing would astonish us more than any marked change in them, though, even then, we might have great difficulty in saying exactly what the change was

If this is possible with artificial symbols we remember having learned, it is easy to see why the symbols of apprehension never appear as conscious knowledge, yet more vividly and directly relate our knowing to what is known, or, as we might say, our meaning to what it means.

First, they are sensations which are not only vivid in themselves but give vividness to what they signify, the vividness coming into consciousness in the apprehension and not remaining in the sensation. Second, while conscious sensations are thoughts, a sensation which is arrested before it is a thought by itself, and turned at once into its meaning, has no separate realisation. Finally, there are hereditary elements which are still farther away from our own consciousness, and which give a smoothness and rapidity of working which never calls attention to itself.

Taking all these considerations together, it is far more likely that this power of interpretation from symbols was developed for perception, and that reading, or even speaking, was invented because we already had this power, than that we first invented language and the symbols of it, and then developed the power to use them.

(*e*) THE CONTEXT OF FIXED IDEAS

The context of perception we have primarily in the form of fixed ideas, that is to say, ideas which are at once called up by the situation and cannot be separated from it, and which call up other ideas inseparably connected with experience of similar situations. In short, what is meant here by a fixed idea is an idea which has a context out of which it cannot be taken.

From no theory of perception can heredity be omitted. Many attempts have been made to confine this to merely physical transmission of impulse and physical capacity. But, for example, instincts, in the sense of a fixed order of doing things, cannot be so explained, and can only be by heredity of fixed ideas. And there is no place where a mere physiological explanation is less adequate than in the contribution of heredity to perception. It is not a mere question of the power of having sensations, though even to have them in working order for perception is much more than physiological. But the rapid

THE FORM OF PERCEPTION

perception, especially of the lower animals at the first moment possible, presupposes a fixed context of ideas ready to come into operation, which must have been developed from the first sense, in the living creature, of contact with a reliable environment and the first pushing of its knowledge farther afield than actual contact.

However much of the individual equipment has been built up by heredity, even sensations belong to the individual, not merely as within his organism, but as within his mind, and therefore, the context for dealing with them, from which fixed ideas arise, must also be within the mind.

The presupposition of a power of perception which yet gives no knowledge of anything till it is perceived, would then be that fixed contexts are hereditary as determined instincts, while free ideas are hereditary only as adaptability. The ideas of animals, we may suppose, are wholly fixed, not in the sense that the living creature has no power of modifying them, but in the sense that it cannot take them out of their context and look round them and put them in another context or use them without any fixed context. Thus their perception is more in working order, while man's has a greater career before it.

In any case, the first question of the context of perception concerns fixed ideas. They are not wholly fixed, for even the lower animals seem to have an increasing power of enlarging them and acting more freely towards them. But, in everything connected with perception, even for civilised man they are fixed in the sense that, while perceiving, he cannot take his perceptions out of this context; and for primitive man, they remain a fixed context out of which he can take very few of his particular experiences and look round them and put them in another context. Especially he seems to require exactly similar conditions of sequence in events and situations in space before he can live again through any experience.

Perception, whatever else there may be that goes with it, is an individualising attention which yet does not take its object out of its whole context of awareness. It is an aesthetic task of individualising, but not isolating The details, as it were, cannot be lifted out of the picture. Thus perception works with a body of fixed ideas, in the sense defined above, as ideas which cannot be taken out of their context, but which draw their context with them.

(*f*) ONENESS OF THE SENSES

One important effect is the continual stirring of one sense by another. It is not association by happening together or by any other kind of connexion, but is just that the experiences have never been taken out of what we may call the coherence of happenings. It is based upon the general coherence of awareness, and not upon associations, which are based upon it.

The higher animals use different senses for different purposes, but probably this does not mean that they can isolate a special sense more or less completely as we can. They may even depend chiefly on one sense, but this does not prove that they isolate even it. Rather the reason why the special sense is so much depended on would appear to be that it is the sense which has most fixed in it the experience of the other senses. Thus a dog's smell or a stag's hearing has a context of other members of their species and men and things. The African native, Dan Crawford says, finds his way in the trackless forest, without landmark or sight of the sky, by a sixth sense, or rather by all his senses working as one. Our isolation of a sense is a work of understanding, rather than of perception, that is to say, it is for grasping the practical significance of a particular aspect of a subject, rather than for apprehending it.

In spite of all our development of free ideas, perception remains, even for us, in a context of fixed ideas: and our senses are much less isolated than our conscious attention to particular senses, for purposes of understanding, leads us to suppose Some measure of this oneness of the senses may be physical. The clearest example is that we cannot rightly taste, unless we can at the same time call into action the sense of smell, but it may be that every sense draws with it to some extent all the others. Hearing perhaps calls up the largest context of experience, and the pleasure of music may have something to do with its resonance in all the senses. Again the vivid sense of a solid resistance in all we see may mean some stirring of the sense of touch. As all our senses are in the last resort senses of touch, having been developed from it to extend its power of prediction to remoter environment, it is probable that the general sense of touch may be specially active with all our senses, and may be important for the conviction of solidity or resistance which accompanies all perception.

Yet the main link between sense and sense is the context of fixed ideas. This is plainest precisely in this relation of sight and touch, because what goes with sight is not merely a general sense of resistance and impenetrability, which might be only a general stirring of the sense of touch, but there is also an immediate distinguishing of various touches by sight which could only be from a context of ideas from many past experiences. On this the reality we ascribe to things seen largely depends. We can scarcely see anything without some sense of how it would feel. Even a cloud has its quality from the idea of resistance or non-resistance, while the sight of it does not stir any idea of how it would taste or smell.

This is overlooked because we think of touch mainly as giving pleasant or unpleasant sensations. In this sensuous form we use it in taste and smell, yet even by them we can have the most varied information regarding which, except as information, we are neither pained nor pleased. But in sight and hearing, when normal, we have no sense of physical contact giving sensations of pain or pleasure, yet the information of touch, being embedded in our vision, enables us to go about our business, knowing what we can penetrate and what we cannot. And all the senses carry with them a similar context With this context of fixed ideas, apprehension moves across the general field of awareness, as a brighter light which is the focus of illumination of the whole. This alone is strictly perception, and what is usually called naive perception includes besides a great deal of understanding and explanation, which is not the same kind of direct testimony.

Though this alone is what we consciously experience as perception, behind it there must have been a general awareness, which, at the beginning, could only have been a dim discrimination in the sense of touch. Many living creatures do not seem to have passed beyond this stage. Yet, low as the stage is, this awareness may not have been a mere imperfect kind of knowing, but have had some direct effectiveness within its own sphere and for its special purpose, which, though lost to consciousness by our wider interests, may still be of the utmost importance for the relation between sensation and awareness.

(g) SPACE AND TIME

This context of fixed ideas is not of mere customary associations, because the order of experience is not of mere accidental accretions, but is a coherent system with a continuous and consistent meaning. Association is, therefore, a superficial name for this ordering of our knowing, because, at least if we are sane, the order reflects the meaning we experience. What we call the laws of association is a mixture of the context of apprehensions and of their relations made by reasoning: and much of our difficulty about perception and our whole naive dealing with the world comes from accepting Hume's account of the senses as giving mere discrete facts, with a sort of reasoning from customary conglomeration as the only way of grasping the connexion of things, and not as something already there in the coherence of perception. Because Kant's criticism did not go back far enough, he landed in the incredible position that the mind of the perceiver imposes all its order upon the chaotic sense data: and many have not gone as far back even as he did.

Even fixed ideas are ideas, and though they are only to be escaped by further experience, and, when no further experience, as with time and space, is possible, are not to be escaped at all, they are still a thinking together of experience, as we should still think together a conversation even if we never had but one and were unable to think apart from it.

The fixing of ideas in a context of space sheds light on the fixing of all ideas, because all alike are fixed by the habitual context of experience, and the only difference is that, as the time-space context never varies, it is most fixed.

As a starting-point we shall take Prof. Ward's view of the extensiveness of some sensations. This he regards as the basis in experience of the idea of space. Extension is, as it were, a patchwork of extensive sensations, which is ironed out flat by our abstract idea of space as uniformity in all directions He thinks that two stamps stuck on the skin are felt as a larger sensation than one, and a bath than dipping the hand in water. And this seems so to us certainly. But is it so as pure sensation? Had we not already ideas of larger and smaller surfaces, by which to interpret them, would they be marked by anything except a doubtful difference in the quality of the feeling in the former case and a more evident one in the latter?

This is confirmed by the nature of simple apprehensions, and the more so the less they are mixed with judgment and reasoning. To a child a big man does not differ from a smaller one by so many inches, but he makes a quite different kind of impression; and a large flock of birds is not so many more birds than a small one, but is an individual object of a quite different quality. Wherefore, although Ward has the weighty support of William James, it is far more probable that extension and space are interpretations of different qualities of sensations by means of motion, than that they are made up of extended sensations. This presupposes, of course, that time is a form of our experience, because only motion in time could give any idea of continuity, and therefore influence perception of extension. Yet time and space, as we have seen, are present, in a qualitative way of great importance, in all awareness, before they have any place as measurable quantities. Thereby all extensions in all perceptions are parts of space, and space is not made up of a patchwork of extended sensations.

Time, being a form of our experiencing as well as of our experiences, does not, in respect of the correspondence of our meaning with the reality of the universe, cause the same difficulty as space, because both may equally be within time. Time by itself, as thus directly experienced, is not quantitative. Its measurement, being by space and the periodic nature of movement within it, such as the hands of the clock and revolution of the earth, is, but such measurement is plainly the work of reflexion and judgment, not of perception. Time, for perception, being just the order manifested in the continuous progress of meaning, as when we follow a discourse, is therefore more directly the form of our awareness than space. In our use of it by measure, it is merely a fourth dimension of the environment of any point-observer, which the higher mathematics can calculate along with the three dimensions of space as one unifiable set of relations.

Time we do not perceive. We only experience it. And, in the strict sense, we no more perceive space than time. The perspective of what we may call our private space is not itself extended Perspective in a picture is not a mere imitation of perspective in our field of perception, but is the same, only less perfect and with different accompaniments which tell us that it does not prophesy real remoteness in the same way. We do not see distance but interpret the signs of it, often judging wrongly. A landsman at sea, for example, underestimates invariably, because his interpretation is largely by intervening objects used as signs of distance, and not by sums of spaces which by addition make up the space between. Even the appearance of size in these objects is qualitative, giving information about what motion in time is necessary for reaching them, and continually changing, as we move and need to be informed of other conditions. Not only colour, but size and shape thus alter incessantly Yet so far is this from being perplexing or from giving a sense of unreality, that all prediction, all utility of the information depends upon it.

But if we had not already an idea of the form and size and appearance of the object at a distance, the changes would not

THE FORM OF PERCEPTION

give us the required information. This comes up in a fixed context with the perception, and is mainly dependent on the peculiar way in which the sense of touch accompanies the other senses and especially the sense of vision. Extended vision, on this view, is an interpretation of motion which derives its significance from touch. Thus, however much we may have enlarged its application, distance is originally a calculation of sequence in touch, and the ground of all idea of quantity, therefore, is interpretation by motion in time.

Yet, in measurement of it, more is implied than the convenient arrangement of information in what we may call one room. It assumes an idea of space which, as we use it, is a purely mental structure of equality of measurement in all directions· and, therefore, is of the understanding, and not of apprehension.

Space, as we thus use it, science now finds to be an undue simplification. But simplification by the understanding is not peculiar to space. The understanding simplifies all relations and this, though its value for practice, is its danger for theory. Yet, if it be true that mind is developed, not by the mechanical arrangements of environment, but wholly in response to its meaning, a simplification which works exactly for ordinary purposes must be true objective meaning as far as it goes, even if it be not adequate for the whole reality of time-space. Ideas which spring spontaneously from what is fixed in our general awareness, must depend on something in the form of the reality of which we are aware. What space exactly is even the higher mathematics cannot say, though, as we shall see afterwards, it is important that mathematics can only treat even space with exactness when reduced to the purest symbolism, which cannot be pictured either by sense or imagination. Yet the enormous impressiveness of space, both for sense and imagination, must represent a quality which belongs to the meaning of the universe. Even if, in the end, it be not material fixed quantity, it is at least fixed idea, and is fixed, not only by experience, but by the fact that we have no other experience by which to escape it.

Prof. Alexander regards time-space as the matrix of all reality, from which all else in our experienced universe "emerges".[1] In order to make a start at all, he has to assume that it has qualities. But this is precisely the all-important step from motion to meaning, which nothing in the mathematical conception of time-space justifies him in taking. Even if our contention that the ideas of quantity are developed out of quality were not correct, this would not alter the fact that, apart from what it signifies for mind, it has no qualities. Though Prof. Alexander repudiates the Cartesian method, if there were no preparation of expectation from it in his own mind and in the minds of his readers, the whole elaborate process of reasoning would not amount to any more than the ancient view that what is first is not the spiritual but the merely organic.

But, while time-space is not a matrix of reality, and in its spatial aspect at least, in spite of the arguments to the contrary, does not even seem to belong to all our experience of reality, it is a fixed form of our perception in which, as we have seen, in a very impressive qualitative way, the unity of the universe reflects itself. It is a context out of which nothing can be taken. Wherever we move, there is always the same context of endless extension in three dimensions; and we must always conceive everything as in a time which stretches to infinity before and after What Ward and James regard as the extensiveness of sensation is merely this context of the fixed idea of space, and what James regards as the extensiveness of every moment of time both before and after is due to the context of the fixed idea of time.

[1] S Alexander, *Space, Time, and Deity*.

CHAPTER XI

SENSATION

(a) THE PHYSICAL AND PHYSIOLOGICAL MEDIUM

ARGUE as we may, it is impossible to conceive sensation except as in a mind, or as other than a mental activity No doubt it is a response to physical stimulus, but it is not a mere transformation of the physical. It is not even a particular response to a particular stimulus, but is a particular aspect of the whole unified feeling responding to a particular aspect of a whole unified environment.

At the same time there cannot be any dubiety that there are both physiological and physical phenomena between the mind and its object. Whether we regard environment as essentially material or as essentially mental, we must still accept this mediation; and, what is more, we must still regard it as physical and physiological.

For aught we know the whole physical medium may be nothing but vibrations or forms of motion. So far as present knowledge goes, this seems to be an adequate explanation of what carries sound. The wave theory is no longer regarded as embracing all the facts of light, yet, as it affects our sense of sight, light is probably merely by vibration. But the more the physical vehicle is reduced to this simple mechanical form, the more certain it must be that the purely mechanical aspect is not itself the whole reality. The true significance must be from a system of meaning, within which the vibrations are symbols of a reality which is also a system of meaning.

That motion, in the form of vibration, is capable of conveying by symbol endless meaning is not difficult to realise when we consider what can be done with a very simple series of black marks on paper. But we do not need to resort to such a parallel, for in hearing we know that it works with the qualities of pitch and tone which are just vibration: and sound is the means by which we most definitely convey meaning, nothing being more wonderful than the wealth and variety of what it conveys. The sense itself is sufficiently wonderful, but the order of sounds which conveys meaning, and without intercourse with which hearing would be an unimaginable development, is more wonderful still, or, at least, it is more widely and intimately a part of the meaning of our universe. Wireless telegraphy has extended our knowledge of its range, showing us that sound waves are being constantly distributed to vast distances with every variety of meaning carried on their margins. We are so impressed by man's cleverness in discovering and using this phenomenon that we overlook the more marvellous nature of what he has discovered That this was merely waiting patiently for him to put it to its first use would be very flattering to Mr Marconi, but however important 'listening in' may be in the economy of the lives of those who like it, that something even more important has always been served by the order in the economy of the universe is much more probable And though we have not yet been able to apply in the same way the higher velocities of light, there is every reason to believe that they carry, more rapidly and more widely, meanings still more varied and wonderful

It is possible that the other medium, the functioning of the nerves and brain, is also merely a system of vibrations, but if so, once again the reality must be in the system and not in the mere vibrations Moreover, the system cannot be the mere organisation, but the organisation must itself be a system of the mind that knows, which again must be determined by the meaning of the environment it knows Thus the function of the brain would be to give the symbols of this meaning a form suited to the mind's capacity for being aware of them, in short to be a kind of receiver

The close interdependence of the physiological and the mental series is a matter of everyday experience, and scientific research has established it in much greater detail This seems to some physiologists to afford sufficient ground for regarding it as a law of exact parallelism. As the brain and its thought cannot be observed together, such a law, however, cannot be demonstrated, and the facts so far known go a very short way to make it even probable. There is no more proof of absolute parallelism than, for example, that, because we cannot think without words, there is an absolutely exact parallelism between thought and language. Speech also is a very wonderful instrument, but we are not dependent on it to that extent. Even the assertion which has sometimes been made, that a man's vocabulary is the exact measure of his mind, cannot be maintained. A mind with many ideas is, as a general proposition, likely to have a large vocabulary by which to express them, and, if it have not, its thoughts will undoubtedly be hampered and less explicit, but, however useful adequate expression be for adequate thinking, there is no approach to rigid parallelism. So also, a higher mind is likely to have a larger and more perfect brain and would be hampered in acting as a higher mind without it; and the dependence both for reception and for expression of feeling upon the brain, being of a longer, more intimate, less artificial development, is also doubtless greater than that of thought on speech. But, when it comes to exact and absolute parallelism, it is no more probable in the one case than in the other.

Supposing, however, that such a parallelism could be demonstrated, it would settle nothing. One would still be first in principle, and be the creative factor, just as speech and thought develop together and in mutual dependence, yet it is thought, not speech, which is creative. Nor is this a mere illustration, for, if mind is the creative and controlling factor in any kind of organisation, it is likely to be so in all.

The organ which is of chief importance for sensation is the brain. Were it merely concerned with a series of intensities, distinguishing impacts only quantitatively, such an elaborate organisation could not possibly have been needed. More than one cell may be needed to determine the quantity of a sensation but the vast number of them could only be required by the vastly varied qualities of all sensations Moreover, the impression of size is not given by the number of cells called into operation, nor do the sensations which determine space seem to depend on the positions occupied by the corresponding cells in the brain.

That feeling is the way mind responds to its environment is an ultimate fact which has merely to be accepted, but the contention here is that sensations are not direct responses to individual impacts so as to be effects of which the vibrations are the causes, but are themselves interpretations within a system of meaning, and that the nervous system is determined by this system of meaning.

Conscious bodily feelings all have to do with the welfare of the body and its activities; and painful feelings, which call immediate attention to injury, are much more acute and challenging than pleasurable, which merely inform us of what is normal. As a whole, they seem to be determined entirely by what is advantageous for our bodily existence. Therefore, they are felt according to their meaning in a system, and not according to the measure of external impact.

The sensations by which we perceive are still more plainly within a system, and do not seem to be stirred in any way essentially different from the way in which feeling is swayed in an audience entirely under the control of a speaker. Feeling does not necessarily exist in material things without, any more than it necessarily exists in the soul of the speaker, but the message must be about things which have their meaning from feeling, in the one case as in the other. Nor can we conceive any universe which could be a cosmos on other terms.

(*b*) THE FUNCTION OF INTEREST

The development of sensations does not ever seem to be in advance of interest. Thus in the sense of colour, we can, even within the comparatively short space of human history, trace the development of sensation in response to the expansion of interest. In so developed a language as Latin the colour of the sky is also the colour of the sombre way that leads to Hades, and so copious and precise a language as Greek has a limited range of terms for colours, of no very great precision. In the languages of some primitive peoples there is no name for blue; and in still more it seems to be very indefinitely distinguished from green. This means that the sensations of sight are less developed than ours towards the higher velocities of light. Yet in the struggle for existence the savage depends more on good sight than the civilised, and there is no reason to suppose that he has not at least an equal physical capacity for developing its range. What he lacks is the interests by which it could be developed. The interest of animals in colours is probably confined to food, sex and danger signals, and the interest of very primitive peoples may not be much more extended. But blue is not of much value for these ends. Something of artistic interest is required for developing the sense for it, just as even in ourselves an eye for the finer shades of colour seems to develop with an interest in seeing them.

Though this is not an example of a sense being created by meaning, it is an example of the enlargement of its capacity which shows how it may have developed from mere sensitiveness to light into the seeing of the meaning light conveys. And this applies to all the senses. While we are very ignorant of ancient music, there seems to be ground for believing that the progress of music indicates development in the sense of hearing as well as discoveries in the art of appealing to it. Some ancient dishes and some savage delicacies suggest a similar development of the sense of taste. Touch also in some trades can become a means of the most delicate discernment. The odours which some peoples tolerate might suggest the same about smell, though this is more doubtful because familiarity makes us less conscious of any smell. Possibly W. H. Hudson may be right in thinking that, though we still judge by it more than we recognise, in this sense there is retrogression among some civilised peoples, precisely because we are not so dependent on it for information.

On any theory, colour presents the largest problem, because the mind seems to create so much more out of the symbols, there being no natural affinity between a mathematically calculable ratio of vibrations and the colours of the spectrum. Even granting, as has been suggested, that there may be something more direct in the pure sensations of light which disappears from consciousness by being subordinated to their uses for perception, colour still remains a problem of which no real solution has ever been offered, unless we were to take seriously the suggestion that we are taught how to interpret it in another state of existence. But, apart from the difficulty of the animals sharing with us in this heavenly education, the whole reality of our present world so depends upon it that both science and common sense are not likely to waver from the conviction that the learning takes place in our present environment, and from it.

We must start from the conviction that colour does actually belong to this environment, and that, let us say, violet is the reality, and not, except as the symbol of it, a very high rate of vibration. Yet if the symbols in their context belong to the same system of meaning as the colour, our perception is only a re-creating of a meaning which exists apart from us, as we re-create in our thought, by intercourse, the thought of our fellows. No doubt this presupposes meanings already in our minds, some of which may be hereditary. Yet all of it has been learned at some time simply by reaching out from the living creature's own thought to what is beyond. The same effort is always required in all our intercourse with reality, and colour may be just the most marked example of reaching out through the senses to what is beyond. Something of this harmonious meaning we have in all colours of nature, and there are a few artists of special discernment who help us to interpret it upwards from one basal, rather neutral tint like the colour of the soil. Few of us may be conscious of this, but the efficacy of environment in our perception is by no means limited to what we consciously discern. Perhaps we still lack the interest which may some day make colour a simpler, more connected, as well as a more adequate language.

But all our senses, and the sense of colour in particular, raise the question whether the physical medium does not establish a more direct relation of understanding, somewhat as speech may establish a direct connexion with another mind, so that the knowledge of that mind becomes the interpreter of what is said. This may be the truth of the new Realism· and though we can hardly hope to establish it, it is a possibility not to be ruled out. But this can be better discussed later on.

In any case, interest is first. and some understanding of that can be won from the history of language. No language has ever been formed by attending to the process of speaking. Every language, and with this doubtless every power of speech, has been developed purely by attending to meaning. Afterwards we may have a science of language and discover the complicated physiological development of the organs of speech, the complicated way in which sounds are produced, and the very long perplexing story of the development of the particular symbols used in various languages. But of none of these things do we think when we speak· and, what is more, no one ever thought of them in the whole development of language All development of the means for expressing meaning has been achieved simply by attending to the meaning itself. Even now few of us know anything about the physiological and philological organisations we use so freely, and our use of them is not always improved by knowing more about them. In learning another language we have to make more use of them, but we never use it freely till we can afford to forget our rules: and perhaps we never speak it as well because we have not learned it so directly from meaning, but must depend on rules of the understanding.

As speech has been developed by concentration upon the meaning to be expressed and not by thinking about the means of expression, so perception has come by interest in what is to be perceived and concentration on it, and not by thinking about the senses and all the other apparatus of perception. Thus the important aspect of sensations which determines all development in the use of them is that they are symbols of meaning in a field which has one meaning, and it does not concern any question of their physical or physiological basis, because even this basis depends on meaning, and not meaning on it. We have already seen that comprehending and still more explaining are very far from being the best kinds of knowledge for all purposes: but here we have something more which must have a general and decisive bearing on every question of human development, and possibly on all evolution. Perhaps all organisation is just a physical embodiment of a system of fixed ideas, developed in dealing with the meaning of environment. But this would raise the whole question of evolution, which we are not at present discussing.

(c) QUALITY OF SENSATIONS

Even the quantities of perception are continually changing according to their message: and there is nothing in perception like Locke's primary and secondary qualities, as though the primary were more certain and stable because they depend on quantity, and the secondary more subjective and volatile because they depend on quality. All alike are at once quality and information about environment, and the rest is imported by the understanding.

This does not mean that there are no quantities in the qualities, but it does mean that, for perception, quantities have meaning and are qualities. Quantities as quantities can only be understood as mechanical cause and effect, whereas quantities as qualities can be understood as meaning from what is known to a mind that knows.

We have seen how marvellous, in their definiteness, variety and attraction, these qualities may be for minds specially equipped for perceiving them, and how deep and moving is the feeling Wordsworth calls love, which we may describe as oneness of feeling in oneness of awareness.

The first and most important consideration is that the interest which sustains awareness is not mere pleasantness of sensation, but can be maintained against unpleasant feeling. It is doubtful whether sensation even begins as mere pleasure and pain and not as some objective interest in environment. The usual explanation of the infusoria swimming out of an unpleasant liquid is that the unpleasant sensation acts as a mere physical cause. But already there seems to be a life impulse and some dim choice of environment, and pleasure and pain as conscious sensations may only be developed out of them afterwards, as rapid and effective ways of guarding the life in dealing with environment. But, if sensation ever began as pleasure and pain, it ceases to be as soon as it becomes the means of objective information. It is not even selective of pleasant things, but is a possibility of being interested in all things, with an interest sustained by life itself. We may call it the joy of living, if we remember that even life's joys may be overridden by it, and that it is not merely subjective, but is an emotional challenge of reality dominating all its particular manifestations as well as life's particular responses. Love, as Wordsworth calls it, may not be the right name for all its working, but if it be the right name for the full communion of spirit with its environment, it may be what most sheds light even on the first beginnings, the poetic glory in the splendour of the world only crowning what began with the infusoria. Sincerity of awareness would then be the prime requirement of all perception. This may only be another name for love of one whole reality: and the history of perception from the beginning may be the story of the achievement by living creatures of this sincerity in dealing with meaning and value already existing.

Something similar is not wholly absent from conscious subjective feeling. Prof. Ward agrees with Bentham in thinking the pleasure of push-pin as good as that of poetry if you like it as well, the quality being entirely from the object and not in any way in the pleasure of the feeling the different objects stir. But the feeling and the object which stirs it are not so separated. Feeling in this sense is an idea as well as an emotion; and the emotion depends on the idea and the idea on the emotion. The mere fact of inventing a special name for such a feeling seems to show that mankind has regarded it as different in quality. If so, this would be important, because, though we may not from conscious subjective feeling argue back to the nature of sensations which give us awareness of objects, a right understanding of the former might shed some light on the latter. Even were it certain, instead of being extremely dubious, that the sole difference in subjective feeling is purely in intensity of pleasure and pain, it would still be inconceivable that the sensations which give us such enormously varied information about our environment, do not themselves have varied qualitative differences, but are merely quantitatively distinguished by intensity of pleasure and pain, which, at least so far as we experience it, is no mark of them.

The qualitative nature of the sensations behind perception would, however, be confirmed if even conscious sensation cannot be all mere quantities of pleasure and pain.

The sensations by which we are aware we cannot test, because, precisely in the measure in which they are objective information, they are never conscious subjective feeling. But we have some test with sensations which come partially into the field of conscious feeling while still functioning partly as objective information.

By importing into them standards of measurement from their objects, which means, by use of the understanding, we can think of them as having quantitative degrees of intensity, but, as pure sensation, these different intensities are differences of quality quite definitely distinct. We speak of getting hotter and hotter, and we think of what can be measured by a graduated scale of quantities. If, however, we isolate our sensations from the idea of a fire or a thermometer, the sensations of being frozen, chilly, tolerably warm, comfortably warm, hot, sweltering, burning are of different qualities, which, taken entirely by themselves, we could never have arranged in any scale of quantities. The scale does not belong to the sensations themselves, but to the interpretation of them by the objects to which we attribute them. It might even be argued that sensation as sensation has quality, whether we are perceiving through it or not. Though we can speak of toothache as becoming more and more painful, as if it were a mere graduated increase of violence, the stages are really of quite different quality, and the increasing painfulness itself is a difference of quality. In any case, the moment we try by it to learn which tooth it is and what is wrong with it, the sensation becomes definitely qualitative. This would seem to show that quantity is from the object and quality from the feeling, and not, as Prof. Ward argues, quality from the object, while the feeling is merely quantitative.[1]

(*d*) SENSATION AND AWARENESS

A state of mere sensation cannot be brought into consciousness by itself. Sensation as a kind of knowledge is conscious, but the sensation, which, though not itself an idea, is the source of all our ideas of the world, is beyond our knowing. Did we attend only to sight and hearing, in which, when normal, sensation is turned entirely into information, we might even argue that perception has no such ground as sensation at all: and the new Realism seems to regard sensation rather as an accompaniment than as the link between our knowing and what is known. But, though with normal sight and hearing, there is no sense of depending on any intermediate sensation, the fact that sensation comes up as a conscious knowledge and not as information when sight and hearing are not normal, shows that it is there, fulfilling another function than conscious feeling, even when unrecognised. Besides we have no right to confine attention to only two senses. When we consider the senses in what we may call their order of objectivity, what we discover is that sensations disappear as conscious feeling, in proportion as they are turned into conscious perception, so that, in the strict sense, not only have we no recollection of being in a state of pure sensation, but we never are aware of the sensation by which we are made aware of any environment. What serves this purpose comes into consciousness only as objective awareness and never as subjective feeling. In healthy sight this is so rapid that there is no accompanying trace of sensation to

[1] The treatment of feeling in Prof. Ward's *Psychological Principles* seems to me the least adequate part of a work which, so far as my knowledge goes, is still the most important contribution to psychology in the last generation. He used to admit in our discussions that I was not the only one who had found here a stone of stumbling. From Mrs Ward's biography of his son, it appears that he also had been among the doubting.

be detected. More frequently in hearing we might seem to recall some faint shadow of it in the pleasantness or unpleasantness of sounds, even though in actual hearing they seemed entirely objective, and it is more easy to hear music purely subjectively as feeling than to see a picture in the same way. Yet music ceases to be sensation in proportion as it becomes really music.

Smell to us is largely a matter of pleasant and unpleasant sensations, yet, when we are using it to detect a dangerous gas or, as a druggist does, to distinguish drugs, the meaning overrides the sensation. To a dog it is almost entirely an objective sense, so that he does not seem to be affected by the pleasantness or unpleasantness of smells. Taste is usually mainly a matter of pleasant or unpleasant sensation, but if we were dying of thirst and were doubtful about whether the water were poisonous or not, it would become an objective sense, and the question of its pleasantness would fall at once into the background. Touch may be entirely conscious sensation, but we can trace the disappearance of it as feeling as we use our fingers to give us information. This is important, because, in the sense that what we judge by is in contact with the sensory, all senses are senses of touch.

In this way we can see that sensation does not disappear, but is turned into information. Sensation only becomes a knowledge of its own as it ceases to be the means of objective knowledge: and, broadly at least, we can lay it down as a principle, that the more we are conscious of sensation the less value it has for objective knowledge and that the more it is turned into objective knowledge the less it is known as sensation. But it must still be sensation, whether known by itself or disappearing into other knowledge.

Nor does the original objective reference wholly disappear when sensations become conscious feelings. Taste is the sense we most use by subjective preference, but even it belongs to a system interpreted by all the senses, and it is very rapidly responsive to what is objectively good or bad. It would be difficult for anything to taste well that was loathsome to sight or gritty or slimy to touch, and an unhappy experience of a food can change desire to disgust.[1] What we mean by a natural taste is just what has in it hereditary wisdom. A poison occasionally met with may taste sweet, but, were we in continual danger of it yet escaped to add to the stock of human discrimination, probably we should develop an instinctive dislike which would operate more rapidly and surely than an objective judgment. This as a matter of fact we have done with things putrid, though the dog, which flourishes on them, regards them as peculiarly toothsome. Thus like and dislike, instead of being independent feelings apart from objective perception, would seem to be summaries of experience, which have their utility from being more vivid, more rapid and more insistent, so that, in the end, they are only special manifestations of what we may call the joy of life, the unified emotional state by which we respond to a unified experience and so perceive it.

That pleasure and pain in themselves are not ultimate is still further seen in the fact that in the healthy mind, especially if youth be added to health, feeling is a continual reaching out to objects of interest, and the arresting of it at pleasurable or painful sensation is rare and fleeting. Normally, satisfaction or lack of satisfaction depends on the meaning for us and the challenge to our action of the objects of which sensation makes us aware, and not on the awareness of the sensations themselves. Whether they are pleasurable or painful is rather a reflexion afterwards, and, even so, is not apt to be dwelt upon by a vigorous, objectively interested mind. So far from being the only possible motive for action, it rarely is present, especially in youth or to anyone who remains reasonably young in mind, except under some stress which, even if it be pleasure, gives a sense of compulsion and not of freedom. In the normal mind subjective pleasurableness is subordinate to the interest of a lively awareness. Goethe says that we ask the birds and the boys, not the philosophers, how the cherries taste,

---

[1] This seems to show that the objective relation of sensation to a world of meaning is the original, and sensation as pleasure and pain a rapidly working system developed on the basis of it.

but we should also get, from the boys at least, a far more vivid idea of all the properties of cherries as objective phenomena. Nor is this an unimportant part of the enjoyment of the taste. It thereby becomes nature's feast, not an isolated gastronomic item.

The tendency of feeling towards action is sometimes insisted on to the point of making will a mere consequence of emotion. But this bent of sensation towards perception comes in between, and, for a mind not given over to sensuality, alters the whole situation, so that in the entire process of apprehending an object and dealing with it, feeling may never appear as subjective emotion, but may function all the time simply as objective information and interest.

If we could get behind awareness of sensation either as information or as subjective feeling, it is possible that we might find some special quality of response, something quite unlike sensation as pleasurable or painful feeling, which is disturbed and limited as soon as it comes to be subjected to the service of a higher faculty: and this may be very important for the relation of sensation to the impressions of the senses, and for the relation of these impressions to such a reality, let us say, as colour. It may be that at one stage of the development of life this direct sensation was alone; that in our own development it at one time played an important part; and that at all times it may be sub-consciously more active than we know. Sensation may thus be, far more simply than we can realise, a response to the witness of the reality about us.

But, however this may be, it is not what is most important. This is that sensations are of different quality and pass the frontier of our minds as meaning, and one very illuminating fact is that even conscious sensations do not maintain themselves apart from or in conflict with the general meaning of experience. As we have seen, the pleasantest sensation may turn to vehement dislike, if it has had unhappy consequences. Thus a passion for strawberries and cream has been turned to utter repugnance. If there be a physiological reason, it is not physiologically caused· and the explanation is not reasoned

SENSATION 199

fear of consequences. What has happened is that the sensation has fallen out of its proper context. This is the essential point Sensations have meaning because they are in a context. Thus, even if the individual sensations have a more direct relation to their object than we know, the deeper reason why they have meaning is that they are in a system of meaning, somewhat in the same way as words are, and so are determined, not by pleasure or pain in themselves, but by an interest which governs their whole activity and makes them effective as response and not as subjective feeling.

(e) IMPACTS

Even sensations, as they function in perception, are not themselves psychological facts directly apprehended. They are psychological inferences from sensations which are perceived but do not function in perception. And that the sensations which do so function are due to impacts is not even a psychological inference. Even in touch we should not know it except by observing the objects with which our bodies come in contact, and in the other senses we have not even this experience, but depend for our information on the researches of science.

Our own experience of contact and the researches of science must be accepted, and both trace all senses to the sense of touch. But if they are the objective means by which we perceive an objective world, contacts cannot be mere discrete impacts, and possibly impacts may be a very imperfect description. If they stir sensations which are symbols of a meaning at once changing and consistent, they must also be in the same system of meaning, and that not as it were fixed printed words.

Sainte-Beuve speaks of experience as a book at any page of which we may begin and read with appreciation. But, in that case, it would be like a book of extracts, varied but disconnected, which is exactly what it cannot be. The singular thing is that we can join in anywhere and at once find the connexion. The only parallel is joining in a dialogue, which though it be in the middle of what had a beginning and will not be complete till the end, we can join in intelligently, as it were by good-will on both sides, though here there is something more, for we are what we are by what has already been said. We have also to consider that every spot at which we are planted is the centre of a universe, with, as relativity indicates, a complete relation of four dimensions to every point-observer.

Because of the finite powers of our mind we cannot deal with incessant change, but must stereotype a great deal. Even in speaking of impacts we do so, our conception not being of the ceaseless change of one varying impression, but, as M. Bergson puts it, a sort of cinematograph series of pictures which change so rapidly as to deceive us into the notion of one unbroken experience. Yet it is one unbroken change of reality we perceive, a stream ever flowing past, so that, as it has been expressed, we never can put our foot into the same water though it is the same river. The mere fact that the result is that the universe is for us one world of rational discourse would alone show that the impacts with which it communicates with us are not merely fixed and mechanical.

This leads us to the question of the nature of physical law, which must wait till we come to it in due place. Yet, when we come to it, a weighty consideration will be that we have not only to do with knowledge, which we have largely stereotyped for the convenience of our limited intelligence, but with a knowing which depends on a ceaseless, continuous and connected manifestation of meaning from the world we know.

CHAPTER XII

VALUE AND VALIDITY

(*a*) THEORETICAL AND VALUE JUDGMENTS

IF our knowing is knowledge only as we establish securely the frontier of our minds and allow nothing to pass except as our meaning, and if knowledge is right meaning in our minds by active interpretation of a meaning that is the true reality, much judgment is embedded in all our knowing.

Man uses two kinds of judgment, and his perception of the world is human because he consciously uses both.

These are sometimes distinguished as judgments of value and judgments of reality. But to this there are the objections that the division is not on one principle and that one part does not exclude the other, because a judgment of reality may be a judgment of value and a judgment of value a judgment of reality, or at least this is a question which is open to discussion, and should not be foreclosed by the form of the division.

Possibly there is no division to which objection might not be taken, but the least objectionable is into value-judgments and theoretical-judgments, though it would be plainer, if less precise, to call them judgments of quality and judgments of quantity. This latter, which is at least a general difference, is what, at all events, most concerns us, though a theoretical-judgment may only be quantitative indirectly. An example will most simply show the difference. It is a value-judgment that violet is the most beautiful of the colours, it is a theoretical-judgment that it is the highest light vibration within our power to see.

As has been maintained from the first, no division of our problems is absolute but only convenient. As our minds have developed by continuous active interpretation of our whole environment, all our dealing with it concerns our knowing, and that we can impress our meaning on it is not only a very important test of our meaning as a true interpretation, but makes us see the world differently, because, though we do not perceive by any kind of understanding or explaining, as we understand and explain our standpoint becomes higher and our horizon wider. Yet explaining, which is the chief business of the theoretical-judgment, is so much more concerned with necessity and freedom that we can leave it over till we come to that problem, and confine ourselves here to understanding the value-judgment. Though also of the first importance for freedom, it is so intimately connected with knowing and knowledge and its bearing upon freedom is so much according to the world we know, that it falls here to be considered. The part of it, however, which is usually included under the name of conscience, though the division is arbitrary, we shall leave over, because, though some repetition may still be unavoidable, the need for it will at least be diminished.

The first question which all our knowing, if it is meaning, raises, is whether a value-judgment is merely individual preference or may be concerned with an objective reality.

The mere fact that man cannot see the higher range of colours until he has developed the higher values with which to perceive them, is itself evidence of the latter. When the Greek saw the beauty of the wine-coloured sea and the Hebrew the marvel of the morning changing the earth as clay under the seal, it was a higher way of perceiving and not merely a higher way of being pleased. Or suppose that we were to reach a still higher value, and it gave the interest which developed perception of a still higher range of light and we found it still more beautiful than violet, would not the value belong to the essential meaning of the colour and be its deepest reality?

One reason why a theoretical-judgment seems to be objective as a value-judgment is not, is that it seems to be public meaning, while a value-judgment is taken to be purely private. But we have seen that our knowing depends for being knowledge, first of all, upon being our own genuine private meaning. Public meaning which merely traverses our mind is neither knowing nor knowledge. For matters of understanding and explaining, social intercourse is a weighty confirmation. Yet it is not confirmation as it replaces our own judgment, but only as it widens interest and directs inquiry to enable us to extend and revise our own judgment.

In a sense our perceptions are more strictly private meaning, because we cannot compare in the same way with others the values which give the meaning. Yet there is also a sense in which they have a still wider public meaning and a still surer way in which their values are tested. All perception of all living creatures from the beginning has been developed by interest, and interest has embedded in it value-judgment; and their perception has advanced as, by sincere living in their environment, they have tested its values. They do not merely prefer one thing to another because life is what it is, but life is what it is because the values of environment are what they are.

So long as life works with fixed ideas, though these values are thereby limited in range, they are guaranteed as natural, because, if the ideas were wrongly fixed, the species would no longer survive. But with man's freedom, though the range is vastly greater, the unnatural becomes possible. The animals doubtless have fewer brains, but they do not put an enemy into their mouths to steal them away. Yet, that one man's meat is another man's poison is so within a very limited range; and there are natural tastes without which there is no normal relation to the world. As Lotze says, even poison and an organised body belong together, like a good thought and a bad in one mind, else there could no more be physical than moral disaster.

A true value-judgment is thus a judgment of reality, and, what is more, no kind of judgment ever was formed except from knowledge which derived its meaning from value, nor would man take the trouble to form any other kind of judgment except for value already determined.

As a judgment of quantity is independent of our preferences and more fixed, Locke thought measurable quantities such as shape and hardness were primary, and qualities like colour secondary; and Hamilton seemed to think he was arguing for realism in perception when he supposed that the shape was impressed directly on the sense and so directly on the mind. But in actual perception shape is as changeable as colour, and by this very change in a qualitative way we judge distance.

Just because quantity is our way of managing the world, any judgment of it is specially convincing; and this kind of theoretical-judgment has added enormously to man's power of impressing his meaning upon his environment. But, at times at least, it has been at the cost of limiting the meaning which environment manifests. And the first task, even for managing our world, is to be sure that we actually see the world and the fullness thereof. For this the first question is, whether we are so living in our natural environment that we can expect to have the normal natural values by which we could perceive what is highest and greatest in it. And with this may go the further question whether the reason why so many see nothing beyond the Natural is not just that they lack the right values of the Natural itself.

(*b*) NATURAL AND IDEAL VALUES

No section of psychology is so inadequate as the treatment of feeling. Partly the reason is that feeling is an ultimate element in experience, and cannot be explained by anything else: but partly it is due also to the idea that feeling is merely passively caused, so that the feeling of a mad man would be as true a response to his impressions as that of a sane, and he would be mad only because he is in the minority. But seeing the world with the madman's *idée fixe* is very different from seeing it with the activity of what is here called fixed idea.

As Plato says, call mind activity and you will not be mistaken. The activity of the will proper, directed to possessions to be gained and evils to be escaped, is generally recognised, but responding to impressions justly and completely is as truly an activity as altering the world for our benefit. We know our environment only as we rightly live in it, and we rise to the height of its meaning according to the kind of persons we are.

But nothing, as Kant says, proves so much what we are as what we enjoy; and the writer of the Proverbs said the same before him and said it better when he declared that "a man is known by his praise". Therefore, no value is purely individual in the sense that anyone's value may be purely personal vagary, yet his sense of his environment remain justly and penetratingly natural. Even the fact that sugar is sweet in the mouth is in some sense an objective fact, and Thackeray's reply to the young man who contemned the sweets he himself was enjoying, that it was early to have sinned away his privileges, was a just rebuke.

But if right values are right knowing, there is no break in principle between natural and ideal values. Nor is there in practice, for higher values of the Natural already manifest the ideal. Both may deal with the same facts, and may differ with different situations, and there may be uncertainty and even mistake about either, although there is an entirely different way of judging what we take to be of sacred obligation and what we take to be merely of expediency and convenience.

Any order we may ultimately discover is only a fuller interpretation of the order already embedded in sensation: and if what rational man expresses as the standards of truth, beauty and goodness, are not fancies of his own mind but the very order of reality without which he could not be rational, even if he were not aware of anything of the kind in perception, it would still be the real order of the world he perceives and of the utmost importance even for his sensation. As the Supernatural is one thing if it is manifested through the Natural, and another if it is wholly apart and the Natural a mere temporal illusion, so the Natural is one thing if it manifests the Supernatural, and another if it is merely physical.

Nor is this mere conjecture. We have seen how spontaneously something akin to the sense of the holy arises from the form of awareness. Just as spontaneously something akin to a sacred valuation arises with the form of apprehension and plays a leading part in our realisation of ourselves and also of the objectivity of our world. Perception with man is not mere animal perception: and even animal perception would never have existed had there been no more than an animal perceives.

With supernatural values, moreover, we find a still further expansion of our environment. The moment we see them as what should be, we know them as claiming absolute allegiance. Nor is the sense of their presence ever wholly absent from any finer perception, which is always a reaching out to 'worlds not yet realised'. What we have called the undifferentiated sense of the holy may be no more than a vague sense of their presence, like the vague sense of the material environment felt by lower forms of life, or the vague wonder of higher creatures as they apprehend something new and strange. But just as even the dimmest discernment of the material world has waiting to be unfolded the whole marvellous world known to our higher senses, and no discernment might have existed had this not been the unknown environment, so with our first rude beginnings with the Supernatural, we enter what doubtless has a scope and a perfection beyond the wisest of us to sum up as the true, the beautiful and the good, which yet may be the source of every kind of knowledge we have. While only as we are aware of our environment have we knowledge of it, we must not conclude that nothing but what we know has any significance for our awareness, for it may be there as the wisdom of our teacher, which, though we do not know it, is the spring of all our knowing.

Though all perception concerns meaning, and therefore the reality of natural values, the reasonableness of the world has to do with ideal values, which we speak of as the true, the beautiful and the good. If faith is what we act on, no one ever really convinced himself that they are the mere opinions of a certain smooth-skinned biped, and of no significance for the constitution of the universe. The moment we begin to live in the world as a rational universe, we assume their validity.

Beauty is related to the sense of the holy, goodness to the judgment of the sacred, and truth to the reality of the Supernatural. But the sense of the holy rightly becomes a general attitude of reverence, and not merely an occasional stirring of the sense of awe; and sacred obligation a general judgment of our whole dealing with life, and not merely something fixed in certain material embodiments; and the Supernatural the question of one ultimate reality or rather of what is ultimate in all reality, and not merely of a diffused but only occasionally manifested potency. Wherefore, before we can consider the beautiful, the good and the true, we must ask what are the unities with which they are concerned.

(c) LOGIC, ETHICS AND AESTHETICS

The standards of ideal values are the problems of logic, ethics and aesthetics, if we take the terms widely as meaning right valuation in thinking and acting and feeling. Yet nothing is more misleading than to expect these sciences, or however we name them, to be able to lay down definite and fixed rules. As this is what standard usually means, we should rather speak of norms, recognising them as only concerned with the attitude which faces in the direction of right verdicts. Logic has to do with right thinking and ethics with right acting and aesthetics with right feeling only in this way of one attitude of one individual dealing with one reality.

Prof. Ward regarded all life as mind, and this from the beginning as one going concern of thinking, feeling and acting. At all events, the human mind should respond with all its thought and strength and heart to one whole environment. We may distinguish truth in thinking, uprightness in action and sincerity in feeling: but we might call them all truth, for truth in the fullest sense would include all, or all a good will, if by this we mean rightness in all our ways, and not mere right action; or all sincerity, if by this we mean the simple response of feeling by which knowing is approved as wholly concerned with knowledge

Definite standards are often affirmed on religious grounds But it is of their essence to be by our own judgment, in view of our own situations. What we do not ourselves see may be fact, but is not in any ideal sense truth, what we do not ourselves judge right is, by that fact alone, not goodness, what is not our own judgment of beauty is merely an echo of fashion, and not a perception of reality.

Yet all ideals have religious quality in three respects. First they are all free, not merely in the sense of not being overridden by anything else, but in the sense that their sacredness gives us a right to stand on our own feet in their strength alone. They are all of an infinite reverence, in the sense that their end is to discern, not only what is not yet realised, but what may have no limits of possibility. They are all supernatural in the sense that loyalty to them is concerned with a worth beyond all merely natural values. Because of this very' quality, the relation of religion to them is just to give independence and courage and the sacredness of personal responsibility for seeing what our whole environment really is and, by living in what is highest in it, seeing still farther what it promises. Expressed scientifically, it is that reality is its own sole witness and may not call any other into court; expressed religiously, it is "I will hear only what God the Lord will speak".

The wrong way of relating the Supernatural to truth, beauty and goodness is to set it over them as an external, legal, infallible authority, and make truth what has been thus revealed, right what has been thus required, and, if there be any place for beauty at all, it is only in its austere aspects as a handmaid of the sterner disciplines of faith and practice, and whatsoever things are lovely are left no standing in their own right, nor any reason why they should be thought of and sought for their own sake.

The very idea of truth as a search, in which no goal is ever more than the starting-point of another race, to which the nature of reality without and of our own spirits within commits us, for which no labour is too arduous, and in which courage is humility before the witness of reality, disappears, and submission to what we are told masquerades in its place. Even were this infallibly correct information, it would not be truth. A whole infallibly revealed encyclopaedia could be received without ever challenging us with the absolute claim of truth and without showing us that only in loyalty to it have we any absolute worth.

Even more plainly the authoritative dependence of morality upon religion has corrupted both morality and religion. At one time Paley's account of morals, as doing good to mankind according to the will of God and for the sake of everlasting happiness, was regarded as the right relation; and Shaftesbury's attempt to show the independence of morals as a requirement which shines in its own light and carries with it the absolute claim of goodness just because it is good, and its own sanctions for the spirit that discovers its own blessedness in this service, was denounced as a subtle form of atheism which undermined religion by denying its chief practical utility. Apart from such gross eudaemonism, religion has constantly been used to reduce morality to a narrow and formal legalism, which deprived it of all its true character as an insight and an aspiration and a reaching out to worlds not yet realised; while religion also ceased to be a faith in the unseen and eternal which is an inspiration and a challenge, and which alone makes it truly religion.

What specially concerns us here, however, is the witness of right feeling. As beauty could not be brought within this rigid scheme, we have had it preached from both sides that religion and beauty are radically hostile. But this has always meant a narrowing of the scope both of religion and of aesthetics. Religion as authoritative belief and legislation does not any more misinterpret its own sphere, than art for art's sake misrepresents its. Art so conceived does not pass beyond the production of things pleasing to the senses, whereby sensuousness degenerates into sensuality, and whatsoever things are lovely in the highest sense have no more real place in it than in hard dogma and austere moralism. The true search for beauty is the search for unity and harmony and perfection in all things. As it requires responsiveness to the higher feelings which respond to life's deeper meaning, our greatest equipment is unity and harmony and perfection in ourselves, with our bodies subject to our own spirits. Then we can stop short of nothing less than the hope of a life harmonious with the universal order; whereupon the sense of beauty and the sense of the holy are not far apart. Religion without this aspiration is not religion; and art without it is only what Montaigne describes as "turfing the grave", mere distraction to help us for a little to forget the 'bondage of corruption'. Aesthetics, so understood, has to do with all form and harmony in all things and all true response to it in feeling, and is thus necessary for all higher knowing. It belongs to science and morals as a striving after harmony in thought and action, as well as to art, though in a less direct if not less effective fashion. Especially it belongs to life and so to religion, though by few things has it been limited and stereotyped and formalised more than by having imposed upon it narrow or external or sentimental or traditional forms of piety. But, though true religion is a concern to respond truly to all the witness of reality, a wrong relation to the Supernatural does not prove in the least that there is no Supernatural, or that any absolute value could be maintained in any other sphere.

None of the treatises on the sublime and beautiful have in them much to help us, because they are, mostly at least, determined by the rationalist view that everything must be justified by the understanding, whereas all our argument has been that it must be determined by the true nature of our whole environment, and that means by intuitions and anticipations which go far beyond what we can set in the clear hard light of the understanding. It concerns primarily what we have suggested about perception, that it is like personal intercourse when speech is more than a set of symbols to be interpreted, something beyond the mere expression of the speaker and the sympathetic response of the hearer, when every word has in it something of the whole mind of the speaker and some direct sense of it in the hearer. It is a judgment of values, but it is what all judgment ought to be, essentially an insight.

From this we must begin, yet we must also realise that we are concerned with much more than the question of art, even though we do not solve our problem till we see in some dim way how our whole experienced world appears to one who is 'of imagination all compact'.

Beauty in this sense is a conspicuous element in the abstract completeness aimed at in the higher mathematics; it is the goal of physics as it seeks to construe the order of the universe; it ought at least to be the inspiration of all study of life. But its fullest manifestation is in the common experience, from which all these studies set out, and to which they ought constantly to return, both to test their results and to keep them from being accepted as the measure of all reality. Most of all, it raises for us the question of the depth and reach of our awareness. This needs the poet's prayer that more of reverence in us dwell, but it is reverence in a much larger and freer sense than is usually given to the word. It is the power to appreciate, which, though it is a little grandiloquent, we can call our full response to the universe.

The importance of this is evident, because it is certain that nothing does reveal itself to us unless we take up the right attitude towards it, and this more concerns right feeling, which means sensitive and sincere and objective feeling, than even right acting or right thinking. We can neither be argued into it nor drilled into it, and there is no narrower education for it than the whole of life.

We readily discern moral insincerity, and spontaneously condemn it; and we know that it is not merely seeing and approving the good, yet following the bad, but it is also inability to see and approve the better. Intellectual insincerity is far from being as readily perceived or as spontaneously condemned, what is regarded as correct opinion being constantly accepted as true conviction. Yet there is a general understanding of the difference between one who systematically faces and one who shuns the disturbing task of seeking truth and truth only. But there are people who impress us as somehow more fundamentally and radically unreal than the conventionally moral or the merely orthodoxly believing. This concerns sincerity in feeling. They never allow life to impress them as it is, but corrupt experience at its source by the absence of simple, direct, whole-hearted response to its witness. It is not a question of having 'inordinate affection', but of schoolmastering feeling to make it say what is desired, or turning it into sentimentality divorced from all objective significance. True sincerity means having neither hard Stoicism, especially towards others, nor false sentimentality, especially towards ourselves. Lack of it is not concerned merely with ourselves and other persons. It goes to the roots of our whole perception of what is true and great in all our environment, natural and supernatural, being the essential and creative sincerity by which our knowing is wholly concerned with knowledge. As to offend in one is to offend in all, sincerity cannot be kept in water-tight compartments, yet for our present question sincerity of feeling is most important.

It is often assumed that, because there is no absolute standard of beauty, there is no norm even of our own attitude towards it. No doubt even this is more indefinite than the norms of truth and goodness. But the reason why there is less certainty about the norm of right feeling than of right thinking and acting is not merely from the nature of feeling. It is still more because feeling is the pioneer in all experience, and, therefore, the higher appreciation of its values is more continuously in the making. Yet genuine pioneering is not wandering at large by undiscerning impulse, but must be directed by a reverence which is a discriminating sense of the holy. This does not mean that it is directly from religion, but it does mean a sense of an environment which is of the quality of the Supernatural. It is not a perceiving of the Supernatural in the Natural, but it is a perceiving of the Natural in the Supernatural in the sense of a value which could have no lower origin. It is, as Schleiermacher expresses it, not from religion, but with religion.

(d) AGNOSTICISM AND VALUE

The test of our higher values is that they are sacred. This means that they belong to an environment which awakes absolute reverence and imposes absolute obligation. If we respond to the former, we start with the conviction that the universe has high mysteries still beyond us, which only our greatest effort and highest progress can even reach after; and, if we submit to the latter, it will be clear that our inquiry is likely to be successful only as we make truth, goodness and beauty our guiding stars.

True humility is reverence before the greatness of reality: and what goes by the name of Agnosticism is not reverence but a dogmatic denial of this greatness, and the failure to see that we are ignorant, not because reality has no witness to itself, but by reason of our failure to rise to the height of its great argument. The sheet-anchor of this Agnosticism is that perception is somehow physically caused, and that the material is the only real, though this is the first point on which, on such terms, we should be agnostic. Thus it is not really nescience, but is a positive affirmation that truth, goodness and beauty are no reliable guides to the nature of reality, being mere sanctions of practical utility.

As a temper it is not characteristic even of the physical science upon which it is founded. True science works with the sympathetic imagination, reaching out in what is felt to be the right direction, with a sense of the endless possibilities of things, knowing that, as it solves one mystery, it is faced by something still more mysterious.

Mystery is not nescience. It is the half-lifted veil of the sanctuary, through which all life's higher meaning shines, and which is the endless challenge to all our inquiries The hold it has upon us is that we know it to be an open secret were we only wise enough to ask it the right questions

But there is a still further reason why we shall never need to weep, like Alexander, for other worlds to conquer, besides the reason that our knowledge ends where the real interest begins and the greater the human mind the deeper the sense of mystery, a wider circle of light always having a larger penumbra of darkness. This is that the world and all its secrets are only a fragment half unfolding a still deeper meaning which, as the development of our interest unfolds, we see ever more fully to be beyond us. Here perhaps is the essential attitude of faith. It is that all this mighty frame of the Natural and man as he belongs to it have their deepest significance, not in what they are, but in the promise dimly unveiled in such imperfect ideals of the true, the beautiful and the good as we are able to reach out after. Only in this sense does religion rightly cherish a sense of mystery. Anything else is mere uneasiness in the dark, upon which any rushlight of scientific fact can serve notice to quit.

(e) TRUE ENLIGHTENMENT

If we have less sense of the 'burden and the mystery' of this unfolding of the Supernatural in the Natural in our enlightened age, is it from our enlightenment, or from our preoccupation with interests which cannot be considered higher or more central? This raises for us the question of how far we, in our time and place, are in a position to be judges of all the possibilities of human experience. In one sense it is not a question to worry about, because we must do our best with the position in which we find ourselves. Besides, have we not great compensation? Do we not live in the age of the world which possesses the wisdom of the past and among the peoples who have added to its riches beyond parallel in former times? And, with all modesty, cannot we say that we are among the enlightened of our generation? Even granting that we ourselves are still only of common stature, do we not stand on an eminence which enables us to look down, not on the primitive savage only, but even upon the seers and sages of other days? Is not the schoolmaster abroad, and did he not reveal to us as babes secrets hid even from the wise and understanding of ancient times? And may there not be some finality in our judgment, for if we cannot weigh anything so big as mountains in scales, have we not weighed their elements with a precision which is more wonderful? And, as far as it goes, this is true. But how far does it go? No doubt we have set out on a far greater voyage, but have we not all the greater need to adjust our compasses?

In explaining we have gone a long way. But is it on the

most important reality that we exercise it? And there is the deeper question of how far it has helped us to be aware of the full, as well as the real, environment in which we live. Again it is a question of interests. Few successes confer such a sense of superiority in judgment as material prosperity, and at no other time have so many enjoyed it. This also gives to life many interests, and it is difficult to question that they help to unfold life's possibilities. Yet, even without going back to an ancient saying about the camel and the needle's eye, we have cause to doubt the real enlightenment of the enslaved preoccupation of this age with material interests. Again, our life in cities is full of interests, and in them we have many wonders of man's creating. But is the distraction of multitudinous affairs necessarily enlightenment, and is the place man's achievements occupy in our minds in proportion to its real importance under the stars? Also by specialising in study we have acquired vast stores of knowledge, but are our specialisms always emancipation? Do we not pay a heavy price in the suppression of other, possibly greater, certainly wider, interests? Many secrets have been wrung from nature in the laboratory about her ways of accomplishing her purpose, but has anything more ever been induced to cross the door-step of any laboratory? May not the erudite person, therefore, be a little high-sniffing in his sense of superiority to those who have lived with nature on ocean and fell and in the vast empty spaces of the earth? Still less can the domesticated pundit, to whom the upsetting of his papers is a calamity, measure his knowledge of the world against the knowledge of those who have lived with courage and insight amid shattering calamities, hazardous adventures and swift challenge to high decision.

The confidence in our power and right to judge and measure is mainly based on our material achievements. But two doubts beset our assurance. (1) Are they the greatest valuation even of material things? Is it their deepest meaning which our science has revealed to us? Does not even the savage have an intercourse with nature which the scientist, dwelling in a world of dead, classified specimens rather than in the actual living world, has lost? Should we not more frequently remember with **how much** loss we pay for our gains? (2) Is even the deepest meaning of material things the deepest meaning of the universe, or even of our small experience of it? Does it not require imagination, adventure, a stirring of 'the heroic that is in all men' for which even our science is not the clearest 'divine awakening voice'?

PART III
NECESSITY & FREEDOM

CHAPTER XIII

COSMOLOGIES OF FREEDOM AND OF NECESSITY

(a) THE TWO KINDS OF RELIABLE SEQUENCE

THE problem of necessity and freedom has, like the last, to do with an experience of seeming to live in two orders. On the one hand, the world has a frame, which is so far at least of a fixed quantity that it is capable of being measured and mathematically formulated as cause and effect, so that the present seems to have been determined by the past; on the other, all our dealing with the world is by meaning, which is of quality, and on which we act, not by impulse behind us but by purpose before us, so that the present seems to be determined in view of the future. Both are reliable orders and the rationality of the world depends at least as much on the latter as on the former. Yet, in the former, cause and effect seem to be fixed sequences of events of the same quantity, determined by laws which are not less effectively laws of what is for not being known; whereas, in the latter, purpose and consequence seem to be of different quality and the reasonableness of the order to depend on knowing and accepting ideals, not of what is, but of what ought to be.

Though all experience teaches us that these orders are not apart, and that there are not two orders but only different aspects of one, they have been even more sharply divided than the two aspects of our last problem, and again each has been exalted into a cosmology, with even greater effect upon practice as well as theory.

The lessons of our last discussion we must recall, because they apply here equally. The first was that, while the reach of our higher perceptions is not independent of our explanations, it is easy to limit even what we perceive by our explanations. The second was that all explanation works with concepts which bring many things under one description mainly by the process of omission; and, as quantity is most manageable for our understandings, we tend to omit all but quantity.

To simplify our tasks by making our explanations the measure of our experience is a danger in all spheres, for the good reason that the practical value of a theory is largely what it allows us to omit as irrelevant to the purpose in hand. Then, as attention goes with practical interest, to ignore the rest is easy. So a useful working rule becomes a theory of the universe, a whole cosmology.

From the time when man could reason about his experience at all, he must have been guided by both kinds of reliable sequence—the way one event follows another and the consequences which follow actions—for, without being in this sense something both of a scientist and a moralist, he could not have been rational at all. But so long as he had only fixed ideas, these sequences were recognised only in the context of experience, and as useful guidance in actual situations. But, as soon as he was able to form free ideas, he began to separate principles from particular situations, and to regard all events under the principle of either action and merited award or of cause and necessary effect. Few achievements of the mind have contributed so much to human progress as this power of affirming general principles: and we ought to realise that the affirmation of a principle of necessity required this stage of free ideas as much as the affirmation of a principle of freedom.

Even civilised man was a long time before he formulated a law of cause and effect, but he only became civilised by formulating a law of action and consequence, or rather, as he conceived it, of action and award. All the civilisation we know anything about was based on this formulation, what most distinguishes a civilised man from a savage being just belief, as a free idea or general principle, in the rational consequences of his actions.

Like the later formulation of cause and effect, this formulation was quantitative. It might almost have been put in the Newtonian form that action and reaction are equal and even that they are opposite, in the sense that good and evil awards are without in exactly the same proportion as good and evil purpose within, and go out into the world and are no more subject to the actions which created them. Even the direct effects of action were brought within the scope of awards, for all that followed mere willing seemed far more like award than effect.

So far as we can trace, this was man's first great generalisation. For centuries he laboured to apply it to the understanding and management of his world: and with it he built up a body of knowledge and practice, the importance of which is not exceeded by anything in human history, not even by the achievements of the Newtonian conception of the uniform quantitative law of matter and motion.

Both have glaring defects as hypotheses embracing all the facts, but, seeing that mere wandering about in life and gazing around us does not lead us anywhere or help to give us our bearings, it is more profitable to push our way along one road which, with any reasonable approach, leads in the right direction. A hypothesis, therefore, is necessary· and if it formulate some common character in the immediately relevant facts, the simpler it is the better it serves. For the time being at least, its limitation and crudeness, its ignoring of all that lies beyond it, may even be a benefit. A formulation is like the conception of the lever. Once we have found it, though the objects we use may have all kinds of other qualities, the more we regard it simply as a rigid bar, the more effectively we can use it; and, for practical purposes, we can ignore everything except rigidity and length. So any formulation which has been abstracted from our experience of reality, if it provide a specially successful lever for dealing with our world, by embodying some general manifestation of it, may be justified by its utility. But this does not justify reversing the process so that, instead of the principle being formulated out of experience, experience is formulated out of it, till it become like the interpretation of the forest by a sawyer in terms of planks. Thus in our day we have a theory which reduces all reality to the absolute equivalence of cause and effect; and in former days there was, by the same method, a theory which reduced it all to the exact equivalence of action and award.

The latter can be regarded as the formulation of the world as freedom, and the former as the formulation of the world as necessity. But though the results are very different in form, it is the same kind of mind which creates both.

(*b*) THE COSMOLOGICAL LAW OF AWARD

The hypothesis of action and award was that all acts are acts of freedom up to the time when actually done, and then they are awarded the exact equivalent of their merit.

That experience should ever have been thought to show this moral equivalence of action and award may seem hard to understand, and some day it will be at least as difficult to conceive how anyone could have imagined that it shows a mechanical equivalence of cause and effect. But both schemes provided useful working theories of a great many facts, the gain from which was so obvious and the possibility of interpreting the facts and extending the theory so great as to make it easy to believe that ultimately the theory could include all acts.

Usually it is assumed that the legal scheme of award was so long accepted because it was held by simple people in a simple peasant life, and so wrought better than it could with our more inquiring minds in our more complex age. But if life was simpler it was less secure, and to be weak was to be still more visibly miserable, and history tells that there was no lack of inquiry. The age when this cosmology was most universally accepted was the sixth century B.C., a time of great mental activity and material insecurity. Moreover, the dogmatic persistence of a theory of fixed mechanical sequence as little covers all the facts, and would also seem to presuppose great simplicity of mind and simplicity of experience. But faith is sustained by difficult victories, not by having nothing against it. And if faith in a righteous order so conceived sustained men against robbery, oppression and wrong, it had no small justification.

The principle had much to say for itself, because it had the two great and notable achievements to its credit of sustained industry and systematic jurisprudence.

At first, action may have meant specially the work of one's hands and award material prosperity. Thus in the Book of Proverbs, which is all governed by this cosmology, we find constant praise of diligence and insistence on its necessary profitableness. Partly no doubt this rested on observing that "he becometh poor that dealeth with a slack hand: but the hand of the diligent maketh rich". Yet the really sustaining faith is that diligence, being practical application to the right objects in the right spirit, is uprightness, and that "the righteous shall be recompensed in the earth". The conviction is that a man's just wages shall be rendered him, and not merely that he will possess useful things as the effect of his work.

Diligence as a condition of any success may seem to be merely obvious. But it is a condition not yet always accepted even among ourselves; and there are peoples who do not recognise it at all. Primitive man would seem to have been capable of great outbursts of energy when he had difficulties to overcome as an immediate object before him, but he was not capable of applying himself steadily to a distant end: and there are tribes not much beyond this state to this day. For mankind it must have been a hard lesson to learn. Considering man's natural state and his natural mind, the wonder is that he ever learned persistent industry at all even for material well-being, not to speak of making it the ground of a higher civilisation and the spring of intellectual and spiritual achievement. Man's industry to-day may be a habit and, from the needs which he has created by industry, a necessity. Then he is able to cut losses and go on hoping for a better result next time. But this does not show how man first learned application, and still less how he attained the co-operation by which he escaped instinctive routine like the bee and developed the arts and founded civilisation. Not the observed results of his labours, which were uncertain, but the idea of a just universe, was his incentive and security. As action and award, and not as labour and work done, man made the formulation which sustained him in face of endless delay, discouragement and disappointment, and which enabled not only individuals but whole communities to possess their souls in patient application. This was a moral principle, based on an idea of justice and held, not by faith in a natural order in which good effects follow good works, but by faith in a supernatural order in which due awards follow the responsibility of free actions.

This is the wisdom which the Book of Proverbs says sought out knowledge of witty inventions. These were the great arts, upon the development of which ancient civilisation rested, agriculture, pottery, writing, weaving, navigation, and the smelting of metals: and, even in our day, have we ever invented anything of greater moment for the advancement of civilisation? How they arose we have no information to prove or disprove. But we know that our arts have required the development of a certain mental attitude, which depended on a faith in the responsiveness of things and in an essential righteousness, assuring, not necessarily materially, but somehow, the enjoyment of the fruit of our skill. We ought, therefore, to ask, what, when there was no organisation of research and no assurance of possession, was the faith whereby men persisted in the labours which led to these inventions, and still more what sustained co-operation in developing them: and as soon at least as we come to written history, we find it in this cosmology of action and award.

The mastery over the Natural thus depended on a faith in the Supernatural, a faith that its awards were as absolute as its commands, that, according to such idea of justice as had then been reached, the heart of the universe is just. No doubt men had also some idea of a fixed relation of cause and effect, but the order of the world which they formulated and upon which they depended was a fixed relation of action and award. And possibly, in spite of all science has done to relate one event to another, this is still a great deal more the ground of the faith by which we can labour and inquire and not be in haste for the result, than we recognise. Science itself is the work of freedom, and presupposes, as the ultimate meaning of things, a different order than its own mere equivalence of cause and effect: and faith in a reliable world, which was the nurse of all science, traces its ancestry back to this early moral faith and the civilisation it created.

The second great achievement due to this faith was jurisprudence—the evolution of law as distinct from mere traditional family and tribal custom; and, with it, there went the creation of the state. This advance upon mere blood and bread associations was the other important agency for producing the ancient civilisation and securing for it stability and progress. All early legislations, from the code of Hammurabi onwards, are religious formulations concerned with action and award; and the idea of justice by which they were determined rested on the belief that in the Divine economy of the world they are in exact equivalence.

To the present day this continues to be the fundamental legal conception. It has long been apparent that the mere idea of law is inadequate for interpreting the religious order, and that persistence in it has only hindered progess. Similarly we are beginning to perceive that it is inadequate for the civil order, and that exclusive attention to it is obstructing our vision of a higher order of the state. Nevertheless, though we may pass beyond it, we may not fall below it: and jurisprudence not only still rests on the old faith, but, till it reaches a higher ground, must do so. It is still a formulation of freedom, as simply what man wills to do, and of the award this merits and which should accompany it; and its basis is still that this is the order of the universe.

Yet, even with these far-reaching practical gains, the theory could not have been so long and passionately defended as the rational order of the universe, had it not also been the challenge and the inspiration for reflexion on the true nature both of action and of award, whereby, on the one hand, speech and demeanour were seen to be also actions, and then the deepest actions to be the thoughts and intents of the heart; and, on the other, reward passed beyond outward peace and material prosperity to social approval, and then to personal worth, and, finally, to a good conscience, not only as a sound moral basis for prosperity, but as itself a reward.

This affirmation on principle of responsibility in a just and ordered world so interpreted, emancipated men from communal thinking and taught independence of thought and action, and from tribal custom and replaced it by universal laws. The equivalence of action and award, though far from embracing all experience, was a concentration on responsibility and righteousness of the highest consequence: and, at that stage of progress, this direct and simple way of conceiving it was not only all that was possible, but was more useful than anything more complicated, for forwarding freedom, enlarging morality and establishing justice.

But this success ultimately enthroned the scheme as a complete cosmology, by the device of making the hypothesis the measure of experience and not experience the measure of the hypothesis. Then, instead of being merely a hypothesis for interpreting experience, needing to be constantly re-interpreted to make it include all the facts, it became the sole reality under all experience, to which the facts had to accommodate themselves.

The practical influence of the theory was doubtless very ancient, but of the domination of it over all experience, the sixth century B.C. was the great period, just as the nineteenth century A D. was the great period of the measurement of all reality by the equivalence of cause and effect. How the view appeared in India, in Persia, in Palestine, in Greece almost contemporaneously has long been a problem. But the communication of ideas may be sufficient explanation, for it was an age of extensive intercourse, and such ideas are a kind of thistledown which fly fast and far and take root easily where the soil is prepared, as it had been by long occupation with the problem of a just universe, with its justice thus simply conceived as a sort of legal bargain.

More or less this cosmology seems to have been accepted

by all civilised peoples. But it was much more modified by humane or prophetic ideas in some than in others: just as the principle of a universal scientific naturalism has been greatly modified by artistic naturalism. In Israel, being influenced by prophetic ideas, it determined the type of monotheism, even in Israel monotheism not being common property or securely fixed in the popular faith before the sixth century. In Greece also, by reason of other influences from which it borrowed, there was maintained with this faith a measure of life and liberty.

But no limitation of idea is ever cherished without limitation of experience. Wherefore, it is not strange that the belief in God tended to shrink to the giver of awards to actions as a kind of destiny. In later Judaism the one God came to be conceived mainly as law working as action and award, in face of which devout souls had great difficulty in cherishing the freer, more gracious conception of the prophets. Among the thinkers of Greece one abstract rule of action and award tended to become an abstract destiny, and the common people, with increasing difficulty, gave it humanity from their more human pantheon. The sixth century sees Xenophanes clearly expressing faith in one God, greatest of gods and mortals. But how far does the belief go beyond the scheme of a justice conceived as the fixed apportioning of action and award? All the dramatists express the tragedy of this fated destiny. What more is even Plato's theory of the Good, and what are his eternal ideas but the pure pattern of it, of which the visible world is the changing, moving shadows? But even these shadows had some reality for Plato as a means of interpreting the real world: and, as in our day, much could be maintained in theory which was obviously not believed in practice.

Buddhism alone made the principle a complete cosmology and accepted it so entirely that it became a rule of life as well as a theory. Not only was it for Buddhism the measure of the universe, but, in the last resort, it was the sole reality. Nothing exists but 'karma', and karma is just the exact equivalence of action and award.

COSMOLOGIES OF FREEDOM AND OF NECESSITY

(c) KARMA AND POSITIVISM

The only parallel in history is the naturalism of the last century, with its cosmology of the exact equivalence of cause and effect, in which motion takes the place of karma as the sole reality.

To put together things so far apart in time and so alien in interest as Buddhism and Naturalism may seem at first sight mere perverse ingenuity. But there are at least three important points of resemblance. The first is that both assume that the order of the universe means a calculably exact and invariable equivalence; the second that, though the equivalence of the one is karma and of the other action and reaction, both take equivalence to be the measure of all reality. The third is that the effect of both alike is to make everything in the universe, except the simple working of a principle of equivalence, mere 'maya' or illusion, so that, in the end, no real existence can be given to the world as we experience it, or to the soul as individual, or to God as personal.

Nor is the temper very different. More recently it has been questioned whether Buddhism is to be regarded as a religion at all, or simply as a rationalistic movement. Though this is mistaken, the religious features of Buddhism were merely continued from the Brahmanism out of which it sprang. Should Positivism ever seriously enter into rivalry with Christianity as a religion, we should have a similar phenomenon. Its religious elements would be borrowed from Christianity, but, like Buddhism, its own contribution would be the same substitution of rationalising for experience, with a very loud profession of rejecting it.

It is true that they start from diametrically opposite points. Though both deal with fixed sequences, Buddhism starts with an act of freedom, while Naturalism begins and ends with events which are only the sequence of former events. But practically this makes little difference. The Buddhist feels himself caught in a terrible, relentlessly unrolling destiny as much as the Naturalist, while the Naturalist, having no considered place for freedom, has all the more to introduce it abruptly, in the same kind of atomic way as Buddhism, before he can begin with anything. The main difference is that, to Buddhism, it is the material series which is a mere epiphenomenon of the mental series; whereas, to Naturalism, it is the mental series which is a mere epiphenomenon of the material.

Both are examples of how much a hypothesis can enable men to ignore: and it may be that we are entitled, in face of the calm and unassailable persistence of our varied experience to say that both are talking nonsense. But it is not Buddhism that is the more incredible, for it is easier to deny the reality of what we think we know than of something which thinks it knows. Yet the difference is less than appears. The world insists on being the sphere in which we live, and the mind on being the sole means of dealing with it. Neither the world nor mind is in the least a mere abstraction. Therefore, both theories must proceed by ignoring experience and working with something underneath it of which the theory is the sole evidence. This allows its absoluteness to be maintained, because the application of the theory turns in a circle upon itself and the perfection of its curve is not disturbed by any attempt to embrace in it the mass of unmanageable happenings in the observed present: and, thereby, both make the concrete world of mind and the concrete world of nature equally unreal. Buddhism, like other reflexions on the principle of action and award, carries the idea of action back to its motive. The essential of action is the thought which determines it: and this presents no problem, because the sphere beyond the present individual life in which it works is so wide, and also, for that matter, so unknown, that it has room for every possibility. Karma, as this exact equivalence of action and award, of thought and happening, can include everything, because what has not its explanation in this present life of which we are now conscious, has it in endless previous lives which we cannot now recollect, or will have it in the endless lives to come which we do not yet know. Nothing social needs to be introduced, except in so far as it is part of the individual's karma. Everything is determined entirely within the limits of the individual's responsibility. "All that we are is the result of what we have thought: it is founded on our thoughts, it is made up of our thoughts." This is the text of the *Dhammapada*, upon which it preaches from beginning to end. "If a man speaks or acts with an evil thought, pain follows him, as the wheel follows the foot of the ox that draws the carriage....If a man speaks or acts with a pure thought, happiness follows him, like a shadow that never leaves him."

Many fine ethical precepts are derived from this reference of all action to thought and of the quality of thought to desire, yet it is wholly a question of award: and, in the end, the sole measure of award is pleasure and pain. Nor is there anything else it could be, for life is just the pleasure and pain of individual karma. Experience, being from it, means nothing except award in pleasure or pain. Nor can experience ever be more than a shadow in any universe reduced to a mere principle of sequence, whether moral or material In Naturalism this principle has made us; and in Buddhism we have made it: but, in spite of the form of freedom in Buddhism, the world is left as meaningless, and all intercourse with it is made as much an oppressive unreality as by Naturalism. Just as a universe without freedom has no meaning, and without meaning no reality, so freedom, without a universe which is not its mere creation, has no meaning, and, without meaning, no reality. As the one reduces the world to a continuity of persistent motion, the other reduces it to sporadic acts of self-assertion.

This we see in Buddhism in the treatment of desire. In an atomic way desires are acts of freedom, being isolated acts of self-affirmation, which may be checked by isolated acts of self-repression Nor is any other freedom possible, because in Buddhism the concrete soul is a mere bundle of such desires, and its world merely their shadows. There can therefore be no idea of freedom as victory by a right relation of the whole spirit to its whole environment. Freedom is merely a distressing exposure to calamity, in face of which desires work like mechanical causes Nor does God count for anything in the story, for if there be gods they too are under karma, as in Naturalism, if they existed, they would be under motion. And the reason in both cases is the same. The world does not exist for any worthy end, either of education by it or victory over it, for which the soul or God could have significance.

Though Buddhism alone carried out the theory of action and award to its logical conclusion, we can trace the practical effect of it in the whole age. The Greek tragedy gave it sublime expression, but there are other evidences of a sense of suffering and paralysis which was all the more crushing from being everyday commonplace experience. High art in any case is not always the expression of the intensest feeling of an age, but rather indicates reflexion when the first bitterness is past. No doubt people then as now, undeterred by any theory from living and loving, retained some practical belief in the real freedom of their souls within and the wonder and responsiveness of a living world without. Yet this theory of moral equivalence was readily accepted because of the practical value of equal bargain in human affairs, just as the modern theory of mechanical equivalence was because of the utility of expecting equal effect from equal effort in managing our world: and within these limits both are valid as well as useful. But, as cosmologies, both discouraged men from looking farther, repressed courage and hope and the high venture of life, and limited and darkened experience even for those who only received them as general impressions from the intellectual atmosphere of their time.

(d) THE COSMOLOGICAL LAW OF INERTIA

Without some dim sense of the reliability of environment, life could not have set out on its great adventure. Instinct in higher forms of life goes farther and presupposes some awareness of a dependable succession. Man becomes rational when he reasons from this as a system of cause and effect. As he advances in knowledge he is able to apply it to ever wider circles of his experience. Yet the application of it in the form of measurable exactness between cause and effect, as a law of universal application of the same form as the measurable exactness between

COSMOLOGIES OF FREEDOM AND OF NECESSITY 231

action and award which had preceded it, was late in being formulated; and it was not affirmed to be the principle of the cosmos till science linked cause and effect together by the idea of continuous motion.

This dates from Galileo's great discovery of the uniformity of a state of rest or motion when left to itself, but the whole bearing of the discovery was not fully grasped till Newton stated it in his laws of motion. From Newton onwards for more than two centuries, this principle of exact equivalence of cause and effect was accepted as the sole ultimate basis of physics, and, in wide circles, as the sole reality of all things. Though by no means Newton's own view, this has come in our day to be known as Newtonism, which means that the equivalence in motion of cause and effect is a complete cosmology. With this alone are we concerned, because only with a sequence, universally applicable and mechanically rigid, does the question of the antagonism between law and freedom arise.

To the enormous successes which have been achieved by the application of this principle of uniform mechanical causation to the interpretation of the world, the last three centuries bear abundant testimony. As soon as it was discovered that any motion which exists sustains itself, and that we have only to account for changes in rate and direction, events which were already known to be periodic, such as day and night, summer and winter, were forthwith explained; and many other events, not hitherto known to be periodic, were discovered to be of this character and to be subject to the same type of explanation.

With ever increasing success the periodic nature of one set of natural phenomena after another was found to be of such regularity that it could be expressed in strict mathematical formulae. Galileo's theory of the pendulum, Kepler's theory of the orbit of the planet, Newton's law of gravitation, Huyghens' theory of light are all formulae of periodicity, that is to say of regular, mathematically calculable recurrences of events. Even the chemical and electrical discoveries, though they have destroyed at least the original simplicity of the Newtonian principle, were discovered through formulations made on the basis of it, and seemed at first not to deviate from it. Thus concrete things were marshalled by abstract thought as uniform motion: and from this it was concluded that this kind of equivalence of cause and effect contained the whole reality of concrete things and ultimately of the universe.

This was the easier that certain conclusions seemed to be established beyond revision and beyond extension, such as the unchanging uniformity of mass under all conditions whatsoever, the mathematical exactness of gravitation as proportioned to the mass and in inverse ratio to the square of the distance, the wave theory of light, and the conversion of energy. The exactness of these theories seemed to prove the ultimate physical reality to be a fixed quantity of matter in perfectly uniform motion. Thereby all cause and effect, all succession of event to event, seemed to be summed up under absolute equivalence of motion. And by this conception all these discoveries were linked to one another, until the whole universe seemed to be a closed system of mathematically calculable mechanical causation, and to be completely accounted for by perfectly elastic atoms of uniform size communicating motion to one another by impact, like balls suspended on strings in a class-room.

Like the notion of interpreting the order of the world by the idea of a perfectly equal bargain, this notion of interpreting it by the experience of exerting effort in proportion to the weight to be moved was so level to the common understanding that it penetrated to multitudes of persons whose knowledge of science never went beyond the encyclopaedia and the popular text-book, and, through them, to many more who knew nothing about science. As third-hand information is the *fides implicita* by which the atmosphere of an age is created, the verdicts of scientists came to be regarded as infallible; and the scientist, in spite of himself, was affected by this diffused influence of his own ideas and came to regard them as much more clear-cut than his science showed them to be. But as what is infallible must be clear-cut, what is clear-cut is apt to appear infallible. So the most modest scientist fell into the habit of speaking *ex cathedra*

As the long, painful groping of man after truth is distressingly fallible, infallibility must be exalted above error by having a unique source of information. In science this unique authority seemed to be found in the testing by experiment. The throne of certainty was in the laboratory. Inquirers in other fields, even earlier scientists, not excepting Galileo himself, varied as his experiments were, had to be content with the world about them, where all kinds of events insist on accompanying the particular event to be studied. But, with the power to select and exclude and to subject even a single aspect of a fact to investigation with instruments of precision, what was included could be regarded as exact result and what was excluded as merely a possible cause of error. The successes of the method have been so great that it was not in human nature to remember at all times, that events, like people, may not behave in the same way in private as they do in company, and that their behaviour, even when most controlled, is not always rigidly according to mathematical plan. Hence the demonstration took to following the Cartesian method of starting from a self-evident postulate and building up on it by nothing but logical reasoning.

This postulate seemed to be found as soon as it was discovered that the Newtonian laws of motion are all reducible to the one law of inertia. Every body continues in the same state of rest or motion, except as other bodies, continuing in the same state of rest or motion, run up against it, whereupon action and reaction are equal and opposite and the motions combine according to their momenta. Before Galileo, it was deemed as necessary to explain how motions were kept going as why they altered. But this seemed to be simple the moment it was called inertia. And as all motions were merely a clash of inertias, it all seemed self-evident. Thus was provided Descartes' desired beginning—a postulate clear and distinct, and thereby self-evident. Moreover, the other condition, that the building on this foundation must be by mathematical reasoning without possibility of mistake, seemed possible to fulfil

Such great and rapid and impressive successes were won

from the application of this principle as to seem to justify the hope that some day everything in all experience would be so brought within its scope that the persistence of inertia would explain how, by the simple evolving into the complex, the world came to be. This varied world was certainly an astounding result, but, in spite of the supposed invariable nature of energy, there is no parsimony of forces, and time for happy accidents in their interactions is unlimited. If the planets evolved by nebular matter whirling till it fell together in a molten ball by this simple law of inertia, why not everything upon them? There was, it is true, the disturbing theory of the degradation of energy, the theory that all energy is running down into a dead level at which it is no longer available for any work, a theory which is supported by the habit of inertia generally. But, as everything was supposed to have originated from a dead level of diffused energy, starting with the nebular creation of the planets, it could be supposed that, when the system at present working has sufficiently run down, it might start to wind itself up again.

These theoretical successes were followed by discoveries and inventions of vast practical utility, which have, whether for good or evil, produced an entirely new order of material production and thereby changed the whole organisation of society. These material victories, being visible, have, even more than the theories, impressed the public mind with the unique importance of mechanism. Moreover, the result has been that multitudes have been so brought together that they see little besides man's working in this mechanical way, and are scarcely aware that there is any other kind of environment.

As with the principle of action and award, so with this principle of a rigid quantitative equivalence between cause and effect, only a sect has accepted it as a complete philosophy. Even its members import, unconsciously, alien elements, but their cosmology is supposed to be that the world and the fullness thereof is only vibration, with every quality of it created by human phantasy, and freedom only an illusion of ignorance of the string which controls the puppets.

Were theory taken as seriously in the West as in the East, this bare skeleton of endless vibrations, regulated only by inertia, would be a worse nightmare than endless change determined by karma, because endless change determined by mechanical process is more paralysing than any kind of moral destiny. Yet, even with a freer faith directed to action, our age has not escaped unscathed. Nor is it necessary to accept the theory as a complete cosmology to suffer the blight of its chilling breath. A vague sense of what science seems to have destroyed of life's meaning and reduced to mere equivalence of quantities withers the courage to live our lives in faith, not only in what is best, but even in what is good. Values seem to have no relation to reality, and ideal values to be mere orchids kept in artificial heat in the Arctic Circle The Natural ceases to be a joy and an inspiration; and the Supernatural, instead of being peace and strength and victory over ourselves, and thereby over all things seen and temporal, becomes a mere distressing uncertainty which we cannot make up our minds to dismiss. It seems folly to talk of purpose; and without purpose, it is folly to talk of spirit in the universe or in any part of it, such as ourselves. The Natural gives, in its values, no gracious, reliable good that is, and the Supernatural no power to realise the good that should be. Under this shadow men can be merry, but they cannot be blessed, they can acquire, but they cannot possess.

Our age is still so far under its spell that we are unable to see how absurd it is to put on such narrow blinkers and, at the bidding of an abstraction, to reduce the glory of the world to a dead routine of motion. Yet it has had no more successes, and it is certainly not a more credible scheme of the universe, than the older formulation of action and award If the victories of the earlier scheme were not so dazzling, were they less important and useful? Was not the creation of law and the state as important for human progress as the invention of explosives and machinery and the introduction of the capitalist order of society? Has the elaboration of the arts of writing, boatbuilding and weaving into the monotype printing-press, the

Atlantic liner, the power-loom, been as important for mankind as the first invention of them? Is thinking things together scientifically as important as beginning to think them together at all? Nevertheless, no one now supposes that the old hypothesis covers all the facts, or is an accurate account of any of them. It seems to us wholly amazing that on a mere theory, even the simplest people could believe that no evil could come nigh the dwelling of the righteous, when openly before their eyes the tabernacles of robbers prosper and they that fear God are despised; and still more strange that this should be used to reduce the world and all its happening to a mere formula of karma, whereby everything is determined by what is wholly unknown, while the obvious influence of the constant interactions of men's own purposes, their society, their experiences and opportunities was ignored.

But is it stranger than the docility which accepts the reduction of the universe and all one's own actions within it to bare vibrations, at the bidding of a theory about uniformity of motion, in face of the fact that no one ever regarded impact as the only reality and the movements of puppets as the only action? If belief is not what we affirm but what we are prepared to act on, it is far more incredible than the other theory, for on that men could, on this they cannot, act. The most naturalistic scientist deals with his world as meaning and not as motion; thinks as if, when he had finished thinking, he would arrive at a purpose and act upon it; and wills as though he did things and not merely registered in his consciousness their being done: while people do seem to have acted as though they really believed that the universe is merely a scheme for adjusting awards to actions.

(e) INADEQUATE THEORY

From what has been said, it might seem that both cosmologies are dead and that we should calmly await their burial. But these simplifications of the moral and physical order are far too useful to the human understanding to be so easily dismissed.

Law, whether moral or scientific, relating things by measure, under the notion either of equivalence of award or of equivalence of effect, still has its application. Even a higher and larger justice than any law could provide would still have to keep before it his connexion between actions and their due rewards, because what we might call a medicinal discipline, taking entirely the place of what is just, would not rise above justice but fall below . The possibility of working for any higher order in the world requires the conviction that the heart of the universe is just: and in practice this constantly comes, in spite of everything that seems to contradict it, to be something very like the principle of the equivalence of action and award.

The equivalence of cause and effect also will always be the simplest and most effective way with the immediately practical physical aspects of the world. Even the Cartesian scheme, though it is no explanation of how anything comes to be, has utility. The new is just the new, and not merely the old with a change of form which does not matter. What does matter is his change of form: and we cannot arrive at it by mere immanence and continuity out of the old. Yet it is a gain for our minds to be able to arrange the new as though it did, because we only understand the new by the old: and it is a useful simplification of this complex world to have it arranged from simple formulae of mass and velocity up to more complex chemical formulae. This may not be in the least an account of how life actually uses its environment or of how anything has ever come to pass within environment, but that does not make the scheme any less useful as a system of classification, arranged conveniently according to mechanical ways, which we understand because they are our ways of working, however little they be nature's. Therefore it is likely that, for many a day to come, the order of the physical world will be conceived under the conception of the exact equivalence of cause and effect.

Not merely do principles not require to be adequate for the universe in order to be of the highest practical utility: they do not even need to be adequate to the particular reality to which they are applicable. The chief task of the understanding is to simplify; and its chief method of simplification is omission: and for a time at least it travels fastest and farthest with a principle which is only a kind of pocket-compass, without regard to the difference between the magnetic north and the true north. Perhaps the very idea of law itself is only a practically useful method of omission.

The earlier principle, which fixed on a simple, very human conception of justice, had sufficient resemblance to some aspect of the actual moral order to stimulate imagination, direct inquiry, master difficulties, subject important elements of experience to human uses, and interpret the whole by a deeper understanding of the springs of action and a higher valuation of its awards; and the newer hypothesis, which fixed on the simplest idea of mechanical sequence, had sufficient resemblance to the actual physical order to stimulate inquiry, direct its course, simplify facts, and work vast changes in human environment. Though no justification for making them all-embracing views of the universe, the history of both shows that a hypothesis is more useful, at least for a time, for being unduly simple and mechanical. Had man been aware of all the complexities of the moral world, when he first started to subdue the powers about him to his uses, he would not have made the same progress as he did by working with the idea of pure acts of freedom and of their consequences as exact material award. The Newtonian formulation is an even more crude account of the world we know, and is more obviously imposed upon it, but in the earlier stages of science it would only have hampered progress had all the perplexities and exceptions and expansions which recent science has added been evident from the beginning. The world as elastic atoms was equally far from embracing all reality, but it presented the regularity required for dealing with the immediate problem of periodicity better than anything less easily handled. So long as the whole reality to be explained is not entirely ignored, but, on the one hand, the awareness of all it manifests is expanding, and, on the other, the hypothesis is being enlarged in the task of explaining it—in short, so long

COSMOLOGIES OF FREEDOM AND OF NECESSITY 239

as it remains just a working hypothesis—any theory will be valuable up to the measure of truth it embodies, and its defects will ultimately be a challenge to further inquiry. Besides, inertia is a very important fact in our dealing with the world, just as reward is, and Newton's laws of motion summarise our knowledge of it in a way which has led to large discoveries about the world of our senses.

These schemes are connected in fact as well as similar in temper. Science, with its equivalence of cause and effect, seems, like King James, to have arrived "like the sun rising in its strength", and to have turned the other scheme into at best "a bright occidental star" already set, like Queen Elizabeth. But in accounting for the scientific era, it is now seen that we must go farther back than Copernicus or Roger Bacon, and give some place to scholastic logic and Roman law and Stoic Fate, as well as to the discoveries of the Greeks. This recognises the development of method and the training of the mind, as well as mere scientific theories. But behind these ways of thinking is the sense of one ordered universe, which goes back to the cosmology of action and award, with its thinking about its universe also by fixed measure. Moreover, though the newer cosmology was concerned with the natural order and the older with the supernatural, it was a change of religious view, a recognition that the Supernatural is in the Natural, and the true religious life right concern with the Natural, which introduced the era of science. The last question about any movement is, what created its interest? And at all events interest in science did not arise till religion found the religious life to be right use of the secular.

The history of science itself, moreover, shows the danger of turning a working theory into a cosmology. The simple mathematical principles of Newtonism, though they had for two centuries seemed adequate for the formulation of all physical reality and had produced formulae of great value for summing up such knowledge as was then available, for a long time fettered the freedom of science. Thus the theory of the atom as a hard impenetrable ball would not have continued so long, had it not seemed to be the necessary vehicle for a mechanical force; the theory of the ether as an even, grainless, elastic medium, and the theory of light as nothing beyond a lateral vibration of it, were so long accepted as adequate to all the facts for the same reason; the conception of space, as a sort of box without sides or cover or bottom, remained unquestioned, because all reality was conceived as position in it and all change as mere change of position; and the struggle for existence seemed to embrace all the facts of life, because nothing was being looked for beyond the old type of explanation. And, when we come to the history of religion, we shall see that the cosmology of action and award had the same paralysing effect on religious and moral progress.

CHAPTER XIV

CONCORDATS BETWEEN NECESSITY AND FREEDOM

THOUGH a cosmology of the exact equivalence of action and award would seem as outworn as the theory that the earth is flat and a cosmology of the exact equivalence of cause and effect at least as incredible, and though the one would seem to exclude the other, in practice we constantly assume that we deal both with a world in which acts are free and their consequences appropriate awards, and with a world in which causes are themselves effects and effects necessary sequences. In our scientific attitude, which even the most unscientific at times assume, fixity is the basis of all calculation and nothing really new is admitted; in our moral attitude, which even the most indifferent cannot always escape, we think of pure acts of freedom which are new creations. The habit of treating the world as though it were at one time wholly managed by meaning and responsive to purpose, and at another wholly by mechanism and responsive only to impact, is, therefore, not due to mere confusion of mind or mere uncriticised inheritance from the past. If science is to help in mastering the world, it must discover continuity in experience in spite of the constantly changing flux of the new; and if morals is to face new situations, it must not embarrass itself with the past, but forget the things that are behind. Wherefore, though freedom would not be free were each award demonstrably adjusted to each act, and though there could be no science were there nothing beyond mechanical cause and effect, both continue to be the practical forms in which laws, whether moral and judicial or scientific, are formulated: and, seeing we always and at the same time work with freedom and necessity, there must be some kind of concordat between them.

(a) PHENOMENON AND NOUMENON

We begin with Kant, because he accepts, without question or reserve, both principles as absolute. For him Newtonism rules absolutely the physical world and Deism the moral. In the world of science the writ of mathematical physics runs with *a priori* certainty; in the world of ethics absolute reverence for universally right ends should rule alone. In the former world all is means, and the sole order the exact equivalence of cause and effect; in the latter all is a realm of ends, and the sole order is action and its just award.

He does not mean that we have half a Newtonian world with all in it determined by the fixed sequence of events, and half a Deistic world with its awards distributed according to acts of freedom. Both are cosmic principles, one having to do with the phenomenal world as we know it, and the other with the noumenal as we act in it. The noumenal or real or ultimate world is free because of its own nature; our knowledge of its phenomenal aspect is made rigid and necessary by reason of the fixity in our form of knowing. Each, in its own aspect, is universally and without exception true, yet the necessity of the phenomenal world does not contradict the freedom of the noumenal world, because the necessity is only created by our way of knowing.

If the real world is the world of freedom and the realm of ends, or, in other words, the world of meaning, it would seem to be plain that, as in ordinary life, we should start with it and end with it. Then the only question would be how any other world could come to masquerade as the cosmic order.

At the moment, however, the Newtonian physics held the field. Hence the view that mathematical conclusions were at once *a priori* and absolute seemed so certain as to dominate all. Kant, therefore, set his problem in the form: Granting the rigidity of mathematical physics, what room is there for freedom? But if the world of freedom is the noumenal world and the other only the phenomenal, surely it ought to have been: Granting that the real world is of quality, of meaning,

CONCORDATS BETWEEN NECESSITY AND FREEDOM 243

of value, and in the last resort of the ultimate values of the true, the beautiful and the good, what is the relation to it of the determinism of science?

Had he made this beginning, so necessary for his position, he would have seen that he was dealing neither with pure reason nor with a theory of knowledge: and then he would not have given the impression that the mind manufactures all its perceptions; that the world of phenomena derives no significance from the noumenal world; that freedom is not exercised in the only world we know; that there is no connexion between the world of scientific necessity and the world of freedom.

Kant calls his treatise *A Critique of Pure Reason*, but instead of being a theory of knowledge by pure reason, it deals only with the theoretical aspect of a reason which is, in all its aspects, practical.

We have already seen how his theory of perception depends on confining attention to the question of how we impose our meaning upon environment, and ignoring the question of how it imposes its meaning upon us.

To the end of making environment less fluid, we employ forms of perception, categories of judgment, and ideas of reason. Space and time in perception are not mere forms of the mind, yet to serve practical purposes the mental forms are simplified into calculable equality in all directions. Though we do not make things individual by our judgment, for the more we know about reality the more we discover individual character everywhere in it, we both stereotype them more than they are in the flux of experience by categories of substance and such like, and make the flow evener than it is by using cause as if it were merely continued in the effect. Finally, ideas of reason we do not merely invent, for the world is an ordered whole, apart from anything we may think about it, but our ideas are more useful for being less complex and more static than reality.

This does not make a Newtonian phenomenal world to which mathematics is *a priori* applicable. Nor does science now ask us to start from it. The more recent thinkers who have dealt with the philosophy of science would agree that the right statement of the problem is: Starting from the world as meaning and value, what is the scope and significance of mathematical forms which seem to make it mechanical and meaningless? At the same time, the imposition of more rigid forms even upon our ordinary perceptions, to the end of making what we perceive more stable for practical ends, does show the beginning of which the laws of science are only the extension. And, with this, we must take the fact—very significant though seldom regarded—that there can be no conception of necessary law which is not a free idea acquired in the free exercise of our minds in the free pursuit of conscious ends. A law is a truth set free from the context of all situations to be available for any situation. And it is of interest and value precisely because the way of dealing with a situation when it arrives is not predetermined. Only because man can take his ideas out of their context and apply them freely in any other context, could he either have created or applied his science. This alone ought to show the absurdity of using physical law to reduce the universe to matter and motion. Yet it also shows how the mind produces the ideas to which mathematics is *a priori* applicable, and how, from both the finite and the practical nature of our minds, our phenomenal world is more fashioned to their application than is the constant changing flux of actual environment.

(b) QUANTITY AND QUALITY

Science, nevertheless, cannot cover all the phenomenal world and be mathematically calculable, if it is thus an instrument of freedom. The question, therefore, is, how is science limited, and how far, even within its limits, does the *a priori* determinism of mathematics hold sway?

The free ideas which most serve the end of managing our environment are of quantity and for this reason, all use of the understanding tends to be quantitative. Physical science in particular, being man's greatest means to this end, is, it is held,

CONCORDATS BETWEEN NECESSITY AND FREEDOM 245

entirely confined to this type of theory. In ideal at least it is the application of a metric system to what is measurable, and only as this is possible is it rigidly scientific.

This measurable aspect of the world is important for us because we are tool-using animals, who by measure cut up things for our use and fit them together for our convenience. But it may have much less importance for the economy of the universe than it has for us; and, even for us, the whole world of experience cannot be brought within its purview. Over the rest physics has no authority. As has been said, physics can only say even about a subject so definitely within its sphere as atoms, that their average behaviour is like certain calculable motions, while, for aught it can show, they may think.

This limitation of science to quantity may seem to offer a way of keeping the peace between science and religion and kindred interests, by dividing their territories after the fashion of Abraham and Lot. If we assign awareness and apprehension, working with quality, to art, morals and religion, and the understanding, in so far as it works with quantity, to science, should we not have the happy state of Germany and England assumed by Bismarck, of the impossibility of conflict between the elephant and the whale? And would there not then be the great gain for ordinary people that quantity and quality are plainer distinctions and easier to keep apart than Kant's portentous phenomenal and noumenal?

But Germany did not always keep to the land nor England to the water. Freedom, to have meaning, must transact its business in the ordinary world, and this largely by use of quantity; and physical law is entering upon a wider career because scientists are asking more insistently how it bears on the world of meaning. Moreover, morals and religion and possibly art might find their tasks surer and more fruitful, did they seriously face the purpose for which environment ought to be altered. Especially if, as has been maintained, it is religion which has given man footing in the flux of experience by the power of the sacred and so put mastery over the world into his hands, it would seem to be the task of religion to make this mastery of environment blessed for man and beneficent for his world.

In any case, order and freedom are so far from being antagonistic that they are necessary to each other: and the most important aspect of this question is the relation of quantity and quality. If this were solved, we might see better the true relation, not only of necessity and freedom, but also of the Natural and Supernatural. Science is concerned as well as religion. As both start with the world as we are aware of it and apprehend it by its own meaning and value, science and religion alike must be tested as they deal with this, the only real world. Practically, therefore, the distinction of quantity is of the utmost importance; theoretically, it is not final.

(c) CONCRETE AND ABSTRACT

The chief difficulty in the way of finding this distinction of quantity and quality a final solution is the claim, in the name of science, that quantity can be determined with mathematical precision and that it determines everything.

The answer given to this claim is that it rests on nothing more than the mere ignoring of the abstract nature of science, and that the advance of science itself shows the unreality of the claim.

During the last century mathematics has made more progress than in all previous ages, and the application of it to science has given results which upset all previous common-sense anticipations of the behaviour of the physical universe. But, while it has affected more than ever before our general view of the world, the result has not been, like the earlier applications of mathematics to physics, in the direction of showing a fixed process by which all things could be evolved out of what is immanent, by any kind of uniformity. On the contrary, it has produced a philosophy of science which realises that, while science attends neither to mind nor to our ever changing experience, it works with mind and deals with the concrete world of our senses, and that a philosophy of the world cannot be built on the omissions of science.

Science deals with our ordinary perceptions, but, as we do in perceiving, it attends to what is perceived and pays no attention to the activity of perceiving. Even what is perceived is not taken as it is perceived, which is as meaning and value; nor in its concrete fullness, which is in a time marked by constant change and newness and in a space filled with a vast variety of objects which change their appearance as we change position. Science attends only to a measurable system which underlies the qualities, and, even in this, mainly to what is periodic and reducible to formulae of recurrence. The justification is that no work can be done without concentration, which means omission. But what is omitted is not for that reason absent. On the contrary, it may affect the result more than if recognised.

The first omission is mind. Though it is the only instrument of knowing in science as in all else, to attend to it is not the business of the scientist. He may not, however, set up as a philosopher on what he ignores, any more than the farmer can set up as an astronomer on his inattention to the sun when growing crops by its heat.

The other omission of equal importance is the varied concrete world of the senses. The mathematical results of physics are necessarily exact because they do not apply to this world, but work with a cycle of ideas—defining one concept in terms of another, and so on round to the beginning—so that its symbol, as has been said, is the serpent with its tail in its mouth. Naturally the results are exact, but they afford no evidence of a mathematically constructed, rigid universe. In practical physics there are never more than approximations Thus viewed, the interpretation would be that, while the mathematical scheme corresponds, in a general working way, with experience, we have no means of proving its application rigid: and that, in this margin, there is ample room for continual increase in the meaning of the universe.

A still more thoroughgoing rejection of the cosmic significance of mechanical law starts from the fact that environment is of infinite variety, always saying something new, always enlarging. Therefore, it is denied that in any sense nature corresponds to a fixed mechanical order. In nature every movement as well as every phenomenon is individual. So it would appear to an infinite mind. But to a finite mind this would be chaos, had not the ingenuity of man hit upon devices for selecting, omitting, arranging, arresting. The result, it is held, has no more actual resemblance to reality than a chart to the ocean, even though it be of the same value in sailing the high seas of life.

Thus even practical physics seems to many at least of the younger mathematicians to be merely a convenient method, like making a straight line with one's eye, and then using the result as an exact test of the eye's accuracy. So far from being a revelation of the nature of ultimate reality, science is taken to be merely a way of simplifying and fixing our information about a world which is endlessly varied and changing, more determined by the nature of our minds than by the nature of physical reality.

In any case, the claims of science are greatly diminished from the old infallibility. Where there was supposed to be finality of knowledge, there are now seen to be little more than facts towards science, complicated far beyond anything likely to be the actual method of nature, something like the cycle and epicycle stage in astronomy before Kepler.

Whatever the end may be, it is now apparent that the order of nature is what Wordsworth calls "something far more deeply interfused" than a closed system of mechanical impacts. Even the atom is an organised world in itself, with an organisation which reflects the whole meaning of the universal order. It is a pattern of energy about which all that can be said is that it behaves in a more or less calculable way after the fashion of certain observable electrical phenomena, and that, though this pattern of energy is of vast duration, seeing that new forms of it are coming into existence, there is always the possibility that they may change still further or ultimately pass away. Fixed material stuff or matter is no longer even a useful hypothesis; and it appears as though the prominence matter has long had in the language of science is like Mrs Harris, the

CONCORDATS BETWEEN NECESSITY AND FREEDOM 249

modern scientist saying with Betsy Prig, "I don't believe there is no such person". With this we have an active basis for a living world of change and, we may trust, of progress, besides the certainty that our best knowledge has no manner of finality or universality of application which would carry us to any general conclusion about what is either possible or impossible in the universe.

The Quantum Theory—the theory that energy is not a mere diffused system of infinite gradation, but occurs in certain definite units—is still only in its infancy, yet already it suggests that nature from the beginning individualises itself, and that mind, with its centre of meaning and its relation to the universe by its own understanding and action, is not a mere incursion into its order. The Theory of Relativity hides itself in mystery from all who have not mastered the higher mathematics, but at least it reintroduces the mind which physics has seemed to ignore, by relating the order of time and space to the observer. In a universal frame of observations which does not merely plant the observer in one isolated spot, it relates the universe to him as a reasonable order at any time and space he may occupy, with light as a means of relating him which, as it does not vary with any rate of motion, remains a dependable uniform medium of communication.

All this the non-mathematical inquirer only sees in a glass darkly, and probably even the mathematical does not yet find it such that he who runs may read. But, whatever it may mean besides, it at least means that the Newtonian world of matter and impact is no longer a possible conception. While we may still be working with energy in the form of motion, it is as patterns which have meaning, and not in mere diffusion which has only impact, patterns which both reflect and contribute to the meaning of the whole.

Physics never did present any hope of getting a complex world out of mere persistence, but to-day this hope is made still more remote by the recognition that inertia is not in the least a postulate. Whether we go all the length with Prof. Whitehead or not, and say that every individual event happens in dependence upon all other events, we only know how events happen in the particular situations in which we observe them and have no means whatsoever of saying how they would happen in isolation. Therefore, inertia as we know it, so far from making a universe, is itself an aspect of the whole, wherein phenomena seemingly worlds apart are found to be in one order. And this order is rather logical than mechanical, because it is by reason of everything having its own meaning as well as contributing to the meaning of all other things. And inertia is part of this coherence of meaning.

Thus recent scientific developments have amply confirmed what Ward said long ago, rather by insight into the trend of science than by its results at that date, that "the advance of physics is proving the most effectual cure for this ignorant faith in matter and motion, as the inmost substance, rather than the most abstract symbol of the sum of existence". The advance since then would encourage him to say even more confidently "that the real world is the concrete, wherein no two things, no two events are ever the same, in development and progress, and that identity and uniformity is a mere device for enabling our finite minds to deal with an experience of endless variety, and that it is truer to say that the universe is a life than that it is a mechanism".[1]

This is as fundamental as it is true, and it goes a long way to solve the problem of freedom and necessity: but does it go all the way? Is the reducing of the universe to the mechanical equivalence of cause and effect, reckoned in motion, to be ascribed to mere mistaking of abstraction for analysis? In thinking so Ward has the support of distinguished physicists and mathematicians, such as Kirchhoff, Mach and Hobson. And, by our own common sense, we see that what science omits it cannot replace from itself or from any other source except experience. Science does not, as it were, take the watch to pieces to see how it works, keeping all the parts ready to be put together again, but ignores everything in its structure except a mathematical relation of mere annotated circles, from

[1] James Ward, *Naturalism and Agnosticism*, vol. I, p. 180

CONCORDATS BETWEEN NECESSITY AND FREEDOM 251

which no embodiment ever could be reproduced. Yet is there not a sense in which this is the watch?

We saw how comprehension reduces an object to a skeleton of its purpose, and explanation reduces this to a formula of its forces. Only by recovering from awareness and apprehension what has been dropped by the way is there any return to the whole object in its whole setting, which alone manifests its meaning and value. Science being simply judgment and reasoning applied to the natural world, the result is the same reduction by the understanding of everything to a diagram and the explanation of it to a formula: and from this there is no way back to a concrete world.

Yet, abstract as science may be, is even a mathematical law merely an abstraction? It serves practical ends, not because it is an abstract, but because it is a free idea, an idea applicable to all similar cases. It is abstract only because, the more we can rid it of the particular, the larger the number of cases to which it can be applied. Though the freer an idea is the more abstract it is apt to be, its freeness, not its abstractness, is what serves a useful end; and it is only abstract because of the vast amount of reality which has to be left fixed in the context in which it is perceived and cannot be transferred to another context. Thus a formula of the proportion of the radius to the circumference is abstract, but its value is that, being free from any particular circle, it is applicable to circles generally And such a free idea was possible only because men had free ends to serve by means of circles and because the human mind was able to move freely round it till it loosened this idea from its context.

Thus physical science depends on the most abstract of all abstractions, which is number, because we could not abstract more entirely from all qualities of an object than to exclude everything except the bare fact that it is a unit. As all exact science is the reduction of extension to units, we might seem to have good reason for saying that a unit is a pure abstraction. But the significance of the unit is not that it is the most abstract of all ideas, but that it is the freest. About everything we say something important when we say it is a unit, because we thereby at once set it by itself and put it in a class: and this is of high importance for dealing with environment. Nothing, it may be, is thus isolated in experience, nor may anything be unchanging, but it suits us to regard it simply as a unit, and mathematics only becomes rigid as it deals with this purely symbolic form. This is a fact which is significant, in view of the place in perception we have given to symbols.

But how far does this idea of the abstract and the concrete meet the difficulties either of freedom or necessity?

On the side of necessity, though there is no mathematically correct lever or time-keeper or circle, the scientist always assumes that the error is in his experiment, not in his mathematics; and there is at least practical utility in this circle of mass, corresponding generally at least to weight, and weight to motion, and so on. Nor is it the mathematician alone who relies on some kind of exactly calculable frame of things. In every common occupation we are scientists of this type, though we be as ignorant of it as M. Jourdain of talking prose.

But, on the side of freedom, the mathematician's sense of freedom, like the sense of freedom of the airiest philosopher, is not something which he thinks has doubtfully to insinuate itself into the interstices of the fixed and necessary. On the contrary, he knows that the fixed and necessary no more interferes with his initiative than the dependableness of the electric telegraph affects the freedom of the messages sent by it.

We begin to recognise that the scientist, like the rest of mankind, has to work with the best knowledge at his disposal and with his own limitations in dealing with it, and that this comes much short of infallibility. But is it not by mathematics that he attains such certainty as he has? And is there any other human instrument equally reliable? Nature, it is true, provides no exact examples, but in cases of doubt the question concerns the experimental application of the calculation and not the calculation itself. How is this to be reconciled with the fact that it is just one of the ways in which we exercise freedom, that it depends upon the general intellectual progress, and that, like other ways of dealing with life, it is to be measured by its contribution to human culture?

(*d*) SYMBOL AND MEANING

The answer here offered is that this rigidity does belong to the symbols behind meaning and that to our knowledge of them is due our power of imposing meaning upon our environment. We have already seen the possibility that the whole material system may be radiation as an ordered system of vibration: and in that case, without mathematical rigidity it would be chaos. Thus science would be exact in dealing with light as a series of vibrations, yet have to appeal wholly to experience for the meaning of light as colour.

Obviously, the mental forms with which science works would be of no value, unless they correspond in some useful way with something in the order of reality. Science may, like writing, omit and fix, but even this must be done with respect to the reality. It does not select and arrest at random. Thus quantity could only be a useful way of managing reality, if it have significance for the meaning by which it makes itself known to us, just as writing would be useless unless its symbols correspond generally with the sounds by which meaning is expressed in conversation. But in writing the rigidity of the symbolism is essential for expressing the freedom of the meaning: and this rigidity increases with the freedom of the idea.

This is not a mere illustration of science, or even a parallel to it. We have seen that speech is an extension of the same exercise of mind as perception. In the same way science is an extension of speech; and the most useful instrument it has fashioned for its purpose is transmission of speech by writing, an invention which is an illuminating example of the method of science.

From the first, writing must have required some measure of free idea, but its earliest beginnings were still fixed with the meanings of words, and the symbol depended on being fixed in the natural context. Thus there was a sign for each word, and the sign was a picture of its meaning. Simpler signs followed, which were symbols, not pictures. But the symbols were still only a means for recalling the picture, and so the object the word meant. Thus they were still fixed in the context of meaning. Science, strictly speaking, only began when abstraction was made from all meaning, and attention was directed solely to sounds as symbols, quite apart from what they meant. This science set itself to simplify. Many sounds which are impressive in speech are both singular and varied, but they were ignored, and only the fixed and recurrent were regarded. These were analysed into syllables: and syllables being fewer than words, a syllabary became a simpler form of writing. But this would not have been possible had not abstraction been made from all naturally fixed context of meaning, and the symbols set free from everything except fixed relations between themselves as members of a system. By further abstraction, vocables were found to be fewer than syllables. Then nothing was required in their symbols except to be distinct from one another. Finally, all meaning can be conveyed by two symbols, such as a dot and a dash. In themselves they are detached from all meaning and convey none. They do not even suggest any sound. Their value consists entirely in being in a system which has value in relation to a meaning already existing, with the symbols fixed and the meaning free.

In the same way science ignores all peculiarities of circles, though one may mean the moon and another a watch-glass, and considers only the relation of the radius to the circumference. Having established the proportion, there is no need to measure any circumference, but only its radius. Thus science goes on till everything is being reduced to point-events and their four relations of time and space. But what is the former except a syllabary, and the latter except a Morse code? The former tells us nothing of what circles may be or of the uses to which they can be put; and the latter, if we ever came to be able to use it, would only have meaning in a system of thought which gave it meaning. In itself and by itself, it would be at most dot and dash without the Morse code. This the higher mathematics to-day is making evident. It only professes to become rigid as it becomes pure symbolism, and it warns us that we leave this certainty behind the moment we attempt to turn the symbol into picture, which is when we turn it from symbol into meaning.

If this be right, the idea that all reality is contained in the laws of motion is on the same level of intelligence as the notion that all English literature is contained in twenty-six vocables. Yet in order to maintain that reality is meaning and meaning free, we do not need to deny that the symbolism of the meaning is of measurable, mathematical precision. If one type of mathematics is found not adequate, the scientist does not say that we must allow for pretty Fanny's ways, but he confidently seeks another, and acknowledges any inexactness as proving that he has not found it. Even the dependence of our ordinary calculations on space measuring equally in all directions must have a basis in fact. It may neither be a picture of actual room nor a scheme applicable to the universe, but it does seem to be rigidly reliable for its own purpose, and, therefore, to be a dependable symbolism of meaning, as far as it goes. Even the search for something beyond our naive views of space and time is only to make our trust in them more assured. A straight line may not be our old conception of the shortest distance between two points, but just because of our certainty that it expresses ordered meaning, we are fairly confident that it will continue to be the most direct way home. Freedom has no use for it being as incalculable for the sober as it sometimes is for the inebriated. Fixity, so far from excluding meaning, is necessary for receiving meaning from environment and for imposing meaning on it. The reason why man seeks to get behind varying meaning to fixed symbolism is that he finds it reliable; and more especially, that, when he has found it so, he can make it express his own meaning. Yet the certainty with which science enables this to be done, neither determines what meaning we wish to express, nor does it limit or determine in any way the meaning the environment itself expresses through the symbols.

With symbols alone mathematical science deals, and has nothing to do with determining the meaning which by them environment imposes on us or which by them we impose upon it. Thus the sounds of which writing is symbol are themselves also symbols. And only with sound as symbol, and not as meaning, does science deal. Nor would all that science knows about it alone enable us in the least degree to pass to any meaning. But knowing from experience what sounds mean, we can, as it were, make them talk our own meaning. Thus a person without music could construct an organ by pure calculation of quantities which would play accurate notes: and, however much more the musician may desire, were this calculable result not reliable, the rest would not profit. Whether he know it or not, the musician depends on a mathematically calculable relation of vibration to meaning, and the more perfectly this is embodied in his instrument, the greater his freedom in playing what he will. Yet the music is the meaning which, as a musician, he intends to convey, and is produced directly from his meaning, and in entire independence of mathematical calculation, even his use of quantity being as pure quality. Therefore, we start at the wrong end when we take the reality to be quantity and meaning a mere accompaniment of its order. The true order of reality is meaning, else there would be no universe, but only a nightmare of dead vibration—colourless, soundless, in short meaningless: and nature, it may be, is no more concerned with number and measure than man, when inventing speech, was with calculating pitch and tone. The calculable order in nature, as in speech, may only be because the meaning of nature gives order to its symbols, so that the symbolism of motion may be calculable precisely because what it expresses is a rational universe.

Yet we should not need to trouble about it unless the meaning were not fixed. The work of the understanding, more particularly its most pre-eminent device the laws of science, is necessary for the very reason that experience is not reiteration, but, though rationally continuous, is in unresting flux and change. So it is that we need these short cuts to keep pace with it. The making of these short cuts, moreover, is by free ideas; and we should never have dreamt of them except as the means of achieving free actions.

With this we may also take the idea of cause. As we direct our attention to it, we are only concerned to have a calculable result. But we distinguish cause from effect because it is a means of achieving an end: and we have made this distinction because we have found the world a place in which nature can be made to fulfil our ends. Thus cause and effect may be continuous as symbols, as breath and sound are, but they are not continuous as meaning, any more than an idea and the sounds which express it.

Suppose we had a mathematics which could deal with all the vibrations of light in a sunset as it could with all the mechanism of an organ, we should still no more include the whole changing meaning of the sunset than the music of the organ. We should have a sequence in which the recurrences might be of the utmost importance, but in which, if there were nothing but recurrences, the order by which it becomes rational could not exist. This is the true natural order and it is of the dullness of our souls that we use our science to measure the pipes and miss the music of the spheres.

Science serves its purpose precisely by its limitation. Its justification is that it extends a process of arresting and stereotyping which has already begun in perception; that it enlarges man's practical management of his world by isolating quantity from all else, both the mind that knows and the varied meaning by which it knows; and that it goes behind all meaning the world manifests to find the means whereby we can make the world speak our meaning. Thus it is an effective instrument precisely because it is not fitted to provide a cosmology.

CHAPTER XV

EVOLUTION AS A PROCESS OF THE NATURAL

(a) PROGRESS

WITH attention concentrated on periodicity and the explanation of it by Newton's law of gravitation regarded as the ideal of all theory, the exact equivalence of cause and effect as inertia seemed to include everything, for the reason that what did not so return upon itself in secure routine was out of the picture. Thus it came to be affirmed that science has so far proved, and, as a necessity of its progress, must assume, that the world is a closed mechanical system. But in such a universe there could be nothing really new: and this problem became insistent when life on the earth was found to be in evolution, and that this pointed, both backward and forward, to change not as recurrence but as progress.

The interest in history, which came in with Romanticism at the beginning of last century, directed attention to the question; and the idea of an evolution which was organic came to dominate philosophy. But so long as this seemed to assume continuous addition and to be outside the recognised scientific explanation, it stirred little interest among scientists. Only when Darwin seemed to show how evolution too could be included under inertia did scientists become interested. So much was this the case that to this day the whole idea of evolution is sometimes ascribed to him, though it is at least as old as the ancient Greeks and had been a familiar idea among thinkers for at least half a century, and even the idea of evolution by descent was not new. What was original was the theory of variation and elimination of the unprofitable by the blotting out of the unfit. For Darwin himself this was brought into operation by the activity, preferences and purposes of the living creature. But as these reach forward and cannot be brought within the scope of a science which only looks backwards, their importance for the theory was ignored or explained away, and all was ascribed to accidental variations and elimination of the unprofitable by the struggle for existence. Then, as variation without subjective selection is mere accident, and selection without purpose mere elimination, there seemed to be a self-working explanation of the same type as inertia. So Darwin was framed in Newtonism and became Darwinism, as different from Darwin as Newtonism from Newton: and the very newness, which threatened to prove a stricken field for the theory of the universe as a closed mechanical system, was turned into a triumph so great as to seem to justify the confidence that some day the mechanical explanation would cover the whole field of knowledge and dispose of every suggestion of freedom as exploded superstition

To this Huxley gave classical expression. "Anyone who is acquainted with the history of science, will admit that its progress has, in all ages, meant, and now, more than ever, means, the extension of the province of what we call matter and causation, and the concomitant gradual banishment from all regions of human thought of what we call spirit and spontaneity."[1] The banishment is some day to be complete, not only from Huxley's own sphere of biology, but from the sphere of knowledge, feeling and action, into which, under what he took to be Hume's guidance, he often made excursions. Ultimately from the Newtonian science no secrets will be hid, or, if to it all thoughts be not open and all desires known, it will know the machinery by which the strings of the whole puppet-show are pulled, which is even better.

All that put Darwin's theory in motion—the purpose of the living creature, its will to live, its subjective selection from environment, its choice of partners—instead of being the positive, directive, creative elements of evolution, were regarded merely as results. This seemed the more convincing that biology and physiology had concentrated their interest on the structure of the organism As this has many mechanical

[1] T. H. Huxley, *Method and Results*, 1894, p 159.

aspects, the rest could be assumed to be mechanical, only waiting for more skill to prove it. From this it was an easy step to the further assumption that, like other machines, it functions just as it is constructed, and that its supposed purposes are merely part of this functioning.

But there can be no progress unless the gains are conserved, and this presented a further problem. Heredity, the supreme conservation, seemed at first easy to include under inertia as mere continuance. But this continuance has the appearance at least of being increasing inheritance from experience, and experience is by meaning and not mechanism.

Yet once again a threatened defeat seemed to be turned into victory, when Weismann transferred the story of heredity from the purposeful activity of ancestors and inheritance of the fruits of their experience to the accidental adventures of the reproductive germ. The germ, according to the theory, reproduces itself from itself, keeping its structure mechanically intact within itself, unaffected by the experience of the individual except in so far as the individual prove a good or bad, safe or dangerous host, or rather hostel. As the individual is produced from the reproductive germ better or worse equipped for the battle of life and the germ shares its fate, the germ undergoes in the individual the process of elimination. But it is not otherwise affected, there being, in technical language, no heredity of acquired characteristics.

Some appearance of a law more rational than accident is afforded by ascribing the variation to the union of two germs. But in the last resort, this also is by accident.

Thus a theory, wedded to periodicity and the mechanical equivalence of cause and effect, kept its routine, yet seemed to get on the march with an evolution which could create all living creatures.

(*b*) PROBLEMS OF EVOLUTION

The scheme bristles with difficulties, and it is often assumed that it is only necessary to answer them to prove it true. But no theory of evolution is more than a hypothesis to explain the

EVOLUTION AS A PROCESS OF THE NATURAL

world and all that is therein as we know it, and the real test is whether it is adequate to this task.

In that case the real test is the way the theory meets four problems.

1. It must explain organism in its due place in the whole long history of progress. A theory of evolution ought to be an account of it in its place along with all else.

2. It must recognise life's characteristic way of dealing with environment, which is by meaning, not by impact.

3. It must show, not only how progress in life is enlargement of meaning, but how it is ever increasingly meaning for the living creature itself.

4. If it ascribe the evolution to the environment, it must be to an environment of a quality to produce all that has evolved.

I. THE PLACE OF ORGANISM

The first point is that the evolution of the organism should be taken in its place in all evolution For his special purposes, the biologist may ignore what precedes and what follows and treat organism as a mere cross-section in reality. But it is an arbitrary limitation, and for a theory of evolution wholly misleading.

The relation of life to what is beneath it, biologists, it may be thought, cannot be accused of neglecting. Do they not deal with the problem of evolution mainly as a history of origins: and in this do they not very fully realise that the supreme task is to bridge the gulfs between the stages, and more particularly between the organic and the inorganic? Is not their supreme hope to be able to break down entirely this frontier, as has already been done with the frontier between chemistry and physics? Is it not thus that life is to be shown to be comprehended in its physical structure: and if this is then reduced to a uniform Newtonian behaviour of equivalent cause and effect measured by motion, what more can be required to link up life with what is below it?

All evolution is one continuous story, and the more we know of it, the more closely linked together we may find all the stages to be. But no linking together makes things the same. What obviously becomes a new kind of reality is no less a new departure, because we cannot draw a line and say, Here it departs. As Bergson says, we are none the less on a new line because the points were so well fitted that we could not tell where we took them. Chemical action is not mere dynamic action, however closely we find them dovetailed, nor is organic action inorganic, however shadowy be the boundary between.

Seen in its right position in the whole evolution, moreover, this vagueness of the boundary between the organic and inorganic may lead us in the opposite direction from the extension of the mechanical. If we cannot tell where we pass from the inorganic to the organic, this may not prove both alike mechanical action, but, on the contrary, may show that we do not know what is potentially in anything till we see what comes out of it. Physics could not predict chemistry, but, with the knowledge of chemistry, the problems of physics are enormously extended; and though we have no knowledge of chemistry which would enable us to predict, apart from all experience of similar events, that a chicken can come out of an egg, knowing that a chicken does come out of an egg, we are faced with a very complicated problem in chemistry. For this reason we have rather to carry the possibilities of the higher development back into the lower than to find the higher a mere difference in form of what we are able to discern in the lower.

Still more, the story should be carried forward. The very lowest form of life, if with it the adventure has begun which leads to the whole organising of spirit with its attainments of purpose and knowledge, may not be treated as though it had no potentiality in it to be more than itself. We are already on the way to the higher organisms, which, in all their multitudinous functions, have the meaning of the whole in all their parts, and police their own frontiers, so as to suffer only what serves their own ends to cross them, yet ever enlarge the scope of their relation to a wider world, which is thereby made ever more perfectly their environment. Then, beyond organism, as part of the same story, is conscious mind, which, so far from being determined by submission to the invasion of outward forces, seeks, by meaning for its own feelings and by its own activity directed by its own knowledge, to understand and rule its whole environment as one ordered universe.

All science starts from this world of mind and dwells in it so constantly as to be able to overlook the fact, but the world of the scientist is no more deduced from beginnings than the world of the artist. Beginnings are deduced from it, and any account given of them must afford promise of returning to its fullness again to be of value. Just because physics has more recently been facing this fact, it regards the atom with far less confidence as mechanism than biology regards the organism. Even the seemingly mechanical behaviour of the atom the physicist realises only to be an abstraction and an average, under which all kinds of individual differences may be hidden, any one of which may be the starting-point of a new development.

In contrast, some biologists at least explain obvious individual activities by reducing them to forces like strains in material or other equally far-fetched dynamical analogies. But no analogy from inorganic materials, such as is used to explain how the plant lifts itself up towards the light, can be an explanation of any aspect of living organisms beyond their physical constitution and recognisable dynamical actions, or, in other words, of any aspect specially due to life.

Attempts are made to show that when low forms of life swim out of an unpleasant liquid, they are not managing motion by meaning, but are merely being moved by some force which accompanies what we judge to be unpleasantness, so that motion creates a semblance of meaning. The explanation is extremely unconvincing and if life does come to manifest itself by managing motion by meaning, the gain of the delay is not apparent. When we come to meaning, we are, in any case, in the sphere of mind, not matter; and we come to meaning when we have the vaguest action, upon the dullest feeling, directed by the dimmest ray of the creature's own knowledge. This is no longer the blind thrust of forces, if there be such a thing. How is it more scientific not to begin with this at the beginning of life, if we have later to take a flying leap to human consciousness and the mind by which we know everything we do know, science included? Here also, as in all developments in which it has any part, mind is first in principle. What we find it doing in our own experience when we learn any language or art, we find it doing throughout, which is to lead the van in organic development, yet never to be able to leave the inorganic behind. This is its early as well as its universal character, pointing already to the intimate connexion between the Natural and the Supernatural.

When we consider whereto life grows, mechanical explanations do not even stave off the question of the relation of life to mind and purpose. While life may very well use more mechanical processes than we know, and almost certainly uses them more simply than we have yet discovered, no living creature is a machine. We may be longer than we thought in entering the territory in which life acts after its own peculiar unified, purposeful manner, in response, not to the impact, but to the value of its environment: but when this is entered, it is precisely life which makes the dealing with environment not mechanical. And if life be thus developing towards mind and purpose, and if nothing can be known concerning it except from this its high achievement, is it not more rational and convincing to carry mind and purpose as far down as we can than to carry up mechanical explanations to the utmost limits of plausibility?

2. LIFE AND MEANING

This brings us to the second point, which is that life works with meaning not with impact: and this again goes with the further fact that evolution works with function. There is not first structure which then proceeds to function in fixed ways, but the living creature has ends for which it desires to function, and this determines at least the direction of the evolution of the structure.

Even Darwin himself was not fully aware of how much the mind of the living creature, its preference and its purposes,

EVOLUTION AS A PROCESS OF THE NATURAL 265

meant for his theory; and his followers, in so far as they saw it, sought to escape all it involved. But the whole scope of what is thereby assumed has more recently been made plain, and, on reflexion, becomes ever plainer. Evolution cannot move a step without the creature's purpose and functioning: and the more they are ignored, the more they are assumed. Thus the botanist has never been as satisfied with the theory as other biologists, for the good reason that the directive energy of the oak is not as present a help in time of need as that of the eagle.

The quality of life is that, if its origin is backwards, all its striving looks forward. It works with meaning in front, not with impact from behind. It functions for ends and not from mere mechanical necessity: and in this its kinship is with mind and not with matter. Structure and function develop together, but in principle function is first. The living creature does not first develop a lung and then get out of the water on to the land, but, having an object to gain on the land which it is ever striving after, it develops the means of attaining its purpose. This organic development again makes possible wider purposes, and, in seeking them, the living creature develops a still more effective organism. Even if the actual elaboration of the organism be done by selection from variations, it is mind which directs the selection into a definite channel, and does not leave mere elimination by survival to work all round the horizon. And it is not by any means certain that there is no other power at work except accidental variation and the elimination of the creatures whose variations are not profitable for survival. There may be a definite power in life itself to make its own organic adaptations. In any case, the concentration upon the physical structure by which life manifests itself, which alone has given colour to a purely mechanical account of life, can no more be justified in face of known facts.

Mere inertia represses variations and does not produce and develop them. No length of time accorded to its working could produce the new, and much less all the fullness of life. Unless something were pushing upwards, it is not within the limits of rational faith that this ordered world and the purposeful and, in ever increasing measure, intelligent life upon it, should have been by selection working with nothing save blind destruction, from variations provided by nothing but accidental throws of unloaded dice.

It must be in the extremest degree improbable that life, the characteristic of which is to deal with meaning, should advance wholly without influence from the meaning of its environment. Weismann's theory, which confines the story to the germ, only emphasises this difficulty. The germ is the new form of karma, which hands down the determination of the new life by the old, having the same irrational relation to the present as the old karma, and differing from it only in having a more irrational relation to the past. Learning from experience has no direct meaning for life either as cause or effect, but everything depends on the mechanical structure of the germ, so that it produces experience, not experience it.

This theory has been described as only making a small photograph of the difficulties. It is not an explanation by positive knowledge of the germ, but merely a hypothesis about the enormous abstract possibilities of the infinitely small. As these possibilities are admittedly great, something might still be said for the theory, did it afford any help towards the explanation of a living creature, developing as a special characteristic individual and dealing with its environment by means of its own knowledge and purpose, and with a heredity which works at least as if it were from the knowledge and purpose of its predecessors And now the theory of amalgamation of the male and the female germ, which alone gave the theory of variation some kind of reasonableness, is more than doubtful, seeing that a living creature, like a frog, has been produced without it. Moreover, if the male germ is only a stimulus which can even be dispensed with, must there not, seeing that the male is as important for it as the female, be some other carrier of the heredity than the mere physical germ?

Even life impulses, such as food and sex, are probably not to be explained purely physiologically, more especially as their acting is concerned in the production of the physiological process and cannot be the mere result of it. But instincts proper, such as hiding from enemies and nest-building, are functioning for ends, which operate at least as if they were by a heritage of fixed ideas, learned from circumstances and only requiring similar circumstances to call them into operation. That what at least looks like action upon meaning has never at any time had action upon meaning play any part directly in creating it, but that it is due to an elaborate physiological structure which functions in this way because of an elaborate arrangement of atoms in the reproductive germ, brought about by blind selection from variations which have merely happened, is a way as far round about and as little persuasive as the Buddhist circular road of karma, when the direct road of learning from experience lies so straight and plain before common sense. It is natural at least, if not necessary, to believe that life advances by what is characteristic of it, which is by action upon meaning, and not by what is not characteristic of it, which is by being thrust forward by accidental happenings like a dead thing. As life works with meaning and not by impact, that heredity is not a transmission of meaning, but a mechanical structure accidentally developed and only negatively selected, would require a great deal more proof than a theory, the sole justification for which is that it is mechanical, in a form which even physics is finding to be less and less adequate for solving its problem.

Heredity must be in some form memory of meaning. Considering how individual it is, the suggestion of race memory is not very convincing. But memory as a sustained and active pattern of energy is to be distinguished from recollection, and may be a feature of all forms of reality.[1] Not only may a plant have some kind of memory, but, for aught we know, an atom may have memory within the circle of its revolutions. Any kind of fixed idea at least must involve some measure of memory of meaning, and any heredity dependent on meaning is most simply explained as a scheme of fixed ideas. Perhaps

[1] Memory which is not recollective is sometimes said to be mere retentiveness. But its character is to be continually active, and not merely to be stored up

all organisation may be just a physical expression of a system of fixed ideas, which has been evolved from environment by education. This idea of more than a merely physical descent may seem absurd to those who have studied life only biologically: but at all events it does not, like Weismannism, reduce all experience to irrational accident; and it makes some suggestion towards explaining how heredity, besides securing the immense complexity in unity of the living organism, can go on, as the conditions arise, expanding mental characteristics as well as physical.

This suggestion of the inheritance of fixed ideas further affords some help towards understanding how recollection as well as feeling depends on the body. While the body would depend on memory, not memory on the body, recollection, requiring a system of fixed meanings whereby we can, as it were, pull the net of past experiences, would depend on the first incarnation of memory in the organism. Though with free ideas we create another system of relations by which we pull this net still more effectively, even then we depend largely on the system of fixed ideas, and those expressed in our physical frame are especially necessary for the contact with experience to which recollection is, in a singular and selective way, attached.

This view would also explain the failure of experiment to discover the inheritance of acquired characteristics, without landing us in the incredible position that all living creatures are born with amazing powers to deal with life, which yet do not depend directly on the experience of their ancestors. The simple explanation would be that only fixed ideas are inherited and that the experiments are not sufficiently extended to cover the fixing of ideas.[1] Free ideas, on the contrary, would only be inherited as adaptability, which would explain why man, of all higher vertebrates, is born with the least immediate capacity to look after himself and the largest adaptability.

By confining ourselves to biology, it might appear that all the victories of knowledge have been with structure and not

[1] If, as has been said to be shown by experiment, an element of skill in dealing with a situation becomes hereditary after several generations, this would be proved.

with function. But all life's meaning is the victory of function: and, even if we limit ourselves to special scientific conclusions, the assertion is no longer true, that nothing has been won from the other side. The extent of the cures by suggestion and psychical-analysis of complexes may be doubtful, but that there are such cures can no longer be denied. And the plain presupposition of this power of mind over body is that the organic functions, however many mechanical operations they may use, are, in so far as life is essential to them, subconscious mental functions.

Physiology ought to carry chemical and dynamical explanations as far as it can, yet, if this be a fact, it is not scientific, if to be scientific is to be alive to all facts and ready to accept any theory which will explain them, to refuse to consider the possibility of explanation by subconscious mind as well as unconscious motions. To refuse to consider any possibility is merely the old habit of making theory the measure of reality; and it may be that physiology is now being retarded by Newtonism as much as physics was in the last generation.

In any case, the unity of an organism is much more like the unity of mind than of a machine, and, what is more, it has come about by the living creature using it as one for its own purposes by response to its own feelings and by direction of some knowledge of its own, which, as Ward expressed it, is already mind as a going concern. Anyhow, if mind does arrive, it is not a convincing procedure to suppose that organism develops as a machine, and that, at some stage, mind is planted in it to direct it, somewhat as a rider may be dropped on the back of an unbroken horse, or as we might suppose that a steam engine had no connexion with an engineer, but that when it became too complex to run by itself, an engineer arrived to manage it. On this line there is no stopping short of the absurdities of psycho-physical parallelism, with its notion of consciousness and will as a light and a policeman having nothing to do with directing the traffic. It runs mechanically by trolleys, but for some ornamental reason they appear when a certain stage of complexity is reached.

But here we may seem to be trying to prove too much. If life works with quality and looks before, and physical science only with quantity and looks behind, would not evolution be outside the scope of science? And considering what science has done in the matter, is not this absurd?

That science has made great discoveries about organisms and the physical elements they use, and that, by after reflexion upon the career of life, it has had much to say about evolution, is not to be denied. Yet strict science stops precisely where life begins: and, even if science should produce living matter, this would still be true. Life as we know it, however physiologically, chemically and physically we may interpret the result afterwards, has no more been so developed than language has been produced grammatically, philologically and phonetically, because such explanations can afterwards be applied to it. Life no more developed its forms from the advance of chemical action than speech from the development of the throat, but both developed by the same power of receiving meaning from environment and impressing meaning upon it.

If the exact boundary between the organic and inorganic is uncertain, the vagueness is never due to there being a kind of life which acts only mechanically. The characteristic way of dealing with its environment which life employs is by meaning: and where this begins, life begins. But doubt arises as much from the fact that there is no environment which is not of a quality to convey meaning to mind and receive meaning from it, as from uncertainty of the exact point where the particular response of life begins. Therefore what is proved is not that life continues to be mechanical, but that there may be nothing in nature wholly confined to the mechanical order.

Yet, as life is response to meaning and not mere motion from impact, however akin the inorganic be to it, it is perfectly distinct in principle, and, as evolution makes this increasingly evident, no dovetailing of the organic into the inorganic in the least proves the contrary. Even should the chemist succeed in producing living protoplasm, or even a living man, he would only have produced by mind, working on nature, what mind, working with nature, is doing continually. But is this more than providing the conditions to which life attaches itself? Seeing that no laboratory could ever be constructed to exclude the possibility of what is not physical entering into the combination, no shadow of disproof that man is a living soul could be given: and if this man proceeded, as rational man does, to determine his life by meaning and purpose, and did not act as a puppet, the entrance of a non-mechanical reality would be certain.

3. MEANING FOR THE INDIVIDUAL

The third problem which a theory of evolution has to meet is that evolution is increasingly meaning for the living creature itself. Not only is organism a stage of the unfolding of the meaning of the universe, not to be understood except in its own place in the whole story, but the most characteristic aspect of this unfolding of meaning has to do with the individual life, which works with its own meaning, and advances by making a clearer distinction between itself and its environment, as well as by wider and more intimate interaction.

We may take the beginning of this long story to be the atom, the unit of energy in which nature individualises its work from the start, yet does not isolate it; and the goal, so far at least as our vision goes, to be the ideal of freedom as complete moral independence, with an understanding of environment and a victory by it and over it which makes us know it as our universe.

The history of evolution has two apparently opposite but really united developments. One is the development of its individual frontier, ever more perfectly policed; the other is a freer and ever expanding traffic with the universe across it. Life is not individual merely by being in one particular creature. From the beginning it is in some way individual as a self, acting for itself and not merely by itself. And the more perfectly it does so, the wider is the environment it can touch, so that, the more perfectly it is itself, the farther it can reach beyond itself.

The problem of how the individual goes beyond itself has

always been recognised as both difficult and important: but the self has been so far from being regarded as a problem, that its selfishness, instead of requiring explanation, has seemed to be the only motive which fits in with universal mechanical causation, because a selfish motive is forthwith identified with physical impact. But a very little consideration will show that the kind of isolation necessary for the exercise of selfishness is, for the theory of universal mechanical causation, the most insoluble of problems.

In the first place, the most selfish motive has no resemblance to a physical cause; in the second, calculated selfishness is not mere blind following of selfish motives; in the third, rational self-interest is not merely calculated selfishness. Even were it true, as is affirmed, that no other motive than self-interest could be rational, or for that matter possible, self-interest is still not mere passive submission to selfish motive, selfish motive is not an impulse in the psychological sense, and impulse is not impulsion in the physical sense. The very weakest submission to impulse is not of this purely physical type; and self-interest is not of this type of submission at all.

The self-interest, for example, of Utilitarian Ethics repudiates subjection to the immediately pleasurable or painful, and insists on regarding our individual good in all its breadth, as interpreted by experience in all its bearings and as measured by the future as well as the present. This in no way comes under the principle of the equivalence of cause and effect, but, as a matter of fact, is the old principle of the equivalence of action and award. Moreover, it is this principle in its primitive form of outward action and material consequence, before the merit of action was carried back to motive and its awards carried forward to losses and gains of the spirit. Yet, even in this crude form, it is an alien phenomenon in a world of universal mechanical sequence. In such a world, selfishness, so far from being the ultimate explanation, is very much in need of being explained: for how can the individual be a world which isolates itself, in a world of matter and universal fixed causation which admits of no isolation?

On this ground of self-interest as a postulate, the survival of the fittest looked like an ultimate explanation. But it is an explanation which does not accord with a world either of mechanical or of rational process. As James rightly says, Darwinism does not deal with any fixed, universally progressive thrust forward, but with the individual and his influence as what he calls "a ferment in the race".[1] Thus it is neither of the Newtonian nor of the Hegelian type, but places the emphasis on the individual, for which neither of them has room. Darwin himself makes plain the long, painful, laborious evolution of the living creature's individual frontier, and shows that the struggle is just to defend it against an assailing and levelling environment. Some measure of this independence belongs to the lowest germ, and the later conscious struggle for survival is still more definitely for the self. Yet only when the self arrives at self-consciousness can there be self-regard in the strict sense, or even genuinely purposed selfishness. In this insistence on the development of the individual frontier in the struggle for survival, Darwin has made a great contribution to our view of the universe, but it is in the direction of freedom and not of process.

For Darwinism environment is everything, yet not because it is positively creative of anything, being only invoked to blot out what cannot maintain itself against assaults. But the individual selects its environment by what it finds friendly to the kind of self it is, and deals with it by active meaning and purpose. As life progresses it at once excludes more effectively the unfriendly and extends more widely the range of the friendly. This better policing yet ever freer opening of the individual frontier is the essential achievement of evolution, reaching out through its whole course towards conscious intelligence which can prove all things and hold fast that which is good.

This struggle for the expansion of life is as real and as important as the struggle for survival, so that, from the first, life has in it the promise of the prophetic ideal of absolute independence in the power of one's own vision of truth and right,

[1] William James, *The Will to Believe*, p. 226.

with complete possession of all things through finding life's real requirements, until the whole universe is in a sense our organism, every part of which our spirit may pervade

The evolution of life is like the evolution of a house, which grows in hospitality as it becomes increasingly wind and water proof. First its organism is a cellar, dark and confined, yet ill-defended. Its barricaded entrance opens only to touch, yet, little as is admitted, it is ill-selected. As life develops, it builds higher and opens all the windows and gateways of the senses till its organism is a home, hospitable to friendly meaning yet better protected against mere assault, its windows, as it were, open to the air and the sunshine and looking out upon the whole horizon yet excluding inclement weather, and its doors on the latch, prompt to be open or shut according to the nature of the caller.

Thus the more the individual's home is secure, the more it enables him to be a citizen of the world. Yet, thereby, he is not less but more individual. Indeed, only as a possible citizen of the world can he achieve a self-regard which shall be really comprehensive and all-inclusive, not mere weak submission to immediately insistent interests but a deliberate and purposeful policy of self-interest

The perfection of selfishness, which cares for nothing, except as the possession of it gives personal pleasure and the avoiding of it spares pain, and for nobody, except as he is either to be feared or made useful, is so far from being the only ultimate explanation which does not need to be explained, that it is perhaps a quite impossible achievement. Yet the highly creditable approach to it occasionally made is by no means the natural result of any kind of universal order, and certainly not of any scheme of fixed mechanical forces, which, as it were, having no islands but, being a shoreless sea of hurtling interactions, has no place for this highly complex power of individual isolation.

The perplexity is obscured from us, as most perplexities are, by familiarity. We are all interested in ourselves, and realise at times that interest in our family, our friends, our class, our trade, our politics, our art, is only an extension of this interest. Therefore we seem at once to understand why anything was done when we say it was to gain pleasure or avoid pain. But this has no relation to an uninterrupted diffusion of inert motion, and is indeed a very wonderful thing to happen in any universe that is interacting and interdependent; and deliberate self-regard is still more wonderful, still more alien.

Selfishness is an abuse, but it is an abuse of man's power to be a self-conscious, self-determining individual without which, so far as we are concerned, nothing would have any value or disvalue. Moreover, this abuse in its calculating fullness is possible only by what man has achieved in the sphere of the Supernatural, and not merely of the Natural. In short, it is an abuse of the essential form of freedom. And frequently it is so quite directly: as great commercial success, though it may be spiritually disastrous, may be the fruit of self-denial and industry acquired in the service of the sacred demands of religion.

Whether this determination by interest for the living creature itself requires in biology the theory known as Vitalism, depends on what is understood by the theory and the ends it is expected to serve. But, if the alternative is that the organism is not different from a mechanism and that life is not the cause of the difference, we have merely the old trick of determining fact by theory and not theory by fact. The whole commonsense experience of mankind is a much larger and more convincing experiment than any possible series of experiments in a laboratory, which, moreover, is about the last place where life might be expected to manifest itself in its fullness and just as life. Learned terminology has always assumed the right to confer impressiveness, yet that the unity of an organism is not primary and determinative of its whole constitution but is mechanically compounded of the sum of its parts, and that the actions of any higher animal are determined by physical stimuli, not by its own intelligence, is as much nonsense in technical language as in the language of the market-place.

Descartes started people on several wrong lines, and this

was one. Everything new is new, and has its own new way of acting. And, in so far as Vitalism affirms this of life, it is not only saying what is true but what ought at this time of day to be a platitude. Science never really crosses the boundary of what is due just to life itself, for the very simple reason that life works, even with the physical forces, as meaning for its whole self and not as mere impact on some part of its structure. This is the real problem, which in the usual biological discussion is at once assumed and overlooked.

The real question is whether the Vitalist is not making the usual biological mistake of judging organisms within artificially determined limits. Perhaps only for this reason does he distinguish so sharply between life and the evolution of the inorganic, on the one hand, and the whole evolution of mind, on the other, and regard it as a *tertium quid*.

Possibly, however, biology cannot escape in the end even this *tertium quid*, in a form very much like the savage idea of the soul. Even physics is very much in need of an idea of forms which can maintain their pattern through all changes of material, yet are not mere self-enclosed motions but are responsive to all things; and the need of biology is greater. The materials of life are pre-eminently to be described as the corruptible, but the forms of life continue in all expansions and changes, and reproduce themselves in new embodiments. This does seem to require a form which determines the material and is not determined by it, a unity determined by unity of function, which again is determined by unity of purpose, which again is determined by unity of mind.

The mere putting of function in the foreground of evolution changes entirely the standpoint. It is the assertion that the structure is the creation of mind acting as a monad, and the denial that it is the creator of life's co-operative unity. And with this goes the power, increasingly demonstrated, of suggestion over bodily functions, which seems to show that there is something before function, as well as that function is before organisation. There are still biologists who claim that science has shown all notions of souls to be ghosts of superstition, but in point of fact, they have so far done nothing to provide a substitute. Whether Vitalists bring this that is before function forward in a way to be helpful to biology, biologists themselves must decide. Yet that there is something not only with which life acts but for which it acts, we do not need the biologist's kind permission to believe. Ultimately it becomes a question of a world of value within, corresponding to a world of absolute value without, and of all this means for the goal of life and the meaning of the universe. Where the biologist will admit its first appearing is his own concern, so long as he does not deny that it has come when we know all worthiness in living to be determined by it. At the same time, the rational explanation would seem to be that, from the start, life has set out on the adventure which leads to this goal.

So long as the physical is taken to be the only certainty from which all else has to be inferred, the spiritual will always seem to be problematical, and there will always be a certain plausibility in accounting for the idea of a soul by mere reasoning from dreams and shadows and confusion between memories and percepts and such-like. But we must account (1) for an active, organising form whose continuity does not depend on continuity of material; (2) for something which works with meaning, not impact, apart from whose meaning we know nothing; (3) for something which is in advance of its natural environment, manages it, and is not merely its product; (4) for something whose values are the world's meaning, by whose highest values the world is understood and managed, and which itself shares in these values.

4. ENVIRONMENT

A view which regards evolution as by what is essentially education, in the end depends as entirely upon environment as a purely physical theory which regards environment as turning structure blindly upon the lathe of time. But, if progress is by reaching forward to fuller meaning, the environment must be such that the value is there waiting to be realised.

The moving force may be in the individual, not the environment, yet it is the environment which produces as well as responds to the individual, and this by reason of the meaning it has for him. That it not only has a place for individual selective expansion, but is not really known to anything else within our experience, must be a very important fact about environment. Only on these terms is it known as a universe at all. And nothing makes a purely naturalistic account of evolution plausible save the ease with which this environment, in which all true values, natural and supernatural, are already effectively present, is assumed, not because the theory is entitled to the assumption, but because it cannot emancipate itself from the assumptions on which all life proceeds.

Ages as well as individuals have concentrated upon particular problems. While this has been to the great advancement and diffusion of knowledge, both the concentration upon the new knowledge and the extension of it as mere information have their dangers. What fills the attention is apt to fill the horizon and appear as greater than it is, because it is nearer the eye; and surer than it is, because interest sets what maintains it in the limelight and what detracts from it in the shade. Then what fills the public stage draws the popular interest, until people who have never inquired into its grounds receive it as accepted· whereupon mere diffusion is taken as support. Thus what may be only a useful working hypothesis becomes a creed, and an orthodoxy is established which accepts phrases without too curious inquiry about their meaning and none at all about their evidence.

The concentration of last century upon evolution is an example of both. Darwin's own theory, were it to become as dead as many at present hold it to be, would still have contributed largely to our knowledge of organisms and continue to be a stage towards any better theory of evolution that may ever appear. But Darwinism, as a blessed magical word having in attendance other blessed magical words like environment and the survival of the fittest, has been a mere device for

EVOLUTION AS A PROCESS OF THE NATURAL 279

dismissing life's deepest problems, and especially about environment and fitness.

Environment cannot be too much emphasised, because in some sense life is the product of environment and its progress is towards a wider and higher fitness for it. But it is an environment which both challenges and rewards life's adventure, for life does not develop passively from environment, but only as the individual living creature learns to deal effectively with its challenge and opportunity. This still leaves us with the problem of environment itself. To dismiss it lightly as also the product of evolution is to regard evolution as creating all things out of nothing, without any suggestion of how it has such a word of power. As the word of power must have been in the environment, and not in mere disembodied evolution, to dispose of environment as also the product of evolution is mere turning in a circle If we regard our whole environment, 'fitness' may rightly be used for learning how to dwell in it· but what is the higher environment which makes fitness to live in our lower environment the power to make it suit us and not merely the suiting of ourselves to it? And if we speak of fitness as higher, it is the appreciation of the nobler values of a higher environment.

Life may have made its first start in the primeval slime, but if there was any headway made in it, the cause was that the slime reflected an ordered universe, offering a challenge and a possibility, and was not a mere mixture of earth and water. Living creatures, as they advance, play an ever larger part in their own development, but they continue to depend on finding an environment still beyond them and equal to their growing needs, and they find it because they are in a universe which visibly or invisibly has potentiality for growing intelligence and more subtly adjusted activities. It responds to the growth of the living creature by providing ever increasing meaning for it, and not by mere increased complexity of dead impacts. In an environment without meaning and response to meaning, there could not be life, and still less its evolution In respect of reaching out to meaning and groping after purpose, all life is of the nature of mind, and could not prosper in an environment which had neither meaning and purpose in itself nor could respond to them in us. While man is the only creature we know that has consciously entered into this heritage, it may be that this sheds light, not merely on an order to be accepted in freedom by the creatures which have developed far enough to realise it, but on the whole process of evolution, at all events of life, by the measure of freedom attained and for the fuller attainment of it. Then we can say of the universe that it is an order in which everything has worth for itself as well as for the whole, and that this is a worth inseparably natural and supernatural, though progress means the increasing emancipation of the latter.

CHAPTER XVI

EVOLUTION AS A PROCESS OF THE SUPERNATURAL

(a) SELECTION BY ENVIRONMENT

IN any theory of evolution environment must play a leading part, but selection by environment must mean an environment big enough for the task. Even if it select only by destruction, the selection would still be according to what it destroys. A purely chaotic one would destroy purely chaotically, and one of mere inertia would keep levelling down, not raising up.

The theory which works with a process of the merely Natural is exposed to both difficulties, because inertia is both chaotic and levelling. By using the Cartesian Method, not merely as a method of inquiry but as a method of creation, it picks up unconsidered trifles by the way till it has accumulated a universe. The result is not a very inspiring universe: but as a creation of all things out of next to nothing by chance variation and mere negative elimination in an environment which is itself nothing more, it would be a very brilliant result, and not the smallest part of the wonder would be any moral achievement, even at its lowest valuation of considered self-regard. We used to have doubts about Satan falling down from the crystal sphere of the ideal, but now we seem to be required to accept the still more difficult belief that somehow he has managed to fall up to it. A creature of mere fighting ferocity and dexterity, with no footing save in a world of brute forces, has evolved, if not into an angel of light, at least into something decently human, ascending, not by means of any ladder of higher environment but by throwing out of himself spider's threads into the void. But whence this thread? Why should man body forth from himself any dream of what ought to be? What made him take its claim to be sacred, and proceed to impose it at once on himself and on his world? What above all holds it so firm that, when he puts the weight of his whole experience on it, he finds the worth both of his own self and his true environment?

The theory we have now to consider, fully meets these difficulties because it works with the Supernatural as universal potentiality which has already in it all the ideals, all the harmony, all the order that may ever be evolved.

If we regard the method, we may call it Idealism. The best known form of it is the process of Universal Reason, of which Hegel took the individual mind to be like the pattern of the heavenly temple shown to Moses on the mount. If we regard the result, it is Scientific Pantheism, because this universal substance or reason is all things, and all is made manifest by the cosmic process

It, too, works with the Cartesian Method, but with something very like Descartes' Perfect Being to put it in motion. As there is an unlimited blank cheque upon potentiality, there is no parsimony in respect of the values it can provide or any doubt of their absoluteness. and the only question is whether it provides them in a way that makes them true ideal values, and by the kind of dealing with environment which is our actual experience.

As it is the old question of the individual and individuality, which has already been discussed, we can here confine ourselves to asking what is contributed to the problem of necessity and freedom and how far it is a solution.

(*b*) THE TRUTH IN THE CONCEPTION

While this form of pantheism has a scientific aspect as an explanation of all change by the becoming kinetic of what is potential, its real appeal is to the sense of the changeless amid change, which affords the peace of calm contemplation.

This Spinoza calls *amor intellectualis Dei*, and is what caused him to be described as a "God-intoxicated man". In spite of the fact that his system is a mere intellectual mechanism, supported by a mathematical form of reasoning which is a mere illusion of proof, this outlook or temper, in contrast to the

EVOLUTION AS A PROCESS OF THE SUPERNATURAL 283

striving of Rationalism, explains his appeal to a concrete, poetic mind like Goethe, and how a Romanticist like Schleiermacher could speak of "Spinoza's holy shade". The more we consider his system, as they did, in opposition to the mere individual striving of Rationalism, the greater its justification, because its merit is in recognising three considerations which Rationalism had ignored.

1. All things interact.

Lotze compares the effect of things coming together in one universe to ideas coming together in one mind Spinoza's solution denies the most intimate experience of this inter-relation we know—the interaction of thought and extension—with the result that his theory is a purely mechanical scheme of one substance with the emergence of modes and accidents running parallel; and the improvements upon it, such as Leibnitz's monads, still leave the universe a sort of Greenwich Observatory with its electric clocks, and do not bring us any nearer the interaction in which everyone believes, if belief is what we act on. Nevertheless, the merit of the theory is that it presents a problem of the first importance for necessity and freedom.

2. If we have universal standards, we cannot have merely individual minds with purely individual relations.

This problem was more fully realised by Hegel, and, by making everything of the nature of thought, he escapes trouble about parallelism. Yet his solution of pattern and web is not really less mechanical than Spinoza's substance and emanation. This has already been discussed under the theory of knowledge: and to it there is no need to return, because action is merely a manifestation of the process of thought and raises no further question. But, while the true relation of action to ideals may be precisely what calls this easy solution of supernatural process in question, the problem of the universal validity of standards which are neither inferences from the Natural nor enforced by natural consequences, is as Hegel raised it, and, again, is of the utmost importance.

3. Morals is more than rule and resolution

What truth is in the theory is once more to be appreciated

only as a reaction from Rationalism. In theory, Rationalism regarded morals as stern resolution on formal, legal imperatives; in practice, it was negative and incapable of inspiring any generous or boundless ideal: and in both it lacked serenity of spirit. In contrast, Spinoza saw, in his own way, that the servant of the Lord should not strive. The solution he offered was extension of contemplation from finite distinctions to the harmony of the Infinite: and this intellectual love of God, as alone virtue and blessedness, he offered as peace. Though this is the peace, not of victory but of being hypnotised into mere unity, it still contains the truth that morality is a new creature, a new creation by a new outlook and not by a series of resolves according to imperatives.

These three conditions—the interaction of all things, universal standards of absolute quality, a relation of peace to the eternal order—may not be overlooked in considering this problem of necessity and freedom: and no solution which ignores them can satisfy. Because it has these truths in it, Spinozism has reappeared in many forms. Leibnitz's monads are a mere variant; McTaggart's planetary system of souls merely replaces one substance by one system, which badly needs something to systematise it; Prof. Lloyd Morgan is merely Spinoza turned biologist. Hegel, in spite of his heroic attempt to escape from Spinoza's pretence of mathematical demonstration which merely returns upon itself, by creating a new logic which may have room for struggle and failure as the way of progress, aims also at peace in the arms of the universe, and secures it also by determined metaphysical process. Nevertheless, so long as this is set over against the striving of rationalistic deism, it is always illuminating, and often convincing.

(c) NECESSITY AS FREEDOM

The solution offered by all these schemes alike is that necessity, widely enough contemplated, is freedom. The question now before us is how far this accords with our experience of a world which is a challenge and an adventure, in which the way of failure is broad and the way of victory narrow. The system has room for any amount of evolution, but has it any place for the only kind we know, which is by what we choose and follow, and for the only means at our disposal, which is by individual hazard? The question, in short, is whether the scheme exalts necessity to freedom or merely reduces freedom to necessity. This is again the problem of the individual, but it is with new emphasis, because it concerns the responsibility and worth of his freedom.

What Hegel meant by "the truth of necessity is freedom", is that the necessity is more and more spontaneously from within, and less and less imposed from without: and this is the only possible idea of freedom in a system of determined cosmic process.

But the real problem of freedom is not that by becoming products of a higher environment we win independence of a lower. It is still more, how we win independence in the higher. Even if necessity were wrought from within to the extent of making us wholly independent in ourselves, it would still be only the appearance of independence. The reality would be determined place in the system. The result might be far more wonderful and stable as part of the whole operation of the Supernatural as Universal Reason than as the mere impact of motion, but necessity is not turned into freedom merely by changing it from fixed mechanical to fixed mental process. Freedom is not mere emancipation from the outward dominion of the Natural. It is also by our own choice and determination, our own responsibility, which may be for evil as well as good, in face of the Supernatural.

Of all problems this may be the hardest, but once again we have no right to determine what exists by what we can explain. We have to take what we find in experience: and what we find there is that, though we cannot be free in falsehood and brutality and doing our own gross pleasure, we cannot be free by any kind of influence which merely makes us shun them, or which merely implants in us correct facts and amiable sentiments and decent behaviour or even the highest truth and beauty and goodness. We are free only as, in independence, we choose truth and beauty and goodness as at once our most real world and our genuine selves. On such freedom all worth in either our world or ourselves depends.

(d) RESPONSIBILITY

Our first question must be what meaning, if any, can be given to responsibility, if there is no other freedom than what we may call an intellectually emancipated necessity.

Conceptions of necessity, we have seen, only arise with free ideas and as tools for our freedom. This alone should show that freedom is not even the highest kind of necessity. Yet necessary laws are such effective tools that nothing else is so convincing to our understanding. The moment, therefore, we use the understanding on the question of freedom, answering dialectic by dialectic, we are apt to be drawn into a quantitative, which means a necessitarian, answer.

On this scheme of supernatural process the necessity is of character; and freedom is understood as meaning the absence of any other determination such as the mere diagonal of impulses. We are asked what action there can be except action according to character· and there is a sense in which the significance of any action is that it reveals the character. But, if our character is just the manifestation in us of the process of the cosmic reason, it is as much determined as it would be by mechanical impulse, and then there is no reason for regarding the Cosmic Reason as other than itself determined.

Determinists, such as Calvin, have thought that they could regard God as free, with all his creatures under the necessity of his will, yet responsible to him. But, if we have no experience of freedom in ourselves, we have no reason for believing in freedom in God. Nor can all Calvin's great subtlety of argument avail to persuade us that we can at once be the helpless tools of omnipotence yet responsible for evil; nor does his burning religious conviction that the glory of God requires all things and all persons to be determined by his decrees, deliver us from the sense that such a God is not a father but a process.

This McTaggart accepts, but seeks to give a place to the individual by conceiving the cosmos as a system of souls. As order depends on the system, he does not attempt to ascribe any responsibility of the soul to God, if there be a God. In any case, as God includes all, he would just be the system. Nor does McTaggart attempt to ascribe responsibility in any direct sense to the soul, which just is what it is. But he considers that responsibility still has a meaning and a practical utility: and, as he is a worthy successor of Calvin in subtlety of dialectic, we shall not do injustice to the subject by limiting ourselves to his arguments.[1]

The first question is what character, in such a system, means. Natural disposition is one thing, and character, if it be moral achievement as well as moral asset, another. Wherefore, if it be all determined, we should not speak of being determined by our character, but of being fated by our disposition. But, as Cervantes says, "Everyone is as God made him, and often a great deal worse". Disposition is as God made him, character the better or worse he makes himself. And this is so because, as Cervantes says in another place, "Everyone is the son of his own works", which could hardly be, if his works were merely the necessary outcome of what he already is.

In that case the primary responsibility is for our character, but what is it if we are fated by disposition? Responsibility to ourselves, McTaggart says, is merely from the sense that what we are is ourselves, and not from any possibility of making ourselves different. Remorse is not because, being what we are, we could have acted otherwise, but is distress to find what poor creatures we are Apparently it is a sort of pain taken from looking at one's bad teeth, merely because they are bad and not because of our neglect; or it is as a wife might be ashamed of her husband because he is hers, though she knows she cannot alter his ways. But remorse for the predestined is rather an unfair thing for predestination to cause, and surely we ought to reason ourselves out of it.

Responsibility to others he takes to be merely a recognition

[1] J M E. McTaggart, *Some Dogmas of Religion*, pp 141 ff

of the right of society to punish us, if we are objectionable members of it. The old idea was that a sheep-stealer was hanged because he might have chosen a better occupation, and there is a more modern idea that it would not be justice at all unless this were reasonably within his power. But apparently the man was a predestined sheep-stealer, and the sole ground for hanging him the inconvenience of losing one's sheep; and this is the less adequate as a reason that this inconvenience also would be predetermined.

Responsibility to God he thinks is not to be admitted on any view: for supposing it were any advantage to make a man free, if God is omnipotent, he could also have made him perfectly secure.

On any scheme of pantheistic process, as God is just everything, he is responsible for all and nothing could be responsible to him, but McTaggart supports this his real reason by argument about omnipotence. As omnipotence ought to be able to create a creature it cannot destroy and then destroy it, it could surely unite perfect freedom with perfect security.

But, even if, to be omnipotent, God must be able to make black also white, he might not choose to do so, and it would be a doubtful improvement on the world if he did; or omnipotence might have a good deal of meaning without being all-inclusive potency. Jebb says that it was the glory of Pericles to be able to rule men with wills of their own: and to be able to do the same, we might think, would at least not detract from God's omnipotence. But apparently, to be omnipotent, he must cherish the mind of a parish beadle who thinks nothing rightly done unless he does it himself. Then we might, like Tartarin on the Alps, have the joy of adventure, with the assurance that a benevolent arrangement made accidents amusements: and were this the actual universe, the secure working of process might have something to say for itself. But the actual world seems to be for those whose joy in climbing is real hazard precisely because it is an adventure of freedom.

Here we have the essential question. What, McTaggart asks, is the gain of freedom which could compensate for its possible ills and calamities? The answer depends on whether we prefer a living leg which can suffer and break, to a weldless steel tube which can do neither. Is not freedom the gain of spirit over force, of value won over compliance imposed, of truth we have ourselves seen because we sought it at the risk of calamitous error, of beauty we have appreciated because we triumphed over baser satisfactions, of good we have ourselves chosen because we faced the world, the flesh and the devil? But escape from this hazardous adventure is the attraction of all pantheistic process. Its real appeal is not to reason, but to the great mother-complex of humanity. What it offers is the serenity of the unchanging when our view is wide enough. The system of souls is only a rather poor substitute for Spinoza's one Substance, and the tendency to amelioration, which is illogically cherished, would joggle it out of order as much as a tendency to degeneration. The only security is of mere system, and that is secure only in absence of change. But there are minds to which it is a very powerful appeal that, the more appearance is change, the more reality is the unchanging.

Hegelianism, being a philosophy of change, may seem to offer another kind of peace by guaranteeing that change will be progress. Yet the security is still because the change is merely from the potential to the kinetic. In spite of all effort to show how this may be an adventure, venture does no real business. Hegelianism is all a philosophy of history, but it is with striving and calamity and all the hazard of strenuous or slack living emasculated into a necessary stage of a process. In one sense, we could admit that the process of reality is the same as the process of thought, but not in this way of providing intellectual peace by thought as an abstract potentiality of all things, which, out of its mere form, effects such change as creates a universe, and gives moral peace merely by feeling ourselves carried in the arms of the universal reason.

(e) PROCESS AND EVIL

For us, unfortunately, this shining goal of hope is shadowed by the sad fact that, in the only evolution towards it we know, many are called, but few chosen. Whatsoever chances or deliverances there may be outside of ourselves, the victory of freedom has such appalling casualties that many besides McTaggart have found it hard to see how it could ever compensate for the loss and pain and evil which it at least allows, if it does not cause. Nor is he the only one who, in face of this kind of evolution, asks, why this waste? Why should each individual struggle upwards with a liberty which admits of multitudes falling down disastrously when their hearts fail them or pleasanter paths attract them? Why not have carried the whole crowd in their places upwards on a secure cog-wheel railway of cosmic process?

Unfortunately the loss and the pain and the evil are there: and, unless the compensation for them is in freedom itself, there is no interpreting the universe, by us at least, as rational: for, if calamity is not the reverse side of enterprise, of the hazard of achieving the heights, but belongs to process, it is ineradicable from the universe as such. The world we know, if it is wholly a necessary process, is a cog-wheel railway, but the result as we know it is unhappy for its passengers at the best, for it seems to have the fixed habit of spilling them into the abyss. And being process, how can it amend? In contrast, the way of freedom, though its final justification can only be its goal, at least saves life from being a dull as well as a ghastly nightmare, because, with it, there is a universe of living interests while, without it, there would be no more than a Punch and Judy show with conscious and sensitive puppets. And supposing an infinite mind contemplating it, could we expect him to be eternally interested in making it pirouette around him, however graceful and intricate he could make the performance? Calvin's predestinarianism, Leibnitz's monads, McTaggart's planetary system of souls are nothing more: and it is all as ghastly as it is dull. Nor does Hegel's process of Reason add

EVOLUTION AS A PROCESS OF THE SUPERNATURAL

anything to its cheerfulness: and his buoyant optimism naturally ended with Schopenhauer's pessimism. Though Hegel's idea, that in history we see in the furnace what is now built into life as cold and commonplace, was a great contribution to the whole method of studying history, in the end real history has no place in his intellectual construction. What masquerades as history is a show staged by dialectic, not history as a record of man's slow, laborious, often mistaken, constantly discouraged learning from experience by the real hazard of dealing with environment.

The Supernatural is an order of freedom, not only in the sense that its sacredness means the right to be recognised as the sole absolute worth, in loyalty to which alone our own worth can be realised, but also in the sense that it is ours to reject as well as to choose, and that its worth cannot be merely implanted, but is worth only as it is of our own free acceptance. Even a life manifesting all the requirements of the Supernatural, yet in accord with them only by process, would be still a mere natural order, or rather not natural but mechanical. However we may explain it, we can only live rightly in the Supernatural by a character won by a freedom which is free to be false and base and corrupt as well as true and gracious and good.

With this independence, we do not return from the possibility of choosing the higher merely to the lower. If we renounce its victory, we fall back, not to the wise instincts, the unconcern and fitting action of the lower creatures, but to positive falsehood, and gross delights, and doings that are vicious, and the deliberate sacrifice of others to our passions and our greeds. In short, we return to the unnatural, not the natural. We only abide in the Supernatural as we choose it, but this shows that the Natural is one thing as steps upward, and another, even at the same point, as a glissade downward.

Wherefore, even more sharply than truth, beauty and goodness, error, coarseness and wrong-doing raise the question of the true nature of our environment. This doubtless is what ought to be, but the quality of it appears in the permission of what should not be. That the Supernatural is not only an order of freedom in which we are free as we belong to it, but that we can only be in it by a freedom which may reject it, must be itself the most illuminating fact about it: or if this be too dark and difficult to be called illuminating, no view of our environment can be right which ignores it as a fact or which makes it less than a positive choice of the lower in preference to the higher sphere offered us.

When we call this rejection of the higher 'sin' we are using rather a theological term than an ethical. But this is right, if we are dealing with a wrong relation to environment, and not merely with crime or shortcoming against a legal enactment. It is not the breaking of any kind of law that is at stake or an irregularity or slowness in a process, but a failure to be worthy of our highest environment. As our question is the significance of this fact for our knowledge of the true nature of the Supernatural, this theological aspect of it as sin is our concern: and its relevancy for this end appears from the fact that all theories of sin are theories of the Supernatural.

(*f*) NATURAL PROCESS AND ITS THEORY OF SIN

Theories of sin, being nothing less than theories of the universe, their proper classification is into Naturalistic, Pantheistic, Acosmic-mystical, Deistic, Theistic. About the Theistic alone is there any perplexity, because, as it covers vastly different conceptions of God, it covers vastly different ideas of sin. But here we are concerned only with the first two.

The ease with which this classification can be applied may come mainly from the fact that theories of sin are mostly intellectual constructions, to fit into views of environment held on other grounds, and are not derived from consideration of actual human experience. But this does not prevent success or failure in accounting for the actual fact being a crucial test of any view of the world, of the Supernatural first and the Natural afterwards.

Even on the view of the universe as physical process, it must be admitted that there are some rampant lies and degradations

EVOLUTION AS A PROCESS OF THE SUPERNATURAL 293

and brutalities, which, not without a measure of plausibility, are called sin.

This is ascribed to irregularity of development. But natural law, as Naturalism understands it, allows nothing irregular. All is determined, and neither direction nor distance can be astray. Irregularity means that insight has gone ahead of mastery. But this is impossible if organisation is the outcome of mechanical law, and insight of organisation. Moreover, there is no right to speak of better or worse, but only of more or less fitness for the struggle for existence. No reign of purely physical law has any room for sin as disloyalty to the true order of the universe and to our true nature as part of its process. It cannot account for anything being esteemed good or evil, and still less even for the illusion of choosing between them.

But it may be said that we have to do with a natural evolution in any case, and that this, however we conceive it, does away with all the absolute distinctions between right and wrong and duty and disobedience, upon which anything resembling the old idea of sin could be based. And so far as theories of sin were theories of an immediate creation in the image of God, and of transgression of absolute imperatives adequately proclaimed by conscience or revelation, they are disposed of by this change of outlook. Yet no theory has any right to affect our view of experienced facts. It cannot determine that there is nothing ideal in life by a material account of life's origin, or that no value is absolute because the approach to the experience of it is shown to have been slow and hesitating, or that, though our responsibility is only for the stage at which our evolution has arrived, its claim may not be imperative.

First of all, we must take seriously the idea of evolution It is not a mere question of slow change, but of direction. Absoluteness of particular acts may be affected by slow realisation, but not the absoluteness of the direction in which we are facing. In the end this must put right and wrong as infinitely apart as the old way of expressing it as heaven and hell.

In that case, evolution itself makes absolute distinctions precisely by the effect of change. If there is a continuous change for better on the one hand or for worse on the other, the roads are as absolutely different in direction and in the end the goals as infinitely apart as any categorical imperative could make them, so that, although in a different way, we have as much right to speak of the radically bad. The idea of evolution changes this radical difference from an act to an attitude, but certainly takes nothing from it.

All evolution of life is by venture on a higher environment: and this process can neither be reversed nor stereotyped. Life may have started in the water, but the creature that has learned to live in the air, if it return to the water, does not become a fish but a corpse. Even to keep where it is, the creature must courageously maintain what it has gained or it disappears. Thus, even in the Natural, turning a deaf ear to the call of the higher is a crisis and not merely a deficiency.

This may be regarded as a natural law, but if, through all life, the challenge of environment is always in front as a call and an opportunity and a bar of judgment, the Supernatural is only a higher bar of judgment by being a sacred call and a decisive opportunity.

Thus, while we are responsible only for our stage of progress, if it is progress into an environment which is of absolute value, our responsibility for our own stage also becomes absolute.

For our whole judgment of sin it is necessary always to bear in mind that what ought to be never presents itself as something we merely ourselves manufacture, but is always there waiting to be realised. This aspect of our own higher evolution would seem to show that no evolution is creating higher environment, but that higher environment is the perpetual challenge in front which makes evolution possible, and that loyalty or disloyalty is determined, not by the measure of our progress, but by the quality of the environment of which our evolution has made us conscious.

EVOLUTION AS A PROCESS OF THE SUPERNATURAL 295

(g) METAPHYSICAL PROCESS AND ITS THEORY OF SIN

Metaphysical Process, or in other words, Cosmic Pantheism, resorts to various devices in explaining sin. Particular ill is universal good; or it is a necessary negative stage of the Process of Reason; or evil is a necessity of finiteness as such.

As this is all a logical construction, it only needs a logical refutation.

Even were particular ill universal good, if it is the individual that suffers the pain and the degradation, and the universe that enjoys the good, reason, even as a process, might have been expected to deal more fairly. We may regard pain and struggle as a necessity for achieving good, and the possibility of moral evil as a necessary condition for choosing good in a way that makes it moral, if, for the true worth of the universe, the moral individual must be self-governing, with an independence which must be won and cannot be simply given. Then, we may see that to correct our sins at the moment of their production and suffer them to have no evil consequences, so that we never learn from the harvest how to sow, might be the end of all hope of realising it. We may then go further and see that, if this is to be a commonwealth of good, it might be universal good that all moral beings should live in an order affected by the iniquities of others as well as one in which each is responsible for the effects of his own. But this means a place for the individual which no process of Reason can allow in its universe and continue to be wholly process.

So far as this system is concerned, therefore, this explanation resolves itself into the second view that evil is a necessary phase of the cosmic process. We have already dealt with Hegel's doctrine of the negative, by far the most original form of it. Here we need only add that, while we can understand why there is pain in striving and remorse for sin if the purpose of the individual is a real agent in progress, no explanation of it as of necessary process of which the individual is only a vehicle, can make this other than a useless callousness and cruelty. Nor is there any reason why process should ever change its ways and give us a hope of blessedness beyond: and, as a historical fact, pantheism is always changing from the cheap optimism of saying all is good to the equally cheap pessimism of saying all is evil.

This explanation, therefore, also passes into the next, that evil belongs to finiteness as such. Why persons should suffer and do wrong as no other creature does, merely from being finite, does not appear evident, more especially as they are plainly less finite So far from sin necessarily belonging to the finite, if, as on this scheme, nothing is more than superficially finite and all is the unfolding of the World-Spirit for its own artistic satisfaction, and individual mind is only the mirror in which it reflects itself, there would not seem to be any possibility of pain in the process and much less of moral evil. What is assumed, while it is denied, is an individual who is in some true sense isolated in the universe, having his own struggle and being in charge of his own destiny, and a universe which is only to be understood aright by him as he determines his purposes in it, losing it as he slacks and winning it as he girds up his loins, in short the very views both of the individual and the universe which make any theory of it as the thrust of mere process, even if it be the process of Reason, entirely inadequate.

The only possible explanation on such a view is that evil is not a reality, but only appears to be so from the narrowness of our outlook. If we took the description by itself, it might be expressed in Browning's words.

> The evil is null, is nought, is silence implying sound,
> What was good, shall be good, with, for evil, so much good more,
> On the earth the broken arcs; in the heaven a perfect round

But Browning's verse is not to be taken by itself, for he is speaking of the failure and defeat of the strenuous will and of how, like William the Silent, by constant defeat, it finally overcomes. By turning defeat into victory we can make evil nothing, but not otherwise. To persuade ourselves that it is not there to be encountered is only, as James says, trying to take a perpetual moral holiday. Evil, moreover, whether physical or moral, can only be regarded as unreal by putting all earthly things into the same category: and then there is no environment which either challenges or rewards our enterprise, and God is a mere empty name for abstract unity.

Whether we consider the matter positively or negatively, therefore, we see that, if we are to speak of evolution as organic, whether we conceive this as physical or metaphysical, it is not just development of a structure out of a universe which is merely a potency behind it, but that the emphasis is on function with a challenge before it. The vital significance is the relation of the individual to environment, as freedom in respect of the Supernatural as much as of the Natural.

CHAPTER XVII

FREEDOM

(a) THE WILL TO LIVE AND THE WILL TO LIVE BETTER

Even the question of freedom of indifference, freedom to make a decision without any particular motive except the necessity of following some one line of action, should not be lightly dismissed. Buridan's ass does not stay starving because he is equidistant from two equally attractive bundles of hay, and we do not fail to meet the difficulty of being able to travel only one way at once because we stand at the junction of two roads which are equally attractive.

William James's argument for it is not merely another example of his pleasant habit of enlivening his pages with subtleties. It is both true and important, because it shows that a decision of the will is not a mere wavering of the balance according to the weights put in the scales, but that there is something deeper and more decisive, even if it be merely the will to live.

The will to live is the fountain-head of freedom, and its stream is the will to live better. But this concerns the possibility of living for higher ends and whether we can because we ought.

Though it does not, as Kant seems to think, cover the whole problem, the first element in freedom is the power to set up an absolute claim with which pleasure or pain, profit or loss, convenience or distressful consequence have no common measure. This may be limited to decision between right and wrong in overt actions, and, even for them, may be largely negative, saying, Thou shalt not. But no greater power has been given man than to say no to the flux and passing appeal of life. Wherefore, the power to obey even negative precepts, which moral laws mostly have been, is an essential of positive freedom.

This negative freedom, even if confined to actions, may be decisive for the whole conduct of life and determine in the end much more than actions. Till a man has sinned away this power of saying no, and become flotsam on the currents of desire, his action is not the mere mechanical diagonal of their forces, and such desires as love of right and love of unjust gain are not commensurate in such a way that they could so act. Then a steady course of right choice makes it easier to choose aright again, and the result is character, and not mere natural disposition.

Much psychology to-day finds no such power as volition, action being a resultant of feelings. But, if there is no free action to influence them, the feelings can only be instinctive. By using instinct to include both life impulses—such as hunger and sex, and also the habitual actions of a species—such as nest-building and migration, feeling and activity are confused from the start, though they are probably in some measure distinct even in the lowest living creature. This is then carried up to man, and used to explain the normative quality by which mind determines what is taken to be true and right, and acts upon it. But, if we know nothing except by this normative quality of mind, the right course should be to carry mind down into instincts and not to carry up what we take to be instincts apart from mind to explain away mind's normal activity. At all events, no merely theoretical question of origin can determine that we cannot act on reasoned conclusions, if we know that we do.

Kant maintains the form of freedom to be, Act for reverence alone on an absolute or sacred imperative. If, in the strength of the claim we thus recognise, we can refuse to balance right against other appeals and so stand against every persuasion of pleasure or pain, gain or loss, or any other natural advantage or disadvantage, we can do what we ought. But, while action by reverence for a sacred imperative may be the fountain-head of freedom, if there are no tributaries from other well-springs, freedom is confined within a narrow channel, and so dried up within it as not to be a very free kind of freedom.

The difficulty appears at once with the injunction to act from reverence alone. Against absolute reverence no other motive could have any claims. But while we can say 'Let more of reverence in me dwell', we cannot say, by a pure act of will, 'Go to, let me have absolute reverence'. If we have a supernatural environment of absolute value, reverence, as the sense of the holy, is the way of being free from lower appeals, but we must agree with the theory of the process of reason that this is given, not commanded, and also that it has to do with our whole environment. We cannot even win it by determining to live in the Supernatural, for, while freedom is not possible in the merely Natural, its practical task is to deal with the Natural, and only as we rightly deal with it have we any experience of the Supernatural.

Decision by absolute imperative may be an ideal limit or last ditch in moral conflict, and we may not, against any recognised duty set up a plea of incompetence; yet other people besides St Paul, when they come to 'Thou shalt not covet', find little help in what he calls 'a law of commandments', though the judgment of conscience is primarily on the desires of the heart.

(b) DETERMINATION BY CHARACTER

This brings us back to the question of character. A good tree brings forth good fruit and a corrupt tree evil fruit. Yet character is not a mere gift of nature, and the question is, How is the tree to be made good? Plainly it cannot be by action on a mere imperative. Neither can we, nor should we, directly will to be good. Yet character is the effect of our willing: and this doubtless concerns reverence. But nothing is less directly under the control of our wills, or would be more worthless if merely voluntarily assumed.

Moral girding up our loins and even acting upon a hard moral imperative are at times necessary and may have a larger place than most of us are ready to admit There may be wrong objection to this because it is the strait gate. But to mere unrelieved, uninspired resolve according to a moral maxim, there may be the right objection that it is a strait-jacket. Certainly it is not the liberty of the children of God. Reverence is an inspiration and has a wider range, a more continuous operation, a finer discrimination, a more unfettered efficacy than resolution. At the same time, no man is born in the seat of the scorner. The greatest, even for our purposes, is what we reverence, and not what we resolve, but this too is the fruit, if not of purposing, yet of one steadfast purpose. We cannot, by mere taking thought, add to our moral stature any more than our physical, yet it remains true, as Kant says, that there is nothing absolutely good in the world, a good will alone excepted, and that character is good only as it is the product of a good will.

As we either steadfastly choose the higher or find the upward way too exacting and arduous, we are what we are, and of this nothing is of greater consequence than that our reverence is what it is. If this cannot be amended by mere decision, the reason is not that we have no power to change our characters, but that we cannot do it at less cost than loyalty and sincerity in all our ways. This may be concerned with preferring a higher truth or a finer, purer feeling or a nobler righteousness, yet it is one attitude—uprightness of action coming back to sincerity of thinking, and higher thinking to sincerity of feeling, and sincerity of feeling to concern with both truth and righteousness. Thus a good will works in a circle. But the widening of the circle is its victory.

Kant would bring everything within the scope of conscience as universal absolute reason by the view that we always act on a maxim. This might suggest that every act is deliberate, and, probably, in view of the imperative as he conceives it, this is his meaning. Though not true in that sense, there is an important sense in which it is true. As long at least as a man is a moral being, motive is not impulse as mere propulsion. Nor is action à mere consequence of the strongest motive, but is a choice between being an upright or a satisfied person. Such a choice may not be present as a conscious reflexion, but the enormous importance of what is called a complex, and its tendency to degenerate towards physical impulse, show that there is a central normal choice, because the complex is just what is left outside of one decision in some sense conscious, ultimately about the kind of person we determine to be. However, then, we may explain the lower choice, the higher is not just commensurate with it. The whole character is involved and is made better or worse, not as mere disposition which has its natural effect, but as character which is the fruit of possessing the power of decision.

But this also determines the kind of environment in which we shall live, as well as the kind of person we will to be in it, because it involves a unity of choice as well as of choosing. We cannot will anything except as we set our whole mind on it. But then the decisive fact is what we mind. This is the old question of whether it be 'the things that be of God or the things that be of man'. With Kant we can say, this is by reverence alone. But, though this is for him the sole moral motive, he gives no account of it. Rather, he speaks of it as though we could simply say, 'Reverence man as an end in himself', and then conclude this to be the order of the universe; whereas man has only a right to this reverence, if already, by the order of the universe, he has a value in some form absolute in a world of this quality.

Though there is a sense in which we can because we ought, it is, therefore, obviously not in the sense that we can by mere fiat of will, it matters not what kind of persons we are or in what kind of world we act, do what we see to be right, or even put ourselves in the way of seeing what right truly is.

Freedom, to be truly free, must have two victories. First, it must win freedom in respect to the Natural, both in ourselves and in our world; and second, it must win freedom in respect to the Supernatural itself. With the liberty of the children of God so conceived, no one of us is free. At best we are only being made free. Yet only as we are thus free, are we the kind of persons, in the kind of environment, who, in practical experience, can because we ought.

(c) FREEDOM IN RESPECT TO THE NATURAL

This has to do both with our natural selves and our natural world. The two are not apart. The appeal of our world and the appeal to our natural man are so much the same that the difference is merely of standpoint. We have, however, constantly to consider the question of freedom from the standpoint of ourselves and from the standpoint of our world; and the different aspects are sufficiently distinct and important to be considered in succession.

We begin, therefore, with ourselves. The first victory of freedom, without which no other is possible, is over our natural selves, both in the limits which we cannot change and in the bounds we may pass over.

The freedom without which no other is possible is the dominion of spirit over what the Apostle calls the flesh. Without this, we are not truly individuals and have no real individuality we can call our own. But that is not all. To be true freedom of the individual and at the same time our right and worthy individuality, we must deny ourselves altogether, to possess ourselves.

Nothing can meet the clamour of appetite and desire save the absolute claim of the sacred. But in the mere form of what Kant calls the categorical imperative, it could only rule them if they are well chilled already. Freedom is not by any way of repression, nor are the true uses of our natural selves, or the changes of character which make them still better possession, by mere duty as observing moral rules.

On the one hand, control over our appetites may be an absolute requirement, without requiring us to exalt our meals into the sphere of morals. Though in eating and drinking and all that we do we should do all to the glory of God, it is not in this way of moral arthritis. On the other, while rules may determine actions, and this, in certain circumstances, may be important, mere negative rules of 'touch not, taste not, handle not', are not, as much experience besides the Apostle's shows, of any value against the disturbing clamour even of carnal appetite, and still less of what he calls 'coveting', which is the real insubordination of ourselves to ourselves. And with these lusts of the eye and the pride of life, we must take the fear of reprobation and the desire for approval, and all that dominates us as individuals who are members of a herd. Victory over ourselves herein is not possible by resolution, however courageous, but only by finding a better environment waiting to be possessed. Only as we seek a better country can we leave a worse, even though we must also be ready to go out, not knowing whither we go, as the way of seeking it. This steadfast intentness on a better country of the spirit, and not sporadic denials of the attractions of the lower, is a good will. And it has to do both with what we are and cannot change, and with what we may become and should by right doing be changing.

The need of a higher environment for the exercise of freedom may seem to speak rather of religious influence than moral victory, and to be purely of the Supernatural. But while we cannot be strong to do anything without the wide atmosphere to breathe in, we do not accomplish anything merely by breathing, nor are we strong even to breathe, if we do not exercise our strength. Hence morals cannot be merely quiescent religion, even if it cannot be in vigour outside of religion's world of the Supernatural.

The importance of the other aspect of the Natural, the world which is provided for us, appears in the fact that, great as the significance of what we may become is for all we have to do, even our characters are not a right object of our purposing, and the building up of our individuality is no direct object of striving. On the contrary, freedom in respect to ourselves is leisure from ourselves to serve among our fellows in the world. And however much there be in this world that we can alter, much of our higher life depends on our attitude towards what is quite outside our control Therefore, freedom of spirit in respect to the necessary is an important part of freedom, though this also has to be won and is not given.

The problem of the world, as of ourselves, is that it is both to be denied and possessed Even outward, political freedom in it is not won or securely enjoyed save by those for whom freedom is dearer than life, yet freedom is the only security of any life in the world. There is an inward freedom which is itself a life of freedom however imprisoned, yet we can only cherish it as we are striving to emancipate it from outward as well as inward bonds. We are dependent on natural relations, like neighbourhood, family, tribe, for any moral relation in which we could realise our freedom, yet mere natural relations may be in the sharpest antagonism to any right moral relation, and only as we deny them may we have any right relation to our fellows or any power to fill rightly our sphere and use our opportunity. We cannot disembody any ideal, yet, like our bodies, the material embodiment will drag us down, unless we can exalt and refine it. So it is again with possessions. Unless we have possessions we can misuse, life would be no school of personal responsibility, yet possession is the most frequent cause of the denial of the order in which privilege is only responsibility. So also with civilisation. Throughout all history we find a constant antagonism between the material interests of civilisation and religion, and between their allurements and the purity of morals: and the antagonism is the sharper the more the civilisation is elaborate and the religion higher and the morals enlightened. No higher religion or more enlightened morality has been developed in a lower civilisation. The task of both religion and morals is determined by the challenge to give a higher civilisation a higher soul by which it may live. Yet a complex civilisation is seldom concerned with its soul. Finally, in this world, we have no abiding possession, but are strangers and pilgrims on the earth; yet there is no final freedom unless even this fleeting world is in some way possessed by finding in evanescence deliverance from the slavery of the material into spiritual possessions which have the promise of being eternal. Religion and even morality have often attempted to escape from the continual change of time and sense, but then religion becomes mere blank unity and morality mere blank negation.

(d) FREEDOM IN RESPECT TO THE SUPERNATURAL

Freedom in true possession of ourselves and of the world depends upon what is sacred or of absolute obligation; and this depends upon whether we live in an environment which is supernatural as well as natural. Freedom is not true freedom unless it is our own spiritual judgment in face of all in us that has merely natural appeal, nor is it true freedom unless it is our own victory in face both of what is necessary and what challenges our enterprise in our world. But, finally, there is no true freedom unless we have liberty of spirit in face of the Supernatural. And, as we can only find our real selves and our real world in freedom, so also we only find our real Supernatural.

Our dealing with the Supernatural is by the judgment of the sacred and the sense of the holy: and though they are never apart in their working, we shall consider them in succession.

First, then, what is meant by freedom in respect to the sacred?

Hoffding finds the whole concern of religion to be with the 'conservation of values', meaning values regarded as sacred.[1] But while religion has conserved much custom and tradition merely as sanctities, the mark of true and living religion is concern with judging the values which ought to be conserved. Only in its name and by its power have men challenged what antiquity has imposed and their contemporaries revere as sacred, standing alone and often at the cost of daring those who can kill the body.

Both types of religion deal with a world of absolute values. But, to one, what is held to be sacred means what is immune from criticism, and, to the other, what most requires independent thought and care to make sure that it truly is of such value. Though the leaders in this inquiry have been few, and others have followed haltingly and timidly, to them all progress in discerning higher truth and beauty and goodness is due. The reformers of religion, and with it of all else, have been revo-

[1] Harald Hoffding, *The Philosophy of Religion*, Eng. trans. B. E. Meyer, pp. 107 ff.

lutionaries of this type, though in all ages there has been much building of the tombs of the prophets to honour them as tradition and conceal their character as disturbers of the traditional. Above all men they had absolute loyalty to what was judged to have ideal value. But the first and highest loyalty was to the task of judging aright, for the very reason that they denied absoluteness to any human judgment of it.

Because the corruption of the best is the worst, nothing so entrenches any custom, tradition or institution against criticism as ascribing to it sacredness, and nothing has been more used to repress freedom, both by reprobation and by persecution. As this comes from recognising the sacred mainly in material embodiment, the first achievement in emancipation is in making it a free idea with its material embodiment diaphanous. Then the claim of sacredness becomes the justification and the requirement of our own independent judgment, in the knowledge that we are dealing with a sanction in face of which there may be no consideration of aught else, and which is sacred only as it is our own independent judgment in view of its witness alone.

Inseparable from this is the sense of the holy.

The judgment of the sacred, however much abused, may be admitted to be what challenges our manhood to stand on our own feet, forgetting the things that are behind, and reaching onward to what is before. But have any blinkers upon the human mind been drawn so close or any fetter upon human enterprise been so heavy as the sense of the holy? And as awe, as the shuddering of the creature before tremendous mystery, it certainly is not freedom, if freedom means independence.

Kant sought deliverance by deriving reverence purely from the form of the sacred as absolute moral value. But if awe shudders from fear, this kind of moral reverence shudders from cold, the categorical imperative being a dull glow at which to warm itself. Kant here shows the same disregard to the sense of the holy as what gives content to all higher experience, as he does to sensation in his theory of knowledge. Yet we pass from the sense of the holy as mere emotion to reverence as objective regard for what stirs it, as we do from sensation as feeling to its disappearance in information. And there is the same law: the more the impression is an objective witness, the less it is subjective feeling. The same kind of question, therefore, is raised, which is, whether the holy manifests a real environment which has a system of meaning by which what would otherwise be mere sporadic impression becomes of the nature of revealing intercourse.

If this be so, the right use of the sense of the holy is not to be cultivated as overwhelming emotion till all things merge into its dazzling glow, but to be changed into an objective reverence, the witness to an environment of this absolute quality. Only thus is it progress in all finer perceptions and nobler thinking and achievement. Otherwise it makes them merely impious raising of questions.

The sense of the holy may be enslaving, not emancipating, and may impose an abject, not an independent, mind. Though the only way of reaching the highest, like all else in our experience it is capable of abuse in proportion to its possibilities of good: and even when it is not abuse, it may still be stagnation, and not a perpetual challenge to freedom and aspiration.

As reverence, the sense of the holy is the humility which is the fountain-head of all right and courageous independence in seeking truth, and truth only as awe, it is a timid and even a shuddering fear of all enlightenment. As reverence, it is the graciousness, the sincerity, the high responsiveness which gives us deliverance both from the mere pleasing of the senses and the artificial tastes of our time, and makes us both small and great before the austere sublimity of true beauty of form and character: as awe, it is as a cloud of blackness upon the earth and of horror upon our souls, leaving us nothing in which to rejoice, and no spontaneity of feeling by which to appreciate. As reverence, it is the regard for our neighbour and our own souls which gives us independence of the canons of respectability and what we may call traditional divine jurisprudence, enabling us to exercise freely our own judgment of good in face of our own situation: as awe, it imprisons us in traditional rules and formal respectabilities

The sense of the holy is to be cherished as it sets us on our feet in the heroism of truth and joy and following what we see to be right, which is as it becomes reverence. Something similar to it as awe, as the shuddering of the creature before the overwhelming and basilisk-like fascination of fearsome mystery, we may feel in any venture upon a wider and higher environment, and is not to be escaped any more in religion than in any other high adventure. It is the first impression and a necessary beginning. But, as it is there for us to overcome in the physical sphere, so in the spiritual, where it is the high challenge to the spirit to win its freedom in independence of all that dismays. When this is won, it is the supreme emancipation from all meaner fears; and only as it is thus the liberty of the children of God is it truly human and perfectly divine.

The peculiarity of the supernatural environment is that we cannot enter it except as we see and choose it as our own. But, if the work of freedom is in choosing the environment in which alone we can be independent in the enjoyment of our true life, sincerity in seeking the highest has not merely the right to command. It is itself set free from commandment by a higher fulfilment and a higher realisation. Thus freedom is not a succession of independent acts of freedom, but is a clearer, surer, more steadfast choice of the world in which we are free, in feeling as well as will. Only it is then more than feeling. No high judgment of the sacred is possible without high reverence; and it is reverence which, in principle, is the creative factor. But, to be moral reverence, it must be in continual interchange with moral values which, having been detached from the material sacred, are no longer confused with material taboos. Then only can we stand in freedom with a reverence which boldly asks what it ought to revere· and so alone is our world found to be great and our souls inspired to seek after its greatness.

Both the sense of the holy and the judgment of the sacred are ways of living in the higher environment we call the Supernatural, and a right impression and a right judgment, or in other words a right sense of it and a right living in it, are necessary for a right knowing of it. Thus a right response to the highest and a right search for the real sacred—the true, the beautiful and the good, in the wide meaning we have given the words—are necessarily inseparable.

Yet directly no question of truth, beauty or goodness is to be determined by the Supernatural. Nor are they to be determined from one another. We may not reason with our hearts and not with our minds, nor judge by edification, and not by evidence; nor determine beauty on grounds of logic or moral influence; nor decide moral questions by sentiment or profitableness. Religion may not lay down their rules, but also it may not enforce them by external motives. Truth takes on a new complexion when it becomes authoritative dogma, beauty when it becomes the decoration of piety, and goodness when it becomes casuistry with appropriate ecclesiastical awards. Moreover, they become worthless for religion, as well as for themselves, when they are thus from religion. If they are merely enjoined and enforced by religion, we have no test of what the Supernatural truly is. If they are merely commandments of God, they can be no aid to the knowledge of what God is, no ground for saying that he is truth and love and goodness. Nor is there any answer to Satan's insinuation that the best of men serve God only as it pays, if religion directly provide the motive, and right thinking and feeling and acting are not their own reward. We are no more so to defer to religion than to business. If we do, religion becomes business.

Nevertheless, all absoluteness, without which truth is mere useful information, morals mere expedient action, beauty mere pleasing of the senses, is from being in the Supernatural. By no manner of addition of natural values of pleasure and profit can they become sacred and by no manner of exalting natural feelings can they be holy. Nor can we say, 'Treat everyone as an end in himself', unless there is a sphere in which he has this worth: for manifestly he is not so in the merely natural. None the less, only in one way should this be determined by the Supernatural, and that is by living in it in its own order which is freedom. All its worths depend on being freely chosen, and we can enter it only as we are free. The gate may be narrow and the way steep, but we can enter only by our own choice and climb by our own purpose, and know we have found it as we discover that we can do what we ought because a vision of the true, the beautiful and the good is the joy of the Lord which is our strength, and they possess us, and we no longer by hard resolve try to possess them.

In all this it is plain that to separate right acting from right thinking and feeling is to make it not right acting; and also that free-will, as the mere power to act by resolution upon a maxim, is a very inadequate account of freedom. It is all concerned with a good will, but as one attitude of the spirit in face of one reality, which may be described as sincerity before its witness in order to make all thinking and feeling and acting be in accord with it. This is true of all environment, but the peculiarity of the higher environment is that we can only know its witness as we are thus free. We can go wrong through unveracity in thinking, sensuality in feeling or unrighteousness of decision, but all are varieties of the lack of true independence and, therefore, of freedom, this being failure to know a reality which so witnesses in its own right that no other witness has any right before it.

CHAPTER XVIII

CONSCIENCE AND CONSCIENTIOUSNESS

(a) THE SCOPE OF CONSCIENCE

WHILE a physical law is a formulation of what exists, which every exception requires us to modify and which, as a universal law, is disproved by a single exception, a moral law is a legislation of what ought to exist, which is not to be accommodated to exceptions and which no number of exceptions contravenes Also a physical law can be received as a general opinion, while a moral law is a legislation by ourselves, the more reliable the more it is our own judgment and the less it defers to accepted opinion Only as a mark set before us in freedom, has it absoluteness of value and authority. But then it can be the power of freedom to make for a fixed goal against the flood of changing circumstances and their appeals to sense and desire.

But the question is how, in face of any view of evolution, any human judgment can have even a shred of absoluteness. And does not history confirm the doubt? We see the sense of the holy moving on, not alone from one object to another but from one type to another, till what once had sacred value may change into abomination. Is conscience, therefore, more than an impressive name for what is at present approved in practice? Is its halo of sacredness more than a traditional glorification of social sanction—ancestral wisdom at the best, tribal taboo at the worst? If it is continually changing, how can it be the obligatory or more than the convenient? All human progress, nevertheless, depends on setting up this absolute mark, and not fearing disaster in pursuit of it, whereas the sole obligation of enlightened prudence would be to be with Falstaff 'a coward on principle'. Especially, the advance of all human society has been by those who opposed society in the name of conscience, which would have been insane and futile were conscience a mere echo of the voice of society.

Nor, if belief is what we act on, does anyone believe that ideals are mere changing peculiarities of a smooth-skinned biped. We cannot question that, if we think in the right way, our thought will be valid for all minds, and that right feeling and acting have the same validity, involving, moreover, something sacred in man's worth as a person. Nor would there be any possibility of maintaining the ground we have won, and much less of advancing beyond it, unless we could set up an ideal, not as a mere prudential precept, but with a sacredness which makes it a power for fulfilling itself.

As the significance of this is precisely for evolution, we cannot shelve the problem of absolute ideal obligation merely because of the changing. The problem is that its absoluteness has been the footing which, in the flux of circumstance appealing to unstable feeling, has made possible man's special evolution.

The question of conscience so understood is not limited to rules of action, mostly prohibitions, even though the power to say no to the mere flux of impression is the first and greatest victory. It also includes the possibility of a good will, in the sense already given of including right thinking and feeling as well as right acting—mere acting, without guidance from truth as the fountain-head of all virtue and without inspiration by right feeling, not being a good will.

As we need terms both for laws of conduct and for ideals of the whole spirit, it would be a gain if we could distinguish ethics and morals, and not employ them, as in common usage, practically as synonyms. Unfortunately, we also use each term both in the narrower sense of observance of rules, mostly negative rules, of conduct, such as, Thou shalt not steal, or kill, or bear false witness; and for the ideals of all right thinking and feeling and acting.

As this wider meaning is the real scope of conscience or the consciousness of the sacred, and as the sacred is concerned with the Supernatural, we might call it true religion. But this would assume a view of religion not as yet justified, and might even suggest what there is no intention to justify. Failing this, we must resort to the old device of distinguishing words more definitely than in common usage, and confine ethics to the theory of conduct—so that it is parallel with logic as the theory of truth and aesthetics as the theory of beauty—and extend morals to the whole sphere of sacred ideals in all. Should this serve no other end, it will at least enable us to say at once that any identification of religion there may be with morals is in no way an identifying of it with ethics, and that any assertion there may be that the sacred is the manifestation of the Supernatural in no way identifies, after the manner of Kant, the Deity with the exaltation to the throne of the universe of the categorical imperative, and his justice with the equivalence of action and award.

Yet the essential distinction would not be made if we merely gave ethics a narrower application and morals a wider, because, by both we might still understand an obedience which is satisfied to keep within recognised rules. This would only be moralism, whereas morality as here understood is a dealing with the sacred as concerned with every aspect of sincerity, whereby the true quality of conscience is not alone to be an ever enlarging sense of the inadequacy of the attainment of what we see, but also a hungering and thirsting after a fuller discernment.

(b) THE INFALLIBILITY OF CONSCIENCE

But, if this be the scope of morals, can we any longer speak of the authority of conscience? Even ethics, with its universal laws as infallible as reason can make them, has had doubtful success in establishing its absoluteness. How, then, can this be maintained for the pursuit of aspirations only dimly beckoning, and which may have their chief appeal from what lies beyond them still unknown? In face of this, can we any longer say of conscience with Butler that, "Had it strength as it has right, had it power as it has manifest authority, it would absolutely govern the world"?[1] Is not its weakness just its un-

[1] Joseph Butler, *Sermon* II.

certainty? To have such a right, would it not also need to be infallible?

Butler himself did not think so, but, as he has not made plain on what other ground the authority rests, it is generally assumed that he is merely inconsistent. This conclusion the older Intuitional School accepted, and sought to make good Butler's shortcoming by confining conscience to moral principles and regarding them as intuitive and self-evident. Error in moral decision, as well as failure in moral action, was not denied, but it was ascribed to mistakes of judgment in applying principles to particular cases under the perverting influence of selfish and perverse feeling. Thus to the French and the Spaniards the same principle of justice might be self-evident, even though, as Pascal says, there was in practice the comic justice which is one thing on one side of the Pyrenees and another on the other.

But looking is not always seeing and even the self-evident is apt to depend on how we are qualified to see. In order, therefore, to make sure of guarding against error and to convict even the worst sinners of sinning against the light, conscience was affirmed to be innate. This was held to be the essence of God making man in his own image and the true justification for describing duty as the

> Stern daughter of the voice of God.

In accord with this view, it seemed necessary to maintain that conscience could not be educated: and to this contention plausibility was given by confusing education with instruction. Unfortunately, the history of the moral progress of the race, though by no means reaching back to the beginning, goes far beyond the point where it could by any possibility be regarded as a witness to the uniformity of even the most elementary moral principles. Still more serious is the fact that these principles at their best could never be more than a few rigid and mainly negative rules of outward action: and no one who confined the authority of conscience to them would ever come within sight of conscientiousness. If history has any meaning, it might seem to be the education of conscience; and, even yet, is there any more important part of education?

Conscience is no doubt innate, but so is every other faculty, and it is not, for that reason alone, specially infallible. It cannot be instructed, but, while this is of the utmost significance, it does not provide the kind of infallibility which would enable us to say that conscience has a right to absolute authority because it is never mistaken in its verdicts. Reasoning also cannot be instructed, yet is far from infallibility. And, in this respect, it is right to call conscience the practical reason. But that it cannot rightly be instructed, so far from proving that it cannot be educated, is the very fact upon which its education should proceed. Wrongly it can be instructed to accept other people's verdicts; rightly it is only educated as it learns to depend on its own. A point of good form can be settled by information, like the time to catch a train; but to deal conscientiously it is necessary to see for ourselves what we ought to do. To tell anyone what he should or should not do to be truthful and upright, as mere information, is possible and is frequently done, but it is the way to corrupt the conscience, not to educate it. No one else can decide our duty and leave it our own duty: and to suffer our duty to be so determined is, by that very fact, to lack conscientiousness. Even in other departments instruction is not education, but in this it is a usurpation in him who gives and a betrayal of conscience in him who receives.

Yet, so far is this absolute duty of conscientiousness from depending on infallibility of conscience that no one who is infallibly certain that he is right is quite conscientious. To be conscientious up to our light is an absolute requirement, because to walk by our light is the only way of being right, not because, even with its guidance, we may never be mistaken.

For the same reason we should approve the conscientiousness of others, even when we do not approve the verdicts of their consciences. True toleration only begins when we think the verdicts wrong but still recognise that everyone should walk by his own conscience, and not by ours. The reason, however, for this respect for conscience, apart from its verdicts, is not that, if one is conscientious, what he is conscientious about is indifferent, but that a more enlightened conscience can only come from a finer conscientiousness in respect of the light he has, and that there is no other way in which his conscience may be more enlightened. What we have a right to ask from others is not the acceptance of the verdict of our conscience, but a more sincere distinguishing from the pride of their caste and the presuppositions of their traditions of the verdict of their own; and the education of conscience is just into being independent of every other voice except its own, and into a humble yet courageous purpose not to silence it when it makes ever higher demands.

Inerrancy no more belongs to conscience than to any other human endowment. But this does not limit its authority, for, while it does not claim that its verdicts are infallible, it insists on their right to be regarded as sacred. What we take to be truth at once claims our absolute loyalty: and from this we can escape only by finding a higher truth to which to transfer it. Being, in the meantime, our truth, we are true as we hold it against either profit or convenience, and are already false the moment we compare it with any merely natural value. Similarly, honesty concerns sincerity to see and loyalty to follow uprightness, while the most impeccable act as merely the best policy is not honest. Thus, though we are not required to accept any of the verdicts of conscience as final, we should regard all of them as sacred. The highest conscientiousness is in seeking further enlightenment, nor is there any other true conscientiousness. But this very pursuit of more light requires absolute loyalty to the light we have.

The explanation is both the quality of the good will and the nature of the sacred imperative on which it acts. All men are at times faced with decision between right and wrong, in which they may know the right yet not do it. Such a decision may be a watershed for the whole life: and, if it be on the wrong side, may leave only a choice between hardening the heart and lasting regret. But, in most lives, such decisions are rare and become rarer if rightly decided. What is continuous and what most determines the character is the absoluteness of the decision between higher and lower. The imperative of conscience is always to discern the things that excel, and this alone is true conscientiousness, as imperative as to decide for honesty and not theft, and the goals of continually choosing the higher or the lower are as far apart.

(c) THE INDIVIDUAL AND THE CONTENT OF CONSCIENCE

If sacredness is not in the infallibility of our judgment but in the absoluteness of the values with which it has to do, we can see what Kant means when he says that duty depends on a metaphysics not a psychology. But, while any view of the Supernatural as sacred may make duty what he calls a categorical imperative, there is still the question of how far any metaphysics can show what duty is.

With a metaphysics which regards the individual as a mere appearance in the process of the supernatural Reason, manifesting itself in the expansion of sacred values, we can see how conscience might have absolute content, because, in that case, duty is simply metaphysics. The only question then is why our consciences should not be a better mirror of the Absolute Reason. But if, with Kant, we hold the individual to be a true and essential distinction in reality, and his knowing the only knowledge of reality, and his commerce with reality the only way of realising any ideal, and think nothing to be of moral worth except as it is of his own insight, appreciation and decision, there can be no such direct resort to metaphysics. Responsibility both for his rule of life and for obeying it has then an independence which makes an end to the confidence that any individual mind so mirrors the Supernatural.

This distinctiveness, through worth in independence, or, otherwise expressed, sacredness in freedom, we shall call the form of the individual, using form in the technical sense of the character of being an individual apart from the kind of individual he may happen to be.

In contrast to his successors, who thought the denying and

transcending of the form of the individual the security of all that is absolute and universal, Kant derived from it something very like the old infallibility of conscience. Merely by his own legislation, determined by his own worth and a similar worth in others and following his own reverence for this worth, the individual, he held, determines absolutely what shall be of universal application.

The form of the individual, we might say, is Kant's metaphysic of ethics. And, in this, it is like the rest of his metaphysics, because the form of mind as individual plays a similar part in his theory of knowledge. As from the form of the mind of the individual he derived all that gives order to the content of the Natural, so from the form of the conscience of the individual, whose worth is independence, whose sacredness freedom, he derived all that gives moral order and shows experience to be a moral cosmos. Thus, as the form of extension is the ground of exact *a priori* mathematical conclusions, sacredness is the ground of absolute *a priori* categorical imperatives.

The essentials of the practical reason or conscience, which he so derives from the form of the individual as of sacred worth, may be thus summed up. (1) An absolute end: Treat every individual as an end in himself and never as mere means to other ends. (2) An absolute rule: What fulfils this end is a categorical or absolute imperative (3) An absolute test: Test each judgment by its fitness to be a law universal, that is, for all individuals so valued (4) Absolute independence: Our absolute worth confers as a right and demands as an obligation responsibility for our own beliefs and actions. (5) Absolute motive: Act only from reverence for this sacredness alone.

The first and most obvious criticism is that this does not provide more than the generalities of the intuitional school. The second is that its rules also are merely negative in spite of the positive form. They are: Do not treat man merely as a means; do not make your rule of life convenience; do not look at things selfishly; do not be merely an echo of other people; do not obey mere impulse and self-interest. The third is that it provides no way of dealing with the special relations which arise out of the individuality of each of us.

The ideal that everyone shall have scope for his duties and protection for his rights is important for their exercise, but not for their determination. That everyone ought to be equal in respect of duties and rights does not mean that everyone's duties and rights are the same. Though the ruler also is a subject of the moral order, the duties of the ruler are not the same as of the subject; though the parent should reverence his child as himself, his duty to his child is not the same as the child's to him. To treat all persons like ourselves is not to treat them all alike, but to realise that their individuality is theirs and not ours.

In the same way, though we are all required to deny and possess the world, we are not all required either to deny it or to possess it in the same way. The virtue of wisdom is concerned with right dealing with such differences, and wisdom the ancients took to be the sum of all virtue.

When we look down the ages, it is obvious that exactly the same things have not been sacred: and, even for ourselves, there are situations which, under certain conditions, challenge all our consecration, which, under other conditions, are of mere secular import. Obviously the sacred is relative to the conscientiousness of the individual and the significance for it of special conditions.

Here we have the old problem of individuality. Nothing is taught of how we are to treat everyone, not as an individual in general, but as one person in particular; of how we are to fill our own particular place in the world with our own special responsibility; of how we are never to fall below duty yet never to walk in the fetters of mere rules.

Nor is this a merely theoretical objection. This type of ethic sprang from what was the right and high concern of Rationalism with man's freedom, as a responsibility for his own beliefs and action. But it had also the narrowness of outlook and the negative temper of the movement. Hence responsibility for one's own beliefs constantly shrank to the mere superiority of not believing unless overwhelmed with evidence, and for one's own actions to doing nothing except it was required by undeniable rule. There was no humble sense that every truth we miss is spiritual loss and every opportunity we let slip moral failure. Not the sense of high responsibility for all truth and all righteousness but negation, was the crown of emancipation and virtue.

More serious minds, like Kant, set themselves austerely to the task of going as far as reasoning would carry them and the categorical imperative demand, but even they failed to see that these are mere empty forms unless we are humble seekers after the truly sacred in the whole world of men and the infinitely varied possibility of the Natural. There was no sense that truth should be the fullness of all that is, beauty the response to all perfection, and goodness the ideal of all that should be; that finite man, with all his highest knowledge, insight and aspiration, is only reaching out towards them; and that no knowledge, insight or aspiration in all the ages is irrelevant to the task. And the reason was that man's long dealing with the Natural, which is the essential experience for filling the forms of the sacred with the whole range of truth, beauty and goodness, was omitted in the scheme.

Even Kant did not achieve the humility of realising the feebleness of human striving in face of the endless possibilities set before us: and the ordinary Rationalist, with his abstractions at second-hand, had a still shallower assurance of being a superior person, on the ground of what is not believed, not admired and not accomplished, till it almost seemed that the crown of worth would be to believe nothing, revere nothing, achieve nothing. True independence is a search for truth, an insight, a vision, a pursuit of what, as it were, must be caught on the wing. But truth was expected to be a sort of tame domestic animal to be led in on a tether of ratiocination. If there should happen to be truth not amenable to immediate individual demonstration, so much the worse for the truth, and not so much the worse for the person who misses it. But if every truth we do not see is our loss, still more is every beauty we do not appreciate our limitation. While we may not gush when we do not feel, nothing proves so much what we are as what we reverence. If we persuade ourselves, as Rationalism tended to do, that the universe is rather a commonplace affair and we must not admire anything in it except by rules of aesthetics, we merely unite prosiness and pedantry. Nor is it any less loss to miss the fullness of life and service because we can justify ourselves for not seeking it, by its failure to conform to our narrow and mainly negative imperatives.

Thus Rationalism became—what it professed most to despise—a protection against the appeal and challenge of all experience. Its form of freedom, instead of being a call to fill itself by seeking all truth, responding to all beauty, realising in action all good, in humility before the world's vast treasure-store from the past as well as the present, in confidence that it is liberality as well as liberty, was used as though the purse were itself coin. Nothing was more contrary to the real challenge of the movement than this satisfaction with the emptiness of one's world and the barrenness of one's soul, but it is precisely when the challenge is a high demand that it is possible to feel superior in merely having made it.

True freedom is courageous sincerity in face of all reality, but is also humility before its witness. It is freedom as it gives independence of human opinion, but also as it gives reverence for all true human experience, and is the pursuit of truth as the search for all that is real and of goodness as the following of all that is abiding, with the discernment of something beyond both, only to be seen as it is a joy to the pure in heart. In nothing less are we truly free, but also in nothing less can we know what the requirements of freedom are. It requires independence, but, so far is this from the airy vanity of being emancipated, that it would be the most appalling burden, did we not also find in it the one promise of all that is highest and most blessed. When it ceases to be the pursuit of this vision in humility, it becomes a mere pose of superiority to the need of earning one's spiritual living. Thus the rationalist temper shuts off the long, dim, challenging vistas in which we may lose ourselves, by a wall of formal laws, about which the only question is whether it is perpendicular and won't fall, and so is merely one of the ways of evading life's insistent and endless challenge.

(*d*) THE INDIVIDUAL AND CONSCIENTIOUSNESS

But, because a form cannot fill itself, it is not, therefore, of no value as a test of the experience by which alone it can be filled.

If we are face to face with an ordered world, with its absolute values more and more manifest, as the sense of the holy becomes more objective reverence and less the mere emotion of awe, and if the question is not a conscience which shall lay down imperatives but a conscientiousness which seeks more and more perfectly to learn what true values are, the form of the individual is such a test as Kant conceives it. Though the form of the sacred can no more evolve the supernatural order than the form of extension the natural, yet, as correspondence with the form of extension is the test of all natural law, so is correspondence with the sacred worth of the individual the test of all supernatural ideal, granting in both cases that we have experience of an environment that has these forms and that we are concerned to know it and live in accord with it

In his theory of ethics as in his theory of knowledge Kant gives the impression that the form can itself create its content. But unless we are living in an environment in which each individual is an end in himself, it is vain to think him so, as a mere abstract maxim of conduct. What is offered as an inference from morals is already its basis. Granting, however, that there is a Supernatural in which the individual lives as he pursues absolute values or, as it is expressed in the old form, one which requires us to 'love the Lord our God with all our heart and with all our mind and with all our strength, and our neighbour as ourselves', even the negative rule, not to use others as less than ends in themselves, is a valid and useful test. With a positive devotion to sacred values as moral, a positive response to an ever higher sense of the holy as reverence, a positive steadfast, courageous following the highest road we can discern, 'no thoroughfare' is not mere prohibition but positive direction.

Not only Kant's, but all moral laws are at bottom prohibitions. This may be their limitation, but it is also their power. The spring of all man's progress and mastery has been the power to say no to the flux of impression and impulse. By itself, this would have meant nothing; with the will to live better, it was both power and guidance for what might be far beyond any possible conscious aim. As we advance, we see farther, yet we are also more conscious that it is not far. Even the wisest and best see no final goal. On the contrary, it is the quality of ideals not to be final, so that what is absolute can never apply to any verdict of conscience, but only to conscientiousness in following the upward road, to always choosing what excels But on that road warnings against bypaths are true direction. Thou shalt not, for fear or favour, follow falsehood; thou shalt not lose the love of the lovely by taking sensuality to thy heart; thou shalt not turn from the high road of right to keep the sunny side of the street, are rules which, taken as the end, have set up a mere negative perfection, satisfaction with which is not morals but vain moralism. Yet negative rule, as warning against departing from the positive way of high purpose, is constantly the only form of conscientiousness possible for us at any moment, for the good reason that we often never know more than the road which is not to be taken. Wherefore, as long as a positive conscientiousness is giving it content, even the negative test, thou shalt not come short of the absolute worth and independence of the individual, is valid and imperative.

This form still justifies the basis in principle of the insistence of Rationalism on the duty as well as the right of determining our own beliefs and deciding our own actions. Its absolute valuation of the individual as an individual with this high task on his hands and apart from all he otherwise is or knows or possesses, as what Kant calls an end in himself, may not say more than the old saying "Unto this last as unto thee". Nor may the deciding of our own duty impose more than "Fear not them that kill the body". Yet once again we see the importance of stating a truth definitely, systematically and on principle, and not merely as an isolated intuition. When once seen, there is no going back on it. Truth is not truth, received merely as accepted opinion; goodness not goodness, determined by the approval of others; beauty not beauty which merely reflects the taste of our neighbours. Without independence, we may have facts, but we have not truth; we may have fashions, but we have not beauty; we may have propriety, but we have not goodness. This does not provide any ideal by itself, but if we are seeking truth, beauty and goodness, it is the direction which keeps us to the narrow way toward them.

Such direction is not infallible law nor even final norm. But if, in loyalty to the absolute requirement of the sacred, in courageous freedom following its guidance and trusting its power, we stand on our feet and allow experience to speak to us, and if we seek clearly to distinguish its true and abiding reality from its material and passing forms, and to use the world as the corruptible which may have in it the purpose of the eternal, and thus to face experience in all its possible reach, we can hope to find what justly claims absolute value because it is our true environment in which we find our true selves. If this is there only waiting to be discovered, then what it has to teach us, and not our mere rules, is what gives true content to conscientiousness, if there is the sacred form of the independent individual to contain it.

This applies, moreover, to learning from the past as much as to learning from the present. No one builds merely on his own foundation, but on the apostles and prophets of the race. Yet we build only as we ourselves are apostles and prophets, which means as we also deal in freedom with this foundation. Only as we search for the truly sacred and give reverence to nothing else, only as we maintain the true form of freedom as independent and autonomous good will, and do not submit merely to what makes an emotional or edifying appeal, can progress and tradition rightly embrace each other.

We can then understand how our ideals may be concerned with everyday secularities in which no conceivable rule could be guidance, yet be, in certain conditions and relations, of absolute worth, with the worth of our own spirits dependent on it; how much of life may be merely natural, and what is sacred to-day be secular to-morrow, yet, while it is sacred, require an absolute loyalty in view of its significance for our present progress; how none of our judgments may be final, yet any may be absolute; how many of them are from the past, yet the measure of them be their free direction for the future. In all this the goal is the full and all-embracing liberty of the children of God, and the absoluteness of the claim in the end is the absoluteness of the worth of our freedom. Thus the real choice is not between two rules, but between a free and an enslaved self, and between one environment in which we can and one in which we cannot maintain our freedom and victory over the Natural. It is between a self which maintains its independence at all costs and a self bribed or terrorised out of it, and between an environment in which we have security by victory over what is by what should be and one in which we have ease by merely reposing in the arms of what is. Thus conscientiousness is one attitude of the spirit in face of the witness of one reality not only of the attained but of the attainable.

(*e*) ABSOLUTE GOOD AND EVIL AND EVOLUTION

But it may still be asked how even this absoluteness of conscientiousness is to be found consistent with any idea of evolution. Does not the mere idea of one phase moving into another by almost invisible changes make an end of absolute distinctions? Is there any longer a determinate frontier between true and false, good and bad, beautiful and base? Besides, do we not find that these supposed absolute norms have themselves been developed in the course of recorded history?

Without absoluteness, nothing is sacred; if nothing is sacred, there is no real morality; if there is no real morality, progress is a meaningless word; if progress is a meaningless word, change is an aimless process. With this many seem to be content, and yet the absoluteness is there for us the moment we deal seriously with the unrealised. The difficulty arises from what is a frequent cause of trouble, which is a lack of thoroughness in the change of standpoint. While the emphasis is transferred to the unrealised, to the idea of progress, absoluteness, it is thought, could only be determined by a finished standard. But if it is a question of what we are facing, evolution sets the goals as absolutely apart as any infallible imperative of right and wrong.

What this absoluteness means we can best see from the breach of it; and this appears most clearly in relation to an evolving experience.

Sin, regarded as a breach of rules clearly revealed either from within or from without, is a breach of a perfection known and attainable. By some subtlety this could be related to the kind of evolution we have spoken of as elaboration of structure It would be only a metaphor to call it a breach of perfection, but if not a perfection which could have been attained, it would at least be what, for some reason, we might have expected. This, however, leaves no meaning in what Kant calls radical evil.

Similarly in any scheme which proceeds from the idea of the whole, sin is only the ragged edges when we separate a part from the whole. Seeing this is still irregular development, it also explains sin by lack of a perfection which, though not attained, has been seen. But plainly, if this depends only on the measure of our evolution, sin can be no more than undesirable remoteness from hoped-for progress and there is again no possibility of regarding it as radical evil.

But if the emphasis of evolution is on function and purpose, the radical distinction is not in the achievement. It is in the choice of our way and sincerity in following it, and in the quality of the environment which is opening for us.

Then sin is radical evil, not because of any absoluteness in our knowing or doing, but from the sacredness of the environment, in choosing which we realise our true worth, and in rejecting which we turn this possibility into unworth, which must be absolute loss. Thus sin is just the higher aspect of all failure of life to lay itself open to the witness of its environment and to brace itself to venture upon it; and the difference from any other evolution is in the environment of absolute quality of which man has become conscious and in which he may realise in himself absolute worth and failure as absolute loss. This not only makes sin radical evil, but, as a breach with this environment, every sin is a sin against the whole law, understanding by law not a statute, but the order of an environment to be realised ever more fully by sincerity in insight, in aspiration and in consecration.

Thus sin can be used, as it is in the New Testament, for everything which comes short of the only blessed order, which is the whole mind of God; and what makes it really sinful be the insincerity which turns away from seeking it, called in the Gospels hypocrisy. This is the sin against the Holy Spirit, which is another name for every appeal of the sacred. 'It hath never forgiveness', not because there is any sin that cannot be forgiven, but because it calls good evil and evil good, and so turns its back upon the manifestation of truth and the claim of duty, and not merely because it is radical evil, in Kant's sense of the breach of an absolute imperative. Such a breach, once committed, is really for Kant irreparable. Here nothing is irreparable except self-banishment by insincerity from the environment in which the spirit may recover purity and peace.

St Paul is taking the same view when he defines sin as resisting truth in unrighteousness. From this root, he says, springs perversion of the intellect. Thinking themselves to be wise, they become fools, priding themselves on the rankest superstitions and idolatries. As the outcome of 'vile affections', meaning the corruption of all simple and natural feeling, even the body is debased by unnatural vice. Finally, men are given over to a 'reprobate mind', not only doing evil, but approving of it as good, thus setting up a society ruled by evil as a law universal. On this view of sin, as not merely transgression but a turning away from the purpose of realising the whole mind of God, he holds that, so long as hypocrisy is this root of evil, no number of detailed reformations will ever make the soul other than an unweeded garden, and his doctrine of justification by faith is just the assertion that nothing will deal with the situation short of a relation of entire sincerity to the Supernatural.

Sin, therefore, is used for anything which comes short of seeking the perfect order in absolute conscientiousness, or in other words the whole mind of God known or unknown. From it is distinguished conscious transgression. Yet it is sin, not transgression, which should determine our whole view of the question, because it places the emphasis, not on failing to do what our conscience demands, but on failing to respond to the whole call of aspiration and opportunity to be conscientious towards our whole higher environment and what may be realised in it.

No genuine pursuit of truth, beauty or goodness ever thought it was creating its universe. We are not left to a mere toss-up to choose between a Deity who is in process of creation and one about whom we can say he is there to be found if we seek him with a perfect heart. Every ideal affirms that, in some sense, our supernatural environment is more truly active than the world of our apprehension, and is always offering itself as a world to be possessed and not to be created. Therefore, the only final sin is the hypocrisy which is the denial of aspiration after its value and the rejection of the responsibility and service of its freedom. This has to do with the absoluteness of conscientiousness which is never satisfied, and not with an infallibility of conscience which we may overtake and think all our works very good.

CHAPTER XIX

THE IDEAL AND THE REAL

(a) FREEDOM AND ENVIRONMENT

WHEN mind becomes conscious and interprets its environment by reason and proceeds to manage it by considered and deliberate purpose, environment is found to be neither adamant nor putty, but an ordered and reliable universe, giving conscious meaning and responding to conscious purpose. It is an environment the order of which we only discover as we are free, but then our freedom enlarges the more we understand its order. Only as we can stand on our own feet over against it are we able to think it together as one rational universe, but then its scope for our enterprise and its response to our management are endless.

So far as we know, only man, among living creatures, has achieved such intercourse with his environment as reveals this its responsive quality. But awareness of an environment, though a supremely important expansion of it, is not the sole relation: and the reason why any living creature advances may be because it is in this kind of responsive universe however great be its ignorance of the fact

The freedom which is aware of this kind of environment, at once independent and responsive as we are independent and responsive, depends on sacred or absolute values Without them even the most natural experience of the Natural lacks its true human quality. None of our most ordinary experience can be wholly apart from it and remain human, but more particularly, freedom, working with sacred or absolute values, is the only vantage ground from which we can consciously be aware that our environment is a universe. The realisation of it as a complete scheme intellectually conceived is an after-reflexion, but it is first morally felt because of our ideals being effective in it. The fitness of ideals of truth, beauty and goodness to direct human conduct is not all, but a world which responds to them, which, under their light, takes form and unity, a world which opens its bosom as it were to the independent insight of truth and the responsive heart for beauty and the decision of righteousness, a world in which what ought to be is in some way more real than what is, is alone a universe.

But this presupposes more than that the Supernatural is real. The problem it presents is that the Supernatural must also be the reality of the Natural. On the one hand, there is no embodying the Supernatural apart from the Natural, and, on the other, the Natural is ready to become our possession and unfold its treasures as, in the power of the sacred, we stand over against it and above it. Then, the moment it becomes a possession, it becomes a challenge, and this, not by what is in it, but by what is beyond it. We might even say that, as a challenge only, we possess it.

As has been said, the ideals by which we know and conquer our world are not, like the physical laws by which we manage the material part of it, inferences from it, which we are to keep on adjusting to what is, but the essential quality of the standards of the true, the beautiful and the good, is the unrealised which is to be realised: and they cease to be standards the moment any attempt is made to infer them from facts or to adjust them to facts. Yet when we accept their claim and, in the power of it, assert our independence in the face of all happenings, environment does not resist, but only then fully responds Even our natural environment it has enabled us to feel with a sensitiveness beyond the nervous system, to perceive with an insight beyond the senses, and to use for ends far beyond the mere maintenance of our animal existence As our feeling has risen to reverence, the world has had for us higher and fairer meaning; as we have made truth our guide, it has unfolded to us its secrets, as we have walked in righteousness, it has accepted our dominion or given us securer possession of our souls in face of its denial.

We may not say of so vast a universe that all things were made for man. On the contrary, the greatest marvel may be that everything in it has an end of its own to serve, and is made for itself. But we can say that, in so far as man has realised this sacred order, he is realising his true environment as well as his true self within it. And this alone gives meaning to evolution as progress. Progress has no meaning, if evolution is mere adaptation to the struggle to keep physically alive in an environment of value only for that end. What we consciously or unconsciously mean by progress is advancement into a life measured as higher by ideals, which is freer and fuller adjustment to an environment which is also higher because of the larger scope for following ideals.

(b) A JUST WORLD

In some way we must hold with Kant that the Supernatural is the supremacy of the moral order. But what does this precisely cover? Must it mean that, like Kant, we fall back on the old view that the final order of the universe is the exact equivalence of action and award? This would be an efficacious working form of the Supernatural, all the more that plainly it includes the Natural under its dominion, but is it the true moral order, the real Supernatural, or the right relation to it of the Natural?

By affirming a moral legislation with just awards as the moral order, Kant has often been accused of falling back upon happiness as the moral aim and so upon utilitarianism as the basis of morals. But he does not make happiness the basis of morality. On the contrary, he makes morality the basis of happiness, which is a wholly different matter. It concerns the question of a just world: and that cannot be evaded by any theory of morals. The legal view of this justice as law and award may be wrong. In face of history and our highest intuitions of goodness, it is wrong. But a morality which is not a fantastic illusion requires a moral world in which to function; and, to be a moral world, it must, however much it be beyond a merely equitable world, not fall beneath it

How necessary this is we shall see if we consider an attempt at moral theory without it. A consistent attempt to think out the consequences of a world in which there is nothing save the continual skimming of superior persons, as a *crème de la crème*, by survival of the fittest, we have in Nietzsche. Its truth is in being an assertion of the form of independence, but its error is in being a perversion of it which cannot give a morality, and, what is more, which does not even give the non-moral success it promises. The animals whose gifts for life were mainly tooth and claw are found only as fossils in museums.

But Huxley attempted to build a genuine morality on the same theory.[1] He also held that the order of progress was the struggle for survival, and that man has outrun all his rivals by possessing a double-distilled essence of the trickery of the ape and the ferocity of the tiger. Being, however, a sane and common-sense person, Huxley persisted in thinking that kindness and consideration, and even helping lame dogs over stiles, and respect for the rights and liberties of the weak, are virtues, not vices. Yet by what saving conversion man turned his ape and tiger career to affection, friendship, loyalty, uprightness, reverence, humility, we are left to guess. The most extreme Methodist form of it would seem necessary. But this requires another order to be converted into, while here the natural order remains unregenerate. Man, therefore, we must suppose, has arrived at the stage of becoming moral on the business principle of seeing that a success, won by pre-eminence in fraud and violence, might most comfortably be preserved by honesty and consideration. As, however, the struggle for existence is still the way of progress, this betaking of humanity to morality suggests that

> This neither is its courage nor its choice,
> But its necessity in being old.

It is Hobbes's theory modernised by Darwinism, which does not improve its working. To Hobbes individualistic pugnacity was destructive, and concession for the sake of peace was progress, but this is mere retiring from the fighting-line. Nor will it work without what Hobbes called a social contract, such as we call a combine. Even Hobbes's form has been dismissed as unhistorical, though something could be said, on

[1] *Evolution and Ethics.*

his view of it, for regarding civilisation as a social combine to give and take for security. But if civilisation itself is a product of rivalry in fighting for one's own hand with trickery and ferocity, when did it arrange to change its ways?

It is better to have a mind not fettered by mere intellectual consistency than to deny plain facts in order to be consistent: and Huxley is not the first wise and sensible man who has maintained his balance by sacrificing logic. Yet the better way, when facts refuse to fit into a principle, is to realise that the time for revising the principle has come. Holding on to both, *C'est magnifique, mais ce n'est pas la guerre.* To talk of morality in a non-moral universe is vain. The mere claim of any demand to be sacred is a claim that it belongs to the ultimate order of the universe: and in some way this means that the universe is just.

But, as it plainly is not so after the formal and legal justice of the equivalence of action and award, the question is whether this view of moral law is not also as narrowly conceived and as much applied beyond its proper sphere as the view of mechanical scientific law; whether it too has not become blinkers, preventing us from seeing both the fullness and the freedom of our true and complete environment. With abstract law alone, whether physical or moral, we never arrive at more than an abstract force or an abstract regulation. Till we escape Kant's limitation here, we cannot appreciate his contention that only in freedom can we find the reality of the universe, for only then has it the meaning which could make it a universe at all. The question of God is, as he saw, the question of the moral order, but is it the question of this kind of moral order? In the history of religion the question of a righteous order is essentially the question of God, but it is also the question of finding righteousness more than a legal equivalence of action and award. Yet the old need of a just universe still remains.

Kant's Realm of Ends, being measured by his mere negative form of not controverting the absolute and universal, is nothing more than the exaltation to the throne of the universe of this abstraction. But a just universe, so conceived, can be no other than the old exact equivalence of action and award. And as it works with absolute moral values, it cannot stop short of the awards of heaven and hell, conceived in terms of blessedness and misery as nearly absolute as material things can be. It is law, and the breach of law is crime, and the fitting award of crime is punishment.

As this must be by the natural order, which, as Kant conceives it at least, cannot be assured by itself, God must be introduced to look after it: and, as his function is confined to this task, he becomes a mere abstraction of the moral order in the form of the equivalence of action and award.

In spite of Kant's anxiety to avoid any such presentation, such a God is an individual. But just as the whole Kantian philosophy fails to show man as a person, so with God. Laws are laws as they are impersonal, and a judge administers them as he is an incarnation of them in an individual and not a person. The idea of God as a person may be inadequate at best, an assertion only that he cannot be less than our highest way of dealing with him, and not that he is no more than we can conceive as the highest. But the least adequate form of it is that he is one individual, standing over against each of us as other individuals; and the least adequate form of the relation is that we impose laws and he sees to their consequences.

(c) THE NATURAL AS AWARD

The chief reason for this purely administrative view of God and the merely external relation of action and award is that the Natural is regarded as merely added to the Supernatural It is not seen to be so transformed by its partnership as to become other than a merely material award and be itself higher environment.

But, if the sacred manifests an environment which is ever beyond us, and which unfolds endless possibilities of freedom to sincerer feeling, truer thought and a more upright will, progress in realising this higher environment is its own reward, and part of the reward is the transformation of the Natural, so that ever more and more it is responsive to our souls and not merely sustaining for our bodies. Then a just world is very different from a world in which evil action is awarded physical ill and good action physical well-being, and is a world of endless possibilities, in which we live in the environment in which these possibilities may be realised in a higher individuality, which also is a true moral reward.

(*d*) THE IDEAL AND EXPERIENCE OF THE NATURAL

While experience of this environment has to do with a sense of the holy which is ever being refined from awe as emotion to reverence as perception and from the material embodiments of sacredness to true moral values, we determine its content not by absoluteness either of feeling or value, but only by experience of it as we live rightly within it, an experience, moreover, which is largely transformation of the Natural. No high purpose ever conceived itself as the revolt of a pigmy creature of a day against a Natural ruled by the mere compulsion of pure physical necessity, but the higher the ideal the greater the certainty that it has to do with an environment which is the deepest reality, and which, amid all change, gives assured footing in the abiding. Yet it is not there simply as unfolding itself out of the Supernatural. Though the essence and quality of the Supernatural is to be above our present knowing as well as our present realising, it is attainable as a possession and a power only as we continually strive to attain and set the mark still farther forward.

That this is by dealing with the Natural and not by any process or thrust of the Supernatural, or even by any kind of abstract reasoning about the Supernatural by itself, all history, and especially the history of religions, is witness. So much as to conceive life ethically required ages of hard learning; to carry this ethic to the conception of a law of action and award was a still greater and more toilsome endeavour to master life's problems; to see that no really higher ideal can be embraced in any kind of mere law and that its award is just in entering a world of greater burdens because they are greater opportunities is what perhaps no one of us has fully attained. And all this has been by intercourse with a greatness which admits of no finality, but requires absoluteness of loyalty both in seeking to know and to serve its ever expanding requirements.

In that case it is not strange that nothing has less finality than man's judgment of the sacred. Within recorded history, the ideas of the Natural have greatly expanded, but the ideas of the Supernatural have been transformed. Moreover, the Natural, so far as we deal with it, is the already realised, so that we have a science of it at least up-to-date. But the Supernatural is the still unrealised. Nor is it merely that there can be no achievement within it completed and at rest. No development is more important than the continual exalting of our ideals of what the sacred is and requires. Dimly we see that it means the changing of the Natural from being a mere bondage of corruption into being an eternal possession, but were we able to say, 'Here is what is, what has been, what always will be the fullness of the sacred', the world would have no revelation for us any more. Finality, therefore, in this sense, so far from being essential to our standards of truth, beauty and goodness, would be a denial of their endless possibility. Nothing high is ever seen which is not a call to look for something higher. And yet this fact that every sacred ideal is the prophecy of further achievement does not hinder its being, amid the changing, a fixed goal and even a secure achievement, without which experience would be mere meaningless and profitless flux of events, and at least all higher development would lack the stimulus of possession as well as all direction.

If we realise that absolute value is in our environment of the Supernatural, and that this is the realm of freedom, and that we are not free but only becoming free, with freedom as our goal and not our present achievement, we should not be discouraged from seeking a higher response to it in truer reverence, and a higher judgment of it in a truer sacred, or a nobler more adequate conception of the Supernatural, because what was once holy for men has become the ordinary, once sacred the commonplace and profane, once the Supernatural the merely rational or even the irrational We should see that this was the way in which man realised even the Natural, and that, in the material form, he was following the light of the Supernatural. Progress means that what once required high and sacred endeavour has become the ordinary and accepted both in the world and in human relations, while the holy and the sacred have moved on to a higher plane, with the still higher as both promise and power of attainment. The Supernatural thus creates ever greater freedom and is fuller environment for it: and, were we capable of fixing it at any point as universal determined laws, and so lose sight of the challenge to set up and pursue the infinite and eternal, we should no longer be in it. Wherefore the call is neither to faint nor grow weary, even were it certain that we are only a little farther on our way than the most primitive savage. Yet we can know, as he does not, that the direction in which progress is to be sought is neither to accept nor to escape the Natural, but to make it more diaphanous for the spiritual. Even the sacred cannot be wholly disembodied of material form, but we advance as the material ceases to be vehicle and becomes spiritual symbol.

The sole final disaster is to turn aside from this way. That this danger is both great and common the history of peoples and individual experience alike bear witness. It is not that man is not religious, but that he uses religion to evade the enterprise of freedom and is not willing to be the kind of religious person who is ready to go out not knowing whither he goes, except that it is to follow the highest and that this road leads to the mount of wider vision.

It is an essential aspect of all environment, that, in the deepest sense, everyone travels through it alone: and of our supernatural environment that no one is a truly religious person till he realises the utter loneliness of his spirit in it and desires to hear nothing but what it says in this aloneness, and not to seek deliverance except by so bearing himself as a free man and not a slave in face of it that he finds harmony with it to be harmony with all men and even all things.

That religion has often been used to keep men compliant

members of the herd is written large in history, and the ecclesiastical mind still tends to use this measure of its success. Nor is it doubtful that to invest traditional beliefs and institutions and rites and customs with sacredness is a powerful means to this end. But the testimony of history is equally that nothing except religion has given man power to stand on his own feet and hear only what God the Lord will speak, and to face all opposition, all social reprobation, all danger by its requirement and in its strength.

(*e*) THE PERSONAL

But the testimony of history is also that nothing less than the consecration of mind and will as well as feeling will suffice.

One way of uniting absoluteness with advance is to make it all a matter of feeling. All ideals, it has been maintained, are mere aspects of what Wordsworth calls love. But nothing in either the Natural or the Supernatural can be won from the mere idea of love, for the very good reason that love, if it is anything more than liking, is only a short name for the necessity and freedom of all our ideal relations. We only truly possess what in this sense we love. Yet progress has been made, not by cultivating our emotions, but by thinking and acting as well as feeling rightly about all environment. For this reason we cannot separate our experience from our explanations: and this applies to the Supernatural as to the Natural. No ideal is quite apart from our conception of the Supernatural, from our theology, for the good reason that, as our environment is of a nature to be used by understanding, we cannot help seeing it in the light of our explanations. Wherefore, if our theology is perverse or inadequate, we must continue to try to think things better together as well as to experience them more fully and more deeply.

But it is plain that we cannot think the ideal and the real together, as it were on the same plane. If we learn from experience, it is by setting a mark beyond it, yet, if we say the ideal is the real, it is that this mark can be realised.

This standing on the ground of what is and reaching out

from it to what ought to be is only possible for a person, and is in the measure in which he is independent; but this presupposes a universe which responds to such independence and is only really known by it, which means that it also is in some true sense personal.

Such a learning by intercourse has a parallel only in our experience of persons. We know them solely as they manifest themselves through our physical environment, but, through it, they manifest more than the physical, and this again we discern to be not so much a manifestation as the key to all the manifestations. All friendship is a reaching out to the person, who is himself both the revelation and the prophecy of fuller manifestation. Is it not by something similar—something known by experience, but discerned as a revelation and a prophecy beyond it, which yet is the interpreter of all that is in it—that man sets up his ideals? And, however inadequate the description may be, have we any better name for what this manifests than a person?

Even physical reality is made up of units which are, in a definite sense, individual: and from this all the infinite variety of the world is derived. With life we have an individual unity which is not a mere sum of the parts, but is in all the parts. The progress of life is not only an increasing individuality, but is the seeking, on its own, of its noblest place in the universe, and the enlarging thereby of the meaning which the universe has to it as an individual. No form of process as the thrust of environment explains an evolution which is by ever bolder individual adventure upon the meaning of its environment and finding thereby an expanding meaning in it, which affords scope for still higher adventure.

With self-consciousness we come to the more complete individual we call a person. A person has a new kind of awareness of self and mastery over self, and with this an awareness of environment of a kind which enables him to think it together as one universe, and to have a mastery over it whereby it changes to his purpose under his hand and reveals new aspects to his spirit. Instead of finding a hostile or merely dead response, the more he is able to confer, the more abundantly he receives. Seeming chaos is turned to order, seeming menace to a smile to laugh with, seeming obstacles to a challenge to make them the means of victory. Then an environment, which was only pleasure and pain for the advancement of the animal life, becomes a joy, and it may be an agony, for the advancement of the spirit, both alike being seen to be good, if, with Ruskin, we do not wonder at what men suffer, but at what they lose. And is this not because there is always something in all our experiences interpreting itself in a way at least like personal intercourse?

A still fuller meaning we give to the idea of God as a person when we realise that the Supernatural itself is an order of independent persons, an order which we may reject and which only in freedom we receive as our own. Absolute values of truth and beauty and goodness are not dependent on our acceptance of them, yet they are not a mere divine ether, in suffusion in the universe and breathed into individual spirits as a sort of breath of life. They are true and beautiful and good only as they are chosen by persons; and their value is in the worth of the persons who in freedom choose them and are themselves thereby made true and beautiful and good. An order which is thus a realm of the free children of God, and not a theatre of even the most admirable puppets, and has its values in even the imperfect accord of their freedom, and not in the most perfectly correct opinions and gracious sentiment and impeccable behaviour imposed on them, is at least not better expressed by anything less than the mind of a person.

But the full significance of what should be meant by God as a person depends on our success in passing beyond mere imperatives for life and a mere Legal Potentate for its environment. When we pass from fixed imperatives to ever expanding ideals and from legal equivalent to freedom, in an order of freedom which has the reward of placing us in a higher environment, we experience what has no parallel except in intercourse with persons. This ever reaches out to a reality beyond their intercourse, which at once gives fuller meaning to all our experience and a fellowship with what is beyond the mere incidents of our intercourse. Then, still more concretely, we can speak of God as a person who, if he is not the Supernatural, is manifest through it. Nor is this manifested only in the good. If sin is not mere transgression of law, but an insincerity in our whole relation which prevents us from reaching out to the ideals beyond experience by which alone higher environment is rightly understood and lived in with ever growing freedom and emancipation, it also is of the nature of the failure of personal intercourse.

One other experience, if it be real, would enable us with still greater fullness and concreteness of meaning to speak of God as a person. This is forgiveness. In all higher religions the question which has given both poignancy and tenderness to the idea of God, is whether to the sinner there is restoration and peace.

The difficulty comes from the form of freedom. If there is a rejection of an order of absolute value, must it not be what Kant calls the radical bad: and if all good is only what ought to be, can there be any compensation for evil? How then can there be any undoing of it? In any form of process there is no place of repentance, though sought carefully with tears. In any legal scheme, there can only be condonation on promise of amendment or by some kind of legal arrangement. But, if the essence of sin is estrangement from our true environment, there is at least the possibility of forgiveness, in the sense of what we mean by it in our human relations, which is neither overlooking nor condoning wrong, but the restoration, in spite of it, to the fellowship it has wronged. Then we can at least go forward to consider men's thoughts about it with hope: and, if we find forgiveness a real and transforming experience, we shall be able to speak of God as a person with the certainty that we are not merely seeing the reflexion of our own faces, but know that our own forgiveness of others is a reflexion of the highest perfection which is kind to the unthankful and evil.

Yet, if we rest here, instead of making it a starting-point for further search, we can land in as grave stagnation and misunderstanding as anywhere else. Especially, though the place of the individual, as we have seen, is of supreme importance for determining the quality of all environment, the idea of the individual and even of a person can be used as the most barren substitute for our real experience of environment God is merely a potentate with laws and purposes who stands over against his world, as a proprietor over against his estate. Then the Natural is divorced from the Supernatural and the Supernatural is just the abstract individual.

When the Natural is thus excluded, experience has no language in which to speak to us. Hence the great problem is the relation of the Natural to the Supernatural. In the history of religions we shall find it continually in such a form that there is a sense in which the idea of God is secondary to the idea of the world. In fact we do not with any profit form mere ideas of God. We win a true idea of God only as by it we have victory over the world. But this concerns our next problem, which is **the Evanescent and the Eternal.**

PART IV
THE EVANESCENT & THE ETERNAL

CHAPTER XX

HISTORY AND EXPERIENCE

(a) TRADITION

In the sense of being from the lessons of the past, most of the content of all knowledge could be described as historical.

Every living creature is itself a record of the past, and instinct as well as knowledge is in a sense history. But man is distinguished from other creatures by remembered tradition. No one builds anything, not even criticism of what he finds, except upon a foundation already provided by those who went before him. This may be social ideals, customs and institutions, but it has been, in increasing measure, what has been handed down by human memory and then written in books. And, from the beginning, this has had to do with the Supernatural.

Tradition first continued because it was sacred, and interest in the past developed from the concern of religion with the abiding. With the advance of religions, an ever larger place was assigned to remembered tradition, and writing seems to have been invented as a sacred art for the securer transmission of sacred tradition. Finally, all higher religions have sacred scriptures, and in some at least the conserving of tradition developed into a living interest in real history

Like all other human power, however, this can be loss as well as gain. Though tradition is the first necessity for progress, it can also be an enslavement to the past which arrests progress. And naturally religion, being the greatest power for conserving the past, is the greatest also for making it conservative Yet this is only one side, for the greatest power for maintaining tradition as sacred may also be the greatest for assailing it in the name of the sacredness of truth and righteousness

To this importance of the past for understanding the present, Romanticism directed attention and, as an example of the gain, we can compare its organic account of the development of social order with Hobbes's abstract idea of a social contract, which satisfied Rationalism. It clothed cold, dead abstractions in flesh and blood, and gave beliefs, observances and institutions the picturesqueness and dignity of antiquity.

This led both to the primitive type of the authority of tradition which accepts as eternal what is merely antique, and to a criticism of the past such as it had never been subjected to before. On the one hand, the past seemed to offer the shelter of external authority, with certainty of belief and security of practice in a doubting and restless age, and to be the supreme victory over Rationalism; on the other, the appeal to history came into conflict with the principle of personal responsibility for our own belief and action, which Rationalism had set high above question. And, ever since, the individual-rational and the institutional-historical ways of dealing with our higher environment have lived in conflict.

This is a fatal dividing of what is one, and an evading of the vital question, which is, How can we reap larger harvests from the sowing of the past, as we grow, not only in knowledge, but in independence of judgment and freedom of action? Nor is there any sphere in which the question is so insistent as in religion, because it is the quality of genius, and ought to be the quality of religion, to use our historical heritage, not only more abundantly, but ever more freely and by a deeper and more discriminating insight. Nor should there be any conflict if the story of the evanescent is the pursuit of the eternal.

We have no ideals which are from the abstract reason of each individual alone, none that do not embody long centuries of experience in dealing with life But unless we have won standards of value in the present, our heritage from the past is merely the tradition which makes void any direct and immediate word of truth. The excellence of the past we appropriate only as we know how to approve it as excellent in the present, which is as it adds to the content of our freedom without rejecting its form. Hence the historical question is the culmination, not the foundation, of our inquiry.

The value of the past, moreover, depends on the present, in that we do not know the past at all except from its evidences in the present. Any other idea of it is merely an error in perspective, arising from confusing the order of narration with the order of inquiry. Even the grossest obscurantism does not arise from mere prepossession, but much more from the simple and uncritical belief that, because the historian writes in chronological order, he has the novelist's privilege of going back and looking down the ages. Unfortunately, even on the rare occasions when he is an eye-witness of what he reports, he has still no finality of omniscience like the novelist, but is merely a witness, sometimes reliable and sometimes not, to be interrogated in the present with such resources as are now available.

The effect of distance increases this error in perspective. We see an age of faith, because we are too far off to see the doubts which beset it; personalities have authority, because we are too far off to see them as persons; councils are inspired, because we are too far off to see them as mere assemblies of ecclesiastics. The condition which creates haloes is the haze of distance.

Scientifically considered, history is just a theory, true, and only true, so far as it is proved from its evidences in the present. Anything might have happened in the past, and there is no absolute reason why Adam should not have been the first man and lived in a garden, and Romulus been suckled by a wolf and have built Rome, and the first pope been ordained by Peter and been formally appointed to his primacy. But history can only accept what, from its present resources, can be proved to have happened. Romulus might have existed, yet history have to say that there is no more evidence for this than for the existence of Jack the Giant-killer: and any mere tradition, unsupported by evidence in the present, is in no better case. Thus, as a theory of evolution is a kind of historical narrative, a historical narrative is only a kind of theory, which, like any other hypothesis, is to be measured as it most simply and completely co-ordinates the known facts. Therefore, so far is criticism from being an impertinent assault upon secure tradition, that tradition only becomes history as it can endure criticism.

To be empirical, history must be grafted into the present in such a way that we can deal with it as freely and independently as anything immediately before us: and an ecclesiastical scheme of the past has no more right to determine facts by its theory than an evolutionary scheme. The results may be poles asunder, but the attitude of mind which measures reality by theory and exalts theory by painting the background of history to suit, is the same, whether it take itself to be scientific or religious, being in reality neither. History may be what Schleiermacher calls it, the greatest and most general revelation, but this could only be for those who, from the highest achievement of the present, look back upon the past. Even if the tradition be revelation, it is only revelation as it now reveals, which means, as it enables us with more freedom, as well as more insight, to deal with the present. Nothing is settled by saying that there is in religion something traditional and something independent, something inspired and something rational, something of the institution and something of the individual. The question is, how do these things go together? And this is answered only as they can become experiences in the living present, with which we can deal in freedom and by which we can become free because they add to the content of freedom without denying its form. All this is merely to affirm the same method regarding this part of our inquiry as has been maintained regarding all the rest.

To deal with all that experience means for our question would require a discussion of all history. But men's thought about it as found in the theologies of the religions is more than enough to be considered. What follows is not an attempt to write a history of the religions, but only an attempt to discover from them what has been most central in the views of mankind regarding the relation of the Natural and the Supernatural, and more particularly in the form of the evanescent and the eternal. This is a necessary part of our subject, because they are great experiments in living which we may not ignore, seeing we can pass beyond them only by passing through them.

(b) ANTHROPOLOGICAL

That the present determines our knowledge of the past and is not to be determined by it except in so far as the past still lives in it, applies as much to the kind of history we call evolution as to the ecclesiastical. It is the same kind of misuse of dogma as the ecclesiastical, to think that we can determine what has evolved by our account of its evolution. We cannot, for example, say that the survival of the fittest produced everything, and then say that everything must be such that the survival of the fittest can produce it. As men have the same hasty love of finality in all spheres, the scientific view of history, that the past is to be determined from its evidences in the present and that the present should not be determined by any theory of the past, is as apt to be overlooked in scientific as in ecclesiastical theory. Then history is regarded merely as an extension of the theory of evolution, with the present shorn of any glory which makes too great a demand on the theory.

The application of evolution to religion has two forms—the Anthropological and Religious-historical, and by both it may be applied dogmatically as well as truly historically.

The anthropological has in our time most dogmatic authority. First, it meets the present interest in research and the faith, which often goes with it, that, from mere accumulation of facts, light will shine forth. And if multitudinous facts alone could shed light, religion ought to be illumined. But, unfortunately, facts enlighten only as we are able to ask them the right questions: and that depends on the knowledge and insight we bring to their interpretation. Second, it offers the kind of explanation of religion by its origins which the last age most favoured, all its theory being in some form theory of evolution. And anything so intimately a part of history as religion naturally lends itself to this kind of explanation. But again we must remember that a theory of evolution is, like all other theory, valuable only as it covers all the facts. And what these are must be determined by what we take religion to be and not by how we think it originated.

But this does not mean that, at the stage we have now come to in our inquiry, we have nothing to learn from the light which painstaking labour has shed on the early stages of religion. Yet, in using it, we must keep two limitations in mind.

The first concerns the beginning. Looking back from a knowledge of what has come out of any beginning, we may dimly discern what was in it: but we cannot determine what was in it, and much less what was not in it, merely by contemplating the beginning. The second concerns the course of development. We have no right to assume that it does not add as well as unfold. To start from the quarry and say what the edifice will be, and still more what it cannot be, is beyond human insight, both because the potentialities of the stone are only made known by the using and because the building is more than the stones.

Looking back from what religion has become, we have a right to say that it must be rather blear-eyed research which does not find any more in its beginnings than the grossest material motives and the crudest fears. But, supposing that religion had this low beginning, to argue that it must remain the same is like denying that there may be good fruit on a good tree because its roots were first planted in rotting manure. Obviously the result depends on the life of the tree itself, and of this the evidence is the fruit it produces. And, in point of fact, conclusions about the nature of religion are not derived from anthropology alone, but from the perspective given to it by a theory of evolution.

This has been already discussed: and the question is not whether we should begin with this study, but whether it has any place in our inquiry. A man is not necessarily honest because his ancestors were Lowland farmers who bred their own cattle, nor dishonest because his ancestors were Highland reivers who appropriated them from others. Superstitions are superstitions and truths are truths according to what they in themselves are · and this is not to be determined either by their origin or by their development. On the one hand, the highest truths have often had low beginnings; and on the other, the grossest superstitions have sometimes been the debasing of a purer faith.

From this Mr Jevons concludes that "It is a misconception of the function of the science of religion that it can prove anything of the truth of religion one way or the other"[1] If 'prove' means 'demonstrate' we must agree. Nothing can be demonstrated for or against the truth of anything by its history. Yet this does not mean that its history sheds no light on it. Kant's philosophy, for example, is not proved right or wrong by any fact about his life. But the infusion of Scottish blood and the home of a poor and pious saddler did something to make him a different man, and, therefore, a different thinker, from what he would have been had it been Italian blood and the home of a wealthy and worldly nobleman.

(τ) RELIGIOUS-HISTORICAL

This applies equally to the type of historical study for which we have not yet invented any better name in English than the clumsy translation of the German—The Religious-historical.

The truth of religion can no more be determined by its course than a biography can prove from the events of a man's life what he has become. But, looking back from what religion now is, we may find valuable light shed on it by its history, just as, starting from the man himself, his character is illustrated by the way he dealt with the events and circumstances of his life.

The Religious-historical School does not settle its account with religion merely by religion's low beginnings, but recognises that, in this, religion is not different from anything else. Its adherents believe in religious progress as much as in scientific, and even regard religious progress as of unique significance in human history. Most of them would readily admit Schleiermacher's contention that religion is the central interest in human nature and the supreme driving force in human history. Moreover, they, for the most part, accept his view that historical

[1] F. B. Jevons, *Comparative Religion*, p. 108.

religions are organised round some special view of the universe; and all regard them as of quite different value from the Natural Religion of the Deist, which is a mere wraith of scientific and ethical disquisitions. By the conviction that the religions are actual schools of experience this study of religious history has been inspired: and much that is interesting and valuable has been done.

Yet here again we must draw the old distinction between the results of an inquiry and the views based on it. With the general attitude we may disagree and of what has been described as *der kaltblutige Historicismus* we may disapprove, and still have to be grateful for much of the work even of the chilliest.

No general description which could be given would be just to any one writer. But the broad impression made by this school is that history is something more than the prophecy of all that the Supernatural will unfold and all that man's progress may embrace, only to be known as prophecy from its fulfilment. The attempt is rather made to show that every phase of religion so arises out of the conditions of the time that the whole story of religion can be so told in its course, that we might be able to describe it throughout as organic evolution. And it might then seem that from this we can determine what is abiding and what is not, though with the limitation that, as everything is constantly in motion, nothing is abiding except in a relative sense. Thus, on the one hand, nothing is ever admitted to be quite new, but only to be a sort of re-arrangement and change of emphasis of ideas; and, on the other, there is something of minimising all the way along and nothing very inspiring and stable at the end.

Troeltsch, who may be taken as the most eminent representative of this school, dismisses both Scientific Naturalism and Hegelianism as outworn and unworthy of discussion. Yet the general outlook of the school retains something of both as a background. The idea of evolution still tends to be the unfolding of structure by mere re-arrangement of what already exists, not the reaching out of mind to its higher and wider environment.

It is still rather by the thrust of process from behind than by prophetic anticipation and striving for what is beyond. The prophet himself is so absorbed into his conditions that his soul's venture and his world's response seem to have little of new revelation. In short, it is a question of history making man, not of what man has made out of history.

The chief reason at least is that such historical study of religion finds in the religions little more than views of the universe as opinions. And opinions frequently are and can still oftener be explained as being merely a new kaleidoscopic arrangement of the old. But if religion is man's dealing with a true environment, his world expands as he advances, and he advances as it expands. Themistocles said that neither would he have been a great man if he had been a Seriphian, nor his detractor if he had been an Athenian. So we may say that neither would man have advanced if the Supernatural had not been his environment, nor would it have challenged him to higher adventure had he not by his nature belonged to it.

Yet no school has been farther away from the old, rather blatant contention that religion has always been a mere drag on the progress of ideas, or from ascribing progress merely to the advance of civilisation. As its study of religion is both learned and serious, it has seen ever more clearly that higher ideas and ideals are religious, both in their source and in their significance, and that these ideas and ideals are the only abiding bequests from the vanished past.

(d) PROPHETICAL

Though the traditional, the anthropological and the critical-historical ways of dealing with the religion of the past are poles apart in their results, all alike deal with religion as though it were mainly theory or dogma. And for this there is the very good reason that the monuments of past religion, uninterpreted by living religion in the present, hand down little save what we may call intellectual fossil.

Merely traditional religion makes this plain by calling itself Orthodoxy, which can only mean right dogma. Mere acceptance of tradition can be no more than not denying a 'form of sound words', and cannot be 'right belief', if belief mean a living conviction upon which we cannot help acting.

Anthropology, also, as a purely external study, whether of the present ideas of still primitive peoples or of the past of those now civilised, yields only fossils of traditional doctrines: and judging from this alone, Sir James Frazer is right in saying that "Magic, religion and science are nothing but theories of thought". Without illumination from living religion in the present, any living religion that was ever in them is wholly beyond recovery. Hence it is easy to conclude that religion is merely outlived ideas. But, though we may not thus reason from the dead to the living, we can reason from the living to what may have been the life of the dead, at least to the extent of being certain that not even magic, and much less religion, ever was mere theory of thought when alive.

The Religious-historical School, being both learned and open-minded students of history, would, in theory, at once admit that religion is much more. Yet, in practice, religion is very little more even to them than theologies, and their explanation of progress in religion constantly shrinks to mere change of opinions, different rather in arrangement than in substance. Thus the history of religion comes to be presented, not as a long endeavour to know a higher environment by learning to live rightly in it, but as a series of curiously confused speculations, which gradually come to be better ordered.

Nor does any kind of history of religion by itself provide more than theologies: and there is a sense in which no other history of religion is possible Moreover it is a very important history, the most important of all human records, when, from the life of the present, we can see in it man's long, long thoughts about the permanent and the evanescent in his experience. Then the theologies are no mere intellectual statements about the Supernatural, but are at least relics of the faiths by which men have sought so to live in the Supernatural as to have victory over the merely Natural, either by escaping from it or by winning from it some abiding possession. The living faiths, as they kindled man's hope and enabled him to face overwhelming events and set up ideals in dealing with his unideal fellows, would be the true record, were it there for our reading. Instead, we have mostly to be content with creeds about them; and even the meaning of them we may know imperfectly and understand less. Yet it makes a vast difference in understanding if we keep it clearly before us that, so far as theologies ever were alive, they were not intellectual inferences, but the outcome of the greatest of all experiments, which is the endeavour to live rightly in our whole environment—natural and supernatural, the seen and temporal and the unseen and eternal. Whether this was at any time rightly endeavoured is not to be judged by speculative consistency but by consistency in dealing with the world's problems and hazards.

Only as we try to look over the whole course, from the highest point we have reached by the best use of history and experience, can we hope to gain such understanding. Nor will even this suffice, because the direction of the road is only to be known by what lies still beyond the highest achieved, even the world of freedom which ought to be. To stir the anticipation of it is the essential work of prophecy: and all true, we might almost say all living, religion is prophetic.

Even from this vantage ground, much of our study of the history of religions may still be stumbling amid shadows. Yet we shall not doubt that it tells of the growing knowledge of a higher environment, known because man is assaying his powers to live in it: and we shall not, for all his gross blundering, lack some measure of esteem for his search. Nor can we fail to have some confidence in the reality and worth of the environment which challenges him to undertake a task at once endless and absolute.

Then we shall know what is relevant for our inquiry amid the multifarious facts of history, as a biographer does whose subject is still alive. How the subject has come to be what he is tends to be of prophetic character, by reason of the insight it gives into the man himself and his possibilities. And a like prophetic character belongs to all true understanding of real religion, because it is the essential quality of true religion to go against appearances and to reach out to the unrealised.

Yet just because, looked at from the prophetic standpoint, the history of religion is seen to be the story of the achievement of freedom by finding in the Natural the eternal meaning and purpose of the Supernatural, it has all freedom's hazards, and is no story of even, guaranteed progress. And the greatest hazard is of bad religion, because bad religion, by misusing the absolute sanctions of the sacred, may turn into the worst enemy of the freedom which is the goal and measure of true religion. Error, then, becomes mere divergence from the orthodoxy of the tribe, with the absolute sacredness of the true turned into the absolute authority of the accepted.

Were it the first consideration that there should be no divergence from what God knows to be true, and correct belief more essential than the right way of believing, or were action as God judges proper, anyhow done, better than truly conscientious behaviour which comes short of it, man's long groping amid error and evil would be a mere scandal of God's inefficiency. But if seeing truth is essential to its worth as truth, and deciding right to its worth as righteousness; if all spiritual possession, to be true possession, must be won by the soul that learns to be in accord with it; if this freedom is an essential relation to the Supernatural as well as the supreme possession of the Natural, not only religious history, but all history may manifest meaning and purpose, and its course be so confused only because a large part of it tells how men weary of the long and strenuous endeavour, and how the power who rules over men and societies never suffers for long any resting-place on this road. On this view of its goal, man's devious way has moral if not rational justification; while, if it is to be measured by the extent to which he is guarded from error and evil, it has neither.

CHAPTER XXI

CLASSIFICATION OF RELIGIONS

(*a*) STANDPOINT

EVEN a classification of religions merely by distribution and date, going from China to Peru and from the earliest known antiquity until now, shows how universal and ceaseless has been man's concern with the burden and pressure of the unseen, and how it has been for him like the burden and pressure of the water which buoys up the swimmer. Religion, however, is so much concerned with value that such a treatment of it leaves us little more than the camel's pride, whose supercilious aspect, the Arab says, is due to knowing the hundredth name of God, while ninety-nine only are known to man.

In any case a classification by value is necessary for our purpose: and precisely our question of the relation of the Natural to the Supernatural provides its principle, and our method of doing the best we can with such knowledge and judgment as we can command is the justification for applying it.

Any classification by value must be judged from above: and the first question is our right to assume that we stand on any eminence which entitles us to undertake the task. Though we may pretend to escape this assumption by arranging religious ideas in a logical or ethical order, even this requires a standard either of the true or of the good, which means that the course is judged by what is taken to be the goal. But does not this assume that our standpoint is something of a Pisgah for looking over the promised land?

Three reasons, however, justify the attempt

The first is that there is no use pretending that we can look out upon the world from any other standpoint than our own. As has, through all this study, been maintained, it is the merest illusion to think that we can transfer ourselves to some absolute standpoint or do more than look out from the highest standpoint we can reach with our best equipment of knowledge, experience and ability.

The second is that, if we are honest and inquiring persons, the position we occupy is the position which seems most to have approved itself to us. Therefore, even should we speak from a particular religion, if this has approved itself to us as the best we know, we could not be freer in any other, or even in none. The utmost we can do is to judge with our best and most sincere and instructed judgment· and this we exercise, not by coming down from such conclusions as we have won to the plain of studied nescience and suspense between yes and no, but by considering all our inquiries as inquiries about the validity of our own views, with readiness to alter them should new light on them require it. Thus a classification from our own standpoint may be at once what alone is possible for us and a test of where, in the end, we have to place our allegiance.

The last is that if we look to the positive marks of progress we may, without excessive vanity, have some reasonable assurance of the right to regard much in the past as at best stages towards even such an outlook as we have attained. Measured negatively by the minimum of follies and crimes, what we may too hastily call the savage state compares favourably with the highest civilisation. There are baser and more degrading civilised idolatries than fetishism; there are among us economic injustices more unjust and in the end more brutal than among the head-hunters, savage promiscuity is not as vile a market of human beings as civilised prostitution. The noble savage of the eighteenth century has since then rather had the gilt rubbed off by greater familiarity with his ways, yet our larger life provides, if not grosser materialism, something much more unnatural and debasing· and perhaps the savage has nothing to teach us about unscrupulous selfishness or evil dexterity. That the Western World is entitled to say 'I am Sir Oracle, and when I ope my lips, let no dog bark', is, we may admit, in any case too freely assumed; and if progress is to be measured by greater security, in a garden of Eden better walled around against the Serpent that whispers of knowing evil as well as good, with no other dangers than stagnation, it is baseless and not merely over-confident.

But if progress is to be measured by positive good, by a fuller awareness of a higher environment and the possibility of a juster relation to it and greater achievement in it, with a clearer call to adventure into the open, we can hardly question our advantage. Nor is this called in doubt by the fact that evil is thereby made more definitely immoral and degrading, for the more definitely immoral quality of evil is itself a mark of progress, being made possible only by rejection of recognised good.

This test of progress as achievement, or still more as the recognition of higher possibilities, is, more than anything else, the standard which gives a religion its place in any classification according to value.

At the same time, though we may, with this positive standard, classify religions with some degree of confidence, it does not follow that this will enable us to arrange them in any order of even upward evolution: and the best we may be able to do is to put our dependence upon the past in some kind of better perspective.

(b) INTELLECTUAL AND ETHICAL PRINCIPLES OF VALUATION

Before the Romantic Movement introduced the idea of historical progress, religions were divided simply into true and false. A true religion was one possessing the revelation which gives correct theological and ethical information. Though Orthodoxy found this in a special inspiration and Rationalism in the light of nature, both alike assumed that the standard of truth was correct idea, all difference from which must be error. Therefore, while all religions might be false, obviously only one could be true.

As study and intercourse increased the knowledge of other religions than Christianity, this sharp dichotomy was seen to ignore the many shades between the blackness of error and the white light of truth. As some religions were at least **truer than** others, religions were arranged in an order of value by the amount of what was regarded as truth in this sense of the right information which could be extracted from them, as a mine is measured by its ore and the rest regarded as waste.

Not till Schleiermacher, under the influence of the Romanticist interest in variety and individuality, protested against this dividing into gold of rational ideas and alloy of absurdities, was there any attempt to study the religions as individual and organic.

The other great Romanticist thinker Hegel classified the religions according to value in the order, Natural Religions; Religions of Intellectual Individuality; The Religion of Absolute Spirit. This is merely a form of his conception of evolution as cosmic rational process mirrored in the human mind. As a scheme it is rather for drilling facts than for analysing them: but, as an affirmation that religion is the most essential factor in the creation of rational experience, it has never had full justice done to it.

Though Schleiermacher did not attempt a classification, his view of the religions, as special intuitions, has proved more directly helpful than Hegel's in the study and even in the valuation of them, because from him can be dated all serious attempts to grasp them as organic wholes. Moreover, he made plain that other matters besides ideas were important for progress in religion.

The whole of religion, he says, is the sum of all relations of man to God, apprehended in all possible ways in which man can be immediately conscious. Each religion is thus a special intuition of the infinite, the whole in some sense always present, but appearing differently grouped from each point of view. "The only way for a truly individual religion to arise is to select some one of the great relations of mankind in the world to the Highest Being, and then, in a definite way, make it the centre and refer to it all the others."[1] Thus the centre of Judaism was retribution, and of Christianity reconciliation. From this it follows that religions are divided into higher and

[1] *Speeches on Religion*, Eng. trans., p. 223.

lower according as they have or have not founders, because a religion without a founder lacks an original, inspiring, creative idea, while a religion with a founder is precisely one which has as its source such an intuition. Moreover, all religions with founders have written revelations, whereby the creative moment of vision continues to work against the tendency to deaden, stereotype and formalise.

While all these intuitions are real, they are not all equally central: and on this difference religions, might be classified according to value And as reconciliation is the true centre of all other relations to God, Christianity, of which it is the organising intuition, is religion raised to a higher power, a religion of religions, and not merely a religion among religions.

Hegel's idea of Christianity as the religion of Absolute Spirit means much the same. Moreover, both alike might be said to rest this finality on the central nature of reconciliation, with the same idea of religion as the way to harmony. Hegel's idea of reconciliation is intellectual harmony with the universe; Schleiermacher's is artistic. Schleiermacher tends to reduce religion to mystic oneness, and Hegel to metaphysical oneness. Yet, for all this difference, for both alike reconciliation is such a harmony with the universe as assures peace. Neither gave any due place to religion as a practical relation to environment, or to reconciliation, not merely in thought or feeling, but as an actual victory over life's evil and evanescence. By thus overlooking the active task of reconciliation in relation to the Natural, both emphasised the mere idea of unity in such a way as to tend at least in the direction of pantheism. Thus in the end both Hegel's rational cosmic process and Schleiermacher's aesthetic mysticism, though they evoke very different feelings, are in idea not very far apart. As any classification of the religions on the basis of either would be on this idea, it could still be described as theological.

But the study of the religions turned attention to their concern with life: and in consequence the principle of valuation tended more and more to become ethical on the basis of Kant's moral view of religion. The fundamental distinction was between Religions of Nature and Ethical Religions, as made by Tiele: and the aim was to show that the history of religion is the story of raising for the Divine the ethical temple of universal humanity.

The first objection is that we do not thus arrive even at morality in the large sense we have given the word, but only at Kant's ethical legalism, with universality as the standard of its imperatives; and the second is that, while a religion must have a higher morality to be a higher religion, a religion is a faith and not a morality. Even morality becomes more than ethical rules of action just by reason of a faith which gives it a kingdom which is above law, and which sets it free, not only from law, but from all striving and crying. This is the truth in Hegel and Schleiermacher, and we may not lightly set it aside and return in this arid way to Kant. Religion is primarily a peace and not an energising, even if it be an active peace of victory and not a passive peace of contemplation

Siebeck seeks to make good this defect by adding to Tiele's division Religions of Redemption. In this class he includes only three religions—Buddhism and Neo-platonism as negative religions of redemption, and Christianity as the one positive.[1]

At first sight this seems to be an advance, because it recognises the most essential element in religion. But to find redemption only in the highest religion and nowhere else, is to miss what is characteristic of all religion Not the highest only, but all religions are religions of redemption. And what distinguishes religions most of all is the kind of redemption they offer, which is, in other words, their conception of the relation of the Natural and the Supernatural.

(c) A NATURAL AND SUPERNATURAL PRINCIPLE

All religions are both theological and ethical because redemption has to do with being redeemed both into the Supernatural and from the Natural, and this always carries with it a special kind of dealing with the Natural, which depends on the special kind of faith in the Supernatural This distinguishes all

[1] Hermann Siebeck, *Lehrbuch der Religionsphilosophie*, pp 50–51, 101 ff.

religions both from mere speculation and from mere rules of action.

What marks a religion is its faith: for even morally, a religion is distinguished not by its ethical practices, but by the faith on which it bases the conduct of life. Yet that this faith is always concerned with some mastery over the evanescent in the Natural, by means of something at least more abiding in the Supernatural, distinguishes it from opinion and even from dogma.

As genuine mastery can only be by what is real, we have still to say that the first question about any religion is how far its theology is true: and, from this, it might seem to follow that we ought to return to the old theological classification— Animism, Polytheism, Pantheism, Dualism, Monotheism. And certainly the religions are much more distinctly set apart by these differences in their theologies than by such a difference as natural and ethical. Even Buddhism is still primarily a concern with the Supernatural, if only as law and not as Deity.

The criticisms of such a purely theological classification might be met: but, even if it could be made logically watertight, it carries no cargo. As the really important mark of a religion is the attitude towards the Natural, no religion is marked mainly by mere theological ideas as ideas. The attitude towards life which the ideas represent, and not the holding of them as mere dogmas, is what makes them religious. Moreover, it is the fact that the religions are convictions in face of the Natural which gives value to their history.

A plain example of the difference is the doctrine of immortality. As a purely intellectual opinion, it can be assailed by an argument like dependence on a corruptible body, and it can be defended by an argument like the unity of the soul which has not parts to disintegrate; or it can be dismissed because death is 'the country from whose bourn no traveller returns', and led home again in triumph because Spiritualism has established communication with the other side. But when we meet it in the religions as the faith which has been, negatively, victory over the fleeting, and, positively, the power of an endless life, it is not held by reasoning at all. It is the achieved conviction that what has absolute claim has eternal validity and that life is so emancipated by this loyalty that it is no more bound to time and sense. Then, just because it is a long experiment in right living, it may not be dismissed by mere argument.

A still plainer example is the idea of God. It is explained as merely the projection of man's highest ideals. But 'projection' is a question-begging word, because it assumes that our ideals are mere human preferences. Suppose that the ideal is in any way, even the most empirical, the reality of our world, would belief in God be made more certain by being divorced from it? What gives value to the history of man's search after God is just that it has been for firm footing amid the flux of changing impressions: for what could be better evidence that his search has not been in vain than that thereby he has won victory in large measure over his world and seen beyond it the challenge of spiritual heights to be possessed, still only on the far horizon? As has been already said, it is not a mere question of the world as it is being God's, but of what God signifies for the world. Thus, in Christianity, faith in the Father and the victory over the world which makes all things in it work for good are one—the world's evil being faced in the faith and the faith being proved by turning the evil into good. And equally significant is the fact that Buddhism, which is the one religion that has no concern with God, is the religion which has most renounced all idea of victory over the world by any kind of possession of it.

Thus monotheism, in the mere sense of having only one God, can go with all kinds of religious types; and the value of the faith is according to the religious type, and not according to the mere intellectual achievement of saying, God is one. Man could, in some sense, say this from the beginning when he happened to be thinking of unity and not of anything that divided it. But it was not in any sense that makes all experience reliable and ordered: while true monotheism is just a faith won in pursuit of this end.

Deism and theism, for example, may not seem far apart merely as theories. But we see them to be wholly different attitudes toward life when we consider how they arose and how they are maintained. The Deists established their view of God by inferring from the world that it is the best of all possible worlds. The prophets won their faith, in face of the certainty that this is a very evil and calamitous world, by finding in God the meaning of it and the hope beyond it which gave them the assurance that it was, even in the moral evil which had to be conquered and the material evil which had to be used for this victory, one moral sphere and one spiritual end. And this faith they held by finding strength for their tasks and peace of heart in spite of the stress of conflict. Thus, while deistic monotheism was only a metaphysical idol, to be worshipped in comfortable circumstances, the prophetic monotheism was victory over the world and possession of it in all circumstances.

To this central significance for any faith in the Supernatural of the way in which it is won and held in face of the Natural, the whole history of the religions bears witness Nor does it concern merely the manner in which the Natural and Supernatural are related, because the way they are distinguished is equally characteristic. When the Supernatural is submerged in the Natural, we have idolatry, when the Natural is submerged in the Supernatural, we have pantheism; when they are set sharply apart, we have deism; when they are related by some kind of moral victory, we have at least some kind of theism.

Looked at in this way, it is plain that the theologies are different conceptions of redemption from the evanescent. By itself, the Natural is the evanescent, and what man seeks in the Supernatural is the abiding All religions, even the lowest, seek some kind of redemption from the evanescent, though it be only an effort to fix natural good. Therefore, the problem of all religions is the evanescent: and their quality is determined by their way of dealing with it. But their way of dealing with it is their idea of the Supernatural: and, in this sense, the dea of God is secondary to the idea of the world. As the evanescent sets the problem, man's relation to the Natural is primary. While strictly there is no before and after, in principle the moral aspect of faith is before the theological. What makes a history specially the history of religion is the theology, but this is religious only if it is a theology of redemption from the evanescent. As this combination of the attitude to the Natural and the theology of the Supernatural gives its specially characteristic form to each religion, it seems to be the natural principle on which to classify religions according to value. The test is, then, the worth of its view of redemption, measured both morally and theologically.

Like any other principle of classification, this can justify itself only as it succeeds in introducing order and in simplifying what otherwise is chaotic and complicated. Yet there are limits set by the subject itself. It is easy to impose an order of the most rigid application, as Hegel does, but it is much more difficult to discover an order which manifests itself, for this may not, in any perfect measure, exist.

In the first place, though the religions are distinguished broadly by their conceptions of the relation of the Natural and the Supernatural, the principle does not divide religions sharply from one another, and it also shows that no progressive religion is strictly one. But, as Siebeck says, the most important element in any religion is what it is tending towards. And, more particularly, it is so for our purpose, which is not to note the conservative elements, but to learn what man has discovered of the eternal in his environment from strenuous living in face of the evanescent.

In the second place, no principle, even if it be comprehensive, ought to show an order of even progress if no such even progress has taken place: and part of the right function of a classification might be just to make plain that there is more than one direction of change, and this not necessarily towards progress. We shall find great difficulty in placing certain religions. and one of the chief uses of our principle of division will be to make clear that there is more than one type of religion, and that it is a problem of the utmost difficulty as well as importance to determine which is the true line of advance. With these reservations the following classification is offered.

(*d*) A CLASSIFICATION ON THE NATURAL AND SUPERNATURAL PRINCIPLE

I. Redemption by seeking the abiding in the Natural through faith in an animistic force indefinitely many and vaguely one. This includes all primitive religion.

If any religion could be called a religion of nature, it would be this. Yet, even this deals, not with nature itself, but with a potency in nature which is also above it, at once universally diffused and in its whole effectiveness localised in particular objects. Even at this stage, religion is, in some sense, ethical. Its moral commands and its moral awards may not appeal to us as ethical. But, as we have seen, it is not the business of religion to provide a full and right understanding of the scope and application of morals. What it does is to place morals in the sphere of the sacred. And no lowest savage, nor any primitive man we know of, ever acted towards himself, his fellows or the world about him, as though the Natural were his sole environment. If we are to call it a natural religion, therefore, it should be only in the sense that the blessedness is measured by natural good and that its ritual, which is mainly magic, is concerned with persuading the Natural to be both more propitious and more permanent, and not in the sense that it regards nothing beyond the Natural.

II. Redemption as the management of the Natural by faith in the Supernatural conceived as individual spirits who rule over various parts of the Natural. This includes all polytheisms.

The conceiving of gods in man's own image used to be regarded as the origin of all religion, and was often assumed to be also the end. When perplexed by this uncertain world, man, it is said, thought of wilful beings like himself behind it. Then, from political unions and other causes, he arranged them into families, taking different names to be synonyms for one deity, and so, by reducing their numbers and setting one over the others, arrived at monotheism.

If God were merely a question of theology and not of practical victory, this might be plausible, but, even then, it would not accord with history, which tells us that it was a great and difficult victory for man to conceive gods in his own image. Polytheism is far from being the simplest of all stages of religion to understand. Why did man thus break up what he must always have known to be in some sense one experience? And this is the greater difficulty that, however we explain it, at least Polytheism Proper has always gone with great progress in material civilisation and with very remarkable advance in mental culture.

III. Redemption either by accepting the Natural in its wholeness as the Supernatural, or by excluding the Natural wholly from the Supernatural, as illusion.

The former, which is Cosmic Pantheism, differs from the Religion of Nature more in dialectic than in faith. Its unity is the old diffused power, its way of dealing with life magical; its oneness of all things a sack to hold primitive animisms and every other kind of belief.

The latter, which we can call either Acosmic Pantheism or Acosmic Mysticism, alien as its idea of the Natural, as all misery and all illusion, is from the primitive mind, nevertheless arrives at this conclusion because it judges the Natural purely by natural good, seeks to get back to the mere sense of awe, and regards the Supernatural as a mere self-enclosed unity, which are all primitive characteristics, differing only in being conscious and reflective, and not instinctive and unsophisticated.

IV. Redemption by distinguishing sharply in the Natural the secular from the sacred, and in the Supernatural the power of good from the power of evil. As this is dominated by the idea of the material sacred, redemption is primarily by observing ceremonial laws—ritual and ethical. Therefore, all this class of religions could be called Legalistic Dualism, though, as the good in the end triumphs, it tends to be monotheistic. It includes Zoroastrianism, Priestly Judaism, and, because of its general nomistic form, Mohammedanism.

This type of religion raises very clearly the question of a just world, as well as of just acts, but it still measures justice by the polytheistic conception of what is good in the Natural; and, as this is material, it is still concerned with taboos, and very imperfectly distinguishes the ritual from the ethical, setting moral goodness and wickedness so far on a level with ritual purity and impurity that both are observance of ceremonial precepts. Thus its essential character is ceremonial-legalism.

V. Redemption as reconciliation to the Natural by faith in one personal Supernatural, who gives meaning to the Natural and has a purpose beyond it. This alone is true monotheism, because it alone embraces all the Natural in God's meaning and purpose. It includes only Prophetic Judaism and Christianity, so that, if we unite them, we could call it all Prophetic Monotheism.

No religion is wholly of this order, and it may be that, if we looked deep enough, we should find something of it in all religions, or at least, throughout the whole history of the religions a reaching out towards it.

As no religion is hermetically sealed against any kind of religious influence, neither the above classification nor any other is absolute. But the first advantage this has over those which deal with religions as systems of ethics or systems of theology is that it keeps before us the essential fact about the religions, that not one of them is concerned with mere rules of conduct about the Natural nor with mere systems of ideas about the Supernatural, but that all are concerned with the environment in which man lives and by which he lives if he is to live rightly, their faith in the supernatural environment never being determined, at least religiously, by mere theory, but always by the exercise of it in face of the natural.

The other advantage is perhaps not essentially different. It keeps before us the fact that no religion deals with the Supernatural apart from the sense of the holy and the judgment of the sacred, neither of which is ever exercised altogether apart

CLASSIFICATION OF RELIGIONS 371

from the Natural. Moreover, as a religion advances from awe to reverence and from the material sacred to the ethical, the effect on the conception of the Natural is as evident as the effect on the conception of the Supernatural.

As this double interest belongs to the essential nature of religion and nothing so distinguishes the religions as their characteristic ways of dealing with both, something might be said for the general scientific value of a classification based thereon. But here it is sufficient justification that it serves our special interest in the relation of the Natural and Supernatural, and, in particular, that it brings out the fact that there are two types of development. The primitive and mystical is one, and the polytheistic, legal and prophetic the other: and this deeply concerns our subject, because it depends on views of the Natural, either as the veiling or as the unveiling of the Supernatural. In other words, the former seeks the eternal in one unchanging reality which the evanescent as illusion only hides, the latter in the meaning and purpose of the evanescent itself.

Long and possibly clumsy titles, however, would be required to bring out this double aspect, so we shall simply divide into Primitive, Polytheistic, Mystical, Ceremonial-legal and Prophetic, understanding, however, that each includes a special attitude towards the Natural as well as a special conception of the Supernatural. Thus a primitive mind is as much manifest in its primitive view of the Natural as of the Supernatural. Polytheistic might seem to be the least adequate term, being by derivation theological. But it is plain that there is just as much a polytheistic attitude towards life as a polytheistic theology, and that neither is apart. As no better term seems to be available, it will serve if we bear in mind that this interaction between practical attitude and theological thinking is what is signified.

CHAPTER XXII

THE PRIMITIVE

(a) BEGINNING AND ORIGIN

In seeking to get as far back as we can, we should keep apart the questions we have already distinguished as the beginning and the origin of religion, meaning by beginning the earliest form in which the religious interest manifests itself, and by origin the rise of the interest itself.

No facts known to us carry us back anywhere near even the beginning of religion. Though, upon such as we know, speculation may possibly build a fairly probable hypothesis, it is misleading to identify theory, even if based on facts, with actual proved facts themselves. Yet this identification alone gives colour to the idea that we are informed how religion begins.

The origin of religion is not within the range of history at all, but is merely further speculation beyond the already hypothetical conception of its beginning. And this is still more dubious when the origin assigned is also some kind of speculation, such as reasoning from shadows to belief in souls. Apart from this belief being too universal to be due to mere reasoning, reasonings of any kind are unlikely explanations of primitive ideas. Animism, totemism, fetishism or anything similar might be early, if not the earliest, manifestations of religion, granting that there was already some sense of the holy, some judgment of the sacred, some belief in a reality beyond the senses waiting to be manifested. But of the origin of the response to the Supernatural we can say no more than of the origin of the response to the Natural, that it is from environment to minds akin.

All that history can possibly deal with is the beginning: and even to an absolute beginning no research brings us anywhere near. Nor are we likely to make much out of such beginnings as we know, if they are summarily disposed of as gross superstitions and delusion or the 'whole monstrous farrago'. This is merely a relic of the unhistorical standpoint of Rationalism, which is the more wonderful that in religion in particular the savage is supposed to reason to his follies in the manner of an eighteenth-century philosopher.

(*b*) HISTORICAL PERSPECTIVE

As everything now comes under the sway of evolution, we might have expected religion to be recognised, among other forces, as an element in progress. But it would appear to be man's chosen field for being stockish as a mule or for working off his crazes. And religion undoubtedly is the most conservative of all forces: and the rationalist judgment, that what is retrograde is wrong, is useful in its place. The place for it, however, is not history, for there it merely becomes a cheap way of saving inquiry. History has to recognise that to conserve is a very important part of progress, and that for this, the importance of religion can hardly be overestimated. But history has also to recognise that religion can be the most revolutionary as well as the most conservative of forces. Either interest may be used to produce bad religion, yet neither provides the least justification for condemning religion wholesale either as stagnation or as craze.

Part at least of the cause of this judgment is due to the readiness with which savage religion is, without criticism, taken to be primitive, merely because it has not progressed. But, even if we find something similar in the early stages of religions which have progressed, we may not forthwith assume that it ever was the same, any more than, let us say, blood when coagulated is the same as in circulation.

Another part of the cause is what we have spoken of as the structural view of evolution, which makes ideas and ideals wholly its effect and not at all its cause. As soon as we see function to be first, we understand Hegel's view that the structure of our thought and of our society is built of the ideas and ideals which were fashioned in mental and moral conflict, of which religion was the supreme inspiration.

This may seem a very large assumption with which to approach anything so crude as primitive religion. But, if we are dealing with the beginning of the history of man's faith, and if his higher faith is the spring of all his higher ideals by giving him understanding of his highest self and his truest environment, can we start on any lower plane? Is this reverence for man's poor groping face to face with the Supernatural, which is at once his perplexity and his hope, other than the necessary attitude of humility before the possibilities of reality? Are the dullest, most routine, most restricted notions the true measure of any possibility in the universe?

Ugly, irrational, immoral facts abound in the history of religion, and they should neither be ignored nor ascribed to something other than religion. But to interpret them fairly, we should consider them in historical perspective. Then, in many cases, it will appear that evils which religious conservatism has retained were once progress and that their evil is only seen because a purer religion has arisen to condemn them. For example, temple-prostitutes were an abomination to the prophets, but even to-day there are savage tribes among whom they would signify restraint. The sense that any licence is monstrous when connected with religion shows the success of religion in laying the foundations of the family and a higher social order As another example, there are very obtrusive facts which justify Sir J. G. Frazer in speaking of religion's blood-stained track'. Yet, if we look at the same facts in historical perspective, it is not difficult to see that they justify Mr Farnell's view that religion is the spring of all regard for the value of life.

Again, regarded historically, it is not to the discredit of religion that what is scarcely wrong in a purely natural state undisturbed by higher emotions and higher claims, may become calamitous iniquities when done in defiance of a higher nature and consciousness of the requirements of a higher environment. If the splendour of man's noblest success belong to religion, it is only part of the nature of all possibility that the enormity and ghastliness of man's failure should also belong to it.

Evils have had great power and long life given to them by being regarded as sacred. From the nature of its absolute claim, while religion is the ground of all that is truly good, it is also that alone which makes anything radically bad. These higher possibilities of evil are among the clearest evidences that, at no stage at which we know him, is man the product of the merely Natural.

(c) RELIGION OF NATURE

The type of religion we are now to consider is sometimes called the religion of nature. As all religions spring from a sense of awe which the merely Natural does not stir, demand loyalties which mere natural preferences cannot require, and look to some order more enduring and purposeful than the mere succession of events, no religion can be described strictly as a religion of nature. Yet we find now, and we may assume it for all races at the beginning, what, for two reasons, we can speak of as a religion of nature. The first reason is that redemption is looked for in the Natural, and not from it; and the second is that the unities are only fixed unities of apprehension, and not free unities of reflexion, unities fixed in their experienced context, not unities capable of being compared and combined

The first point is that, though the Natural is, by its very quality, the evanescent, this was a late discovery, and the simplest mark which distinguishes higher from lower religions is that the lower religions seek permanence in the Natural, and the higher know that no quantity or quality of it can give satisfaction or afford security. The second point is that, while it was the footing religion gave man in the flux of experience which enabled him to set free his ideas, this was a long and laborious, and, to this day, not always successful task, and that all understanding of primitive religions depends on recognising that their unities are still mainly fixed unities of apprehension and not unities of reflexion at all. Natural good and unities of fixed idea, therefore, we take to be the tests of the primitive

Savage religions are as modern as our own; and they have extensively, even if in less degree than ours, been subjected to many influences. On general or historical grounds, therefore, we have no manner of right to regard them as primitive. We cannot even be sure that they are not debased forms of higher faiths; and, even if we could be sure that they are what they are only by stagnation, the stagnant is never the same as the adventurous. The awe of the adventurous is not the same paralysing dread, its sacred is not the same taboo fixed by fear of consequences, its Supernatural is not the same irrational potency. All we can say is, that man is still primitive in religion when he is concerned with the security and continuance of natural good only and his unities are determined by fixed ideas of apprehension, not by reflexion

(d) VIEWS OF PRIMITIVE RELIGION

We begin with the more generally accepted views, because, if they are not all the truth, in the main they are true. Yet, in estimating their value, we must constantly bear in mind that partial truth may be as misleading as positive error.

1. "Primitive religion is not determined by reasoning or theory, but is an emotional response, stirred by the task of warding off actual or imagined dangers and of furthering well-being."[1]

This is perfectly true and also important, but says nothing which is in the slightest degree peculiar to religion. There is no other beginning of any kind of knowledge of any environment: and if this reduces what is taken to be experience of the Supernatural to mere phantasy, so should it of the Natural, because, as we have found, not even a colour can be seen till it comes within range of practical interest.

2. "The world was first divided into the dangerous and the safe: and out of this were developed the ideas of the holy and the profane."

This is not history, but hypothesis. In so far as it is merely

[1] The statements are summarised from B. Ankermann in *Lehrbuch der Religionsgeschichte*, vol. I, pp 131 ff. References to ed. 4, editors A Bertholet and E. Lehmann

a suggestion that the deeper experience first became conscious through the lower, it is probably true, because all experience of higher environment is by a higher experience of the lower. But we know of no religion which first divided the world into the dangerous and the safe, and then proceeded to transform this into the holy and the profane. What is thought holy or profane is often found determining the safe and the dangerous, but where do we find what is thought safe or dangerous determining the holy and the profane? Every religion, from the lowest, has some kind of belief that there is a reality beyond the visible Natural, and this by a sense of awe which is not mere fear and by the absolute claim of the sacred which has nothing to do with the profitable. To ascribe this further reality to the Natural is easy if we take the Natural as we experience it, that is with reverence and sacredness. But when the Natural is reduced to the appeal of pleasure and pain, with the safe and the dangerous judged wholly by them, how could it even be the occasion of any feeling of absolute worth or any judgment of absolute demands?

3. "With this distinction of sacred and profane, man won three victories over the mere flux of experience. The first was that death is not an absolute end, but a part of man continues to exist; the second, that his conduct is not measured by the immediate situation, but has a relation to a wider society of the living and the dead; the third, that there is an invisible reality, which, though of uncertain and various manifestation, is more continuous and more reliable than mere material events, and is akin to man himself and responsive to his purposes, whereby purposes, otherwise impossible, may be realised."

Ankermann holds that the tap-root of all primitive religion is the cult of the dead and magic. This in the main is true, but only if we do not take primitive too radically, because, while some feeling about the dead as still alive may be strictly primitive, the cult of the dead is not. The more fully recognised form of it as ancestor worship depends on the development of the family and the handing down through it of property, which is not a primitive state at all. Possibly magic also is not strictly primitive. Yet, if not strictly and exclusively primitive, the cult of the dead and magic, at any stage we know, are characteristics both of a primitive bearing towards the Natural and a primitive belief in the Supernatural.

(e) THE PRIMITIVE UNITY OF FIXED IDEA

"The absence of system", Ankermann says, "remains the hallmark of this type of religion." If system mean thinking things together, its absence marks the primitive mind in all it does, and is no special mark of religion. Though no people we know may be wholly at this stage, though perhaps no creature could be called man that did not in some vague way reason, in the sense of seeking abiding relations amid change and coherence among events, the primitive mind might be described as prelogical. Again, though no savage may be without mechanical skill, and possibly no human stage have been wholly without it, the primitive mind, which in general measures environment as it agrees with immediate desire and not as it affords opportunity for fashioning it to a greater purpose, might be described as pre-mechanical. Finally, though no savage may be without some sense of absurdity, yet, as in the main his emotional response to life is determined by immediate impression, the primitive mind might be described as pre-humorous. In short, the primitive mind is still one which, broadly at least, accepts environment as a destiny not as a challenge.

Yet there is no religion which does not work some kind of mastery, if not in action, at least in feeling, over the flux of experience, in a way which makes a great difference of mental victory between man and the lower creatures. and the belief in an abiding soul which links man to the larger society of the living and the dead, and in a mysterious potency which responds to him, is no small part of the difference.

Before entering on this we must first consider what the primitive unity is, because it is not the absence of unity but the dominance of its own unity which most explains the primitive mind.

A reflective unity, requiring a free idea of unity, movable

from one object to another, is not possible for minds which cannot abstract. But the absence of reflective unity—which, just because it is reflective, is never a closed circle—allows fixed unities of awareness to dominate. Because these unities are fixed in the context of situations, they readily close completely around their contents. Though, as we have seen, they are the unities by which perception works, they are not the unity of one rational and ordered universe which may in the end embrace all perceptions, but each immediate unity of awareness is a universe.

As such unities belong to all human perception, the minds of most people are more primitive in their dependence on them than is usually recognised. A statement like Mr Tansley's is not the psychology of ordinary humanity and much less of primitive humanity. "It is impossible", he says, "to overemphasize the overmastering desire of the human mind for some kind of unification, for having a single consistent or seemingly consistent scheme, which appears to include and reconcile contradictory things."[1] The love of unity alone is true. The account of it as a reflective inclusive unity is so far from being true, that human energy, in all ages, has been largely devoted to excluding from its unities of awareness what contradicts them. Some one's reflexion may have created them, but, held in this way, they are unities of awareness.

Men can thus enclose themselves in unities which make up their universe, in science as well as in religion · and the result differs from the primitive mind, not in being more progressive, but only in having a greater inheritance from the past In spite of Hegel's mechanical use of his order of ideas for explaining the cosmic process, he remains fundamentally right about the essence of progress being the breaking up of mere fixed unities of awareness. Yet his merit is largely discounted by the way in which he makes what professes to be a unity of reflexion into what is, in all essentials, a unity of mere awareness Polytheism, with all its defects, divides to conquer, whereas pantheism remains essentially of the primitive type of unity.

[1] A. G. Tansley, *The New Psychology*, p 135

All belief in determinism is of this type. For example, when Santayana says that "Belief in indeterminism is a sign of indetermination", because, apparently, if our own wills were unified we should believe in this kind of determined unity in nature, he is quite right in ascribing it to man's love of unity. But it is of the kind which, in order to save its unity, is prepared to exclude every disturbing fact or element.

Again, on the religious side, we are told that the normal perception is of the world of single vision, the mind and senses only coming between us and reality. Blake is thought to have said the last word when he declares that "If the door of perception were cleansed, everything would appear to man as it is—infinite". As a matter of fact this seems to be exactly how primitive man perceives the world, the power to isolate individual things and regard them in their places and relations being a late and difficult achievement.

The difference, then, between the primitive and the civilised mind is not the absence of all sense of unity, but a sense of unity which, being still continuous with the fixed unity of apprehension, is a world by itself, with the focus of attention as its centre and an indefinitely extended awareness around it as its universe. As this awareness is of what we have called the undifferentiated sacred, we have here the source of the two most characteristic elements of primitive religion—the animistic and the magical.

(*f*) THE ANIMISTIC

For long it seemed too obvious to need proof that religion arose from a simple argument from man himself to persons like himself, only more powerful, behind the mysterious changes around him. Then, by a little further reasoning from shadows and dreams and such-like, and in particular from the change which comes over life with death, he was supposed to have conceived the idea of ghosts, and, from this, of gods, and, by a little further inference, of one God.

But, while man's first idea of the continuous amid change was doubtless derived from consciousness of his own life, and there was never any stage we could call human without it, a conception of the soul, as the unity of life behind all its manifestations, which might be thought to continue as a unity when these manifestations ceased to be visible, is a free idea, and was a comparatively late achievement: and the anthropomorphic view of gods, which could not have anticipated it, is now known to be very far from the beginning of religion.

As all free ideas depend on reflexion, reasoning may have had something to do with the idea of the soul. But, seeing that this idea is probably the fountain-head of all free ideas, the reflexion must have been on some experience, and not from mere reasoning. The soul, moreover, has always been connected with the Supernatural, and no mere inference in the least explains the value of the sacred which has always been attached to it.

Bergson may be right in thinking that a direct sense of life is a heritage from man's animal ancestry. The animal, he argues having no instrument but its body and no way of managing it but a direct consciousness of its life, has a much more direct consciousness of life than is possessed by civilised man, who uses tools and has turned his attention outwards to managing by them his world. The explanation of the universality of the 'inanimate' among all primitive peoples would then be that man does not lose this direct consciousness of life till he begins to use tools and turns his attention from his life in the world to conquering the world for his own ends.

Whether this be all the truth or not, as far as it goes it is at least much more probable than that he started from no direct impression of any reality, and arrived at a belief in souls by reasoning about shadows. In that case it would have been from the first a unity of reflexion, whereas the essentially primitive works with unities of perception. That he turned this into a unity of reflexion by reasoning is another matter from supposing that he made it all of nothing, especially if it was his first impulse to reflective unity.

At first the dead had to be thought of just as they lived, in a combination of what has been called a life-soul and an image-soul. Yet, even with this, man began to free his thoughts from perceived situations and the mere connexion of happenings, and to conceive both his fellow-men and the departed as forming one moral society, with at least the possibility of the growth of a moral tradition. The importance of this for the development of the human mind is not seen only because it is not realised how much, in all other ways, man's ideas were still fixed, and how only by what was valued as sacred in the soul did his ideas begin to be free.

Until then, unity had its focus in some material object, with an indefinite awareness of the Supernatural around it, as every pool reflects the whole sky, or as every point is surrounded by space, so that primitive thinking seems to have many worlds, yet never quite fails to live in the world as one. Primitive man, when looking at his whole world, has no more difficulty in thinking of it as one with one spirit in it, than when he is considering himself or his neighbour as an individual. But, as he cannot take this unity out of its context and think the variety of the world under it, when thinking of any particular object he ascribes to it a soul, or when thinking of the various aspects of his own life, he regards them as carried on by several souls.

This at least helps to explain what seem to us opposites in his religion—one something like the idea of one God, and certainly of one power, and the other the sense of the whole potency of an unseen but supernatural power felt in many things, even the most trivial. Have not we, too, something of the same sense when we simply lay ourselves open to the impression of nature? Our world varies with the focus of attention, but the same indefinite awareness is around any point of our observation.

A still closer parallel to this dim awareness at any point of one whole potency, we may conceive to have been the first sense the living creature had of its physical environment. Before clear perception, every touch must have been awareness of one undifferentiated universe with its whole potency at every point. Or it is as we might see the sunshine, by which in the end all objects are distinguished, without distinguishing any object, but just seeing at every point the wholeness of the sunshine.

Thus a fetish has all supernatural potency, because, for the moment, it is the focus of awareness of the Supernatural; and all magical practice depends on the fact that its horizon, so to speak, is not measured by the rationality or the importance of the performance, but every performance is like an infant looking at anything on which the sunlight strikes. Moreover, there is a sense in which, both in the Natural and in the Supernatural, every point of interest is the focus of a universe.

(g) MAGIC

The significance of magic will be evident if we realise that its use is for peoples whose ideas and feelings are fixed in special contexts, and are in particular inseparable from the context of mass-impression. What magic ritual does is to stage the situation according to the desired result, with the traditional sacred setting in which the higher emotions are fixed, and with the solemn assembly to be, as it were, a sounding-board for it. Minds lacking free ideas cannot escape situations, but they can fashion the situation to give the effective fixed context.

While with this mimetic victory an unprogressive people might remain satisfied and stagnate in it, for progressive minds freedom of staging would be a step towards freedom from all staging.

Magic, it is true, would then cease to work, because its efficacy depends on minds which have their ideas fixed in accustomed contexts and are imperfectly shielded from the passage through them of crowd-emotion. But it is by this possibility of progress, and not by what remains as the mere terror of neglecting any possible security, that the significance of magic should be judged. Irrational it may seem to us, and it is in a sense both pre-rational and pre-mechanical; yet with it man had his foot on the ladder by which he rose to reasoning about his environment and to managing it.

We saw that in perception there are three unities—the unity of the knower, the unity of the known, and the unity of the feeling as a link between. This in primitive religion takes the form of a soul one amid all change, of a potency present in fullness in particular things, and of magic as working by a feeling which has something of absoluteness from both. But here we see the limitation of this form of unity. The permanence of soul is mere oneness of being, without relation to the growth of the spirit; the permanent in environment is mere oneness of power, without value for setting up higher purpose; the oneness of feeling is mere awe without help for attaining higher or more discriminating reverence. So magic may become the merest routine of traditional practices, which, though tradition is man's first equipment for progress, is his supreme device for evading the labour of it.

Magic, however, like all else in man's development, should be judged by its use not its abuse. At its creative stage, it is religion, because its effective setting is sacred tradition, its feeling is at least akin to the sense of the holy, and its power of the nature of the Supernatural. Nor does the fact that, with much repetition, the rites are no longer accompanied by any emotion call in question this function of creating the desired idea clothed in the sustaining religious emotion, because the sense that all the proper securities have been taken is a very sustaining kind of religious emotion.

How far this is connected with ideas of the *mana* type may be doubtful, though it is unlikely that they were ever quite absent. Magic might even be described as mysticism in the fetters of fixed idea, because both alike work with the sense of the holy as awe-inspiring in itself, as an infinite of undifferentiated feeling and not as it manifests a varied reality.

Savage religion has remained stagnant, because it remains at the level religiously of the unity of fixed idea, and this largely because it has shirked the adventure of managing its world, and continued to live as a dependent upon the bounty of its environment, concerned only with persuading the power behind to a favourable mind.

When this unity is disturbed, devices are sought to banish from the mind the invasion of distracting thought. Here we find the explanation of the use of drugs, the whirling madness of the religious dance, and the religious orgy: and higher efforts after ecstasy, however different, seek the same end. Also we have the explanation of the extraordinary tests of endurance at initiation ceremonies and such-like, which again have the same aim as the mystic's asceticism. In neither case is the aim moral. It is to maintain a shell of sheltering unity and prove the power to exclude everything disturbing.

This has a basis in the experience that endurance, to the exhaustion of all nervous energy, does give this curious satisfaction of maintaining one's soul in unity and winning a victory which is peace, and it has the more power that it is part of an essential truth, the truth that we can lose our souls in distraction of attention and the wanderings of desire But the real point about these doings, from a drugged medicine-man or a whirling dervish up to a Yogi and a Christian Contemplative, and from a savage feat of endurance to the saint's maceration, is that they are all regarded as religious for the same reason that they are an exalted dismissal of the conflicts of life. That the savage, never having begun to worry, attains success more easily than the saint, makes no difference in principle Both are concerned to abide in one undisturbed unity of awareness which leaves the Supernatural one undifferentiated potency. But this does not call in question a real experience of the Supernatural any more than not looking at what is under the sun calls in question the reality of light.

(*h*) PRIMITIVE MONOTHEISM

From this we may have some understanding of what has been regarded as primitive monotheism That there is among very primitive peoples a belief in one power, and that this is sometimes conceived as a creator, who is benevolent and even morally good, has been proved by an increasing weight of evidence. Lang's evidence may not prove that "many savage tribes are as monotheistic as many Christians", but it certainly shows that there is something very primitive which is wholly different from polydaemonism. This evidence has been gone into more critically since, but, if it proves less, the evidence can no longer be dismissed or thought of no importance. The belief in a 'power' is possibly earlier than belief in 'powers': and throughout all polytheisms this never quite disappears. Not only is Lang right in finding it behind Yahweh and Allah, but it is plainer in Brahma and still more in an idea like Tao. The fact is that polytheism is neither primitive nor something to be assumed, but is a dividing up of experience very much in need of explanation. As the explanation has to do with property, it is to be noted that this belief in one power is most evident in simple communistic societies.

Human experience cannot be thought of without some sense of the unity of environment both natural and supernatural: and this doubtless is the source both of pantheism and monotheism, though more of the former than of the latter. In itself, however, it is neither, not being a reflective unity of any kind, under which a varied experience could be thought together, but a unity of awareness not yet divided by individual conflict of duty or rights, and is neither rationally nor morally a thinking of things together. In any case, it is not, in the least degree, the victory over environment which marks a true monotheism: and pantheism, though it may be an effort to return to it, differs precisely by the fact that this effort is made by reasoning and reflexion. That the belief tends to pass into the background with the multiplying interests of civilisation, is only what is characteristic of all unities of awareness. Yet unity of awareness never wholly disappears or ceases to be an impulse towards realising that this world is not mere disparate experiences.

In perception, though the sense of one awareness fades when attention is turned to many particulars and there seem to be merely many objects, the awareness still remains a general dim background of one reality. In a similar way, the unity of an undifferentiated awe of one sacred reality fades as this reality comes to impose special tasks and interests, till there seem to be merely many Supernaturals, yet the unity of awareness here also remains a continuous, if dim, background, never quite failing to impress on man that his thoughts and his tasks belong together.

When this unity is brought forward again by reflexion, it

works either as a summons to make life one by meeting its endless challenge and relying on its endless resources, or as the promise of a shining temple of unity from which can be shut out all that distracts, and which has made religion to appear at times the supreme mother-complex of humanity and not the supreme challenge to come home with our shields or on them.

(*i*) RELIGION AND MORALITY

The question of the Supernatural in the Natural is always in some form moral. A religion, when it is purely formal, may have no concern with morality; and a morality, when it is purely conventional, may have no dependence upon religion. But there is no living religion which is not in some sense moral, and no aspiring morality which is not in some sense religious.

The first reason why they seem so easy to divorce is that religion is regarded as merely creed, and morality as merely conduct. Even so, they are not as easily separated as is frequently assumed. The creed may become mere traditional dogma, but the reason why it persists is often that it still has a bearing upon conduct. A morality may be mere good form, but even good form is usually parasitic either on the dead trunk of the religion of one's ancestors or on the living stem of the religion of one's society.

The second reason why the interdependence of religion and morality is not seen, is that they are wrongly related, both in theory and practice. The sole relation of religion to morality is taken to be the providing of rules of conduct and motives for following them: and primitive religion has not our rules of conduct, nor is its good moral good in our sense. Throughout the whole history of religion, moreover, external rules and motives of fear and self-interest are found, which should not be regarded as moral, but as conflicting with the true moral rule and moral motive of doing what seems right to our own conscience and for the sole reason that it is right.

It is necessary to distinguish what religion provides for morality **directly** from what it should provide only **indirectly**.

Directly, it provides only the sphere in which persons have absolute worth and duties have sacred obligation. As, without both, there is no morality, no morality that is truly moral is non-religious; and as there is no religion which does not provide this sphere, there is none which is non-moral. But ideals and motives religion should provide only indirectly. When, in the name of religion, rules are laid down by authority and enforced by hope of bliss and fear of misery, we have neither religion nor morality, but the Natural masquerading as the Supernatural. Indirectly, nevertheless, the growth of all higher ideal and the sway of all nobler motive is dependent on how the relation of the Natural to the Supernatural is conceived, so that a higher morality is closely interwoven with a higher religion and there is no form of religion in which there is not some beginning of a higher value for man and his society and some measure of better rule than impulse and better motive than fear or favour or any form of self-interest.

We may easily underestimate what man received even from his animal ancestry, because there is no Natural wholly divorced from the Supernatural, and a state of nature is not a chaos of every creature fighting for itself. But in man at any stage, the sense of the holy, however sunk in mere awe, the judgment of the sacred, however fettered in the material, and the sanction of the Supernatural, however beclouded by magic, make man's conduct in some sense moral, a standing above the mere flux of impulse and circumstance, and an estimate of himself, his fellows and his ultimate environment which is not measured by material advantage.

As far back as we can go, religion has some element of the eternal in it, some ground in a worth in man himself and his fellows which is not physical and does not end with the grave, and some continuity of influence, if only in reverence for his ancestors and the assurance that his own influence some day will abide with theirs. The moment that some things are sacred, man has begun to live in the world which provides for him the substance and the sanction of his ideals and the change appears as much in the quality of his disloyalty to them as of his faithfulness, for it is no longer nature but vice. Much that is vice to us is still nature to more primitive men, but there is no religion which does not draw the distinction somewhere, and this in a way to show that both the individual and his society in some degree measure the Natural by the Supernatural.

Only when we consider the whole of the above classification of religion can we fully see how man's dealing with the Natural according to his idea of its relation to the Supernatural determines the content of his ideals. But there is no form of religion in which this process has not begun. Primarily it is by higher values in himself, his society and his environment, but it is also by some growth of helpful tradition, which provides both rule and motive. Therefore, as there is no purely natural religion, so there is no purely natural morality. Both alike deal with the Supernatural· and to it man attends so much for the good reason that it is the environment which is of the highest importance for his life and progress.

CHAPTER XXIII

THE POLYTHEISTIC

(*a*) GODS AS ANTHROPOMORPHIC INFERENCE

So long as religion is explained by notions we can imagine man to have thought of most easily, few problems in its history are difficult, and polytheism is one of the easiest. From the days of Xenophanes it was thought to be nothing more than the vanity of man in conceiving gods in his own image. Later it was ascribed to concern with the causes of things conceived after the pattern of human wills: and sometimes all religion was thought to begin and end with this theory of causes. In our day inquiry has shown that the ability to conceive gods in man's own image was a late and difficult achievement. Religion, however, is still ascribed to quasi-personal causes in the form of vague centres of supernatural force, nameless and little distinguished.

Originally, it is supposed, they may have been what Usener calls *Augenblicksgottheiten*, deities of the moment. Then that, if for some reason one bulked more largely in attention, it absorbed the others, and so the gods were formed as rain out of mist. The chief way of rising out of the ranks was to receive a name, as when Tommy Atkins in general becomes Lieutenant Atkins in particular. Or, as the name first came from the function, it is as when the ancestral anvil is forgotten in the name of Smith and the owner is on his way to a peerage. Thus progress is conceived to be from a polyzoic or lowest animism, or animatism, through a more individual polydaemonism, to a therianthropic polytheism, in which, if the likeness was still to four-footed beasts and creeping things, the god behind was conceived in the likeness of man, until, finally, we arrive at anthropomorphic polytheism, or polytheism proper, with reverence for beings in human form, but above human power.

This theory has the consistency of a rational construction, but there are facts it fails to cover. For example, Augustine ridicules the tribe of numina invoked to prosper a marriage,[1] and, in the official state prayer of Rome for the crops, there is a series of divine performers each named by the function. But how could this be the first stage towards a higher polytheism when it presupposes an elaborate society in which the functions of individuals have become highly specialised? Like his worshipper, the primitive god was concerned with all aspects of life, so that, if he ever was, as is in a high degree improbable, 'a mere god of the moment', he was for that moment at least the sole deity.

Belief in numina is found abundantly even in fairly advanced religions. But, in the first place, that it ever was the sole religion is improbable; in the second, that the belief arose out of intellectual inference from effect to cause is yet less probable; and, in the third, that the higher deities were compounded out of them is still more unlikely.

The numina are only in a very vague way powers. They are not individual and personal, like the polytheistic deities, but rather manifestations of one mysterious, awe-inspiring diffused potency. How this vague unity of awareness, which was felt as a whole at every point of interest, as space at every point of perception, came to be broken up into powers corresponding to a wide range of organised interests and graded values, is a question as difficult as it is important.

There are, however, parallels which at least help the imagination. A university earned its name when its studies were all within the scope of one individual and were all regarded from one point of view. In our day, neither are its studies within the possible scope of one individual nor are they one culture. Instead, a university has become a sort of cave of the winds of many specialisms, each of which is to its devotees the one knowledge, which is not very different from the ancient pantheon. Moreover, the old polytheism had the same justification of being a better way of conquering the world than a

[1] *De Civitate Dei*, Bk VI. 9.

vague unity which included everything but did not carry very far particular interest in anything. A still closer parallel is the stage in the development of every active and interested mind, when life divides into many varied interests, each a unity of imagination, which break up the whole awareness of life, yet raise problems which, if they are faced, may in time effect a harmonious unity of reflexion. And polytheism has the same justification of being a similar stage in human development. Even much maturer persons do not, when engaged in the distracting business of managing their world, always escape from a polytheistic mind merely by professing a higher religion, but the centres of their interests are still apt to be centres of the universe. When the interest is in creed and worship, then God is no respecter of persons and, if the shadow of a heart-shaking war do not intrude, no mere tutelary deity of the state. But when other interests are absorbing, there is a business god who shows a man's worth by his substance, a social god who, like the French nobleman's deity, would think twice before condemning a man of his quality, and a patriotic deity who would have deplorably neglected his business if he suffered any real calamity to happen to the nation. So long, indeed, as managing the world is concerned more with privileges than responsibilities we are all polytheists, with a dim awareness of the universe as the nimbus of each of our deities.

Polytheism depends on a sense of the holy which is still awesome, not ethical, a judgment of the sacred which is fixed in a context of material associations, and an imperfect power of reflexion unable as yet to keep the circle of mere awareness from closing round each particular sacred interest and making it a sort of universe. But this is no longer unchallenged. Truly anthropomorphic polytheism marks a stage new in principle and not merely in aspect, because with it man faces life's concrete, distracting problems as a concrete, distracted individual· and though this may stagnate into disintegrating idolatry, the higher polytheisms show that it may be the way towards the realisation of the unity of a spiritual as well as of a material universe.

(b) PROPERTY AND THE CONCRETE INDIVIDUAL

The rise of polytheism is specially related to man's realisation of himself as a concrete individual, and, in particular, by the possession of private property as the special sphere of his rights and responsibilities. Thus all mystical religions rightly hold individual possession to be the chief cause of dividing the world into separate interests and so of creating separate idolatries; and they are also right in connecting this with man's realisation of his concrete individuality and the management of his own world. But, in spite of the evils which have gone with it, this realisation of himself, and of his world as manageable, has been the first and highest gain for all progress. And in this, private possession has played an important part, for, until man had something he could call his own, he could not use it in any way that was strictly moral or immoral.

There ought to be a higher sphere for individual rights and responsibilities than material possession, and mankind cannot wholly escape the covetousness which is idolatry till it be won But, till it is won, men could not be deprived of the right even to misuse private property without a limitation of moral responsibility which would be greater loss than any possible gain Personal property should not be the highest good, but, so long as men regard it as such, they cannot allow it to be absorbed in the tribe yet continue to develop as responsible persons. The only profitable way of doing without private possessions in material things is what has been followed by the noblest of mankind, to find higher possessions for which all else may be counted loss. But, seeing that it was the first way in which the individual could realise himself, the rise of private property, as the sphere of his special rights and responsibilities, is definitely the stage at which he begins to manage his world and is no more a mere dependent upon its bounty. This marks the discovery of the Natural as the sphere of opportunity and so of rights and duties which are determined, not by what the Natural is, but by what we may make of it: and this is also the beginning of finding deeper meaning in it and a purpose beyond it. Polytheism thus goes with the breaking up of mere unities of awareness fixed by customary experience, which makes possible the search for real relations and challenges the mind to dissatisfaction with mere customary happenings. Thereby man is set upon the endless adventure of thinking and working all his experience together. Hence it is not a mere superstition of bribable deities which makes polytheism and civilisation advance together, but polytheism has its place in man's realisation of his universe because the most broken-up unities of reflexion are more than any mere undisturbed unity of perception.

Moreover, this is also the stage at which the sense of the holy as mere awe begins to change into a reverence which has distinctions in its applications, as is seen in the development of the sense of beauty. Also it is the stage at which the valuation as sacred begins to be detached from its immediate material embodiment and to become moral valuation. Though the relation to humanised divinities seems only to increase chaos, it is a very important advance when unities fixed by interest and the context of happenings are disturbed, and the mind can move more freely in personal forms from which may arise questions about what is the higher reverence and the truly sacred.

What was of importance for freeing the conception of the Supernatural from mere fixed situations was just the individual anthropomorphised and rationalised gods.

Nowhere were they more completely anthropomorphised and rationalised than in Greece, and nowhere is it more evident that this was a humanising of the Natural and not a mere anthropomorphising of the Supernatural. Hermes may have started from the boundary mark or 'term'; and the beginning may have been the carving of its top in the form of a human head. But, forthwith, there was a different kind of protection to one's field from a mere heap, because the Supernatural, as a sort of dangerous fluid, had become the rational and universal protector of human rights. In the same way a city became a new order when Athene stood for human rights and duties within it. With gods of nature giving fertility and protection, man won the confidence by which he could do what his hand found to do with all his might. The gods of the family gave a divine call and sanction to marriage, the duties of parents and the piety of the children. Strangers were differently received when there were gods of hospitality. Arts were differently respected and followed with Apollo as patron, giving them a standing as divine. Especially a sanction was given to all agreements and laws when Zeus became the protector of truth and righteousness.

If we do not realise that ideals are necessary for even imperfect industry, moderately considerate dealing, living together in one state, and having a hospitable mind to the world at large, we can think of all this supernatural structure as mere later decoration· but if we realise that the difficulty is just in conceiving the ideals, we can see that man was so constantly and continuously concerned with the Supernatural because he knew it to be the source of his security and his progress.

(c) POLYTHEISM AND CIVILISATION

That polytheism and civilisation advanced together and have some kind of interdependence is a historical fact so obvious as to require no discussion. This does not by itself decide which is first in principle but if polytheism was the power, however chaotic, by which man moved from mere unity of awareness to unities of reflexion, and this helped to set free his ideas, is it not the religion? In any case, if man found in the claims and succour of the Supernatural an absoluteness of requirement and an absoluteness of the call to venture which the purely Natural cannot provide, the assumption that religion is a mere reflexion of man's material progress and that his material progress had no dependence upon his religion is, at least, a hasty conclusion.

The usual account is that, as man developed in individuality, he conferred more of a distinctive character upon his god, as states were united, local gods were identified and made more important; as the family developed, the gods were united in ties of kinship; as the organisation of the state was perfected, the gods became a hierarchy, with a tendency to exalt the head and make him a constitutional potentate; as the rational and moral extended its sway over life, the supernatural rule was conceived more consistently and more ethically, till finally the supreme ruler was regarded as the protector of the laws and the moral code. In all this, religion, so far as appears from anything ascribed to its influence, is a mere reflexion on the clouds of man's phantasy, following after his better appreciation and use of the Natural, a mere shadow of progress similar to what, on the theory of psycho-physical parallelism, thought is of mechanically effected change. Mankind, however, still persists in believing, not only that thinking does things, but that nothing sensible or for any higher end can be done without it · and if man has devoted such endless interest to religion for the similar reason that he realises his higher possibilities only in a higher environment, his religion may have had as good a justification.

Many religious ideas are connected with agriculture, but nothing more plainly marks the transition from the primitive to the polytheistic, because it is the source of all endeavour to manage environment. When man has to earn his bread in the sweat of his brow, his primitive awareness is disturbed and he no longer sees the field but the individual sheaves. From this disturbing effort to manage environment for man's own ends, there arose the still more divisive claim of private property, and, with this, the individual who realises himself in responsibilities and rights. Wherefore, Buddha was only logical when he forbade his monks agriculture as well as property. The individual with his management and his claims cannot return to any primitive paradise. Such a person may live, not in the world, but in his own world, which is apt to obscure any vision of the other. His family is an economic unit, dependent on his efforts and apt to absorb his interest; his society is a state, which he relies upon for his protection but stands over against with his rights And when these private goods appear the end of all that is sacred, there can be no unified conception of the Supernatural or, for that matter, of the Natural.

It is easier, therefore, to see the material than the spiritual gain of polytheism. Rationally and morally, is it not chaos? If there is religious progress, is not this a mere reflexion of the material? And it does seem so unless we take evolution seriously. But if we do, we must ask by what ideas and ideals man found such footing in the flux of experience as enabled him to refuse its first impressions and reject its first gratifications, and to reason about it and subject it to management. Then, is it not just the faith in which man created civilisation which most needs explanation? Once he had the insight to realise higher opportunity and had achieved freedom of mind to use it, civilisation could arise: and though this offered larger opportunity to abuse as well as to use, it is by the possibilities of a larger freedom that we should judge progress.

A very high religion is not found in a very low civilisation. But this proves nothing, because it is equally certain that no higher civilisation has been created or has maintained itself in vigour without a religion which had at least some elements of what was still higher. We cannot dissociate our ideals from what we are at least trying to realise, nor set up ideals very far beyond our striving, nor strive very far beyond our achieving. Yet we achieve nothing unless our ideals are always beyond our striving.

A full discussion would require a treatise, and when it was done, it would not settle a question which does not admit of demonstration but must be decided by our own way of looking at life and history. A statement of how it appears to one's own mind, offered merely as a suggestion for the reflexion of others is, therefore, the better as well as the shorter way. So I merely state, with some illustration, what seem to me to be the more important contributions of the Higher Polytheism to the development of civilisation.

(d) ELEMENTS OF PROGRESS

1. Polytheism gave a greater freedom of mind, which was a call to adventure upon wider and higher environment and a sense of security in following it.

The Aryan is thought to have embodied his highest sense of the Supernatural in the sky, because when he set out on his journeys the home of his local gods disappeared below the horizon and the sky alone was always with him. But would he ever have set out from the familiar except, as primitive tribes have done, by being driven forth by sheer necessity and kept away by inability to return, had he not already had some way of carrying with him the sense of divine protection beyond the home of his local gods? A material embodiment the stage of his mental development still required, but he must have already won some sense of a Supernatural not fixed in a particular situation, before, by mere courageous expectation of what might await him, he travelled into the unknown and was content to say at the end,

> Under the wide and starry sky,
> Dig the grave and let me lie

The theology and the experience doubtless confirmed each other, but the fact that so many Aryan tongues, far apart from each other, have the 'Day-Father', would seem to show that a faith by which to travel had already been won, before company after company of this race ventured so far afield. Possibly there was something distinctive in the situation, such as the practice of agriculture while the individual still sat lightly to private possession, which helped him to a faith in a real personal power, without losing the primitive sense of awareness of one power. But, in any case, it was his faith in the abiding amid all change which was his freedom and his courage.

This, with some truth, might be regarded rather as a kind of monotheism, than as polytheism. The Aryan arrived in Greece with no real god but Zeus, in Persia with what easily became Ahura-Mazda, and in India with Varuna in much the same position, very much as Israel arrived in a settled land with Yahweh: and the pantheon arose out of the gods of the cultivated land, as it would have done in Israel but for the prophets.

But it is doubtful if there ever was a polytheism entirely without a sense of one Supernatural as a dimly felt awareness. This helped to maintain the higher polytheism against the lower animisms; to make all the gods more and more defenders of truth and righteousness; to enable some thinkers, like Xenophanes, to distinguish God from the gods; and, finally, to subject the whole idea of gods to destructive criticism. On the other hand, the monotheism of Israel, though its origin may not have been polytheistic, had its distinctive quality from facing the task of victory over environment, with the problems before it which had their origin in polytheism.

2. Polytheism, by setting free higher sanctions from local limitations, made possible the formation of a state with universal laws.

When one tribe conquered another, the gods of both were frequently regarded as the same god with different names or were fused together; and frequently the conquered gained by the triumph of their religion what they lost by the defeat of their armies.[1]

This is often treated as the merely natural result of political absorption. But what transformed a collection of subject peoples into a larger state with equal laws could not have been the mere result of annexation. Babylonia and Rome are conspicuous examples: and we see the difference if we compare the result with a religion of the Assyrian type, for which the other gods were mere enemies to be made weak by slaughtering and enslaving their worshippers. Babylonia and Rome were world-empires which did much for order and civilisation, while Assyria was merely a passing world-nightmare. That the reign of mild and equal law was at the time ascribed to religion is itself evidence. The Code of Hammurabi rests the justice of law and

[1] Prof. W. M. Flinders Petrie, *Religion and Conscience in Ancient Egypt.* "A conquered race always subdues its conquerors to its own type after a few centuries of fusion . And what is true of the races is probably true of the religions."

right observance of it upon religion as definitely as Deuteronomy. Nor is it early jurisprudence alone which makes the claim to have divine legislation as its standard and authority, because no law, even to-day, works merely by the will of the majority, but only as it seems to be established by some absolute quality of righteousness

3. Intimately connected with this was the rise of the family as a moral society, as well as a blood and bread relationship.

The handing down of property in the family seems to have been connected with the cult of the dead as polytheism transformed it. It was at once a way of claiming the right of succession and a substitute offered by those who succeeded.[1] By this right of succession the family was made the most important unit of society, with rights and duties towards the members within itself as well as to society as a whole.

To this polytheism gave further support by gods of the hearth and of marriage and gods who protected the family and the family rights, and the relations between the gods themselves as a family. The wife and the family, it is true, were still regarded as private property, but it does not take much insight to see that in the higher polytheisms they were establishing their own rights, so that the family, in spite of the legal position of the head, became more and more a sphere of mutual responsibilities. In all this, changing human relations were made sacred by being regarded as in an eternal order.

(e) LIMITATIONS AND DEFECTS

Even in the very matters in which polytheism was a stage of progress, its limitations and the temporary nature of its benefit also appear.

1 In respect of a wider environment.

Polytheism arose with the beginning of reflective unities, but when reflective thinking was carried farther, polytheism entirely failed to meet its needs When it became at all systematic, it

---

[1] From Prof. A. B. Cook I learn that a *Zeus Ktésios* was made by sealing the offerings to the dead in a jar. This seems to be a clear confirmation of the above view of the place of property.

either settled down into a traditional irrationalism, as among the Egyptians, or was criticised out of existence, as among the Greeks. Polytheism is only irrational when it becomes theological; and one of the reasons why it seems to us such an utter confusion of mind is that we regard its theology as its essence. As polytheism presupposes the absence of thinking things together in one unity, scholastic theologising within the limits of the traditional conception of the gods was probably never any religion by which men lived, and is certainly no religion in which we could imagine ourselves living.

2. In respect of civilisation and the state.

By creating unities of reflexion polytheism showed, what no merely primitive religion has ever done, the power to create civilisations.

Yet in this we have another limitation, because an essential mark of polytheism is that it has no ideas beyond civilisation, and no quarrel with it. It never goes beyond the idea of the state and never shows any power to subject the idea of the state to a higher end beyond itself, so that, when the state becomes moribund, polytheism begins to disintegrate.

The higher polytheisms created the state, but they continued to be shut up in it. They were not only state religions; they were religions merely of the state. The Babylonian gods disappeared with the state; the Egyptian gods, as the national independence vanished, degenerated into what we may call theological superstitions; when the virility of the Indian nation was sapped, the gods multiplied and degenerated into animisms or aspects of pantheism, in Greece, when the citystates ceased to be vital elements of society, the popular religion sank to animisms and the educated became mystical or philosophical generalities. On the other hand, the victory of Christianity was made much easier by the fall of the Roman Empire, and in Israel the foundation of monotheism was laid when Amos denied that the fate of Yahweh was in any way bound up with the fate of the Jewish state. In contrast, polytheism never rises above the imperial idea of the Supernatural, and for those who do rise above it polytheism becomes merely idolatry

3. In respect of the family and society.

While the higher polytheisms did much to secure the rights of the woman under the marriage tie and to establish the family as a social unit, they failed to create the ideals which made marriage a sacred and equal bond and the family a moral society for moral ends. Success in material civilisation tended still further to undermine such ideals as had ruled, and so to destroy itself through sheer materialism. This danger, it is true, besets all religions. Even the highest cannot always save its material civilisation from the corrupting influence of luxury and licence. But a higher religion can set up ever higher ideals, and, like the Hebrew prophet, cherish the hope that disaster itself will work for their victory and so recover what has been lost and make it a higher possession. Polytheism, on the other hand, has always perished with its civilisation, not being able to set up any independent standard of purity or righteousness to save it. Nay it has always itself become corrupted and a chief cause of corruption.

Even the prophets of Yahweh had to face the dangers for their civilisation of intemperance, unjust greed of wealth and callous luxury, fostered by material prosperity and the sense of material security, and they saw, as no polytheism had ever done, that nothing so undermines a people as the licentiousness which such material prosperity may foster. This for the prophets was the crowning evil of their time, a canker at the nation's root, more dangerous than any storm of outward evil which might assail it. So obvious does this seem that it is one of the most impressive evidences of man's inability to see what is before him, if he lack moral and spiritual insight to interpret it, that the prophets alone in the ancient world ever had this insight. Polytheism by itself was always in danger of being what made the Baal worship so detestable to them—the occasion and the justification for sensuality.

Not only does civilisation require a basis in the family, but the discipline derived from self-restraint and the energy sublimated by it are primarily what serve all higher interests. For the finer sensitiveness and higher insight which reach out to higher ideals nothing is more necessary than for man to honour woman, for the very reason that, in physical strength, she is the weaker vessel. And this is so because brute force and the use of others for our own merely selfish ends are precisely what have to be overcome in building any high, enduring civilisation. Yet history and experience alike make it plain that civilisation cannot provide for itself what it needs, but, by its failure to maintain what religion gives, it has constantly destroyed itself.

Purity is not a virtue of nature, but rests on a religious valuation and a life in what is beyond the Natural: and no virtue is so immediately responsive to the growth or decay of religion. Religion is not merely a ladder by which we climb and which may be kicked down when we have used it for this purpose, but remains the pillar and ground of the faith by which life can be made austere and society secure. Some religion man must have, and when he fails to maintain a higher religion, he falls back on polytheism, meaning by that whatever gods there be that protect his body, his family, his property and his state, without exacting much self-denial in their protection. Nor is it very difficult to see that there are many disintegrating idolatries even in nominally Christian states, such as worship of power above righteousness, and of pleasure above purity, and of possession above nobility of soul.

On the other hand, it is equally plain that no true monotheism is ever maintained on a merely natural valuation of man and human relations. Moreover, the supernatural valuation must extend even to those who, by a merely external estimate, may seem to be worthless, if it is to be a sure realisation of our higher environment. If Amos founded a universal monotheism by denying the ultimate religious significance of the state, Hosea raised it still higher by setting as his equal, not only a woman, but a woman who had fallen from everything that would make her a prized possession, thus affirming a truly universal God of all humanity and all the humanities.

If this be the way man has travelled, the question of whether, when he comes to realise that he lives in one universe, he shall conceive it personally or pantheistically is not determined by speculation, but by whether he continue to face the problems of polytheism, or attempt, by delivering himself from his concrete individuality, to return to the undivided and undisturbed primitive awareness of awe and sacredness. In short it is a question of seeking the eternal by a higher possession of the evanescent, not by escape from it.

CHAPTER XXIV

THE MYSTICAL

(a) TWO TYPES OF RELIGIONS

WHEN man arrives at unity of reflexion and begins to think his unities of awareness together, he needs to express his religion in a theology: and the type of theology is determined by the way in which the Natural is regarded. The Natural is taken to be a veiling or to be a revealing of the Supernatural. In the former case, the religious task is to be rid of the illusion of the many and the changing, both in our concrete world and in our concrete individuality, and to penetrate to the one and the eternal; in the latter, the task is to find in the evanescent abiding meaning and endless purpose. The former type seeks, by reflective effort, to recover the primitive unity of awareness as all-embracing; the latter faces the problems of polytheism, in the trust that their solution is a deeper meaning in the concrete world and a higher purpose in the concrete individual. In the former case, the eternal is sought as the unchanging by escape from the evanescent; in the latter, it is looked for in the evanescent as a revelation of increasing purpose in its changes.

As both are reflective, the intellectualist type of mind, which alone studies them, is apt to think that the difference begins and ends with reasoning and speculation.

All theologies, it is true, when traced far enough back, are found to be products of reasoning; and some theologies, especially of the mystical kind, and not least when most professing independence of all human thinking, are merely the imposing of speculative ideas upon experience. But, in so far as any theology is religious, it springs from the deeper ground of an attitude towards experience. It is reflexion on a conviction of the kind of reality man lives in, natural and supernatural A faith to be religious is in the Supernatural, and what kind of faith it is depends on the quality of the sense of the holy and of the judgment of the sacred from which it springs. But it is merely an opinion, unless the faith is determined by what is or is not acted on in the Natural. Were it only to deny the reality of the Natural, all religions are occupied with it and their character is determined as they affirm or deny.

The very lowest religions show that man is not satisfied with the Natural merely as it appeals to his sensations; and, in respect of the face meaning and value of the Natural, as the religions are higher, they are increasingly pessimistic.

This may seem to be merely that 'Man never is, but always to be blest', with the increase of this discontent from the increase of sensitiveness due to the growth of civilisation. And it may be true that, if man's senses had satisfied him, he might never have become aware of any higher reality beyond them. But, without the sense of the Supernatural, discontent with the Natural would never have passed beyond mere animal dissatisfaction, and never have been the divine discontent which sent him out on his troubled career of endless search and aspiration. Though there is never any first and last in such elements of experience, the possibility of the higher environment is first in principle, if it alone can create a truly human discontent and if only seeing and approving the better gives the right dissatisfaction with the worse

Even in religion, however, the pessimism may be rather from the thinness of the skin than the roughness of the world's climate, and may also be cherished as a mark of superiority. Thus in India it arose with a race, which, as superiors served by inferiors, became hypersensitive and not sufficiently occupied. Even Buddha's wail that all life is misery, as Oldenberg says, is not possible for hard-working people, who have to bear another kind of burden. Yet the pessimism was at least seriously acted upon, and was not just indulged in as an additional luxury of the sense of superiority, as sometimes it has been in our fiction and even in our philosophy. But there are also religions the pessimism of which springs from virility, which was also acted upon though to a quite opposite end. The

THE MYSTICAL 407

Hebrew prophets had material and moral justification from appalling calamity and deep-seated corruption; and Jesus thought that he was facing such calamity as had not been since the world began, while, for him, much that was virtue to Buddha was mere soul-destroying hypocrisy. But this was only the beginning of their faith, and the end was at the opposite pole from despair. For the former type, the misery of the Natural justifies self-pity, and the way of escape is to regard the Natural as illusion; for the latter, it is to be counted all joy to fall into divers trials, as the way, not only of victory over the Natural, but of possessing it by discovering its true and eternal meaning and purpose. The question, then, even about the theologies, is not which argument, but which attitude, is right.

By this, and not by mere speculation, are religions divided into two types, with different lines of development. For the one, redemption is by absorption into the Supernatural—the sole reality, which is one, unchanging and eternal: and thereby it is escape from the Natural—the great illusion, which is divided, fleeting and insubstantial. For the other, redemption is by reconciliation to the meaning and purpose of the Supernatural, whereby the Natural is transformed and becomes both revelation and opportunity.

All true polytheism shows the beginning of reflexion, and in all higher polytheism there is such an advance of it towards thinking things together as tends to dissolve the whole polytheistic way of thinking. But the historical result was in either of the two directions indicated above. One was in the direction of pantheism and absorption in the One, and the other in the direction of monotheism and victory over the many.

A plain example is Greece. One section ended in what we may broadly call Fate, and the other in what was at least in the direction of legal dualism. But the difference is seen on the largest scale in the contrast between India and Persia In India an all-embracing monism reduced all the conflicts of the Natural to illusion, *maya*, and all moral distinctions to a universal law of retribution, *karma*, which, and not any external order in which he lives, determines each individual's form of illusion. Hence the Natural is a mere product of the private mind of man. In Persia, on the contrary, while there is at least a monotheistic tendency in the hope of final victory, the way of dealing with the Natural resulted in a sharply divided dualistic legalism, which was ritual, concerned with physical contamination, and ethical, concerned with moral evil. Thus by the attitude to the Natural, religions are divided into two camps.

(b) WAYS OF DESCRIBING THEIR DIFFERENCE

The opposition can be described in a variety of ways.

The usual distinction between monotheism and pantheism seems to make it purely a difference of theory But no one in the last resort, not even the most dialectical philosopher or the most dogmatic theologian, is either a pantheist or a monotheist on mere reasoning. And this is still truer of the religions. While both theologies are products of reflexion, and pantheism in particular even of speculation, what finally determines the result is the view of the Natural, and what finally determines the view of it is the way of living in it. Therefore, what sheds much more light on the questions at stake is that the pantheistic religions are a return to the primitive type, with the main difference just in the fact that they are the product of the reflective and even speculative mind. They work with the unity of awareness, seek to exclude the divided natural world from it, and aim at redemption into the undisturbed enjoyment of the one undivided Supernatural The monotheistic religions, in contrast, continue the problems of polytheism, seeking to achieve unity in the varied world we apprehend. To them the existence of evil, both physical and moral, is so real that the sharp division it creates in the world makes it impossible to regard the present world as any kind of fixed, all-embracing unity of rule Yet this is the beginning of their task, not the end.

Another way of expressing the same difference is that, while the redemption of the one is what we may broadly call mystical, the hope of the other is always, in some form, apocalyptic. As this is the essential difference in their religious content, we may, henceforth, divide religions into mystical and apocalyptic.

Again, from lack of any better device the terms are given a somewhat special meaning. A mystical religion is, as it always should be understood scientifically, one that seeks the eternal behind the illusion of the evanescent; but in using apocalyptic for any religion which looks for a revealing in the evanescent, the term is extended from its customary use, which is for a religion that expects this in sudden catastrophic form, to one that expects it in any form.

Once again we find the decisive element to be the way of regarding the Natural. For mysticism, the Natural is purely the evanescent, a mere delusive veil between the soul and the unchanging; for the apocalyptic religions, it is also the unsatisfying and the evanescent, but even its changes are a challenge to seek in the true uses of them a meaning in them by which they can be possessed, and a purpose beyond them whereby the possession may be blessed. Thereby, most plainly, we are faced not by mere theory about the Supernatural, but by the practical problem of our right bearing towards the Natural.

It is only another aspect of the same distinction that the mystical religions seek to be rid of the concrete individual with his rights and his responsibilities in his special sphere, so as to reach a unity of soul which, as unchanging and undisturbed awareness of the mere self, is without distinctions which could divide it from the Absolute Unity; and that, in contrast, the apocalyptic religions regard the rights and duties of the concrete individual as the essential religious concern, significant for the conception of God as of the soul.

Mystical morality, therefore, is concerned with the submissive virtues, with suppressing desire, with asceticism and ecstasy: and its goal is a Nirvana, in which the illusion of the world is for ever escaped, because the burden of the concrete individual has been for ever laid down. In contrast, apocalyptic morality is far more concerned with what man does than with what he does not do, with his active, positive righteousness: and it looks for some kind of establishment of God's kingdom upon earth, for the most part in the strictly apocalyptic sense of a renewal of all things.[1]

Ultimately, in the apocalyptic religions as in the mystical, we come to the judgment that the Natural in itself is the 'bondage of corruption', its whole character being evanescence, and we ourselves, so far as we are merely of it, enslaved to its changes. The direct way of seeking escape is to deny utterly its reality, to regard it as mere shifting, veiling cloud upon the face of the unchanging heaven. This the mystical religions follow, seeking to exclude the imagery of the senses and to withdraw the mind from life's conflicts, in order to find behind the concrete person and the concrete world the unchanging unity. But the apocalyptic religions do not find it so simple. They seek to discover in the Natural in spite of its evil a revelation and true possession, and in its changes the unfolding of a purpose which is eternal. Thus the Natural is for them at once to be denied and possessed. As this question about the reality, meaning and value of the Natural, and not mere speculation about the Supernatural, is what decides between a pantheistic Absolute and a personal God, the most decisive of all questions about religion is—Which estimate of the Natural is right?

Speculation necessarily tends towards the pantheistic answer. And as the Natural with any kind of recognition of its reality remains a distressing problem, the pantheism always tends to be acosmic mysticism. Pantheism, from its earliest Indian to the latest Hegelian manifestation, starts by imposing the idea of unity upon experience: and the peace of mind it offers, which for struggling humanity is its chief attraction, is the finality thereby assured from the start. But to impose unity upon all things is not to bring all things into unity. As mere

[1] This could be expressed in the opposite way. For example, Stevenson says that nothing impresses him so much in the morality of Jesus as that no one is damned for what he does, but always for what he does not do. But this is obviously only another way of saying that the standard is always of positive aspiration and endeavour, and never of mere obedience to rules and absence of offence.

speculation is just the imposing of unity, the pantheistic solution is already settled by the method. But if we know the supernatural environment only as we know the natural, by solving in thought and practice its problems, this method is merely what used to be called in science Pre-Baconian, the imposing of what we think ought to be upon what is. It appeals persuasively to many both by its speculative satisfaction and its promise of peace. But if the all in any way includes the real, it is not less distressing for being called God. Hence the pantheism of 'all is God' changes constantly into the mysticism of 'God is all'.

Our first task, therefore, is to consider the mystical treatment of the Natural as an illusion which veils the face of the Eternal, and of the concrete individual or particular man as the source of the distressing manifold of appearances, withholding us from the undisturbed unity of the eternally unchanging.

'Mysticism', it must be kept in mind, is not here used, in the vague way mostly found in English writers, for any kind of experience which goes beyond reasoning from the data of the senses. It does not include even visions like the prophet's intuitions, or revelations if they are concrete experiences concerned with man's life in the world. If what is beyond ordinary perception and thought is won by following both to their utmost limits, it is not mysticism in the sense here meant. The essential marks of this mysticism are, first, its attitude towards the Natural, as in no form a manifestation of the Supernatural, but a mere confusing manifold, the illusory evanescent; and second, its attitude towards the empirical personality as the source of the unreal. It is the mysticism for which the task of religion is to rid ourselves of the Natural, both as the world and as concrete personality. Moreover, we must distinguish between even this mysticism as an occasional mood and relief from struggle, and as an abiding attitude of a settled faith and persistent practice, because it here concerns us only as an ultimate view of the relation between the Natural and the Supernatural.

Just because the Indian religions, and possibly only the

Indian religions, take this conception whole-heartedly, they will chiefly occupy our attention.

(c) EARLY INDIAN PANTHEISM

Veda means 'a thing heard', in short a sacred tradition. Even the Rig-Veda, however, "does not present us with any naive outpourings of the primitive consciousness, but with a state of belief which must have been the product of much priestly effort and the outcome of wholesale syncretisms".[1] Nevertheless, we can still see through it 'the vigorous, agricultural, cattle-rearing, fighting Aryan race, with a stirring world of gods, giants, trolls, nymphs, elfs and spirits, who fill heaven as well as earth'. And there is the hope of another and equally strenuous life, when this is over. Outward prosperity is the recognised good, and the ritual and the sacrifice are for procuring it. Yet ritual and sacrifice are not, as later, magical means for controlling the supernatural powers, but are still supplication and offering to persuade and win the favour of the deities, who control men's actions but are not controlled by them.

This religion of offering sacrifices as food to please the gods and increase their power, and prayers to invoke their aid to fill man's mouth with good things, is commonly thought to be purely selfish and material. Then it is concluded that all religion is the same, only better disguised.

But should it not first be asked whether there was in the world anything better at the time; whether we have any right to expect another beginning than a fellowship which helps to make individual good the common good, and a sense of security in material things which could give the mind freedom to consider something higher; and whether there is anything else, save religion, which could have been the source of man's more unselfish and spiritual interests?

Higher ethical ideas did, in point of fact, begin to appear: and, through the ritual, the gods that were of importance for man's higher interests came to be more prominent, and Varuna, 'who is strict against sin while showing mercy to the penitent',

[1] *The Cambridge History of India*, vol. I, p. 103.

came to have a unique position, so that he promised to be like Zeus as Theos or even Ahura-Mazda.

The question is, why was this personal god, who might have replaced all polytheism and become the moral order of the universe, replaced by a pantheistic Brahma, who was not only served by magic, but could be controlled by it? The gods have still traditional existence, but they no longer complete this imperfect world by working in answer to prayer and sacrifice. They are mere tools in the hands of the Brahmans, the priestly caste; and later they tremble at the might acquired by the ascetic practices of the Yogi. Even black magic, to wither and to curse, is right in the hands of the Brahmans. All this is strange, and can hardly be reckoned progress, yet some measure of explanation can be offered.

Much is accounted for by an objective and accurate language made permanent in sacred writings, which had been developed under the influence of an advanced polytheism but now became the tool of subjective and dialectical minds. Magic is systematised in the sacrifice, and ritual made impressive by resonant repetition of formulas in which the familiar cadence of antique words plays a large part. When a people moves from the conditions which have created its language, language with a flavour of sacred antiquity always appears something magical, the meaning being of little importance compared with the feeling it stirs. Such ritual of impressive words, which have magical force by repetition in traditional intonation, is by no means confined to India. Though more effective among some peoples than others, everywhere it has been used to stir the feeling of the undifferentiated holy as awe, which is the ultimate element in all mystical, as it is in all primitive, religion.

Further explanations of the change have been given, and they may all have weight. Thus it is impossible to question either the effect of the sweltering valley of the Ganges on a vigorous northern race, or the influence of the religious ideas of the peoples it conquered, which were doubtless, as they are to-day, animistic. And there is as little doubt about the effect of turning the Vedas into magically sacred tradition, whereby their more primitive ideas, like *mana*, and the power of the shaman won by wild ecstasy and self-tortures and self-denials, and even general ideas of order like *rta*, were systematised and modified, and exalted over the higher polytheistic.

In all this we have a return to primitive ideas: and the cause is that, in several respects, there is an actual return to a primitive state. All persons who escape the burden of subduing the earth, whose wives and children have a position which reduces the family to a sort of clan, who meet life's claims upon them by an easy and gratifying openness of hand when they have, and by priding themselves on their race when they have not, are more or less in a primitive state. Only rights which are responsibilities can maintain a higher. In the Upanishads, for example, there is a most astonishing absence of any such conception. A wife is for the sake of her husband and may be lightly abandoned for the sake of his soul; gifts are for merit, and large possession is good because it is the means for acquiring large merit. Further, a world thus non-ethical and even irrational, is already more or less unreal, because man needs to keep both his reason and conscience in good repair by conquering the world, if they are to serve him well.

Caste then is the most important consideration for our problem, and possibly for the whole situation. The Aryan conqueror lived a Southern planter kind of life, with all religion preaching the curse of Ham and no one writing 'Uncle Tom's Cabins'. The Southern planter, too, had primitive virtues and vices, a stately sense of superiority, the open-handed ways of a chief, set taboos in his own class but laxity with regard to others, superiority to persistent toil and menial tasks. His superiority was too little questioned to create in him the pessimism of the Hindu, yet his religion was an orthodoxy of a magical order, and his heaven a good deal of a Nirvana. There is such a thing as the noble savage in the strictly class-meaning of the word: for any class which has freedom from the challenge of life's tasks and problems has a primitive mind. But, with reflexion, a primitive mind cannot have primitive peace. Feeling, diverted from the joy of knowledge and victory and consciously directed to pleasantness as mere feeling, is never far from pessimism, because, if pain ends with itself, it is able to dominate all other feelings.

Mysticism has always been in some form esoteric, and has on the whole been confined to the classes who were in a position to provide their own discipline for their bodies, instead of being indebted to life's battle for enough of it. Hence it has never had a message for the toiler, so that Indian religion is not unique in having no vision which would enable it to say to the outcast, 'except your righteousness shall exceed the righteousness of the Brahmans, ye shall in no wise enter into the kingdom of heaven'. That all these religions, early Buddhism included, were religions purely of the upper classes, determines their quality. The outcast had to get along with his animisms and lower polytheisms as best he could. Perhaps, as these at least cheered him on his way, one purpose of the ascetic doings of his superiors may have been to achieve his freedom from the worry of a complex life, while maintaining the sense of class superiority. This we may call aristocratic primitiveness, and perhaps no mysticism is wholly rid of the satisfaction of it.

The mere fact of being esoteric is itself primitive, for all primitive ideas are a mark of a tribe, not the basis of a religion for all humanity. The kinship of mystical pantheism with the primitive, moreover, appears, not only in its tolerance of primitive ideas, but in its readiness to absorb them. Neo-Platonism admitted all kinds of animistic superstitions, and would have been empty without them; and even Christian mysticism has not been free from ideas of magic, and it more readily tolerates superstition than the intellectual chill of the criticism which assails it. The mere idea of the One has no control over the many which would challenge man to undertake the task of valuing all things in due order. All this may be summed up by saying that mysticism comes near the primitive culture by refusing to bear the burden of the concrete individual, with all this means of positive conflict with the world.

The difference introduced by a mind which has arrived at

the idea of system soon begins to affect the whole situation; and this becomes plain in the Upanishads.

By this philosophy the magic of the sacrifice was developed into a faith in the One, in which the soul is and which is in the soul, and for which all else is a magic issuing from the One, or an illusion imposed by the soul itself.

The name of the One is Brahma. This name originally was the sacrificial formula; and Brahma is just systematised, exalted, universal *mana*. The first use of this unity of everything with the All was to give rationality and effectiveness and sublimity to the magical rites, and was not separable from them, though they were only truly effective when consciously done in this faith of their relation to the One. But, in time, the knowledge of Brahma and the soul's identity with him came to be a doctrine of salvation by itself: and this was the easier that the Brahman who performed the rites was also a teacher, and tended to become more a teacher than a priest, if we can trust his prayer that pupils should come unto him like a flood.

(*d*) PESSIMISM

With this there went, either as a cause or an effect, or most probably both, the kind of pessimism which did not merely deny the face value of the Natural, but which came to be summed up as "all the elements of life are misery". Asceticism mixed with ecstasy as a way of attaining power was very old in India. Now it comes to be the means of attaining the state in which "conflict ceases when there is nothing but the self". Yet, at first, this is not pessimistic, because in this soul "all things, all goods, all worlds, all breathing things are held together".[1]

This was still optimistic pantheism: and logically, it seems difficult to pass to pessimism, because, if all things are Brahma are they not good, and if our soul or *atman* is all Brahma is it not also good? But, whether we can explain it or not, the passage from pantheistic optimism to the sense that all is unreality and all misery has always been both certain and rapid [2]

[1] R. E. Hume, *The Thirteen Principal Upanishads*, p. 104
[2] "The Western World", an Indian professor of physics once said to me, "plays

Nor are reasons impossible to find. When all is given by process, there is no real room for human achievement. Therefore, feeling is arrested from its natural development into interest in an objective world, where the joy of living can face the darkest problems, conflicts and trials of life, in the confidence of finding a higher value in life and a purpose beyond the present, and is turned back upon itself as mere awareness, as mere feeling, which is the most unstable and may be the most distressing of all things. We see the difference in Buddha under the sacred fig-tree finding all the elements of life misery, and Jesus on the Cross finding them all fullness of life and victory.

To this must be added the idea which went with it, that the world which the objective feelings manifest is *maya*—magic, illusion. We have, even as late as the earlier Upanishads, the old idea of a creator, but now it is as the great magician. Out of his own power Brahma produces the world as the great illusion. This naturally raised the question of how far it is produced by Brahma and has a relative reality, and how far by ourselves and has none. The same difficulty appears in all mysticism More and more it is driven to the idea that the manifold is produced by the self, for if it is produced by the One, and the One is good, why should it not, even as illusion, have a good purpose? Then we have the idea, not of *karma* merely, which is old, but of *karma* as the producer of this illusion. On this view, feeling not only has nothing in itself which is permanent, but it reveals nothing permanent, neither meaning in the Natural nor purpose beyond it. Therefore, nothing can be abiding except what is untouched by feeling.

This is the basis of the Samkhya It holds that the soul is unchanging, uninfluenced, yet is the centre of the world of illusion, an illusion which, on a lower range of knowledge, is real, yet does not concern the soul, which is apart from what happens to the individual and even from what his empirical

---

with pantheism, and perhaps then pantheism may not do much harm, but the Eastern takes it seriously and it sucks the blood" Yet the shadow of Hegel, even in the West, is Schopenhauer.

self may be. This embodies the Hindu ultimate mystical idea, though, as Keith says, it is hopelessly illogical.

When to this doctrine of *maya* and of the soul as Brahma was joined the old *Yoga*, which came down from something like the Dervish, we have a new development of mysticism, which continues to this day, and which raises the most important question regarding the Mystic Way. The unsympathetic call it self-hypnotism. There is asceticism to the point of what seems to us entire stupefaction, such as sitting between fires under the blazing Indian sun, standing for hours on the head, and such-like. Then there are the usual methods of self-hypnotism by regulation of the breath and pressing the tongue on the roof of the mouth, fixing the attention on one object, such as the navel or the point of the nose. Except the Egyptian monks, no Christian mystic has gone to this extreme. But if the way to reality is suppression of sense-perception and rational thinking, the method is justified. The only question is whether such a method does not itself condemn the end, which is pure light without any object it illumines, an ecstasy of completely void awareness. This is Nirvana, or at least a foretaste of it, when the eternal, unchangeable alone remains, and rebirths and all earthly happenings are shaken off from the soul that has realised itself as pure undiluted Brahma.

(e) COMMON ELEMENTS

No Indian religion really departs from this foundation. As Prof. Konow says, "The unity idea of the Vedanta, which equates man with the Eternal, discovering man in God and God in man, meets us continually, alike in the pantheistic and in the theistic systems".[1] "Again and again we meet the tendency to seek, behind all the mysterious potencies and substances, an all-penetrating and all-determining original power. This appears in the Vedic idea of *rta*, in the doctrine of the omnipotent sacrifice, in the Brahma idea of the Upani-

[1] *Lehrbuch der Religionsgeschichte*, vol. II, p. 88.

shads, in the belief in the law of *karma* and the redeeming might of knowledge."[1] The soul may be conceived as all Brahma, as part of Brahma, as alongside of Brahma, and even by being full of *Bhaktas* to have some semblance of a personal relation. But the idea of salvation, as absorption in this oneness, remains the same, and in the end it is mystical and pantheistic of the acosmic type, with a passive and even negative morality.

The general effect morally is hard to estimate, but it does not seem to contradict the Apostle's statement that, 'Touch not, taste not, handle not is not of any value against indulgence of the flesh', or Leuba's view that, so far from overcoming the self, it springs from inordinate self-concentration: and there are competent observers who think that the whole view of the unreality of life creates a callous mind. Love indeed is taught, but it is of a kind which could be satisfied with freedom from any emotion of repulsion.

Finally, there is less difference between the forms of salvation—salvation by works, which means ritual doings, salvation by knowledge, and salvation by love—than appears at first sight. We have already spoken of the three unities of form with which mysticism works. Here we have them. One is the world as one magical potency; one is the self as one knower including all knowledge; one is the feeling which is one all-embracing yet empty emotion. But, from whatsoever point the start is made, the goal is the same, being absorption of the soul in the One. And all alike work with one undifferentiated feeling of the holy, with a sacred which is one unchanging absolute value, and with a Supernatural which is one unchanging oneness.

The likeness of Buddhism to all this becomes ever plainer with increasing knowledge. That it was merely a rationalistic sect of Hinduism, with no soul and no Supernatural, can be maintained by selecting what favours the theory. But it is improbable in itself, and there is weighty evidence to the contrary. The empirical ego is more vigorously denied, karma is

[1] *Op. cit.* p. 148.

raised more fully to a universal and more ethical law of the equivalence of action and award, but the ordinary Indian notions of a true self and of karma working by illusion are not less assumed because they may not be discussed.

The idea of the duty of helping to redeem others, however, gave some measure of reality to a moral world. This was further developed, probably under external influences, in the Mahayana, though even there the inherent fatalism has degenerated largely into ideas like *Feng-Shui*, with the priest little more than a kind of augur of the lucky and unlucky.

Acosmic pantheism lies at the root of all these forms, so that their differences are only of method, and not of substance. One form starts with the holy as one undifferentiated diffused feeling; one with the self as containing all the value of the undifferentiated sacred; one with the real environment as the undifferentiated Supernatural: but all work with the abiding as mere undifferentiated unity, and all come to the same result of a feeling which has no objective meaning and victory, of a self that has no difference of quality or profit from experience, and of a universe which has no meaning or purpose in its changes. In all it is the unchanging oneness which alone abides amid the fleeting.

(f) CHRISTIAN MYSTICISM

In the strict sense, there is no such thing as a Christian mystic, because, in so far as there is use of a historical revelation and of a church, with its cult, fellowship and active service of others, the religion is not mystical. In a distracted age which dissipates the sense of unity and peace, some measure of mysticism may serve at least a temporary purpose of recollection and be a help to recover the forms without which the content of experience may be only chaotic impressions and feverish activities which 'lay waste our powers'.

English writers usually understand by mysticism this mixed form, and even it they do not distinguish from prophetic insight into the meaning of history and experience or intuition of the purpose beyond them, though they are entirely different.

The mixture is defended on the ground that no one wholly a mystic would be out of the asylum; and the use of mysticism for what we may call objective insight is justified on the ground that anything else would be morbid. Ordinary usage, it is true, justifies almost any application of the term, because it is one of the vaguest words in the language, 'mystical' being sometimes only a synonym for 'vague'. Even when more carefully employed, we have only one word for what German distinguishes as *Mystik* and *Mysticismus*. But in any treatment which professes to be scientific, things so very different should be carefully distinguished. What we are discussing here is *Mysticismus* which tends at least to be acosmic pantheism, whereas *Mystik* is almost as wide as religion.

In spite of the difficulty which our practical, objective mind has in conceiving it, there have been many Hindus and some Christians who have been wholly mystics, in this sense of regarding the Natural as illusion and all concrete personality as of the Natural, and of seeking unity of soul with the Supernatural as an absolute, undifferentiated oneness, by ridding themselves of all else.

Doubtless they regarded the world as little more than their asylum, but their fellow-men allowed them to go their way. And, even were the statement that they should have been in the asylum true, it is entirely irrelevant, because the business of all scientific inquiry is to isolate a phenomenon. It would be much truer to say that no one could be wholly a naturalist, and not be in some kind of confinement, while, for certain people, a little more naturalism might do no harm. But just as our business is to ask what naturalism is undiluted, so with mysticism.

With true mystics, even Christian, it leads in the same direction as in India. The rites of the Church tend to become fixed points of magical contemplation. Though the mystic state, in the form of ecstasy, cannot be maintained and there must be a return to ordinary life, which means a return to the common religious call to serve one's fellows, this mystic state is the highest, and such service is for recuperating from the flight into the empyrean and giving vigour to soar still higher, and not for itself. Moreover, the Western mystic is constantly driven, in spite of a confessional faith in God as Father, to something very like acosmic pantheism, which is the only true justification for the view that God is not manifest in his works but is only to be known by direct interpenetration of spirit and passive absorption into his oneness. For this all history and all experience are merely disturbing or irrelevant, or, at best, a means of passing beyond themselves to the true unchanging reality. Intellectual and moral preparations are usually required, but they are only means for ridding the soul of the illusion of the self and its world: and when this is won, the intellectual and moral again disappear. Nor is it easy to escape the view that the empirical self is the one illusion which creates all the rest, for if the world is in any way God's, it must be in some sense real and in some sense good. Thus the general feeling at least is not far from the acosmic-pantheistic, however much formal acknowledgment there be of God as Father.

What this means we shall see if we consider Dom Butler's reasons for confining himself to Augustine, Gregory and Bernard in his account of Western Mysticism.

(1) They were too early to be influenced by the writings of the Pseudo-Dionysius. This means that they had not yet learned the device of how to rise from sense to ideas of negation, darkness, void, unknowing, viewless abyss, in short, the Mystic Way of later Christian mystics. From this point, Butler rightly judges that mystic contemplation passes from being an occasional and unarranged experience into a systematised cult.

(2) These fathers were pre-scholastic. That is to say they lived before mysticism had developed a mystical theology, and become, as Butler expresses it, a science of contemplation rather than contemplation itself, an intellectual system, rather than a religious experience.

(3) Four other reasons he gives, but they may be reduced to one. These fathers lived before the days of visions, raptures, ecstasies, physical manifestations, the large rôle assigned to the

Evil One, and the prominence of women mystics, which is to say before the day of special, cultivated emotions.[1]

But mysticism, as here understood, is what has these features. It is a technique of withdrawing desire from the Natural by asceticism; of preventing the senses from witnessing to it by excluding all images of sense; and then, by suppressing all thinking even as contemplation, of passing into ecstasy. Its theology is of the eternal, unchanging unity, one shining glory of light and light alone. Its highest method is ecstatic union with the One and passive reception of the divine. As all concern with the Natural is evil, the Natural is represented by one spirit of evil As the aim is the dominance of one feeling the readiest vehicle is a certain type of feminine responsiveness, which is by no means confined to one sex.

Nevertheless, even this special mysticism, in spite of the historical continuity of its cult, is far too independent, yet far too uniform, to be disposed of as mere self-delusion working on nothing. That the cult is a device which becomes more elaborate as it passes from one devotee to another, gives it an air of artificiality, which is very far from confirming faith in it as a higher way of revelation than man's best thinking about his fullest experience. Yet it could not have been carried on by any spread of doctrine so widely and so uniformly without some basis in experience.

There is an amazing, a stereotyped uniformity of testimony. In the whole literature of mysticism, when we strip it of its artificial language, this uniformity is of a monotony which is far more like the testimony to a mirage sun than the varied impressions of the world men receive under the light of the actual orb of day Yet, even if we regard it as mirage, we must explain it as mirage, and not as mere psychological illusion.

The suggestion has already been made that it has its source in real forms of unity—of the self, of the world and of the feeling by which the self knows the world. If so, it is just the attempt to have the forms without being troubled by

[1] *Western Mysticism*, pp. 179 ff.

their harassing, conflicting, and not always manageable content.

Returning into one's self is an attempt to abide in the empty unity of mind; the dogmatic system an attempt to empty environment of all but its unity, making it, as it were, a mirror which reflects nothing except light, the asceticisms and ecstasies ways of having one passive, undifferentiated feeling: while the assigning of the incursions of the natural world to the Devil merely shows the difficulty of maintaining the undifferentiated and undisturbed feeling of the holy, which is so often described, in the most superlative and even erotic language, as a state of bliss.

But the fact that mysticism works with real, and even fundamental, elements in experience, does not prove it to be revelation, because, while empty forms may be real subjective experience, they are not experience of objective reality The studied isolation of the form is only a device, which is in itself a doubtful way of dealing with any experience, because experience only speaks to us truly as we deal with it simply, sincerely and objectively. And it may be a very misleading device, if it divert us from the high purpose of winning harmony in the whole activity of our spirit and all the manifestations of our world, and offer us an easier way than dealing with the widest experience of environment as taught both by life and history, by applying our fullest knowledge and all our powers.

Yet we are not here specially concerned with the question of whether the effects of mysticism are good or bad. There is nothing manifesting even the most partial aspects of reality, which, under certain circumstances and with the people who are great and wise enough to choose the good and reject the bad, may not advance our knowledge of the highest, even as there is nothing so complete in itself that it cannot be abused. What we are concerned with is whether this is the right relation of the Natural to the Supernatural.

In the first place, when one material object after another ceases to stir the sense of the holy, till, finally, the holy cannot be connected with any of them, is nothing left but the mere feeling itself, which is unchanging, because it is an empty temple of awe? Or should it mean that we ought to face all life, its common objects, its trials, its conflicts, its problems, its daily tasks, its ordinary human relations, with a finer, more objective sense of the beauty of holiness, responding to the sense of one reverence which embraces them all?

In the second place, when we see that what man has valued as sacred may become merely secular, and even what we ourselves value as sacred duties may come to appear little more than traditional taboos, are we to say that nothing is of absolute value except the hidden, unchanging depth of our own spirit? Or should we, with a more open-minded, sincere and steadfast loyalty to what we see as highest, and more conscientious purpose to see what is still higher, seek to know the truly sacred as the most real as well as the highest, wherein we realise our true empirical selves?

Finally—and this includes all the rest—are we to find the eternal only in what is unchanging, and the sole ultimate reality to be the All-one, into which we enter as we discard the empirical self? Or are we to seek the Supernatural as the Father of our spirits and him in whom all fullness dwells, as what gives meaning to the world and a purpose beyond it which assure that to be called according to his purpose is to find it all working for good?

This brings us again to the view discussed far back in this work, that man is a reasoning, tool-using, humorous being, because his sense of the holy, his absolute value of the sacred, and his faith in the Supernatural gave him a footing in the flux of experience, and thereby means of victory over the Natural. Is religion concerned with carrying on this beginning? Is it to consecrate reason more utterly to seeing the real relations of all things, till man discovers both the Natural and the Supernatural to be one harmonious order; is tool-using in the broad sense for achieving victory over the world for all human good and especially the highest, and finally, is man's triumph over his feelings, which begins as humour, to go on till he win a reconciliation which, in face of all evil, is joy and peace? Or is all this idea of high adventure a mere illusion of our empirical selves, which is the supreme illusion? Is the true religious task of the reason to undo the elaborate web it has woven; of the will to cease from its task of conquering the world and have peace in quiescence; and of the feeling, to abandon its endless effort and aspiration, and, realising that all desire is misery, to sink itself in the bliss of one impersonal and empty awareness? In short, is the right way of finding the eternal to be quit of the evanescent?

CHAPTER XXV

THE CEREMONIAL-LEGAL

(a) COMMON AND DISTINGUISHING ELEMENTS OF
APOCALYPTIC RELIGIONS

BEFORE entering on this subject, it may be well to repeat that the term apocalyptic is here used in contrast to mystic, and means any religion which looks for an unveiling of the Supernatural in the Natural.

The higher apocalyptic religions see as clearly as Buddha that the fashion of this world passes away; that the Natural, with ourselves in so far as we belong to it, is subject to the bondage of corruption; that life, even while it lasts, may be misery. Moreover, the Hebrew prophets in particular knew these facts, not as shadowy and sometimes artificial dogma, but as actual overwhelming disaster. From Elijah onwards they saw the ruin of their civilisation approaching as invasion, political chaos and moral corruption; and the three greatest movements of prophecy, whereby its deepest discoveries were made and its greatest victories won, were due to Hosea, Jeremiah and Jesus, who lived in the days when this conviction became reality. Hosea prophesied in face of the dissolution of Northern Israel, amid the combined horrors of revolution and the imminence of invasion; Jeremiah in face of the unspeakable calamities of siege, famine, pestilence and brutal captivities, by which the Southern fell; and Jesus face to face with the final end of his people as a nation, which he saw approaching with such tribulation as had not been since the world began. Also the prophetic judgment of moral evil was more universal than the mystical, because it was more profound. For the prophets, and still more for Jesus, Buddha's virtues were little more than respectabilities and negations, and the vices he condemned of small account compared with the inward hypocrisies he overlooked.

Even the lower forms of apocalyptic religion, Zoroastrianism and Hebrew Legalism, had their character largely determined by a struggle with nature and cruel foes which was too hard to afford leisure for the luxury of self-pity and too insistent to be dismissed as illusion. Moreover, though these forms still measured blessing by material prosperity and tended to confuse moral evil with ritual contamination, they had a far more real sense, not only of physical but of moral evil, than is found in any mystical religion, because in such a conflict the negations could not be the virtues, nor the affirmations the vices. And with this went a different valuation of the concrete personality.

More than any other religions, the apocalyptic religions learned, in a stern school, how much the concrete personality, in as far as it is in the Natural, is exposed to the chances and changes of time: but, unlike the mystical, they did not end with the concrete person as merely part of the Natural. Though they knew it to be in the Natural and even by the uses of the Natural, they did not conceive it to be merely the part of the Natural by which evanescence and misery lay hold of us. Not merely as some abstract unity of soul, but as the actual character of the individual, they regarded it as itself of the Supernatural, and thereby found the Natural to have a meaning and purpose above the seen and temporal.

At the same time there is a double estimate of the worth of the Natural. The concrete individual and the actual world have absolute worth from what they have in them to be and to serve. But also the concrete individual is radically evil because of the absolute worth he fails to realise, and the world can be made evil by being diverted to the service of the unworthy self. For the ceremonial-legal religion, righteousness was possible though hard; and part of the world only evil: but, for the prophetic, man's righteousness is as filthy rags and the heart deceitful above all things and desperately wicked, and his whole world as he uses it lies in the Evil One. At the same time, while for the ceremonial-legal only part of experience can work for good, for the prophetic all things work together for the true divine fulfilment of what man should be, and nothing is outside of God's rule.

As in all these religions the Natural is thought to unfold a divine meaning and be big with divine promise, they can all, as the term is here used, be called apocalyptic: but, with the possible exception of Mohammedanism, they have all cherished hopes of sudden, catastrophic transformations, which makes them apocalyptic in the strict sense. Though these catastrophic hopes depended for their particular embodiments on the circumstances of the time, they all express the same essential faith that God's will is to be done on earth as it is in heaven: and this deter.nines their ethic as well as their theology. But, with the higher forms, more and more the hope passes from a change in the Natural itself to a change of the heart that uses it, so that the new heavens and the new earth have their newness from righteousness dwelling in them. The failure of Mohammedanism to develop this attitude is only one among many proofs that, whatsoever be its value for maintaining monotheism against idolatry and disciplining masses of men by a morality of legal injunctions, it contributes nothing to any higher way of conceiving the relation of the Natural and the Supernatural, but measures even the bliss of heaven by purely natural good in no way exalted.

Though regard for the concrete individual and for the Natural as his sphere of discipline and duty is thus common to all apocalyptic religions, they are divided into the ceremonial-legal and the prophetic by the difference in the ideal of the concrete individual and in the measure of his possession of the Natural.

The former seeks the ideal in legal righteousness, and measures the good in the world as it rewards this by material prosperity, taking the same view as the Indian religions of what the justice of the world is, with the difference that, with due ritual and ethical circumspection, life will be happiness, not misery.

Though these forms are described as ceremonial-legal, they are not distinguished merely by any kind of ceremonialism and legalism. As both ceremonial and legal elements begin to emerge even in the lowest religions and continue not yet overcome even in the highest, it is not anything distinctive about a religion to have ceremonial and legal elements. But in this type, in the first place, the moral is the legal and the legal is ceremonial precept; and, in the second, this is not merely one among other elements, but determines the whole view of the Natural and the relation to the Natural of the Supernatural.

This view of the relation of the Natural and the Supernatural may be regarded as a development of the problems of polytheism. When with reflexion the many sporadic perplexities become one problem and this becomes the central problem of religion, polytheism disappears: but so long as the distinction of material good and bad is regarded as ultimate, the problem is still the same as in polytheism, and to get farther than some kind of dualism, with the pleasant and profitable alone related to God's will and the rest lying in the Wicked One, was impossible. The final distinction was between sacred and secular, rather materially than morally conceived, the sacred, as it were, being alone God's territory. These forms of religion, therefore, are not truly moral and monotheistic, but only tend to be.

The prophetic religion also regarded natural good and evil as real and important. But, on the one hand, it did not think any of the Natural secure, or at its best as measured by possession and profit, necessarily blessed; and on the other, it believed that the worst might have in it such abiding divine meaning and purpose as to turn its evil into good and its evanescence into an eternal possession.

This change of outlook is like the change from having sensations as feeling to concern with them as objective information, when objective interest puts the mere pleasantness and unpleasantness of the passing sensations into the background. So the Supernatural, like the Natural, manifests itself as a real, varied, concrete, wonderful world, itself the compensation for the tribulation by which its kingdom is entered.

Like other stages of religion, these forms are not sharply marked off from each other. The higher ceremonial stage prepared for the prophetic; and the prophetic was very far from dispossessing even the lower. But there is also a closer relation between them than the mere fact that, in history, they overlap.

THE CEREMONIAL-LEGAL

Even primitive religions may have prophets, who introduce more spiritual ideas into the traditional forms, the spiritual and moral elements of all religions being prophetic. But all ceremonial-legal religions are still further prophetic in the sense of having had known prophetic founders. Moses and Zarathustra may only be dim figures, looming vaguely out of the past, yet, more certainly even than Mohammed, they taught a higher and more ethical approach to monotheism than their followers were able to receive except in so far as it could be incorporated into the general religion in the form of ceremonial law, both moral and ritual.

The direct ascription of the ceremonial-legal system to Moses is doubtless not historical. Much was before, and much grew up afterwards. Even in Deuteronomy Moses is a prophet, whose true succession in Israel would be prophetic. Yet indirectly the legislation—ceremonial as well as moral—could be ascribed to him, in the sense that the inspiration which raised it to a spiritual level which made any admixture with it of the religion of the surrounding peoples a debasing of it, could only have been from his prophetic reform.

What was discovered prophetically was carried on and in some measure made available for the popular religion legally; and the higher ceremonial-legalism produced from the living spirit of prophecy was also, under certain conditions, a protective shell for the prophetic.

But what protects, in time imprisons: and we find both the prophets and Jesus faced with a situation in which the external legal embodiment of religion had to be destroyed if the spirit of religion was to be saved. Yet, forthwith, both the prophets and Jesus were also turned into a new law, which was more moral and even more spiritual than the old, though not less external. As ceremonial precept, and not as personal faith and insight, their higher teaching spread in as large measure as was possible in so inadequate a form, till it became the general creed and the common worship and rules of practice.

Yet the simpler and higher and more personal the living prophetic faith is, the more elaborate must be the ceremonial-legal substitute for it. Therefore later Judaism and Catholic Christianity have a more elaborate ceremonial-legalism than any other form of religion. And even then there is more of the shell than of the kernel.

In this ideal sense it can be said with the Apostle that the gospel was before the law. But, as a stage of progress and in actual historical form, the ceremonial-legal is much earlier than anything to be called prophetic. Thus, though the Jewish Law as we find it was mainly after the prophets, and stereotyped much of their teaching, it is misleading to say that modern research has reversed the order of Law and Prophecy and made it first the Prophets and then the Law. The Law absorbed the prophets because it was already there and was never deposed from its dominion over men's minds, and could not be till men had achieved the prophetic freedom. And the same was true of Christianity. It became a new law, not because this was its true outcome, but because it had only a very partial victory over the ceremonial-legalism of Judaism or even of Paganism which was already in possession.

For this reason we cannot say of any religion that it is purely legal or purely prophetic. Yet if we contrast Zoroastrianism with the religion of the prophets, Pharisaic Judaism with the religion of Jesus, and the general spirit of Mohammedanism with the general spirit of Christianity, a distinction between ceremonial-legalism and prophetic freedom becomes sufficiently clear for a working distinction, clear enough at all events to allow us to consider the ceremonial-legal form by itself.

(*b*) DUALISM AS A PROBLEM AND AS A SOLUTION

All ceremonial-legal religions are dualistic in the sense that they still value good and evil as material prosperity or adversity, and so are led to divide the world into a part which serves the purposes of a good God and a part which is of the powers of evil. And this leads to the further dualism of a sharp distinction between the sacred and the secular, because so long as material good and evil is primary and moral good and evil only secondary, the way to keep in the sphere of the good,

THE CEREMONIAL-LEGAL 433

is strict ceremonial observance and ritual purity Therefore, nothing so marks this type of religion as the domination of the fear of ritual impurity because it exposes to the powers of evil. The result is not only that morality is always in danger of becoming secondary to ritual precept, but as morality is only part of the system for securing natural good and shunning natural evil, it is itself ceremonial precept, more apt to be sacred tradition and material taboo than moral insight and moral motive

There is hardly any form of higher religion in which, in this way, the material sacred and secular have not at some time appeared, and perhaps there is none in which they are not always present. Moreover, something of dualism has affected so many thinkers that a general discussion of the problem would take us too far afield.

Nor is this necessary, because only the difference between dualism as a problem and dualism as an explanation concerns deeply our special question of the Natural and Supernatural.

Whether the distinction of sacred and secular, thus materially interpreted, became a definite theology or not, it was in practical effect dualism, but the theology makes a vital difference. Dualism become a theology is a final solution; whereas, without a theology, it is a standing problem. As few distinctions have been of weightier import in the development of man's thoughts about the relation of the Natural and the Supernatural, we must consider two examples—one of dualism as a final, a theological solution, and one of it as a standing practical problem Zoroastrianism is so much the greatest representative of the former and Judaism of the latter that there is no call to go beyond them. Judaism alone may have been the direct source of a higher conception of the relation of the Natural and the Supernatural, but Zoroastrianism emphasises two essential elements of progress, and what is even more illuminating for our subject, shows two great by-ways into which men turn aside from it.

(c) THE PERSIAN SITUATION

The great contrast between the Persian and the Indian religions is the more striking in that the Persians and the Indians were the same race and started from the same polytheism. The vast difference between them might, therefore, seem to be due entirely to difference in environment: and this might be regarded as showing that man's religion, as well as all that belongs to him, is merely a product of his environment. And if we take environment widely enough and also realise that man's environment is largely as he deals with it, this conclusion may be accepted. But, if it mean his purely physical environment apart from any use or misuse he may make of it, the explanation is obviously inadequate

We have seen the importance for Indian religions of the hot and fertile plains and especially of a subject and submissive inferior race to till them. Without the fruits of its labours, there would have been no need for self-appointed asceticism, nor any complex life from which to flee, nor leisure for the study of contemplation or the enjoyment of ecstasy. And, for the most part, all mysticism has been in the same aristocratic position, trying to make itself primitive. The mystic who was a shoemaker was rather a unique person, and there are few other trades, and least of all tilling the soil, with which contemplation can be so easily conjoined. Are there any small farmers or farm-servants who have been mystics? Buddha thought the mildest horticulture a dangerous occupation for his monks, and doubtless he was right from his point of view Christian monks have even been pioneers in agriculture, but it is doubtful if any of them were mystics, and certainly not when so occupied

In contrast, all ceremonial-legalism was originally a religion of the working farmer Zoroastrianism has him in view continually, and he is as obviously the person with whom the earlier laws and the earlier cult of Israel are chiefly concerned

So as not to be suspect of stating the problem to suit the

answer, I quote an independent witness on what the Persian situation was.

"With bodily strength and vigour went an energetic will, steeled in conflict with a harsh climate and the dangers of the nomadic life on mountain and steppe. Thus the Persians won courage and seriousness. Yet there was also awe before the dark, dread side of existence, which continually showed itself in their ethics and their religion, and which, for their whole spiritual existence, would have been fatal, had it not stirred in them an equally intense striving for light and power and victory over evil." Hence "the wavering between dreamy idealism and pure materialism, which meets us with the Indians, is entirely shut out from the Persian way of thinking, because, from the first, the two sides of reality were grasped in their natural equality of power".[1]

This certainly emphasises the difference of situations, but it does not prove that there was nothing but the situation. Where nature 'is tickled with a hoe and it smiles with a harvest' is not where man has best understood the Natural or most turned it to higher ends. And if this gives men their desires but sends leanness into their souls, and if there is no real entering upon a higher environment except by higher uses of the lower, the thoughts of men, whom life has challenged to strenuous endeavour, are, by this very fact, of value concerning the Supernatural as concerning the Natural. If right thinking is produced not by passively accepting the environment, but by actively discovering challenge and opportunity even in its hardness, a situation which challenges the active virtues and affords scope for their exercise must deserve consideration. Yet not, except by these virtues themselves, is anything ever discovered in any situation, beyond the superficial and material.

It will suffice to take the four Platonic virtues. They are wisdom, which is insight to look beneath the surface of things and direct life to higher ends; temperance, which is active self-mastery over the lust of the flesh, the lust of the eyes and the pride of life; courage, which is enterprise and virile stead-

[1] Ed Lehmann in *Das Lehrbuch der Religionsgeschichte*, vol. II, pp. 201-202.

fastness in face of difficulty and opportunity; righteousness, which is due balance and valuation, with an unwavering regard to the duties more than the privileges of our sphere. The positive exercise of these virtues, and not the mere hardness of environment, is what works higher faith as well as austerer morals.

Yet in principle, it is the faith which is first. As Luther says, it is the quality of faith to be able to go against appearances. But faith is sustained by its victories, and languishes without enduring hardness. It endures as seeing what is invisible: and in all the history of religion such a victorious faith has always looked in the direction of one God, who is the meaning and purpose even of the visible world. But faith in one personal God is only sustained by serving his meaning and purpose as our most real environment. Without this faith, the Natural may be taken to be merely our own illusion, blurring the vision of the Supernatural, and the Supernatural to be a mere diffused sense of the magically holy, like Brahma, or a mere metaphysical abstract Absolute which is little more than unrestricted potency, not very distinct from universal mana.

(d) TWO ELEMENTS OF PROGRESS

Ritual and ethical law, as ceremonial precept, is tradition accepted very much in the primitive way; and many at least of the ritual forms have their direct descent from primitive forms of magic, and still derive their impressiveness from the primitive awesome holy and material sacred. Yet there are two elements of progress of great importance, one whereby the holy is no longer merely awe, and the other whereby the sacred is attached to the good in a way which is at least the beginning of conceiving the good as moral.

First the transformation of awe.

The cause of this was such a faith in the Good Power as enabled men to affirm that no fear, however dread, is ever to be averted by deference to the powers of evil. The circumspection of the ritual, and especially the care to avoid ritual impurity, show how fear still shadowed men's lives but all the more obvious for this was the value of the faith which would not defer to it

It has been said that in religion the devil was before God and in the sense that men were first concerned with appeasing the powers that wrought evil, this is true. Moreover, we have seen that, even in advanced forms of pantheism, such worshipping of Satan is not wholly overcome.

The ideal even of Zarathustra himself may not be very lofty. It is largely governed by self-interest; the conception even of self-interest rises little above the ordinary peasant's ideal of prosperity; if later it advanced somewhat, it was at best bourgeois. But because a religion is not high enough to have developed a higher good than not very enlightened self-interest, is no reason for denying that it made advance when it said, in defiance of all evil power, Thou shalt seek the good thou dost seek only from the Good Power and never by any dealing with the lie or any favour of the might of evil. To seek even material prosperity only by honest industry, especially if industry be accompanied by kindness to living creatures and neighbourliness and austere family relations, is, even in our age, not so universally regarded as elementary morality as to make it impossible for us to conceive an age when it was not a moral platitude but a high ideal which required a high faith to put into practice.

The second element of progress was that, if the sacred was still ceremonial and material and largely concerned with material good, it now became a formulated law. Formulation is itself an advance on mere traditional magical custom, because, for one thing, it must be given some kind of universal validity, and, for another, the lawgiver himself is subjected to known rule as much as other people, and has no longer the arbitrary authority of the magician which rests on possessing secrets unknown to others. Laws which are a revelation from Ormuzd to Zarathustra are very different from the unknown, uncertain, uncanny doings of the medicine-man. They are at least a discipline for all, and are, therefore, in the way of becoming laws of righteousness As the higher source to which they were ascribed in all forms of Zoroastrianism called for the exercise of a more universal moral judgment, there are traces of a morality which rose above mere ceremonial precept, and was positive and not merely negative.

(e) DUALISM AS A THEOLOGY

With these gains, however, we must take the defects which are ineradicable from dualism as a theology offered as a final solution.

Zoroaster, or more correctly Zarathustra, was a prophet of agriculture and civilisation. Armaiti, who is the spirit both of earth and prayer, "chose the pious cultivator, the propagator of life, whom she blesses with the riches produced by the Goodmind. All who do not worship her, but worship the devas, have no share in her good tidings" (meaning earth's produce). "It is as though red-hot iron were turned round in the throat of the devas, when there is plenty of corn" To till the soil well is one of the ways of reaching paradise, one description of which is the fields of the righteous. In the Gathas, where is what is at least nearest to the teaching of the founder, we have prayers such as: "This I ask thee, tell me straight, O Lord, how can I, through the right path, win the reward—ten mares, with a stallion, and a camel?" Nor does the meaning appear to be figurative. Like the Fifth Monarchy men, Zarathustra himself seems to have taught that unbelievers retain, against God's will and only for a time, the goods rightly belonging to believers.

With this conviction that sorrow should keep strictly on the track of sin, it was impossible to believe that the world is all of God. Wherefore, though Ormuzd or Ahura-Mazda, the good principle, created the world, the belief which determined all the ritual circumspection into which the whole religion degenerated, was that Ahriman or Angra Mainyu entered it and marred it. In the end Ahriman and hell shall be destroyed, and believers shall rise from the dead, and everlasting happiness reign, but meantime the chief security is in the punctilious observance of the commands given by Ormuzd to Zarathustra.

Moral good is thus inextricably confused with ceremonial circumspection about material good. Sacred prayer and sacred ceremonial are what aid the good principle, mainly if not exclusively, while the ordeal which admits into heaven is primarily concerned with ritual purity Hence sacred and secular came to be sharply defined distinctions· and as every evil could be explained as neglect of the sacred, there was nothing to raise question about dualism as a complete and final solution.

If the prison-house was enlarged, it was still a prison-house. At first, the sacred literature promised to become the record of a growing religious experience. But the Natural interpreted by the pleasant and unpleasant does not lead to objective knowledge of the Supernatural; and when circumstances became unpropitious and the vigour of the religion began to fail, life once more was enslaved to the holy as awe and the sacred as taboo. Then, with new political influences, the polytheistic feeling, which had never been wholly overcome, introduced, alongside of Ormuzd, Mithra, an old Aryan god connected with the offering and having aristocratic associations, and Anahita a goddess of fertility, probably a form of the Semitic Astarte. and the effect was disastrous, not only for the purity of the monotheism, but also for the austerity of morals. At the same time, truth became merely scholastic orthodoxy, and the lie merely its rejection. Thereby, the sacred was so fixed in the ceremonious as to leave no freedom to inquire what the sacred really is. This result is found in other religions, even in Christianity, but in no other did it become the whole religion. The Pharisees came nearest to it, but they were never the whole of Judaism, nor was it the only element either in their faith or practice

Finally Zoroastrianism never rose above the polytheistic dependence on the security of the state. When it was no longer possible to trust to the state, hope turned to a millennium to replace it more gloriously. For some this was so absorbing as to replace the old Zoroastrian interest in this life which had formerly given the religion its special character.

But the commoner effect of a material hope in the future being to make material provision for this world, when the old national religion fell with the nation and when the millennial hope followed it, little was left but a rationalistic deism which, as it still continued its search for a materially good world, turned to commerce.

(*f*) GOOD AND EVIL AS A PROBLEM

Still more plainly than the difference between the Indian and the Persian religion, the difference between the Persian and the Hebrew needs more to explain it than the situation. Both religions had to do with the stern life of toil necessary to earn a living from a niggardly soil. Yet the results are so far apart as to prove that the way of handling a situation may be more important than the nature of the situation itself. For the Persian, the difficulties of agriculture remained to the end the work of the powers of darkness, and the approval of the good was made clear by 'sheaves, big sheaves'. But the Israelite, with the insight of spiritual genius, discovered that God had cursed the earth with a grudging response to man's toil for man's sake. This view is already a moral interpretation for which dualism never could be a satisfying solution. Moreover, its idea of good and of how this good is to be won is no longer at the mercy of material evil.

The recognition of the radical opposition between good and evil allows no dualistic solution to be as final as the pantheistic. If finality is the only ultimate heresy, this is its value, and the finality of pantheism, which is its greatest attraction, is in reality its greatest defect. Granting that we are satisfied with its kind of answer, there is no question for which pantheism does not suffice Why, for example, throughout the long centuries of Indian thinking, and amid its scepticism about the visible world, are ideas like transmigration and karma never questioned? The plain reason is that, as solutions, they settle every perplexity. Job could raise heart-searching and unanswerable questions about the legal solution, because it could be brought within the criticism of present experience. But, if he had ascribed his misfortunes to the karma of previous states, he would have thought that the unknown past explained why those who fear God are despised; and he would have had an equally complete answer from the unknown future of how the prosperity of the tabernacles of robbers was to be requited. It was a problem only because even his friends did not answer him either from the unknown past or the unknown future, but confined themselves to what might at least be within the limits of someone's experience, and in particular of the transgressor's. Like himself, they were determined to see the goodness of the Lord in the land of the living, and were not satisfied to appeal to the working of a law of retribution, either in former lives or in future.

But it is also of consequence that they did not accept any dualistic solution. On the one hand, they related both good and evil in some way to God, on the other, they did not attempt to explain Job's affliction by ceremonial pollution which exposed him to the evil powers, but judged him to be outside the scope of God's protection for moral reasons.

The necessity of referring all things to God may be comparatively late and due to the influence of the prophets, but, in all the ages of Hebrew religion known to us, there was something of this power of rising above the merely ceremonial to the moral, sufficient at least to keep the dualism, which is implicit in all ceremonial law, from becoming a fixed and satisfying dogma The prophets could ignore it from the beginning, while their work made it a still more impossible solution: and how much the problem of evil was kept open, even in later Judaism, appears from the fact that Ecclesiastes, which raises it almost to scepticism, is canonical, while Tobit, which is the embodiment of what we may call juridical finality, is not.

That explanations from the unknown past did occur even to the Hebrew mind is seen from the necessity, as late as the time of our Lord, of combating the idea that a man is born blind because of his own sin or the sin of his parents. If one's own sin involved a pre-natal state, the explanation may be late and have come from some outside source, but the connexion with one's parents was combated by Jeremiah and Ezekiel, and may have been from time immemorial. Yet such ideas were employed at most as occasional helps to solve a difficult problem, and were never accepted as a final solution, which, for understanding the whole Old Testament, is of the first importance.

The Book of Job is a radical attack upon the theory that the equivalence of action and award is so much the measure of all reality that we can argue back from prosperity to virtue and from misery to vice. Carlyle speaks of it as the greatest of all that is called literature· and that it is literature is itself important, because this means that it is supremely an appeal to life. Though a supreme command of ironical and incisive criticism is no small equipment for assailing a position held mainly by not questioning its assumptions, the power of the book is its positive appeal to experience as we meet it. From beginning to end it affirms that theory must be tested by experience and not experience by theory, and that experience does not show the equivalence of action and award.

Yet the appeal would have lacked persuasiveness had there been no better interpretation on the horizon, for the last word would then have been that the tabernacles of robbers prosper and they that fear God are despised, which would have been no order at all, no vision of any cosmos. What gave courage to look reality in the face, and power to assail a theory so inconsistent with it, was the vision of a higher order already seen by the prophets Thereby, the author of Job could maintain that his position was good religion as well as good science.

At the same time, Job shows that the prophets had not succeeded in replacing the cosmology of the law of equivalence of action and award by their higher conception, and it is plain from later Judaism that no more did Job. None the less, both had a large measure of success Though the old ceremonial-legal religion continued, and, left to itself, might have ended, like Zoroastrianism, in the finality of a dualistic solution, even it never did so settle on its lees.

(g) LAW AND PROPHECY

The Old Testament shows as plainly as the Persian sacred literature that the ceremonial cult was originally concerned with securing physical well-being and averting physical calamity; that it appealed by the awesome holy and the material sacred; that the ritual was put alongside of the ethical and often before it; that the ethic, as well as the ritual, was ceremonial law, which was largely sacred tradition; and that, through material fears and the desire for material security, the religion was exposed to the attractions of polytheism. Later Judaism, though delivered from danger of actual polytheism by a sacred tradition which had incorporated the monotheism of the prophets, if not in its whole moral and spiritual fullness at least as an unquestioned creed, was almost as dualistic as Zoroastrianism. There was the same distinction between the righteous who kept the law, and those who, not knowing the law, were accursed; the Kingdom of God was the rule of the righteous so conceived and the Kingdom of Satan the rule of the unbeliever; unbelief, as the lie which condemns to outer darkness, came to be, as in Zoroastrianism, lack of orthodoxy in creed and ritual.

As much in Hebrew ceremonial-legalism as in the Persian ritual, all this rested on a sharp dualism between the sacred and the profane, which was more material than moral. Yet, just because of the absence of finality, all parts of the Old Testament are very different, morally and spiritually, from the Persian sacred literature No Hebrew religion, not even Phariseeism, failed to maintain some spirituality in the secular and an essential moral element in the sacred.

The source of this was doubtless prophetic, even before the prophets who are known to us by their writings. Yet, from Amos onward, the prophets are in conflict with the whole legal-ceremonial type of piety because of its trust in this kind of sacredness, counting it an abomination that men, who would not cease to do evil and learn to do well, should trust in the solemn mummery of sacrifices and appointed feasts. They even thought that the chief purpose of the destruction of their nation was to make an end of this type of religion, by sending it back to the wilderness where there was neither sacrifice nor offering.

Neither negatively nor positively did they wholly succeed in replacing the old ceremonial-legalism: and that much of the dualism inherent in it remained is shown by the development of Satan from a sort of *advocatus diaboli* of what is still the divine judgment, into the head of the powers of darkness above the world and the organised world-powers within it. Yet the effect of the prophetic monotheism, even as a traditional creed, appears in the fact that, in spite of the large rôle assigned to the evil power, it is still only by God's permission, within limits he has set and for the ultimate fulfilment of his purpose. Thus, though the legal-ceremonial religion never was really able to say that by God and unto God are all things, even evil was recognised as in God's world and remained a problem. And, further, a higher morality, even as a sacred tradition, made it impossible to keep the ritual merely a ceremonial safeguard without interpretation by moral ideas of sin and moral purity Thus, even in the ceremonial-legal religion, faith was in some effective measure a prophecy and morality an aspiration.

Probably at no time was the idea of ceremonial cleanness wholly divorced from some ethical feeling: and so long as this is above the level of the worshippers, it may be both a discipline and an education. Nor does any progress wholly deliver from something of awe in reverence or from some dependence upon material embodiments of the sacred, though the former should be exalted to the sublime and the latter to the symbolical. The Old Testament is, on the whole, a record of progress in both.

An important influence, which is generally overlooked, was the relating of the cult to the history of Israel. The real interest in history, as God's dealing with man and man's with God, is prophetic, but the relating of special observances to events in the national history religiously interpreted, wrought a very significant change also in the ritual. It was thereby set free from the early association with the seasons and the prosperity of agriculture and associated with great events in the history of the nation: and thereby it was freed from mere magical ideas of securing prosperity, and being associated with spiritual deliverances, made more capable of being sacramental of moral and spiritual ideas.[1] New chords of emotion began to vibrate and more moral associations with worship to be formed, till a rite like sacrifice ceased to be of awesome potency and an offering to appease and gratify the deity, and became, in later Judaism, largely a symbol of sin and atonement.

Thus it could be rightly spoken of as a *paidagogos*, though, on deeper reflexion, we see that the Apostle is also right in saying that it was this only in so far as the promise was before the Law, or in other words as the prophetic insight and freedom was working in the ceremonial-legal.

[1] Prof A. C. Welch says that the passover was associated with the event which made Israel the sphere of the self-revelation of God, as Christmas was dissociated from Yule and associated with the event which made the Church a similar sphere, and he seems to think that this disproves my view of the prophetic indifference to the politically and ecclesiastically organised state. Both are notable examples of the exaltation of popular usages by a prophetically inspired ceremonial-legal religion and I certainly do not question the importance for this religion of the ecclesiastically organised state. But the vehicle of revelation for the prophets was not Israel, political or ecclesiastical. It was the prophetic remnant, the few who were themselves inspired by God's word.

CHAPTER XXVI

THE PROPHETIC

(*a*) A RELIGION OF RECONCILIATION

ALL religions are religions of redemption, in the sense of seeking in the Supernatural what is more abiding and more in accord with human purpose than the constant stream of change of the merely Natural; and were both God and reconciliation interpreted widely enough, it might be maintained that no religion is wholly without some idea of redemption by reconciliation to God. Even the practices of magic are exercised because of a faith that they are in accord with the unseen powers. Religions above that stage, though much occupied with appeasing the dread might which sends tempest and pestilence and famine, have some persuasion that the characteristic working of the Supernatural is to befriend man, and that if it work otherwise, there must have been some cause of offence. Of the growth of this confidence the increasingly beautiful forms of the higher polytheisms are a striking evidence, and still more consciously ceremonial-legalism seeks such reconciliation to the Good Power as shall enable men to defy the powers of darkness.

But in none of these religions was there any idea of reconciliation to life as in any sense all of God. Panic, it is true, is no test of the normal in religion more than in anything else, and such horrors as burning one's own children to Moloch were the outcome of panic amid appalling disaster. But the fear which so wrapped the soul in horror was only the exaggeration of a shadow which beset all religions other than the prophetic, in some degree at all times.

The beliefs and actions of the prophets, in face of the same calamities as struck others with abject terror, show a reconciliation to God in all his appointments in the Natural of duty and conflict as well as patience and enduring, which made reconciliation all religion and not merely part of it. As this left outside of God's rule no sphere which does not manifest his wisdom, righteousness and love, it is also alone true monotheism, which is not a mere affirming that God is one, but is the assurance that the world is all God's by reconciliation to his meaning in it and his purpose beyond it. This is what is meant here by a religion of reconciliation, which is also prophetic religion.

On the one hand, as there have been 'prophets since the world began', some element of this prophetic faith may not be wholly absent from any religion. but, on the other, no religion, so far, has lived continuously at the prophetic level and been exclusively and comprehensively a religion of reconciliation. Judaism used the prophets to raise its religion to a higher level of ethical monotheism, but its organised form remained to the end ceremonial-legal. Though this may come to be regarded simply as what God has commanded, it is concerned with the defence of proper ritual and rule against the assaults of the powers of evil· and so long as there is observance of taboo against what is outside not only our mind and purpose but God's, the true prophetic reconciliation has not been won. Nor is this yet wholly absent even from Christianity. Though the faith of Jesus in the Father, which makes all free who accept it, in the assurance that, for his end, all things work together for good, and that his end is his children, remains the leaven which makes it Christian, it is far yet from having purged out all the old leaven.

In its purity, we find this prophetic religion of reconciliation only in the Hebrew prophets and Jesus, though we cannot separate from him the interpretation of his immediate followers, who through him also lived in this prophetic order, as appears from the emphasis they place on a right relation to God by faith in his meaning and purpose, and the subordination of organisations and ordinances.

Again there is in this something akin to the passage from sensation to perception Experience as pleasant or unpleasant sensation is transformed into objective knowledge of meaning and purpose, giving an objective revelation of the Supernatural as our highest and most real environment, which makes the Natural, in relation to it, in a sense all good, and its evanescence the unfolding of a meaning and purpose that manifest the eternal.

(b) PROPHETIC MONOTHEISM

That the Hebrew prophets were the first true monotheists is usually esteemed their highest achievement: and, rightly understood, it sums up all that was original in their teaching. But it is not rightly understood when taken to mean that, by some happy metaphysical reasoning, they arrived at the idea of the Supernatural as one omnipotent and omniscient personality. They were monotheists in the only effective sense of being enabled to face the darkest ills of life in the assurance that God's meaning is in all and his purpose over all. What determines their faith is not a theory of the Supernatural, but an attitude towards the Natural, as a sphere in which a victory of deeper meaning than the visible and of more abiding purpose than the fleeting can be won That is to say, their monotheism and their doctrine of reconciliation are one, because only when man has found in life a meaning and purpose for which he can believe that even the worst works for good, can he effectively say, 'There is one God and Father of all, who is over all and through all and in all'.

The prophetic monotheism is thus not a metaphysical inference, but is a development of the way all life, from the beginning, has advanced into higher environment mainly by recognising through the higher a higher use of the lower. The revelation of the Supernatural was by reconciliation to the Natural. and this was made possible by realising in the Natural the meaning and purpose of the Supernatural. This we see in the way the prophets faced their situation. In others it created the ghastly terror which made them offer to the angry powers the fruit of their bodies for the sin of their souls. Earlier and more vividly than others, the prophets saw the magnitude of the calamity of the fall of their civilisation. They bore their own fullest share and realised with the deepest sympathy the agony awaiting others. They never sought to shelter their spirits from the horror: they never comforted themselves with the thought that particular evil is universal good, they never took the individual personal sting out of their distress by generalising it into 'all life is misery'.

But the more clearly they saw that the Natural, by itself and as man uses it for his appetites and desires, is all evanescent, and, as he abuses it for his pride and ambition, all bad, the more they were taught to look for a deeper meaning and a more enduring purpose in it, which could make its defeats victory, its misery blessedness, its evanescence an eternal possession. Pleasantness and unpleasantness of sensation were thereby changed into perception of a higher world, manifest in the Natural yet above it, which provides values which make another kind of appeal and give another kind of joy in possession. Thus they were able to face physical evil as real and terrible, and moral evil as calamitous and perverse, and yet say that, by his own meaning in them and his purpose beyond them, the Lord God omnipotent reigneth. This confidence that no evil could hinder life from being one moral sphere, and experience from being one triumph of faith, was the essential victory of the prophetic monotheism, and is the sole ground still of any real confidence of one God being in all and above all.

(c) THE PROPHETIC FAITH AND POLYTHEISM AND LEGALISM

This faith in one Supernatural, which is possession of all the Natural, may be professed by societies, but, in its power, it can only be held by the prophet and by those built on his foundation by being in some sense themselves prophets. In so far as it is merely the traditional creed of a corporation, even in Judaism and Christianity a monotheism which is a reconciliation to all God appoints is mixed both with polytheistic and with ceremonial-legal elements.

What marks off a true monotheism sharply from polytheism is its rejection of the political state as a religious ground of trust, and from ceremonial-legalism is its rejection of the national cult as pre-eminently God's service. For the prophets, faith does not depend on nation or church but nation and church upon faith.

Because the prophets dealt much with public events, they are often spoken of as if their central interest was political: and misleading pictures have been drawn of them as great statesmen, and even as expert politicians. But, from the first, all the prophets regarded their civilisation as doomed, and their own nation with it: and their supreme discovery was the concrete individual. To him all appeal is made and for his abiding good alone the world may be found in the end to be of Divine wisdom and goodness, however much evil may be imported into it by his own folly and wickedness. Their monotheism not only embraced the Natural, but found the meaning and purpose of it in the concrete individual, whom the mystical religions take to be the very part of the Natural whereby the evil dominion of desire subjects to the misery of evanescence.

As the Natural will only serve God's end, man, in so far as he seeks a contrary end, may turn it to the most appalling calamity. Yet, as man's own highest good is God's end, the only true evil is diversion from it, and calamity, being designed to show the folly of such diversion, is within God's purpose of good.

But when God's order is thus seen to depend on the relation of the individual soul to him and all security to be by each in his own sphere discerning God's meaning and purpose, outward organisation, either of the political state or the ceremonial religion, becomes subordinate, which subordination is an essential of any kind of universal religion that could be called monotheism.

Yet individual judgment was not for the prophets a mere opinion of the individual. They could stand alone because of God's call and commission to their own hearts and consciences, which they called the burden or oracle of the Lord. In the sole might of this authority in their own souls, they were able, though mostly plain men of humble origin, to stand alone against political rulers; though without professional standing, against religious dignitaries; though mostly of the people, against popular domination. In spite of being sensitive, sympathetic, imaginative spirits, they could, in the sole might of a conscience ruled alone by insight into God's will of truth and goodness, withstand every kind of power which assumed the right to rule over the conscience by violence.

By this sense of being directly taught of God, they could affirm the responsibility of each individual for his own conscience and opportunity, till, in the end, Jeremiah and Ezekiel could reject all tribal and hereditary ideas of morality, and affirm that no one suffers for his father's sins, but only for his own, and that no one is saved from his sins otherwise than by his own repentance. Their interest was in the concrete individual with his personal responsibility for others as well as for himself; impending calamity was ascribed to his failure to exercise responsibility; all securer conditions were expected only from more responsible persons. The prophets were not indifferent to their nation either politically or ecclesiastically, but they assigned to it a subordinate place, not merely because they set God above the ruler, which, in theory at least, none denied, but because they held both the political and the ecclesiastical to be only a means, and not an indispensable means, to God's rule, which was concerned with personal character, human relations and the recognition of privilege as individual responsibility. And, though their concern was still more passionately with their people, not even the people was for them the organ of the revelation of God's meaning and purpose. This was the holy remnant, those who themselves incarnated the prophetic message. These might be a very few, but, as there was no condition except the recognition of the truth itself, their fellowship was, in principle, universal Thus the prophetic monotheism was not merely, negatively, the rejection of a national deity, but was, positively, faith in a universal order of truth, righteousness and mercy, which should direct all men and be served by all.

Yet to estimate fully the religious significance of the attitude of the prophets, we must realise that what they opposed was not merely a state and a church, but was a state with a sacred as well as a secular aspect. As this was the foundation of the ceremonial-legal religion, any question of its abiding necessity for God's purpose seemed to be impiety as well as treason. If the worship as well as the worshippers of Yahweh would disappear with the nation, in preserving the nation his honour and even his existence seemed, to the people as well as the priesthood, to be at stake. Wherefore, it was felt to be ungodly as well as unpatriotic, when the prophets, from Amos onwards, said, "You only have I known of all the families of the earth: therefore I will visit upon you all your iniquities". Nor did the prophets deny that this was subversive, for the most revolutionary part of their message was that the seats of worship would be abolished as well as the seats of government.

The prophets were very far from regarding all religion as good. A religion which sought God's blessing, while disregarding his mind, they did not think to be unreal or to be lacking in zeal, but, so far were they from thinking that it should be approved or even tolerated, that they denounced it as, more than the worst politics, man's most dangerous enemy and God's most hated abomination. The crowning impiety was iniquity and the solemn meeting. The state could rob men of their material rights: and the prophets were so far from making light of them that they were the most daring defenders of even the most material rights of the meanest. But false religion could, by making good appear evil and evil good, rob man of any conscience to which to appeal, so blotting out the light by which he might walk even in the darkest days. More than with the end of the political power, however much it had been abused, the frequent prophecies of a return to the wilderness had to do with the end of this religion and a return to the simplicity and sincerity of true worship. Emancipation from the particularism of worship, even more than emancipation from the religious limits of a nation, shows the universality of a true monotheism, for which the lie that alienates from the truth is never mere departure from orthodoxy.

(*d*) THE RULE OF GOD

Like all great movements, we understand the prophetic movement best by its fullest understanding of itself. This we have in Jeremiah's conception of a rule of God known by one's own insight and accepted by one's own consecration, when no one should need to say to his brother, Know the Lord, for all should know him, and no one need to lay down rules for his brother, for God would write his law on all hearts.

As this could be a present fruitfulness in one's own soul as well as the promise of the full harvest of God's husbandry in the end, it justified the dissolution of states, destruction of temples, loss of possessions, even the casting out of delicately nurtured women and children from their homes and appalling trains of captives in chains, carrying their own spoils to enrich their oppressors.

Like Hosea, he felt bitterly the agony of humanity and was well assured of a like sorrow in the heart of the Most High. But, to him also, it was a necessary ploughing of the fallow ground so as not to sow among thorns. Wherefore, he knew that, for averting what man's iniquity required as a discipline as well as deserved as a judgment, either political or ecclesiastical device was a refuge of lies.

Thus it would be true to say that the prophet interpreted human tragedy even more by the possibility of what is good and great in man than by what is evil and small. He saw calamity to be inevitable, because no evil which could befall man is so great as being protected in greed and pleasant but selfish vices, and in trust in impressive but soulless ritual, and that no price is too high to pay for the freedom which is by true reverence for oneself, one's neighbour and one's God. Thus he could contemplate the destruction of his nation and, with it, of the outward rites of religion, in the assurance that in this rule of God a higher, securer order was waiting to take their place. Like other apocalyptic hopes, the perspective was foreshortened, but if this freedom in right reverence is the end even of the longest vista of human history, the sternness of life's lessons, in view of man's idolatries, has justification.

This kingdom of freedom which, by personal insight and consecration, emancipates from all slavery to custom and lust of pleasure or gain, and so from all final trust in material safeguards, political or ecclesiastical, we can see, looking back from Jeremiah, was the hope of all the prophets.

This faith is in the Supernatural, but as it is by what can be realised in the Natural, some account of the prophetic conflict is a necessary part of the exposition of the prophetic faith.

The story seems to begin with Elijah's distress at appointing Elisha, whose ordinary civilian appearance created the popular story of mockery and judgment. But, in any case, it had begun with Amos, the first whose prophecies have come down to us in writing. He declares himself a plain shepherd and working farmer, no member of any prophetic guild. Nor had he, either in outward appearance or in ecstatic utterance, anything of the dervish or shaman. And henceforward the prophets assail evil as plain men, with calm reason and popular or sometimes poetic speech.

That Elijah should think this more calamitous than either invasion or rebellion has the reason that no nation goes to final ruin unless its society is first corrupt, and that a warning unheeded does not leave this corruption what it was before, but makes it sinning against the light. All the prophets knew that for an impenitent people they were precipitating calamity, as well as heralding it. But they also knew that they had a message for the hearing ear and the understanding heart which would turn disaster itself into a triumph of the spirit. Hence they had a still more difficult task than arresting calamity, though for it too they spared no labour. This was to make all life's sins and sorrows, as well as all its virtues and joys, into one moral sphere of victory, in the knowledge that God's meaning and purpose in them is the liberty of his children. But it also meant that for no regard for their ease would he suffer them to live, either by ignorance or by perversity, in slavery.

(e) SUFFERING AND SIN

While the prophetic faith was concerned with the worth of the concrete individual, it had no more optimistic view of human nature than of outward events. The more clearly the prophets saw that all the issues of life are from the heart, that all worth for man's own soul and all secure order for his society flow from it, the more they felt this well-spring to be polluted and what flows from it corrupt and corrupting. As, however, they thought the heart thus evil from being self-enclosed and not fed from the Eternal, they concerned themselves no more with sins as breaches of ceremonial rule, but with sin as disloyalty to one's own worth and the worth of others, and the possibility of both in God.

In the Book of Amos, the earliest prophetic writing, there is already this view of sin. Amos spoke to an externally religious, but pleasure-seeking and materialised people, as conscience incarnate, but it was the conscience of the herdsman and small farmer of Tekoa, for whom the damning sins are the abuse of power, either in cruelty or callousness. Against the brutalities of war, such as ripping up the woman with child, he declares the judgment of God, but against the brutalities of peace, such as maintaining in luxury and licence the women of wealth at the cost of crushing the poor, he speaks still more emphatically, for the reason that they are done under the cloak of religion.

In Hosea we see still more clearly the valuation of the poorest human soul which changed the whole religious basis of the moral order and left no room for the distinction between the sacred and secular of the ceremonial religion.

Amos spoke as stern conscience outside of the evil, and, therefore, in spite of all his sympathy with weakness, he never quite heard the music which drowned the thunders of Sinai The complete escape from the legal temper, as well as the ceremonial expression of it, came when Hosea spoke compassionately from within the evil because he had suffered bitterly from it in his tenderest affection. The tragedy of his wife's shame and desertion and descent into the lowest depths of degradation, and of his purchasing her out of slavery and pardoning her and nursing her back to life and hope, is no parable, but an actual tale of human agony.

If we know our environment only as we live rightly in it, the question is whether Hosea was doing so when he met the evil which had wrecked his home, made life a desolation and harrowed his soul, with a regard no degradation could destroy and a pardon and succour no need could exhaust. This question of whether he bore himself aright in face of the Natural must first be decided, before we can judge his thoughts of the Supernatural. The lost outward respectabilities seemed nothing in face of the lost inward loyalties. Hence any depth of degradation and agony which helped the erring soul to discover her true loss, he found to be good. By his tenacious affection he interpreted the heart of God: and forthwith the idea of legal equivalent seemed wholly inadequate to God's rule, seeing that the last thing he desired for his erring wife was the just award of her evil life. How could a forensic righteousness, which would have been a poverty in his own spirit, be the righteousness of God? In seeing the calamity which follows sin to be for the deliverance of the soul, he found another key to the mystery of this sorrowful and perplexing world than legal equivalent. He made the discovery that it was in order to realise in his children their true worth that God has set life as the Valley of Troubling for a door of hope; and in this he found that reconciliation to the whole rule of God which is, in the full sense, monotheism.

Yet something more had to be accepted before this was complete. He had to accept without resentment his own share in the misery however unmerited; to be ready to bear with gladness the burden of sin with the sinner; and to be fully rewarded if this helped to work reconciliation. No really sympathetic person ever desired to live, sheltered by his own innocence, apart from all the fellowship of sin and suffering: but Hosea stands out as a supreme prophetic figure, because he raised this to an understanding in principle of God's rule and of our share in it, which we can call an atoning service if by it we understand participation in God's task of reconciliation.

Yet, just because of this penetration to the significance of the heart's loyalty, Hosea's pity, more even than the sternness of Amos, shows sin to be a deep-seated corruption. Few have walked in a darker pessimism about man. Even when calamity drives men to better ways, it is only as the morning cloud and the dew which goes early away. Yet compassion with man teaches Hosea undying hope in God, who desires mercy and not sacrifice, the knowledge of himself more than burnt-offering. As no other good can compensate for missing so great an end and no road be too terrible to gain it, God is alluring his people into the wilderness, that there, when the voices of worldly pleasures and possessions which make them deaf to higher calls, and of greed which makes them unmerciful, and of the rites which they offer as compensation for wrong, have fallen silent, they may hear his voice speak comfortably to them and be willing that he should heal their backsliding.

Micah still more emphatically opposed the whole ceremonial idea of serving God, declaring the worthlessness of the vastest sacrifices that could be imagined. But greater still was the effect of the ideal of what he declared to be God's sole requirement, as doing justly and loving mercy and walking humbly with him. Doing justly was no mere meeting of legal requirement, but was doing to the least as to oneself; loving mercy was no mere abstinence from oppression and wrong, but was a passion for humanity which knew no limitation, by rule, of succour and helpfulness; walking humbly with our God was no mere cringing dread, but was such an exposing of ou souls to the infinite appeal of his truth and goodness that lega merit and the self-approval of fulfilling rules have no place left for them.

Yet again it is to be observed that Micah won this great step in moral freedom, not by reasoning on abstract principles, but by being the great democrat who had taken the poor and the wronged to his heart, believing that God did the same.

Isaiah, like all the prophets, judges sin morally and not ceremonially. With Amos he sees it to be both iniquity and calamity; with Hosea he thinks of it as one who suffers from it and has learned compassion by suffering; with Micah he identifies himself with the wronged, and knows that no mere negative laws will direct aright But he goes beyond all who went before him by the sense of sharing in the lack of truth, and seeing this to be the fountain-head of all evil. That he also is a man of unclean lips, as well as a dweller amid a people of unclean lips, is the secret of the words which tremble and burn as they plead for God, and of the hope of a remnant, not pure, yet saved, though as by fire, out of a sinful state which they are all conscious of having shared, to be the redeemers, as well as the redeemed of Israel. Moreover, seeing that he thinks Israel is only to be a third in God's kingdom with its oppressors, Assyria and Egypt, he is rightly interpreted, when this remnant is afterwards described as a light to lighten the Gentiles as well as the glory of Israel. For one who had so identified himself with sinful humanity, there could be no national limits to the purpose of God.

Probably Isaiah was the first to give this hope apocalyptic form, in the sense of a new world through a rule to be introduced wholly by God But the singular thing is that what might seem to be sheer contradiction—a catastrophic change introduced by sovereign might and a spiritual rule men receive as their own—stirs no sense of conflict. On the contrary, ever more clearly the catastrophic and the spiritual nature of the conception grow together. The reason of this is to be found just in the tracing of all evil to one root of false worship, even as all right rule concerns one loyalty. As God is always ready to give a new world if man can enter it, a change of heart would mean a regeneration of all things. And the tribulations which are always thought necessary preparation, are God's way of working this change.

That transformation comes more by reverence than by

resolution, though that neither is won without labour and sorrow, is true for every individual. But there is also a sense in which it is a truth of history that there is always a higher environment to be entered as soon as mankind knows how to reverence its higher values, and that, while this alone is higher possession of the Natural, it has never been won without the loss and disappointment which wean from lower satisfactions and ultimate trust in the things that pass away.

Jeremiah penetrates still farther into the secret of the suffering which atones, the weakness, strong only in God, which, in an age of violence, is alone invincible, the life, which may be destroyed, but remains more than conqueror. Though feeling himself to be a child and equipped with nothing but faith in God and his working for his own purpose, Jeremiah was called to pluck up and to break down, to build and to plant: and with no support save this call, he was enabled, not only to face the annihilation of Judah as a nation, but to put a spiritual reality, which cannot be destroyed, in its place.

Thus, finally, suffering for the saint, even more than the sinner, was embraced in God's wise and gracious rule, because this rule authenticates itself to the soul who judges sin morally and not materially, shares with the sinner his burden, sees the high ideal of which all come short, recognises his own part in the falsehood which is the source of all sin, and accepts the labour, danger and distress needed to overcome its evil dominion.

(*f*) THE PRESENT AND THE FUTURE

This result was due to the determination to see the goodness of the Lord in all the land of the living, and the refusal to settle the perplexities of suffering and sin by either of the two recognised answers, the one, that there is a secular sphere which is outside of God's working, and the other, that the inequalities of life are explained by the unknown merits of a former life or the unknown rewards of a future.

We begin with the merits of a former life.

In any question of former existence the prophets never showed the slightest interest, nor would they, had it been put before them, for the good reason that they accepted themselves as God had made them and their situations as God had appointed them. Man's talents and dispositions they conceived to be his equipment for doing and for being what God requires of him. Not only were his gifts a call to consecrate them to God's service, but his weaknesses were a challenge to turn them into strength of character by overcoming them, and the desires by which he is tempted material to be transformed into the aspirations by which he follows the road on which temptations are left behind. Man's world was thus for the prophets the sphere in which God had placed him, the experience of which was for his learning and the opportunities of which were for his using, no more to be accepted as they are than his own disposition as he found it, but with the challenge of evil to be vanquished and of good to be forwarded. As the good and evil that befell themselves was thus for a service according to a call which left no merit, the idea that what happened to them was determined by the merits of a former state would have seemed an impiety. For the same reason, they regarded this world as wholly independent of themselves and a reality of God's appointing. Therefore the idea that it was an illusion of their own desires would have seemed merely an ungodly absurdity. Since they had deliberately rejected the whole idea of the equivalence of action and award as the ultimate order of the universe, which the idea of karma was invoked to justify, no conception of experience as fashioned by former merit or demerit could have made any appeal to them.

In respect of a future life, it is plain that even the Natural is not the same if its significance is confined to this one earthly existence, as it would be if it fulfils the larger purpose of being a school for immortal spirits; nor can our relation to the Supernatural be the same if it is only for time, as it would be if it is for eternity. Nevertheless, it was of the highest consequence for the faith of the prophets that they never disposed of the difficulties of our actual experience in this life by leaving them to be settled by the unknown possibilities of another.

Any appeal to retribution in a future life is as entirely absent from their writings as any appeal to the merits of former existences.

That they had no belief in a future life, as has sometimes been asserted, is improbable. Their people believed in Sheol as the place of the shades, and called up the spirits of the departed, the spirits that peep and mutter. That there were such spirits probably they did not deny any more than their contemporaries, but it was a kind of belief of which they could make no use in interpreting God's ways. To appeal to the shades of the dead, rather than to the living God, seemed to them merely impiety and folly.

As they were not ignorant of the countries around them, and especially of Egypt, they must have heard of the idea of a future life in which men's actions were weighed and good or evil appointed them accordingly. But explanation of life's injustices by future award of merit was as little consistent as explanation by the result of past demerit with their views of this life and the purpose of him who has appointed it. For one thing they were realists, who did not think of explaining the known by the unknown, and, for another, they had a different idea of God from an adjuster of awards to actions.

That the belief in a future life sprang from the mere desire to prolong this life and to enjoy fuller material good is probably not true of any religion. The belief was man's earliest victory over evanescence: and it does not appear to have been by any kind of reasoning, but by a direct sense of something abiding in himself and something of enduring quality in what he held to be sacred, which subordinated the immediate to the enduring. When in the mystic religions he turned his attention to the forms of unity, he found a continuity of unity in the soul, which was found in no manifestation of the natural world: and to preserve and realise this unity he made the greatest sacrifices. But it was from the conviction that the soul could find its home in the eternal unity, and not for the continuance of natural good. With the question of future award, the higher polytheisms and the legal-ceremonial religions were both concerned. But this had much more to do with justifying what they took to be the righteous order of the world than with any mere eudaemonistic extension of natural good. On the contrary their faith in this order forced on them the expectation of a judgment which would appoint what they rather feared than desired. Thus, though every hope can be corrupted by lower motives, what made this hope a victory over the evanescent was not the promise of material good, but the conferring upon higher aspirations the power of an endless life.

For this no other religion, except Christianity, did so much as the religion of the prophets. Yet Siebeck begins at the wrong end when he says: "A salvation which lay in the future occupied itself more and more with personal immortality. This gave a new earnestness to the consciousness of guilt and the desire for reconciliation with God, as the holy and yet gracious Father of men. The result was a greater emphasis upon the virtues of gentleness, love, pity, sincerity, in contrast to self-regarding correctness of worship".[1]

But the mere expectation of another life has never delivered men from anxiety about correctness of worship; and if the prophets laid emphasis on the gentler virtues, it was not at the expense of the active and robust. If their view of evil had been that it only waits for another life to redress it, they would never have wrestled with the problems of this life as they did, to interpret them by a deeper meaning and a more enduring purpose.

What the prophets did was not to arrive at a doctrine of immortality, but to make it possible to arrive at a higher faith than any hope of reward, which, once again, was through their way of dealing with the Natural. They did not change the view of the Natural by importing into it a doctrine of immortality, but they made a higher doctrine of immortality possible by showing, in all their interpretation of the fleeting present and all their dealing with it in fearlessness of its natural consequences, that which is eternal. What they thought of persons was not the result of thinking of them as immortal

[1] Hermann Siebeck, *Religionsphilosophie*, p 139.

souls: but the hope of immortality came to be truly personal because of what they thought of persons by reason of the virtues of gentleness, love, pity, sincerity. This made impossible the ritual idea of God as jealously watching the correct observance of ceremonial precept, and the juridical idea of him as a punctilious distributor of awards weighed in legal balances, and inspired faith in the wise and holy Father of all men, from whose love nothing can separate. Hosea did not say of his erring wife, this is a worthless woman in time, but I must think of eternity, and be gentle and loving and pitiful towards her and try to make her realise her situation as an immortal soul. He saw in her, just as she was, what made it impossible for him to be anything other than gentle, loving and pitiful, and, as he dealt with her situation in sincerity, he realised that no situation could ever take her out of his heart and his life. Then he knew also that the same must be true of sinful man and the mind of God. So, by the sense of the abiding worth of every person in the sight of God, he laid the foundation for the faith to which Jesus gave the final expression, that God is not the God of the dead but of the living, that in his heaven there is joy over one sinner who repents, and that his supreme purpose is to seek and save the lost.

Yet this hope of the future was scarcely at all in evidence till after Jeremiah. Possibly his life and teaching were its inspiration, though not because he taught it as a doctrine or lived for a future life. On the contrary, his whole thought and labour were concentrated on the tasks of the present; and there is not the slightest suggestion of concern about his immortal soul. Yet his life was such a triumph over the things seen and temporal that it could not be thought of as ending with them. Moreover, it was plain that the order of freedom by seeing God's truth and accepting his will, in which he lived, is here and now divine and eternal. Thus the argument was not from compensation for the defects of God's rule, but from the vision of an order of insight and consecration, a freedom in God as the end of the world that passes away, but which does not pass with it This came to be regarded as the counsel of God which, just because of its scope, could not be complete in time, but required a hope beyond its earthly manifestation, which is described as being received with glory. In this way living for a divine order in time was the source of a more spiritual hope for eternity.

Thus was laid the foundation of Paul's hope that immortality would mean knowing God's love as God's love now knows us. This hope the apostle did not, any more than the prophets, make a mere faith in the Supernatural. It was the outcome of his vision, however blurred as in a rusty mirror, however much a guessing as of a dark riddle, of the meaning and purpose of the Natural as a love which knew him, however imperfectly he could know it. It was for them that love God and thereby love his children, and are called according to his purpose of enabling others as well as themselves to win the liberty of his children, that all things, however much they may seem to be merely material and adverse happenings, work together for good. Moreover, the good news of God, which was the inspiration of this hope, was not a mere proclamation of God's purpose beyond this life, but was a life in this world which manifested God's meaning in common things and God's value in common people. It was a seeking and saving the lost which showed that no one, however hopeless his state in the eyes of man, is ever banished from the care and love of God, and a turning of earthly defeat and agony and death into victory and joy and the power of an endless life. This was the good news whereby a life which perfectly manifested life's deepest meaning set immortality in a present light.

Thus the hope of personal immortality, a hope which includes the concrete individual with all the experience and character which has become truly himself, is from what is present in the Natural when rightly interpreted and rightly used, and not by reasoning from what is lacking to it, even though what is present be only promise and not fulfilment. This hope was not won by meditation on another life, but by proving in this life that the victory over necessity is freedom and the spirit that is made free, and that the reality of the evanescent is the revelation of things eternal as the spirit's inalienable and abiding possession. The hope of immortality was thus given spiritual content from the true meaning and value and purpose of the Natural. And this, historically, was apocalyptic, not merely in the general sense we have given the word, but in the immediate, catastrophic sense. Logically it might seem that such an expectation should put the idea of eternal life into the background. But the hope was realised as a present possession of God's rule now, before it could be a consecration which was personal without being self-regarding and have spiritual content by relation to the life we know. And to this day, and in spite of all profession of a personal hope, when another life is made a direct end, not passing through God's purpose with the world now and consecration to his will being done on earth, it becomes either material or mystical, generally something of both, a sort of material unity of a spirit which is a material unity with a Supernatural which is nothing more.

It is natural that the more men were conscious of God the more imminent a kingdom of his rule which depended on his working should seem to be. Even granting that man's only necessary part in it is right reverence and pursuit of the true sacred, we may have to learn that even this needs the whole long lesson of human history. But unless we see this rule somewhere at the end of the vista, and so are able to cherish the faith that all right human relations belong to the things eternal, and in face of difficulty never withdraw from our tasks in the world, and in face of discouragement never despair, there is no concrete individual meaning in the assurance that life does not end our participation in God's purpose. Then, even if the hope is still cherished, heaven is little more than a Nirvana.

All this means that what is concretely personal depends on the Natural.

The Natural need not all be personal. But only if it all have personal meaning and personal purpose, responding to us as we attain personal insight, personal values, personal independence of action, has the idea either of God or of man any content which could enable us to speak of God as a Father who cannot be separated from his children, or of man as having his hope in the love from which death cannot separate because life cannot. From this none of the pictures of another state have been drawn, and still less, any idea of the writ of an earthly authority running in it. If our task is, here and now, to realise God's will on earth as it is in heaven, and if we are not distracted from it, the limitation of our knowledge to our present sphere is necessary Yet our concern with God's will now and the personal insight and personal consecration it requires, give the hope that all the truth, beauty and goodness realised in this world will follow us, because what we have won of true freedom will be our true selves. This at least is the hope of which the life and teaching of all prophetic souls laid the foundation by showing God's final order in the future to be continuous with its realisation in the present.

(g) RELIGION AND HISTORY

We have seen the value of sacred tradition as a stage of human development. No progress in dealing with experience is possible till man retains what he has won: and the first form of retention is sacred tradition But, not being real history of experience, it is apt to conserve only as the bulwark of conservatism.

Further progress was made when tradition was committed to writing. It was freed from the arbitrary personal or class domination of oral tradition, and, in spite of a material sacredness ascribed to the writing, which may extend to its cover, it was exposed to critical minds by being public property. Yet its appeal is neither to individual experience nor to the wider experience of history so long as its authority is merely that it is sacred. The writings of pantheistic mysticism are so sacred that they are held to be the principles of the universe, but they do not use experience in any way which could develop into an interest in history. The higher polytheisms, precisely because of their interest in life and the state, have produced the most valuable records of the past, but they also failed to develop any view of a purpose in experience which could make history a religious interest. Something more was possible for ceremonial-legalism. Its relation of laws to historical events was still as sacred tradition, but it was with a sense of historical purpose. And this was so in fact as well as idea. The interest was in law and cult, not in the common life, yet the development of the rites from being merely ways for securing 'plenty of victuals', to being memorials of national events, with associations of higher deliverances, was genuine progress. But, to the end, as in Zoroastrianism, so in Judaism, the sharp distinction of sacred and profane tended to subject everything to purely ceremonial tradition, so that the prophetic 'Thus saith the Lord' of the Spirit of God appealing to the responsive spirit of man tended to become, Thus saith a sacred dogma of external authority.

The prophets so obviously spoke out of their personal experience, in face of man's earthly conflicts, that it was not easy to make their writings sacred, in the sense of what is to be held in awe. Wherefore they remained of inferior inspiration to the Pentateuch. Even more conspicuously the same is true of Jesus. Never has so much effort been made to turn anyone's sayings into sacred legislation, and yet the Gospels persist in being a witness from truth seen to truth seen, to which external authority is alien. Nor can any effort to make Jesus an external law wholly ignore the fact that the whole revelation of the Father is a radical denial that law, either as ceremonial or as ethical precept, is the ultimate divine order.

All external authority of events weakens as we remove from them in time and space. But interest may vanish for other reasons than uncertainty about events The Jew regarded the pattern shown to Moses on the mount as the most authoritative of all revelations. Yet, even had we been eye-witnesses of the event, it would be to us to-day of no more than antiquarian interest. In contrast, the interest of the prophetic revelation is perennial: first, because, as it deals with human experience, it is empirical, in a way which speaks to all experience, and, second, because it set up the final order as freedom in knowing the Lord by our own insight and accepting his rule as our own legislation, an order which we may hope is nearer, but which can never be overpassed. And just because the Gospels are most of all concerned with this liberty of the children of God, they have in them their own witness. Expressed negatively, the reason is that with Jesus the only creed is a prayer, the only casuistry the spirit of love, the only organisation willingness to be first in service and last in honour, the only form of worship worship in spirit and in truth.

If Jesus is in any sense a final authority in religion, it is because he spoke entirely from this witness of the reality, and not by any authority apart from it. What this means is most evident from the change which took place when he became an external authority. The Gospels at once passed into the background, abstract ideas of omnipotence taking the place of the practical manifestation of the Father amid life's secularities, and the sacred becoming once more a sphere by itself In place of God's perfection, which we share as we forgive others, of his gracious dealing, which we know as we love mercy, and of the righteousness of his whole will of love, which we know as we hunger and thirst after it, we have judicial ideas of pardon, mystical mechanical ideas of grace, and rules of belief and action, which are ceremonial, in the sense of rules imposed from without and enforced by fear.

The prophetic attitude to the common life as sacred, appears even in the use of the popular speech as it was created mainly to serve life's common interests, and of illustrations drawn from man's daily tasks and human relations. Of the associations of the family there was much use, and of the religious ceremonial little or none. Even the corruption of society and the turning of religion from a right life to ceremonial doings, though regarded as graver dangers than invasion or revolution, were assailed with simple, sincere, reasoned speech, made memorable and poignant by figure and parallel, mostly from life's common things, and often by poetic form, rising constantly to poetic beauty. The worst corruptions, no more than the gravest calamities, could deprive prophetic souls of the liberty of spirit which garners 'the harvest of a quiet eye'. In quietness and confidence was increasingly their rest amid the worst tumult:

and they did not feel themselves merely striving and crying against even the worst iniquities. This was crowned by Jesus, who used the simplest and most popular speech; had leisure of mind to turn his teaching into parable and memorable saying; drew his illustrations from field and sky, farmer and merchant, creditor and debtor, the house mother and the children's play; was pitiful even amid the sternest rebuke.

The natural order of the sun rising alike for the evil and the good and the rain being distributed equally on the field of the just and the unjust he interpreted as the manifestation of the Father who is kind to the unthankful and evil, a manifestation to be understood by being sons of the Father in this his supreme perfection, by loving our enemies and praying for our persecutors as his children and our brethren. Thus, finally, he overcame the idea of the moral order of the universe as the equivalence of action and award; the putting of ceremonial observances on a level with moral fidelity; the sense of the holy as awe, not moral reverence; the dividing of life into sacred and secular. This, which we may call the secularising of religion, is the reconciliation to all life's appointments, which alone is true monotheism, because it neither identifies anything with God, nor separates anything from his meaning and purpose. Thus it sees the eternal in the meaning and purpose of the evanescent

(*h*) THE RULE OF GOOD AND THE RULE OF EVIL

This should be an end of the idea of a moral world as a manifest material payment of goodness, of thinking that we ought to be able to look at a fruitful field and say, 'here is a good man', and not, 'here is a good farmer'. Yet if the world has in it God's meaning and is ruled for his purpose, any meaning and purpose hostile to his must make the world our enemy. And with this there is a sense in which we are judged by the deeds done in the body, seeing that the final judgment of us is what our deeds, taken as all our doings within as well as without, have made us. In respect of both, in the most absolute sense, out of the heart are the issues of life.

In consequence, Jesus concerned himself exclusively with the heart's loyalties. For the recovery of them he recognised only one condition—the acceptance of God's meaning and purpose. The prodigal is taken home without question and with every display of gladness over his return. But, for all that, there is the condition that he accepts with gratitude the same discipline and duty of his home as he had escaped from to a far country.

This is of the highest moral consequence, being the poverty of spirit from which flow all the beatitudes. And the beatitudes are just a deepening of the old requirements. To do justly is now to hunger and thirst after righteousness: to love mercy is never to ward off claims upon our sympathy by self-regard, callousness or keeping out of the road of misery, or by any sense of personal wrong or even by general moral disapproval; to walk humbly with God is to accept utterly his will as our own, to shun no task to which he calls, nor any trial which he appoints. This means accepting life, yet not as it is but as it challenges us, in short to have that meekness which lives openly and calmly in face of all reality. Thus and thus only is the earth in all its fullness to be inherited. It is as far from being deference to the voice of authority without as to the voice of desire within, for it is a humility before God which is emancipation from all fear of men.

That reconciliation and revelation are thus reciprocal is in a sense the whole story of the evolution of all living creatures. As they live more in accord with their environment they know it better, and as they know it better they can live in a larger accord. With man victory over his environment and knowledge of it go hand in hand, so that the more he is himself an independent person, the more his knowledge is objective. Religion differs only by reason of a higher environment. If reconciliation to the evanescent is revelation of the eternal, and revelation of the eternal a higher reconciliation to the evanescent, that is only as we know all environment, which is by living in accord with it. The faith in this as personal intercourse differs only by the deeper significance a higher environment gives to the personal.

If we would have any content in the eternal, it is from dealing whole-heartedly with the evanescent; if we would have any content in freedom it is by victory both without and within over the necessary; if we would have any content in mind and spirit we must know aright by valuing aright. If so, religion must be a large experience in which we grow in knowledge as we grow in humility and courage, in which we deal with life and not abstractions, and with God as the environment in which we live and move and have our being and not as an ecclesiastical formula. This we realise, as environment is only to be realised, by rightly living in it. It is for our knowing, but only as in the courage of humility we submit our minds to the witness of all that is to be known, it is for the victory of our freedom, but only as we accept the discipline of what cannot be altered and endure the burden of the duty of altering what should be changed; it is to be an eternal possession, but only as we grow in the eternal wisdom through life's changes and do not imagine that any other abiding possession can be in the evanescent. Denying the world does not mean that we do not possess it in courageous use of all possibilities, but only that we do not allow it to possess us.

APPENDICES

A. THE HOLY

APPENDIX TO CHAPTER V

To Prof. Otto's book, *Das Heilige*, is due the credit of bringing before a wider public the primitive idea of the holy and its importance for the study of religion. But he is very far from having been the first to call attention to it. Old Testament scholars recognised it long ago. They knew that the original meaning of *quadosh* was not moral, and there were scholars who regarded the development of the awesome into the moral as one of the chief marks of the progress of Hebrew religion. The knowledge of this prepared me to regard with interest Kattenbusch's view that the essential difference between Apostolic and Catholic Christians was that the former, being familiar with the Old Testament foundations of the teaching of Jesus, thought that to be of God and to be morally holy are one, while the latter received with its converts from heathenism the idea of the holy as awesome and mysterious.[1] This view I discussed in a note published in 1911 [2]

Soon after, I read Windelband's essay, *Das Heilige*, in *Praludien*.[3] The holy is there treated as the ground of all ideals as well as of all religion. About this time I dealt with the subject in Cambridge University Philosophy of Religion lectures. My chief differences from Windelband were in making distinctions between (*a*) the sense of the holy and the valuation of the sacred, (*b*) the undifferentiated and the particularising feeling, and (*c*) the significance of the material sacred in itself and for development. Prof Otto's book[4] I read soon after the close of the war and, when it was translated, I reviewed it in the *Journal of Theological Studies*, April 1924 Of that review only one sentence need be repeated, "Personally I remain much more indebted to Windelband's clear and calm exposition than to Otto's fervour, which often produces more heat than light". At the same time I learned better, though mainly by disagreeing with him, both how to distinguish and to relate the awesome and the ethical, the material and the spiritual.

1 Ferdinand Kattenbusch, *Das Apostolische Symbol*, vol I, 1894, vol. II, 1900.
2 *The Church and the Divine Order*, p. 121.
3 Wilhelm Windelband, *Praludien*, this essay being first published in the edition of 1902
4 Rudolf Otto, *Das Heilige*, 1917.

B. KANT AND HEGEL

APPENDIX TO CHAPTER IX

Many extracts might be produced from Kant's writings which could be read to mean that Kant denies all absoluteness of judgment and regards the world, the soul and God as having place in our minds merely as though they were, and that, therefore, he is the father of all agnostics. But, when they are given this meaning, they are considered apart from the whole system, and the system considered apart from the man who created it, and the man apart from the age in which he spoke. No doubt he held that the ultimate realities could not be either maintained or expressed purely intellectually. But his real world is the intelligible world, the world which manifests itself by absolute values; and what he maintains is that, while no reasoning from the sensuous world can establish them, the assurance of their existence is confirmed by the fact that all our knowledge must proceed as though they were.

This conception of intrinsic value, Prof. Pringle-Pattison says, was the spring of all the German philosophy which followed Kant. "What the German idealists substantially did was to enlarge and complete Kant's conception of intrinsic value by making it include all the higher reaches of human experience "[1] This is what I call the question of individuality, of the endless wealth of variety the individual can present But Prof. Pringle-Pattison thinks success was rightly achieved by discarding the eighteenth century framework of the Kantian scheme, which is what I call the question of the individual : and my contention, on the contrary, is that the essential weakness and failure of all the Romanticist philosophies was in taking the easy road of overlooking it.

Hegelianism is by far the greatest of them just because it does not merely dismiss the problem of the individual, but is the profoundest attempt to account for it on a scheme which, nevertheless, derives all rationality from absorbing him into the process of the Cosmic Reason. The criticisms in the text are purely of this system and the rôle it assigns to the process of the Negative. No one ever had more faith in his system as a general panacea or even in his mystical terminology as the 'open sesame' of all mysteries than Hegel And

[1] A. Seth Pringle-Pattison, *The Idea of God*, p. 38.

it is this system which has most attracted especially the English mind, because it offers a neat solution in terms of mind, as Naturalism does in terms of matter.

For the very reason, however, that Hegel is deeply conscious of the problem of the individual, he is so much greater than his system that he is often most suggestive and stimulating when farthest from being complete or even convincing. Of the man himself the prayer with which Lasson, his new editor, sends out the *Lectures on the Philosophy of Religion* is a true picture, "May this work of the great logician, who is also the deepest mystic of recent times, this work of the methodical thinker, who is also the most assured believer, not be without its working on the restless seeking and dim longing of our time".[1]

Though this is true as regards Hegel, it still does not meet the charges against Hegelianism. "The stress laid on religion", Prof. Pringle-Pattison says, "as the bearer of human culture, and as presenting, in its own form, the substance of philosophical truth, goes far to refute the common criticism that the intrinsic values of concrete experience are sacrificed in his system to a logical abstraction."[2] But if all religion does is to give in popular form what philosophy can turn into scientifically precise statement, the charge is confirmed, not refuted. Hegel, of course, affirms that higher values are produced in the religious arena as ordinary values are in the common life, but if in the end it is the *Begriff*, the philosophical generalisation, which is the abiding essence, the old charge holds against the system, however inapplicable it be to the author.

Lasson considers almost all the charges against Hegelianism to be mere misunderstandings. And, as applied to Hegel himself, it is not difficult, especially after the drastic revision to which Lasson has subjected the text of the *Philosophy of Religion*, to show that they are. Hegel speaks very gravely of sin, and he sets forth freedom as individual responsibility and possibility of abuse; he speaks with a warmth of personal religion which shows he does not regard it as mere philosophical concept, he has a largeness of outlook which is inconsistent with regarding him as the state philosopher of Prussia, and he affirms that the universal is found in the individual as in no society. But the charges are not made against Hegel. They are made against the Hegelian scheme, which is another matter. Though Lasson him-

[1] Hegel's *Samtliche Werke*, ed. Georg Lasson, 1930, XII, 2ter Theil, xi
[2] *Op. cit* p. 38

APPENDICES 477

self has little faith in it, this does not hinder it from being Hegel's own faith. And has it a real place for the kind of freedom Hegel affirms? Is sin what he says it is, if it is a mere process of the negative? Is it not from philosophy, and not from any reformation of religion that he expects recovery from the present decay of religion? Does he not at times speak as if the nation, and Prussia in particular, and not the individual, were the supreme organ of absolute spirit : and does not his system require it of him?

Granting that the individual is a real distinction in the Absolute, the process of the Negative has vital significance, but, as a substitute, it is never more than a pretence at a solution. In the end, it gives no more reality to man's struggle and failure than, let us say, Spinozism. The really great genius expended on the task merely makes the lesson more impressive, that spiritual values have reality only as the spirit has value in a freedom which is an independent system, in some way apart from the universal system as well as within it.

C. THE UNITY OF AWARENESS

APPENDIX TO CHAPTER XI

There may seem to be lack of precision in speaking, sometimes of unity of awareness, sometimes of unity of apprehension, and occasionally of unity of perception. To be more precise, it is a unity of awareness which is around any apprehension and which expands to embrace the whole system of fixed ideas by which perception works The effect is to give all perceptions individual character, but, though at first this seems to be each in its own universe, it is also the impulse to think all together in one universe. The unity of awareness, it is maintained, is related to the sense of the undifferentiated holy, and the unity of apprehension to the material sacred But more particularly the unities of perception explain both the breaking up of the Supernatural and the impulse never set aside of thinking it as one. And the reason would seem to be that this religious quality is in all perceiving which could be called human, because all environment is felt as supernatural as well as natural. The first and most apparent effect is the divisive one of giving individual character, but the impulse to realise environment as one and to pursue this unity by seeking to discover less material relations is also from it

D. THE ORIGINS OF MODERN SCIENCE

APPENDIX TO CHAPTER XIII

No one, in recent years, has dealt more fully with the origins of modern science than Prof. Whitehead, or gone farther back to look for them.[1] But even he has not gone far enough. To go back to the first conception of one ordered world, to the law and the prophets, might have led him too far afield. But to overlook the rise of the kind of religious interest in the Natural which developed scientific interest, is a grave omission for one whose main contention is that the scientific cosmology of the last three centuries was due to lack of interest in the concrete world and its higher values, and that a different scientific outlook and a new type of explanation are coming precisely because a higher interest is enabling men to recognise deeper problems.

The plainest example of his blindness is in his account of the sixteenth century of our era. Between the two great events which marked the age—the disruption of Western Christianity and the rise of Modern Science—he finds no connexion, except that both show the age to have been in ferment. For him the Reformation was a mere loud and bloody domestic broil, which accomplished next to nothing; while the rise of science, coming like the kingdom of heaven without observation, was the most intimate change of outlook the human race has yet encountered.

Even as a mere domestic broil, supposing there were no more, the Reformation had some value for the rise of science. Had this upheaval not been in progress, neither would this transforming change of outlook have been able to introduce itself so quietly, nor would men's minds have been so open to receive it. The estimate is so far right that neither the Reformation, nor the general movement of which it was a part, contributed directly to the new type of scientific explanation. But the movement has a wholly different significance when we ask what created the awareness and interest which provided an unceasing supply of men of genius for the task of investigating nature, and what gave them the faith that things small as well as great might exemplify universal principles. Then we see the significance of a movement which held that religion is victory over life's insistent

[1] Alfred North Whitehead, *Science and the Modern World*, 1926, pp. 1–28.

interests and distressing uncertainties, and not escape from them. The world might still be in the bondage of corruption, but, such as it is, it is our divinely appointed sphere. Justification by faith, theologically formulated, might be an abstraction, but, as a religious experience, it meant reconciliation to God in this world and not merely in the heavens. This meant what we may call a secularising of religion, which required, as Luther put it, that the shoemaker should shoe the Pope as religiously as the Pope should pray for the shoemaker.

This was by no means new, being as old as Paul's saying that all things are ours, and doubtless older. In the north of Europe especially we see it centuries earlier than the Reformation in the carving of natural objects, the daring feats of architecture and the secular uses of the cathedrals. We see it also in the rise of secular literature like the poetry of Chaucer, and still more in the social and political interests of persons like Langland and Wycliffe. But once again we see in Luther's conscious affirmation of the secular life as the religious life, the importance of presenting a truth as a principle and claiming for it absolute value.

An interest thus equipped soon grows up and sets out on its own adventures. Thus the great apostles of this faith came to be Montaigne and Shakespeare, with their endless interest in men and their world. More even than Galileo, they show the awareness and interest which created science, though this at once raises the question why the world of science has become so utterly unlike theirs.

If our previous discussion is right, the reason is not that they were shallow and science profound, but that they saw life whole and science only in part. No doubt science made a great discovery when Galileo 'harped on how things happen', and looked to actual observation alone for the answer. Then only was thought emancipated from Mediaeval Scholasticism, with its ready-made *a priori* complete scheme of why things happen, and men were free to learn from the world as it is. But observation is a high and difficult achievement and requires reach of imagination as well as concentration on detail. Seeing is interpreting. Therefore, imagination is necessary for perfect objectivity as well as for comprehensive awareness. and from lack of it a great deal of scientific theory constantly came short of reality.

Prof. Whitehead's plea is just that science should look again at its world with a wider interest and a deeper insight and his contention is that, in the measure in which this is done, a mechanical abstraction ceases to be sufficient even for the purposes of science. But in that case the first interest for him should be the history of apprehension and awareness which he ignores, not the history of theory on which he concentrates. Had the scientific mind been possessed by Montaigne's and Shakespeare's interest and imagination the new vision might have been earlier, and even now it might be more extended and more penetrating.

E. BIOLOGICAL PRINCIPLES

APPENDIX TO CHAPTER XV

Nothing has been said on physics which could not, were this to serve any useful end, be buttressed by authorities in high respect among physicists, and there is little which any physicist would now call in question. But I knew at the time of writing of no biologist who had given serious thought to the principles of his science whose views were not regarded by most biologists as heresies. Driesch mostly seems to talk sense, but he is a Vitalist, and that stirs the same kind of feeling as was once associated with being an Arian. Prof J. S. Haldane insists on the unity of the organism no more than to the common mortal seems indisputable. But even to his friends it is distressing how, through Hegelianism, he should have fallen from grace. Unfortunately I was too late in discovering Mr Woodger's book for it to be of any use to me.[1] His reputation for orthodoxy should not be better, and this might be ascribed to his having absorbed Prof. Whitehead undiluted, who is more Hegelian than he himself knows. Mr Woodger says that, in comparison with physics, the principles of biology are still in the middle ages, and that we have at this moment no theory of evolution. and he even offers proof But his main criticism is the persistent question: What is really proved? Many years ago, after I had read several books on Reproduction, I went to Prof. Alexander Macalister and asked him if he could tell me what is fact and what theory, or in other words, what does one see in a germ with a powerful microscope. "A great deal," was the reply, "but mostly with the eyes of one's theory." Mr Woodger affirms this suspicion about almost all biology:

1 J. H. Woodger, *Biological Principles*, 1929.

APPENDICES 481

and as the rising generation is adding a chorus to his solo, he will not be so easy to dispose of as a heretic as the men of the older generation.

But so far as my argument goes, it is not very much dependent on the result. I have only made one definitely biological statement It is about reproduction without a male germ, and my inference from it may be quite wrong without much affecting my argument. This has to do with matters in which the ordinary intelligent person has as much right as, perhaps more than, the specialist, my main contention being, first, that life so certainly works with meaning and develops from it, that the vast probability is that the effect is direct and not round about by way of accidental variation of the germ, and, second, that, in any case, mind is the governing principle. Just here Mr Woodger, too, would require to reconsider his view. Biology, he says, cannot go beyond behaviourism. Is that consistent with his contention about the place of thought in life? If we have means in human experience for carrying back mind as explanation, is it still to be heresy in biology to do so? If all life seems to do things because it finds meaning in them, is biology still bound to give another explanation?

F. AN ETHICAL CLASSIFICATION OF RELIGIONS

APPENDIX TO CHAPTER XXI

C. P Tiele's classifications both remain interesting. The one by date and distribution is employed in his *Outlines of the History of Religions*.[1] The other on an ethical principle of value was first given in a larger unfinished work, but the complete form, given in correspondence with Chantepie de la Saussaye, is found in the second edition of the *Lehrbuch der Religionsgeschichte*[2] The former is valuable because it is of such learning and judgment that little advance has been made on it, the second has interest mainly as an application of Kant, being

[1] Trans. 1877 by J Estlin Carpenter An edition, expanded and in part re-written by Archbishop N. Soderblom, has been issued in German and French.

[2] P. D. Chantepie de la Saussaye, *Lehrbuch der Religionsgeschichte*, 2te Ausgabe, p. 12 All other references are to the 4th edition, edited by A. Bertholet and E. Lehmann, 1924-5, and is so entirely re-written as to be rightly described as merely founded by de la Saussaye

on an ethical principle which is mainly judged by the approach to universality. The former does not concern us, but the second is of considerable interest for our study.

I. Religions of Nature.

The interest which governs the arrangement of this group is progress towards the human, and then towards the moral. From a low polyzoic dread it rises to the idea of souls, and becomes polydaemonistic-magical, i.e belief in unseen spirits, with devices for keeping on the right side of them. This develops into Therianthropic Polytheism. Its deities have souls after the human pattern, but still have animal forms The ways of influencing them are still magical, but there is now more of the humanities At this point we can begin to name definite religions. As unorganised forms, we have Japanese, Dravidian, Finnish, old Etruscan and Slav, as organised forms, old Mexican, Peruvian, Chinese state-religion, and Egyptian. Finally, we have definitely Anthropomorphic Polytheism or Polytheism proper, which is always at least half-ethical, and which includes all the old Aryan and Semitic religions.

II Ethical Religions.

These are further described as Spiritual Ethical Religions of Revelation, meaning that they deal with man as a spirit on the one hand, and with the will of God as a spirit on the other. They are divided into, (*a*) National nomistic religious communities, (*b*) Universal ethical religious fellowships. The first class—the National nomistic—includes Taoism, Confucianism, Brahmanism, Jainism, Mazdaism, Mosaism and Judaism, the last two forming a transition to the next. The second—the Universal ethical—includes only Buddhism and Christianity, Islam, owing to its particularist and nomistic elements, being no more than half universal or ethical.

Though this classification is the work of great erudition, it takes no great erudition to see its limitations as an account of the religions Nevertheless, it shows an aspect of the development of the utmost consequence for human progress

G. SOME PRIMITIVE IDEAS

APPENDIX TO CHAPTER XXII

Man's first idea of the continuous amid change seems to have been derived from consciousness of his own life. That any earlier stage we could call human ever existed is unlikely, but there is evidence of a stage at which life was still fixed in the objects, and not yet conceived as separable souls. This stage Mr Marrett would call 'Animatism', and Hobbes before him called it the 'Inanimate'. 'Animism' Mr Marrett would use only for a definite belief in individual souls. And, as there is a great difference between a fixed idea of continuance as life and a free idea of soul, it would be well to have different names to mark the distinction.[1]

Mr Marrett would prefer not to use a term with such disparaging associations as magic for the most rudimentary form of cult, which he takes to be "a genuine phase of the serious life as lived under certain conditions of culture": and he would confine the term magic to the practice of what, for the science and religion of the time, are superstitions.

And it is necessary to distinguish, in what may appear to be the same, what is rising upward by its own venture and buoyancy from what is sinking because it is weighted with custom and vague terrors. Nevertheless, the distinction does not lie in the practice itself, which for two reasons may in both forms be called magic. One is that only when the more primitive form stands opposed to what is higher and has become superstition, do we understand it; and the other is that it is no more than the distinction already made between good religion and bad. In the text I have spoken of the prophets and other religious persons sharply distinguishing magic from religion. But on reflexion I doubt if this is right. Is not their real objection precisely that it is bad religion? There may have been a magic which, as much for religion as for science, was progress, or a magic which, for both, was stagnation. But the reason is different uses of the same thing. As evolution and degeneration in the physical life are in the same environment, and the difference only concerns the uses to which it is put, so with the spiritual.

For Sir J. G. Frazer's view that magic is the fountain-head of science

[1] R. R. Marrett, *The Threshold of Religion*, p 14

there is more to be said than is generally allowed. But just because he makes a clear-cut distinction between religion and magic, and thinks of the invention of scientific devices and not of the development of the scientific mind, he misses the point. All savages have scientific devices as well as magical, and keep them apart. What requires explanation is the creation of an attitude of mind which could become scientific. For this the first stage was the ability to refuse to submit to the mere impression of the situation. But this freedom was won by arranging the situation. And this was first done by magic as religious ritual.

Mr Marrett rightly thinks that the true significance of magic ritual is obscured by assuming it to be mere imitation and by inventing names like 'sympathetic magic'. To suppose that first there is a belief that 'like produces like', and that this generates symbolic ritual is, he argues, putting the cart before the horse. No savage rite, he says, is purely mimetic. His own explanation is that magic rites are ways of expressing emotion with the form due to custom, 'repercussions', vents for superfluous emotion: and that only later, and with the introduction of ideas of the mana type, do they come to be regarded as having power But, in the first place, when were such ideas absent, and, in the second, it is far from being apparent why, if this were all, they should be, as he holds, of the greatest practical value in giving 'hope, courage and confidence'.[1] Mere working off emotion is, on the contrary, apt to be a waste which 'gives too cold a breath to action'. To have this value the ritual must surely generate the right emotion. This it does by staging the situation as is desired, with the traditional setting in which the experiences of higher emotions are fixed, and with a solemn assembly to give them resonance. Thereby, people whose ideas and feelings are fixed in situations, and who are subject to mass-impression, win freedom in handling a situation. By reason of the lack of free ideas, they cannot escape from the context, but they can arrange it to suit. With this mimetic victory an unprogressive people might remain satisfied and thereby be made more stagnant, but, for a more progressive, freedom of staging would be the first step towards a freedom of idea which could dispense with any particular situation. Thus freedom from the context was won by learning to make free with it.

The lack of free ideas is a mark of the primitive mind, and magic,

[1] *Op cit.* pp. 39 ff.

when it ceases to be religion and becomes a routine of superstition, may only make ideas more rigid. When it no more stirs the feelings which originally produced it, but is a purely formal and ossifying ritual, it is moral as well as intellectual stagnation, the lack of moral enterprise being the cause of the failure to achieve intellectual emancipation. But from such a state we have no right to argue the course of a progressive religion. At the same time, it is easy to assume more stagnation and less moral significance in the most retrograde religion than exist. Mere collections of information are apt to be misleading about anything, but are certain to be about what is living and organic like religion. The impression of an observer like Mr Malinowski, who has lived among a savage people long and sympathetically and with full understanding of their language, is very far from being that their morality is of mere natural impulses.[1] And their religion, he says, does not lack individual, personal struggle or prophets to give it higher interpretation. "Religion sets its stamp on the culturally valuable attitude and enforces it by public enactment."[2] Even the occasional licence of festive gatherings has to do with meeting in a moral atmosphere of general harmony and benevolence. From his faith, such as it is, the savage derives all his social cohesion and mental composure.

H. PRIMITIVE MONOTHEISM

APPENDIX TO CHAPTER XXII (*h*)

The chief exponent of this view in recent times is Lang To prove his case he brings forward a great wealth of evidence.[3] Soderblom has dealt with this more fully and more critically; and while he shows that it does not always bear Lang's interpretation, he has greatly increased the amount and the certainty of something very primitive which has at least to do with a power, and not powers.[4] Konow also finds an element in the earliest Indian religion, which he calls 'The

[1] Bronislaw Malinowski, *Argonauts of the Western Pacific*
[2] "Magic, Science and Religion," in *Science, Religion and Reality*, ed. Joseph Needham, p. 61. The whole essay is a remarkable tribute to the important place of religion in the life of the savage and to its moral value.
[3] A Lang, *The Making of Religion*, 1898, pp 210 ff
[4] N Soderblom, *Das Werden des Gottesglaubens*

Power' as distinct from the powers, and which he thinks played an important part in the later Indian developments.[1]

Lang argues that this belief cannot have been a development through a polytheistic pantheon, because it exists most clearly among tribes that have never had the social conditions for such a development. "The maker and ruler of the world, known to these races, cannot be the shadow of a king or chief, reflected and magnified on the mists of thought: for chief or king these people have none." Further he argues that, if it were latest in development, it ought to be newest and most fashionable with advancing material civilisation, whereas it is with such a progress that we find it in course of disappearing.

Allegiance to this God was undermined, he thinks, by the advance of material culture, because the very moral pre-eminence of a God who could not be bribed, proved a handicap in the competition with the ravenous but serviceable ghosts, ghost-gods, and shades of kingly ancestors and their magic and bloody rites, which had arrived on the scene with the rise of animism. The rise of autocratic institutions further fostered polytheism, till the old Supreme Being was obscured or superannuated, or at best enthroned as Emperor-God. Yet, out of the original conception, rapidly being corrupted, the prophets of Israel restored Jehovah, who thus never had an animistic ancestry; and similarly Mohammed found in this faith of the simply organised Arab tribes the basis for his monotheistic reform.

If a belief in one God as a supreme person, as Lang conceives it, existed at the beginning and passed away with any kind of human progress, how are we to conceive the relation between higher views of the Natural and of the Supernatural? Could a truly personal being have been replaced by a theory of ghosts? Would it not have been as easy to give him a soul and make him lord of souls as to make him lord of earth? Again, if he is maker and ruler of the world, why was nothing in it used to show gratitude and devotion, and, if this was merely because it did not pay, are we not taking away from man's religious disposition what we are giving to his ideas? This again would challenge our view of the interdependence of higher interest and higher ideas.

Facts, of course, are not to be answered by argument. In some form, this belief in one power in the main just and beneficent does

[1] "Die Inder," in *Das Lehrbuch der Religionsgeschichte*, vol. II.

exist, and we may not dispose of it by saying that it is unlikely, or that, as it had no cult, it cannot have been important But we ought to ask what this unity is and what it includes, and why there is no cult. And certainly the answer is not that it is pre-animistic.

With this we must take forms like Tao among the Chinese. Mr Soothill describes Tao as "the eternal, ubiquitous impersonal principle, by which the universe is produced and governed"[1] We have a similar idea in the principle which is exalted in India as Brahma Unity is its chief mark: and, if it is not a person, it is personal, being a righteous and not merely a rigid force.

Soderblom holds that there were three original ideas of unity, one a creator or ancestor, one mana, one a development of animism[2] The Chinese Shang-ti he takes to be a development of the first, the Indian Brahma of the second, and the Israelite Yahweh of the third Brahma probably is rightly explained, but Shang-ti is still within the limits of the state, which is a mark of polytheism, and the belief of the Rechabites that faith in Yahweh was corrupted by contact with the animistic gods of civilisation rather bears out Lang's contention that he originally belonged to the simple life of the desert and was not animistic The real starting-point of them all is a unity of awareness, in a simple, communistic state not disturbed by individual possessions. But it is not a reflective monotheism. Two unities of reflexion, however, develop from it—the pantheistic, with its essential element mystical, and the monotheistic, with its essential element moral.

As it is what responds to monotheism, it is easy to think it more monotheistic than it is. Livingstone, for example, says that wise persons in Central Africa agreed with him about good and evil, one God and a future state. But, first of all, a native, speaking from a standpoint given him by a Christian missionary, is a very different person from one speaking from his own. And, in the second place, the same words, especially in this sphere, are often far from meaning the same thing. Dan Crawford, when he is not tempted to indulge in edifying phantasy, shows the profoundest knowledge of the Negro mind: and what he says about the same apparent monotheism is that the language of resignation to God as the Author of All, which has gone

[1] W E. Soothill, *The Three Religions of China*. A clear, interesting and documented exposition of the whole idea is given, pp 46–84.
[2] *Op. cit.* This is the main contention of the book.

the round of the Garenganze for centuries, is a 'dark fatalistic sing-song'.[1] Even in Mohammedanism we have the same, and there have been Christianities which have not escaped. Though fatalism is not necessarily non-religious, even in the form of predestination it is a falling back on a world which produces us and in which our task is accommodation, not responsibility for our own sphere within it But that there was a sense of unity which was broken up by the sense of the concrete person with property and responsibility yet never quite obliterated from the human mind, is not to be denied.

I. THE PRIMITIVE IN INDIAN RELIGION

APPENDIX TO CHAPTER XXIV (c–e)

Prof. Berriedale Keith argues that there is little evidence to show that the Aryans were deeply influenced by the religion of the native races they subdued. But considering how profound such an influence has been in every other case of which we have knowledge, there would need to be very definite proof to the contrary before we could believe India to be an exception. As Prof. Flinders Petrie says, the state religion may belong to the ruling race, but the domestic religion retains the aboriginal type, and the conquered is avenged by this latter becoming more and more dominant over the whole religion.[2] Even if caste had been a very early distinction and had been more successful in preventing mixture of race than there is any reason to suppose it was, there would still have been a state of things such as we find in early Israel, where the young men in a newly-won country were allowed more freedom of intermarriage than in the settled parts Moreover, we find a definite return to a primitive magical type from a high polytheism with an element almost monotheistic, and from prayer and action to magic and passivity, which themselves seem to prove lower influences

Oldenberg, Rhys Davids and Bertholet ascribe the pessimism, which is so marked a feature in the later development from optimistic cosmic pantheism to mystical acosmic pantheism, to climate and its depressing effect upon a vigorous warlike race. Though this was doubtless an important cause, it would not have made the Aryans pessimistic any

[1] *Thinking Black*, p 476
[2] *Religion and Conscience in Ancient Egypt*, p. 24

more than the native races but for their position, which did not require either labour to provide for themselves, or war to keep unwarlike races under, or efficient politics to rule them. A people may rise above these things, but it will fall below them unless it has moral and religious substitutes to keep it in strength. Keith, however, thinks, though he scarcely attempts to show how, that the pessimism also came out of the religion, as well as contributed to it. This is confirmed by the fact that, in the earlier Upanishads, pessimism seems to be a doctrine which ought to be held, rather than one which was acted on, something like many evangelicals' view of life In both cases a lively interest in possession and a determination to make the best of both worlds were very much in evidence. Theoretically, this world is a vale of tears, but, practically, it requires the weather eye to be kept open Yet theory has a tendency to fulfil itself, for when religion, becoming mystical, arrives at the conviction, in principle, that all earthly things are only illusion, the grounds on which the trials of life can be faced in hope and courage disappear, and then theory tends to become practice. Anything like complete mysticism is always pessimistic in this sense and this may explain why it has been so frequently a resort in times of political and social discouragement and intellectual unrest. If it is not a medicine for life's ills, it is at least an anodyne.

A view of the development held by Garbe, and accepted by others, is opposed to the view maintained above, that primitive ideas, especially of mana and magic, continue to affect the theology as well as the practice of Hindu religions This is that the doctrine of salvation by knowledge of the All-one was in direct opposition to the theology of the sacrifice, having sprung from the Kshatriyas, the warrior class, as a revolt from the domination of the Brahman class. "To the warrior class", Garbe says, "belongs the honour of showing how senseless was the sacrifice with its trite symbolism, by opening up a new world of ideas and so working a great change in the spiritual life of ancient India."[1] Oldenberg's reply it will be sufficient to summarise The Kshatriyas appear seldom in the literature, and even they ascribe this kind of knowledge to the Brahmans, it is the Brahmans who follow the ascetic practices, the gradual development of their speculations from the rites can be traced, finally, the Brahma, which becomes the Absolute, is just the indwelling potency of the Veda-word and the Brahman class [2]

[1] R. Garbe, *Beitrage zur indischen Kulturgeschichte* This is the drift of the whole discussion of Pt I, *Die Weisheit des Brahmanen oder des Kriegers?*
[2] Hermann Oldenberg, *Die Lehre der Upanishaden*, pp 166 ff

With this Keith agrees, and he gives further reasons for his opinion. But he causes needless difficulty in his explanation of the development just by failing to see how much the doctrine of salvation by knowledge of the One is closely related with the mana of the sacrifice. He thinks that the Upanishads show that the sacrifice was tending to fall into abeyance, and cites two passages which he regards as definite criticism of the priestly order.

"The sacrifice", he says, "is least reputed in the Brhad-Aryanaka Upanishad where, with a certain insolence, the worship of anything except the self is derided, and the relation of the ordinary worshipper to his gods is compared with that of house dogs."[1] The references do not give the passages in Hume's translation, but probably the first passage is 1. 4. 10, and the passage about the dogs is in the Chandogya. Much obviously depends on the connexion. In the translation, the context of the first passage is, "whosoever thus knows 'I am Brahma!' becomes this all, even the gods have not the power to prevent his becoming thus, for he becomes their self. So whosoever worships another divinity (than his Self), thinking 'he is one and I another', he knows not. He is like a sacrificial animal for the gods".[2] But, taking it with the rest of the Upanishad, this would mean that the magic of the sacrifice does not work unless we know the universal power in ourselves by which it works It is like some Protestant views of the sacrament, which regard it still as a magic saving power, but only on condition of holding consciously in the act certain doctrines. Again we have this passage:

> And on what is sacrifice based?
> On gifts to the priests.
> And on what are the gifts to the priest based?
> On faith, for when one has faith, then one gives gifts to the priests.[3]

In its connexion, this seems to be quite serious After all it is only the same opinion as is held by Chaucer's friar.

> For unto a povre order for to geve
> Is signe that a man is wel i-schreve.

The passage on the dogs Hume heads *A satire on the performance of the priests?*[4] But there is good reason to put the question mark. It

1 Arthur Berriedale Keith, *The Religion and Philosophy of the Veda and Upanishads*
2 Robert Ernest Hume, *The Thirteen Principal Upanishads*, p. 34.
3 Hume, p. 24   4 p 188.

is called the Udgitha or chant of the dogs. They glide in like the priests, sit down together and perform the preliminary vocalising, then sing "Om! Let us eat. Om! Let us drink. Om! May the god Varuna, Prajapati and Savitri bring food here! O Lord of food, bring food here! yea, bring it here! Om". This looks like satire to us, but the connexion is that Om is the essence of the chant. And the chant is the essence of everything and the fulfiller of all desires, superior to the three Vedas, and the immortal refuge. The endless detail is evidently just to give this feeling of diffused power. Then we have a worthless sort of person, but he is a Brahman and knows his business, and all goes off successfully. In this connexion, the dogs come in quite seriously. They are, as it were, priests of the animal world.

More than once we have the statement that ritual doings only provide merit in the other world for a time, whereas the right knowledge rids of all questions of merit and secures enduring bliss. But is it knowledge by itself, or the knowledge which gives a universal scope and power to the magic of the sacrifice? What is the purpose of all the repetitions in connexion with the sacrifice, if not just to exalt the impression of the sacrifice? Moreover, with this interpretation, we can read the two Upanishads, not indeed as a logically united whole, but as an emotionally connected unity.

Keith, judging apparently from the number of references, thinks the ritual fell into abeyance and was later revived But this is probably the same mistake as used to be made about the Epistles of Ignatius. From the silence about the episcopate in Rome and the many references to it in what concerns Asia Minor, it was assumed to be already existing in Asia Minor and not in Rome, whereas the real inference seems to be that it was beyond dispute in Rome and was still a matter of contention in Asia Minor. Similarly, that the question of the ritual becomes more vocal later and that there is more insistence on the duty of observing it, would not prove that it came to be again prominent after a season of neglect, but that it was no longer of universal observance and without question.

The elaboration of detail—connecting the sacrificial ritual with life, the quarters of the earth, the sun—is not to be explained, as Keith does, by lack of power to make general statements, because of such statements there are abundance. It is to give a deepening impression of the mana in the sacrifice and to afford some kind of universal justification for its supposed efficacy. This, working with old ideas of *rta*—the universal order—and such-like, developed pantheism. "In so far as man makes offerings and sacrifices, he becomes the world of gods."[1] But this needs the right kind of knowledge.[2]

At first this is cosmic pantheism and optimistic. "From reverencing the chant as good one gets good." A good tone is the gold of the chant, and he comes to have gold who knows it.[3] This is the usual type of magic. The power is just the usual part which has the potency of the whole; and the mana so controlled is the usual 'splendour, brightness, food', dangerous to oneself when wrongly used, deadly to one's enemy when duly accomplished. "Him who hates us and him whom we hate waste thou away, with his vital breath, progeny, cattle."[4] This knowledge is also plenary absolution, not, as Deussen argues, because it delivers us from the illusion of individual existence and its responsibilities, but far more probably as a purely magical deliverance.

Then we have such a mixture of ideas that the usual device is to ascribe them to different authors. But they are found together in other places than India. Behind all possessions pleasure is the plenum, and the plenum is Brahma. In the Brahma-world desire is possession, even of women. And the Brahman, even after talking of unconscious life in the Brahma, takes his reward of cattle without apology. Moreover, the most amazing and even brutal licentiousness is enjoined, while the idea of Nirvana, which is more than once repeated, is enjoyment in the arms of the beloved woman, when there is no without and within.

About the place Leuba gives to sex in mysticism there may be dubiety regarding Western mysticism, but, regarding the Indian, there is none. Nor is it by any means mere inhibition complex, as Leuba thinks of it Right down to modern Bhakti and Buddhist Tantrism, there are outbreaks of gross sensualism Nor is mere empty feeling, undisturbed by any content, very far from mere sensuality, regardless of all but feeling. In India the most passionate erotic language at least has been used to express the feeling, as with the Sufi poets and even the Christian mystics Keith's contention, that in Buddhism neither the idea of a true *atman* or soul, nor of some kind of real Supernatural, nor of almost any of the accepted Indian religious ideas is really absent, is probable in the nature of the case, seeing Buddhism succeeded as a religion. But Keith also argues that Buddha's view of

[1] Hume, p 85
[2] p 89.
[3] p 80
[4] p 314

the outer world was naive realism.[1] Were he arguing about any other than a Hindu, his reasoning might be convincing. But is not the doctrine of karma alone sufficient contradiction? A world created by desire can hardly be other than a self-created magical world of appearances. It is subject to a law which makes some pretence to be a law of freedom, but which shows its real nature, as almost all Indian ideas of the kind do, as fate. The raising of this to a universal order is perhaps what is most original in Buddhism, if it be not from outside India, as it may have been, seeing that the idea of the Divine order as the equivalence of action, or rather by this time of motive, and award was already a fairly widely accepted conception elsewhere. Though logically it was fatalistic, in the teaching of Buddha it was free and ethical: and, as Buddha himself was a religious person of a fine spirit, opposed to all kinds of excess, Buddhism, at its best, was something of a moral and even a Puritanical reformation. For example, the *Dhammapada*, though its principle is that the life follows the act as the wheel of the waggon follows the foot of the ox, and its rules are somewhat external and legal, presents what we may call the more passive side of morality in a way that is not much inferior to some Christian ideals of the saintly life. But, when we come to ask why the life of each one should be the mere shadow of karma, the answer can only be that the external world has the old Indian unreality Karma is still what Konow calls a magical fluid, forcing the empirical self to create its own magical illusion, so that any reality of re-birth and all that follows is still only this inferior kind of reality. This goes back to magic and magic to the sacrifice, which is another argument against Keith's idea that they are not continuous. It is rather a case of the more it changes the more it is the same.

That we have in the Indian religious books, especially the Upanishads, a philosophy which has all the essentials of Christianity on the one hand, and all the deepest thoughts of the philosophers on the other, as Deussen first taught and Indians like Dutt and Radhakrishnan have since maintained, is true only on Radhakrishnan's ground, that its ideal is of a kind to accommodate itself to anything.[2] This, however, has the drawback of being as accommodating to the lowest as to the highest: while an important part of any religion, and for that matter of any philosophy, is what it denies as well as what it affirms In any real

[1] *Buddhist Philosophy in India and Ceylon*, pp 71 ff.
[2] S. Radhakrishnan, *The Reign of Religion in Contemporary Philosophy*, p. 451.

claim to be a contribution to the problems of philosophy Oldenberg[1] and Keith[2] have not left much substance. Nor is any one, though ignorant of Indian languages, without the possibility of forming an opinion of his own, when he can read a literal and unadorned translation like Mr Hume's, especially if he have a little knowledge of other philosophies and religions. For one who starts with the opposite of a bias towards pantheism, Keith will seem to sum up the situation justly when he says that, "regarded as serious contributions to the solution of fundamental problems of philosophy, the value of the Upanishads must be considered to be comparatively small".[3]

Something more he grants them as a school of mysticism, though the mysticism "is too purely metaphysical, and lacks the ethical and social content of Christian mysticism". This difference, he thinks, is due to the difference between the Christian God and Brahma, though even in Christian mysticism, he adds, the personal deity tends to be merged in an impersonal absolute and the ethical and social to fall into abeyance. But this means that Christian mysticism is different precisely in so far as it has other elements than mysticism; and the same may be said of the later Indian tendency towards a personal deity

J. MYSTICISM

APPENDIX TO CHAPTER XXIV (*f*)

(*a*) DEFINITION

As Prof. Pringle-Pattison complains, the term 'mysticism' is often used for "any kind of protest against formulas and observances, in the name of heart-religion".[4] Even in more serious discussions, it is used, as Mr Rufus Jones does, for "the type of religion which puts emphasis on immediate awareness of relation with God, on direct and immediate consciousness of the divine presence".[5] This is better, yet he omits as pathological what has been most characteristic of historical mysticism—the exclusion of the world of the senses. Dean Inge is equally indefinite. Among English writers, all the more perhaps for

[1] Hermann Oldenberg, *Die Lehre der Upanishaden und die Anfänge des Buddhismus.*
[2] Arthur Berriedale Keith, *Religion and Philosophy of the Veda.*
[3] *Ibid.* vol. II, p. 599.   [4] *Encycl. Brit.* xith ed., vol XIX, p. 123.
[5] *Studies in Mystical Religion*, p. xv.

APPENDICES 495

the welter of quotations and stereotyped phraseology, Miss Evelyn Underhill keeps closest to the exposition of true mysticism [1] Among French writers there is both more precision and adequacy, and Delacroix's definition fairly covers the ground "Mysticism", he says, "going beyond religion, aspires after ultimate union with the Divine, even to the penetration of the Divine into the soul, to the disappearance of individuality, with all its ways of acting, thinking and feeling, into the Divine Substance."[2]

(b) HISTORICAL CONNEXIONS

No one is so independent of material forms as not to be helped by them to deeper reverence. A worthy form is as important in religion as in poetry, and in both cases for the same reason, that it clothes with feeling the bare idea. But just as there are people who read poetry for the mere impressiveness of the language, so there are others for whom a religious service is measured by the stirring of the mere feeling of awe. The ritual does not need to be visible ceremony, a ritual of familiar phrase and familiar imagery being equally effective: but both work as the ten thousand words in a tongue, not as the five with the understanding The intoning of impressive phraseology is, in particular, the ritual of the Celt, who, in spite of his bare outward forms, is far more of a mystic than the English High-churchman. The Welsh *hwyl* and the Highlander's chant are just ways of saying Ah! with the same sense of including everything, as the Indian says Om! The temperament which creates this is probably independent of any historical connexion. Yet, even in this, a descent from a type of Catholicism which was essentially mystical is certain, and its connexion with the East not improbable.

If, as I think, mysticism is related to actual forms of reality and of mind and of feeling, there might be independent origins even of the exercises of the Mystic Way. But historically it all seems to go back to an Indian origin Though it is more than suggested in Augustine's *Confessions*, which itself had its origin in Neo-Platonism, it did not appear as a cult in the Western Church till it was introduced by Erigena's translation of the Pseudo-Dionysius, which was purely Neo-Platonic. With regard to Neo-Platonism, most writers, on both Indian and Greek religions, assume an Indian origin. and, seeing that there

1 *The Mystic Way*.
2 Henri Delacroix, *Études d'Histoire et de Psychologie du Mysticisme*, p vii.

had long been connexion both by land and sea, this seems difficult to question. Keith argues that there is little evidence of literary dependence, but probably even he does not mean to deny all connexion. It could hardly be derived directly from Plato, for, as Edward Caird says, "It is an extreme misunderstanding of the words which he uses about the idea of the Good, when the Neo-Platonists attribute to him the idea of an absolute unity, in which all distinction is lost, and which, therefore, cannot be apprehended except in an ecstasy in which thought and consciousness are annihilated. On the contrary, it is his most fundamental thought that what is most real is most knowable, and what is most knowable is most real".[1] Moreover, this was characteristic of the earlier Greek mind. That even Plotinus arrived at his position by his own genius without any aid, is extremely improbable in view of its unlikeness to Plato's active virtues and interest in the state and human life, and indeed to the whole Greek genius, along with the certainty of Oriental influences at this time in the West. But, in any case, it seems impossible to regard the vagaries of his followers as without any influence from Yoga. The only other similar type of mysticism is Mohammedan, and Prof. Nicholson thinks it was directly influenced both by Neo-Platonism and India.[2]

(c) THE MYSTIC WAY AS REVEALING HIGHER TRUTH

Prof. Leuba treats the mystic's Supernatural precisely as the mystic treats the Natural.[3] It is all purely individual phantasy and illusion. With mysticism he includes all worship of every kind in the same condemnation. But to identify what is designed to exalt truth, deepen fellowship and inspire consecration to service, with what is designed to have unmediated oneness with the Divine only leads to confusion. Some sense of the Supernatural beyond the Natural doubtless belongs to both But the question of whether, through experience of the manifold, we may reach a unity beyond it, is very different from the question of whether, by excluding it, we can have an experience of the One in its nakedness. To write poetry which goes beyond facts is one thing, to think that soaring above facts is poetry is another. To fail to observe this difference is to confuse the inquiry from the start.

1 *The Evolution of Theology in the Greek Philosophies*, vol I, p. 256.
2 Reynold A. Nicholson, *The Mystics of Islam*, p 112.
3 James Leuba, *The Psychology of Religious Mysticism*

The whole business he traces to a mixed inferiority and power complex, auto-suggestion and suggestion by traditional ideas and manufactured influences, with morbid sex impulse playing a leading rôle. Not only is this an incredible explanation of anything so universal and spontaneous as worship, but it does not account for any kind of mysticism. It might cover any case, but not all cases. This distinction he seldom bears in mind, yet it is an essential consideration about any kind of explanation. The wish to win a professorship may explain any particular man's scientific interest but not all scientific interest. So, though modern psychological devices may explain the doings of any particular mystic, or of any particular church-goer, they do not explain all mysticism, and much less all worship.

On his own principles, moreover, there is no reason why the Mystic Way should not be the way of ultimate knowledge. The universe, as he conceives it, seems to be a kind of pantheistic emanation of force, which, in some way, includes the ideal as well as the mechanical. But, if man and all things are thus passively produced, why should not the passivity of the mystic be the way back to the unity in which all multiplicity is rooted? A great deal of mysticism has wrought with just such an idea of the universe: and, indeed, this is its natural cosmology, anything different being merely an intrusion from the other type of religion.

What is impossible to harmonise with the Mystic Way is freedom, not necessity. The long process of evolution is increase of individual quality, leading to personal insight and response and free choice: and no environment reveals itself to the merely plastic soul, all knowledge of it being only another name for the activity of mind. But Prof. Leuba is never so stimulating as when he is inconsistent, which, fortunately for his usefulness, is often the case.

The mystic ecstasy, he thinks, is no more than a sort of luminous vacancy, warmed up by many cross-currents of what we may call transmigrating emotions, which apparently all have a sex basis. This basis might not be anything to their discredit, as the sublimation of sex has been one of the supreme impulses of human progress, and possibly is the way of rising to all higher sympathy. This may be in mysticism, but something at least akin to sex may also be cultivated as mere feeling, which in itself is dangerous, and is the more dangerous for expressing itself in passionate superlatives and erotic imagery. That this has all been morbid, as Leuba maintains, may be too sweeping a generalisation, but morbid elements have not been wholly absent, and gush is not less in danger of unreality for being pious. Moreover, it is possible to maintain that the whole attempt to live in empty forms is itself morbid, seeing we no more naturally and spontaneously have the unity of mind and the unity of environment emptied of meaning and even of conflicting meaning, than we have one precious feeling of love applicable to all objects or to none without the disturbance of any aversions.

Leuba further maintains that the suppression of self is very far from being as complete as the mystic's own impression of it. And this also is true. The activity which follows the mystic state is generally concerned with directing and dominating other people, which goes with the psychological fact that the inferiority and power complexes are often interchangeable terms. Nor is there complete suppression of the world, but merely the imposing on it of a scheme which has become a kind of fixed idea.

Also I find myself not less sceptical than Leuba about any revelation of new truth: and this scepticism is in no way modified by Father Maréchal's defence of the view that, as the Mystic Way is beyond the interpretation of our ordinary methods of knowing and what is experienced is beyond the mystic's own power to put into words, we must simply accept the claim to illumination.[1] Moreover, the defence, that the passive mind is not strictly passive but that what the soul is still belongs to it and that this meets the revelation, confirms the doubt, because in the first place, if the mind is active, even subconsciously, we lose the mystic's assurance of truth, which is that, being passively received, it is no creation of the mystic's own mind; and, in the second, if the mind is active at all, why should it not be so consciously and fully?

Scepticism is further increased by what the equipment of the subconscious is supposed to be. Mysticism in Christianity cannot be separated from other mysticism, either psychologically or historically. What alone distinguishes it, Maréchal holds, is the theology. This is true, but what does it mean? Even Christian mystics, it is admitted, have at times taken queer phantasies for truth, and not infrequently tended towards acosmic pantheism. From this Maréchal argues that only the Catholic mystic, well secured in orthodoxy, can be trusted.

[1] Joseph Maréchal, trans. Algar Thorold, *Studies in the Psychology of the Mystics*. The references are mostly to the sections 149–187.

Apparently the Catholic faith is such an exact map of the supersensuous world that those who have it do not err therein as other less well provided mortals are sure to do. Then, however, they see wonderful sights, like the Mystery of the Trinity and the Procession of the Logos. But should not a really original source of knowledge be its own light, and not require guidance from any theology to keep it in the way of truth? Such dependence rather rouses the suspicion that the mystic sees merely what he already believes. Nor has any fuller revelation won by this way yet enlightened mankind. Many have published what was said to have been so received, but, alas, it has all been pious platitude, of the dullest conformity to orthodox pattern. In contrast, in every religion, any writing ever cherished as a sacred book, has been written by men who were facing life and the conflicts of experience with the highest activities of all their powers of mind. Even the mystical sacred literature is not an exception. Mohammed did profess something different, but the Koran is not a mystical treatise, nor is what most professes to have been received in this way the best part of it. If, then, professions of unique illumination are not followed by anything which enlightens, it is not wholly unjustified scepticism to regard mystic vision as belonging to a well-known order of mental phenomena, in which glow is in inverse ratio to enlightenment. The mind, it is true, does not become empty when the discursive understanding is dismissed, but it is occupied only by what is already fixed in it. Usually this is something on which there has been much meditation. Hence such problems as the Trinity and the Procession of the Logos. But, if in spite of the sense of glowing light on them, the doctrines remain as dark as before, the suspicion is impossible to escape that even ecstatic contemplation is no more than a mirror in which is seen magnified what is already believed.

Another argument is that, as we receive knowledge of the Natural passively at the bottom of the ladder of our knowing, so we may receive knowledge of the Supernatural passively at the top. This does not seem very consistent with the previous argument: and, in any case, it is merely a very ancient error. Our whole study of perception has shown that even the lowest perception is an active interpretation, the meaning doubtless given, but becoming ours only as we actively interpret it as our own. Knowledge is just activity of the mind, and a passive knowledge is a contradiction in terms.

Nor is mysticism much more convincing on its practical side. Dom

Butler values meditation and prayer as they bear fruit in practice. But this is not the attitude of the true mystic, as he recognises. Because the mystic's flights into the empyrean of ecstasy have exhausted him he must return to the world to recover energy for a higher flight, but this is not regarded as the natural fruit of energy and inspiration received from his ecstasy.

Mysticism as an occasional recreation may, however, have a very different effect from mysticism as what William James calls taking a perpetual moral holiday. Though the church benefited more than the world from the services of the Catholic mystics, some of them were capable and efficient persons. We may think that St Theresa might have been better occupied than shutting up young girls in nunneries and tightening the rules over them, but there is no doubt that she was a very forcible character. Probably also we cannot deny an increase in St John of the Cross's practical discernment, any more than we can deny an increase of Suso's distressing sentimentality. But most of the mystics would have been very ill to live with, as good people ought not to be: and the writings of those who carried out the full cult of withdrawal from ideas of the senses, claims of desire, discursive thought, all lack the simple directness of reality. Life's true lesson can be learned only by looking with open eye at all its situations, and by free and independent thinking about its problems, and true victory can only be won by facing all its challenge. For this a God who is merely a temple of unity, into which to withdraw from life's distraction and evil, is no succour. Asceticism and austere morality are only justified if required for our tasks in life. Then they can be genuine self-forgetfulness. As an arranged scheme of self-deliverance from evil, self-sacrifice is apt to be only an arranged scheme of self-exaltation. The only denial of self worth anything is from the challenge of following the highest; and this never calls itself self-sacrifice and much less self-immolation. Nor is love compensation for what distresses as ugly and base, but is an objective end to be set up in spite of it. And higher truth can only be tested as it is, for this end, power and inspiration.

INDEX

Absolute, 116, 326
Action and award, 219 ff., 241, 332, 442
Aesthetics, 210
Agnosticism, 76, 157; and value, 213 ff.
Agriculture, 396
Alexander, 184
Aloneness, 102, 130, 132, 143, 338
Ames, 44-5
Amos, 401, 403, 455
Anaxagoras, 50
Animism, 32, 48, 142, 483
Animistic, the, 380-3
Ankermann, 376-8
Anthropological, 350-2
Anthropology, 56-7, 355
Apocalyptic, 429 ff., 458; religions, 409 ff., 427-32
Apprehension, 181; fixed unities of, 375
Arnold, 130
Augustine, 391
Authority, 100 ff.
Award, cosmological law of, 221 ff.; the Natural as, 335-6
Awareness, 113, 180; unity of, 384, 394, 477; and apprehension, 120-43, 245, 251, a poet's, 124-32

Beginnings, 261-3, 351
Bentham, 193
Bergson, 83, 200, 262, 381
Berkeley, 170-2
Bertholet, 376, 481
Biological principles, 480-1
Biology, 276 ff.
Blake, 380
Brahma, 52, 416-7
Brahmanism, 227
Brahmans, 413, 489
Brain, 186 ff.
Broad, 158
Browning, 296
Buddha, 396, 406-7, 493
Buddhism, 24, 227 ff., 363-4, 419 ff.
Butler, Dom, 422 ff., 499
Butler, Joseph, 314-5

Caesar, 57
Caird, 496
Calvin, 286-7, 290

Carlyle, 82, 126
Cause and effect, 157, 167, 218 ff., 237 ff., 257
Ceremonial-legal, 427-45
Cervantes, 287
Character, 287; determination by, 300-2
Characteristics, acquired, 268
Chaucer, 490
Christianity, 227, 360-3, 370, 401, 432
Church, 13
Civilisation, 219, 305, 401 ff.; polytheism and, 395-7
Colour, 188-90
Comprehension, 121 ff.
Comte, 30, 54
Concrete and abstract, 246-53
Conscience, 301; and conscientiousness, 312-29; content of, 318-23; education of, 316; infallibility of, 314-18; negative rules of, 324; scope of, 301, 312-4
Cook, A. B., 400
Copernicus, 12
Crawford, 178, 487-8
Crawley, 32-3
Critias, 47
Cult, significance of, 21-2

Dante, 125, 142
Darwin, 57, 100, 264, 278
Darwinism, 258 ff., 273 ff., 333
Dead, cult of, 377
Deism, 24 ff., 156, 242, 353; and theism, 366
Delacroix, 495
De la Grasserie, 33-4, 40
Descartes, 51-2, 114, 275; Perfect Being of, 103, 106, 282; method of, 104-8, 114-16, 164, 168, 184, 233, 237, 281-2; rules of, 105
Desire, as act of freedom, 229
Deussen, 493
Dhammapada, 229, 493
Diligence, 222
Driesch, 480
Dualism, 369; as problem and solution, 432-3; as a theology, 438-40
Durkheim, 41-2, 145

Elijah, 454

INDEX

Empiricism, 117, 169
Enlightenment, true, 214–16
Environment, 277–80; experience of, 58–9; freedom and, 95, 302, 330–2; higher, 55, 294, 304, 309, 354, 406, 459, 470–1; and the individual, 278 ff., 297; as meaning, 96, 138; proof of, 51–2, 166; selection by, 281–2; the religious, 58–73; unity of, 64, 142, 146; and value, 337
Environments, choice between, 326
Euhemerism, 47
Evangelical Movement, 11
Evolution, 86, 95, 293, 313, 373; and absoluteness, 326–9; Darwinian, 31, 37; as education, 277; problems of, 260–1; as process of the Natural, 258–80; as process of the Supernatural, 281–97
Existence, former and future, 459–60
Explanation, 121 ff., 218 ff., 339
Extension, 181 ff.
Extensiveness, 214

Faith, 82, 364, 436
Family, 400, 402
Farnell, 374
Feeling and action, 198; as idea, 61, 193; manipulation of, 78; psychology of, 204; and reality, 80; sensitiveness of, 79; unity of, 146; and value, 66
Feuerbach, 35–7
Fichte, 155
Finality, 337
Fixed idea, context of, 155, 176–9; inheritance of, 268; and magic, 384; and reality, 183, 203; scheme of, 172; primitive unity of, 375, 378–80
Fixed and free ideas, 89 ff., 219
Form and content, 146, 152
Frazer, 8, 54, 355, 374, 483
Free idea, science and, 244; soul a, 381
Freedom, 70, 108, 111 ff., 229, 298–311, 497; acts of, 309; form of, 102, 342; formulation as, 221; hazards of, 357; and the Natural, 303–5; and order, 113, 246; and the Supernatural, 95, 306–11; of the will, 89

Galileo, 231, 233, 479
Garbe, 489
Ghost, 32, 48
God, belief in, 24, 26; communion with, 38; doctrine of, 365–9; and moral order, 334; as a person, 335, 341; the rule of, 453–5
Gods, anthropomorphic, 390 ff.
Goethe, 78, 159–60, 283
Good, the, 226; and evil as a problem, 440–2; rule of, 469–71
Greek gods, 394–5; religion, 407, tragedy, 230

Haldane, 480
Hamilton, 204
Hammurabi, 224, 399
Heaven and hell, 137, 143, 335
Hebrew Legalism, 428 ff.; prophet, 173, 407; religion, 441 ff.
Hegel, 132–3, 417; and freedom, 285; his classification of religions, 361; his conception of history, 88, 291; his conception of religion, 17, 27–9, 148–51; his process of reason, 31, 34, 107, 162–6, 282–4, 290, 379, 475
Hegelian type, theories of, 30–5
Heredity, 176–7, 260, 267
History and experience, 346–57; its perspective, 373–5; philosophy of, 289; theory and, 47–57
Hobbes, 47–8, 333, 347
Hobson, 2, 250
Höffding, 306
Holy, awesome, 59, 174, 392; the particularising, 64; and profane, 65 ff.; sense of, 59–65, 205, 306, 336, 392, 474; undifferentiated, 61, 80, 145, 206, 308 ff.
Hosea, 427, 455–7
Hudson, 189
Hume, David, 40, 49–55, 154, his sensationalism, 37, 180
Hume, R. E., 416, 490 ff.
Humour, 84 ff.
Huxley, 259, 333–4
Hypocrisy, 75 ff., 328

Ideal, 326; and experience of the Natural, 326–9; and real, 330–43
Idealism, 282; empirical, 40
Idée fixe, 89, 204
Illuminism, 99–102, 103
Immortality, 24–6, 364–5; and the Natural, 460 ff.
Impacts, 199–200
Imperative, categorical, 294, 303 ff., 319
Independence, 291, 295, 321, 330
Individual, 95, 295; concrete, 409, 428, 450–1; and conscience, 318–26; and individuality, 144–67, 282, 320,

problem of, 151-2; and knowing, 110; meaning for the, 271-7; frontier of, and the Natural, 156-60, 271; and the Supernatural, 160-5
Individuality, 70, 160 ff.
Inertia, cosmological law of, 230-6, 265
Inquiry, field of, 2-14; justification of, 11-14; order of, 114-17
Interaction, 283
Interest, test of, 3-8; insufficiency of, 8-11; function of, 188, 192
Intuitionalism, 315
Isaiah, 458-9

James, 17, 18, 44, 155, 181, 184, 273, 296, 298, 500
Jeremiah, 427, 451, 453, 459, 463
Jespersen, 172
Jesus, 21, 22, 407, 417, 427; as authority, 468-9; religion of, 470
Jevons, 352
Job, 59-60, 77, 440 ff.
Judaism, later, 226, 432, 467; priestly, 370; prophetic, 25, 370
Judgments, theoretical, and value, 202-4
Jurisprudence, 224, 400

Kant, 62, 67, 100, 106, 138, 180, 205, 314, 342, 352, 362-3, 481; and the content of conscience, 318-29; and form of freedom, 298-302; and form of sacred, 307; and Hegel, 475-7; and individual, 161-2, 165-7; his conception of religion, 17, 27-9, 148-51; and moral order, 332, 334-5; Newtonianism and Deism, 242-4; theory of knowing and the individual, 152-5
Karma, 407, 417-19, 460, 493, the germ as, 266-7; and Positivism, 227-30
Kattenbusch, 474
Keith, 418, 488 ff., 496
Kepler, 231, 248
King, 44
Knowing, four types of, 120-4; and knowledge, 110-11, 151-2
Konow, 418, 485, 493
Koran, 65, 499

Lang, 385-6, 485-6
Language, 413; development of, 191 ff.; and perception, 170 ff.
Lasson, 476
Law, formulation of, 437-8; mathematical, 251; moral and physical, 237, 312, 325, 336; and prophecy, 443-5; ritual and ethical, 436 ff.
Legalism, the prophetical faith and, 449-53
Lehmann, 435, 481
Leibnitz, 283, 284, 290
Leuba, 37-41, 45, 419, 496-8
Life, 68, 134, 263 ff., 374; and meaning, 264-71
Locke, 192, 203
Logic, 45, 149, 314; aesthetics and ethics, 207-12
Lotze, 203, 283
Luther, 436, 479

Macalister, 480
Magic, 24, 355, 377, 383-5, 413, 483 ff.
Malinowski, 485
Man, definition of, 82
Maréchal, 498-9
Marrett, 483-5
Matter, 248
Maya, 52, 73, 407, 417
McTaggart, 284, 287-90
Meaning, 154, 157-8, 189, 201; system of symbol and, 174-6, 253-7; life and, 264 ff.
Mechanical cause, 34; explanation, 44, 158; inventions, 234 ff.
Mechanism and freedom, 112
Medium, physical and physiological, 185, 188
Method and problems, 99-117; determination of, 108-10
Meyer, 43
Micah, 457-8
Milton, 125, 142
Mind, as adaptation, 45; prelogical, 94; fullest capacity of, 117; seeing another, 134; unity of, 145
Mohammed, 431
Mohammedanism, 370, 429, 432, 488
Monotheism, 226, 365; and pantheism, differences of, 408 ff., primitive, 385-7, 485-8; prophetic, 370, 448 ff.
Montaigne, 210, 479-80
Morality and ethics, 313-14; growth of standard of, 94; tribal, 451
Morgan, 122, 160, 284
Moses, 431, 467
Motion, 232
Motive, 136, 272, 301
Muller, 56-7, 174
Mystery, 213
Mystical, the, 405-26, morality, 409

INDEX

Mysticism, 144 ff., 434, 494–500; Christian, 420–6; effect of, 424; esoteric, 415; Indian, 406 ff.; Neo-Platonic, 363, 495–6; and revelation, 424
Mystic Way, 422, 495; and revelation, 496–500
Mythology, 174

Natural as personal, 465–6
Naturalism, 156 ff., 164, 226 ff., 293, 353
Necessity, as freedom, 284–6; and freedom, 113, cosmologies of, 218–40, concordats between, 241–57
Negative, 475–7
Newton, 100, 107, 231
Newtonism, 231 ff., 242, 258 ff., 269
Nicholson, 496
Nietzsche, 333
Numina, 391
Numinous, 61

Obligation, 306, 388
Oldenberg, 488 ff.
Omnipotence, 288
Organism, place of, 261–4
Otto, 60–4, 474

Paley, 209
Pantheism, 40, 282, 410 ff.; acosmic, 155, 369; cosmic, 295, 369; early Indian, 412–16; and peace, 284; and process, 288
Pascal, 315
Paul, 300, 303, 328, 419, 445, 464, 479
Perceiving, the child's, 132–7, the poet's child's, 138–40
Perception, 96, 147, 148, 201, 203; the form of, 168–84; and meaning, 157; context of, 183
Periodicity, 231
Persian situation, 434–6
Personal, the, 339–43
Pessimism, 296, 406, 416–18
Petrie, 399, 488
Phariseeism, 443
Phenomenon and noumenon, 242–4
Physics, 10, 262–3; Newtonian, 30–1
Plato, 173, 204, 226, 496
Platonic virtues, 435
Pleasure and pain, 135–6, 193, 197, 229, 449
Plotinus, 496
Polytheism, 368–9, 379; higher, 407; holy and sacred of, 392; defects and progress of, 398–404

Polytheistic, the, 390–404
Pragmatism, 40
Present and future, 459–66
Primitive, the, 372–89; ideas, 483–485
Pringle-Pattison, 165, 475, 494
Problems, the, 110–14
Process, 164, 336; and evil, 290–2; and theories of sin, 292–7
Progress, 93, 338–60, and science, 259–60, standard of, 359–60
Property and the concrete individual, 393–5
Prophetic, the, 446–71
Prophetical, 354–7
Proverbs, Book of, 222 ff.
Psychology, 7, 299; genetic, 30 ff.; and metaphysics, 42–6; and validity, 39 ff.; volitional, 37
Psycho-physical parallelism, 158, 269, 396

Quantity, 192 ff., 204; and quality, 3, 244–6
Quantum Theory, 249

Radhakrishnan, 493
Rationalism, 7, 11, 99, 102–4, 108, 152, 156, 161, 165–7, 284, 321–2, 347; failures of, 103
Realism, new, 191, 195
Realm of Ends, 155, 334
Reason, Absolute, 318; process of, 282, 286
Reconciliation and revelation, 470
Reid, 154
Relativity, 249
Religion, and authority, 209; bad, 14, 17, 74–82, 95, 357, 374, 452; and beauty, 209; beginning and origin of, 22, 55–7, 372–3, conservative, 373; definition of, 3 ff.; as egoism, 36; and environment, 23, 82–6; and history, 116, 466–9; as illusion, 29–46; a mental state, 16–21; and morality, 209, 320, 387–9, as phantasy, 35; and piety, 19; primitive, 54, 92, 372–89; primitive Indian, 488–94; progress of, 9, 86, 92–3, 367; and reality, 28, 245; seat of, 15–28, as social, 21–3, 41; and theology, 23–8; a total reaction, 17–18; and value, 58; variety and reality of, 70
Religions, of Nature, 368, 375–6, 482; of reconciliation, 362; types of, 30–42

INDEX

Religions, classification of, natural and supernatural, 368–71, intellectual and ethical, 360–8, standpoint of, 358–60
Religious-historical, 350, 352–4; outlook, 149–51
Remnant, holy, 445, 451
Remorse, 287
Responsibility, 225, 286–9
Reverence, 299 ff., 308
Rig-Veda, 412
Ritschl, 20, 41
Romanticism, 152, 156–67, 284, 346
Rousseau, 56, 150
Runze, 3–4, 8–9

Sacred, absolute value of, 61; ideal and material, 87, 90, irrational and immoral, 67; judgment of the, 65–9, 307, the material, 90; and secular, 377, 432 ff.
Sacrifice, 68
Sainte-Beuve, 199
Samkhya, 417
Santayana, 380
Satan, 444
Scepticism, 51–4
Schematisation, 63
Schiller, 127
Schlegel, 161
Schleiermacher, 17, 27–9, 161, 352, 361–2; his conception of history, 88, 349; his conception of religion, 148, 151, 212; his type of religion, 35–7
Schopenhauer, 13, 291, 417
Science, 2, 6, 10, 44, 102, 109, 112, 115, 169, 213, 243 ff., history of, 239; origins of, 478–80; and morals, 241, omissions of, 247 ff.; philosophy of, 246 ff., and writing, 253–5
Selfishness, 86, 272–5, 326
Selves, 303, 325
Sensationalism, 37
Sensations, 154–5, 176, 185–200, 205, awareness of, 195–9, development of, 188, and meaning, 198–9, quality of, 192–5
Senses, evolution of, 141, oneness of, 178–80; function of, 170
Sensitiveness, 141
Sensuality, 175 ff.
Sequence, two kinds of, 218–21
Shaftesbury, 209
Shakespeare, 126–34, 138, 140–2, 479–80
Siebeck, 363, 367, 462

Sin, theories of, 292 ff; radical evil, 327; suffering and, 455–9
Sincerity, 39, 100, 131, 317, 322; sensitiveness, unity, 140–3
Soderblom, 481, 485 ff.
Soothill, 487
Soul, 32, 56, 68, 276, 289
Space, 240, and time, 131, 136, 142, 153, 167, 180–4; religious, 144–5
Speculation, 410
Speech, 187, and perceiving, 172–4; popular, 468
Spinoza, 49, 107, 159–60, 282–4
Standpoint, 74–98, 327
Starbuck, 43
State, the, 399, 439, 451–2; civilisation and, 401
Stevenson, 410
Structure and function, 265, 276
Sublime, 210
Supernatural, the, 69–73, and Natural, distinction between, 72
Symbolism, 171, 174–6

Taboo, 55, 92
Tacitus, 56
Tansley, 379
Tao, 386, 487
Tennyson, 137
Themistocles, 354
Theologies, 366, 407
Theology, 95–8, 104, 108–9; four principles of, 101
Theory, danger and necessity of, 147–9; fact and, 54–5; inadequate, 236–40
Tiele, 363, 481
Tool-using, 83
Touch, 169, 179, 196
Tradition, 346–50, 466
Troeltsch, 353
Truth, beauty, goodness, 91, 205, 310, 329, 466; standards of, 208 ff.
Turgot, 54

Unities, 144–7, 379
Unity of experience, 2
Upanishads, 414, 417–18, 489 ff.
Usener, 390
Utilitarian ethics, 272

Valuation, principles of, 366 ff.
Value, absolute and comparative, 67–9, 90; Agnosticism and, 212–14, natural and ideal, 204–7, and validity, 201–16
Vedanta, 418

Vedas, 414
Vedic hymns, 87
Vibrations, 111, 154, 158, 175, 190, 235; system of, 185-6
Vitalism, 275-7
Volition, 299

Walpole, 11
Ward, 181, 184, 193, 195, 207, 250, 269
Weismann, 260, 266 ff.
Welch, 445
Whitehead, 5, 6, 249, 478-80
Will to live, 298-300
Windelband, 15, 474
Woodger, 480

Wordsworth, 129, 138-40, 141, 144, 147, 192, 193, 248, 339
World, deny and possess, 320, 471; a just, 332-5, 469; problem of, 304 ff.; victories over, 377 ff.
Wundt, 31

Xenophanes, 226, 390, 399

Yoga, 418
Yogi, 385, 413

Zarathustra, 431, 437 ff.
Zoroastrianism, 370, 427-8, 433-40, 467; progress of, 436-8

www.ingramcontent.com/pod-product-compliance
Lightning Source LLC
Chambersburg PA
CBHW071220290426
44108CB00013B/1235